Life Science
for Young Catholics

Seton Press
Front Royal, VA

Executive Editor: Dr. Mary Kay Clark
Editors: Seton Staff

© 2016-2020 Seton Press
All rights reserved.
Printed in the United States of America

Seton Press
1350 Progress Drive
Front Royal, VA 22630
Phone: (540) 636-9990
Fax: (540) 636-1602

ISBN: 978-1-60704-143-6

For more information, visit us on the web at www.setonpress.com
Contact us by e-mail at info@setonpress.com

Table of Contents
Life Science for Young Catholics

Preface 1

Chapter 1: Science and Life 3

Chapter 2: The Chemistry of Life 14

Chapter 3: The Cell 28

Chapter 4: Single-Celled Organisms 46

Chapter 5: The Fungus Kingdom 64

Chapter 6: The Plant Kingdom 78

Chapter 7: The Animal Kingdom 96

Chapter 8: The Human Integumentary System 114

Chapter 9: The Human Musculoskeletal System 122

Chapter 10: The Human Respiratory System 132

Chapter 11: The Human Circulatory System 140

Chapter 12: The Human Digestive System 154

Chapter 13: The Human Urinary and Reproductive Systems ... 170

Chapter 14: The Human Immune System 180

Chapter 15: The Human Nervous System 190

Chapter 16: The Human Sense Organs and Endocrine System ... 202

Glossary 215

Index 239

Image Attributions 243

Preface
Creation and Life

Genesis, The Creed, and Life

Did you know that God is "Life"? Mankind did not know God's Name until He told Moses at the burning bush. God called Himself "I Am Who Am," which means that God is Being, or Existence, itself. God is Life. Jesus declared the Name of God for Himself when He said, "Before Abraham was, I AM." Jesus also declared Himself to be "the Way, and the Truth, and the Life."

God has shared the gift of life with mankind, and with many other creatures for the good of mankind. God said, "I call Heaven and Earth to witness this day, that I have set before you life and death, blessing and cursing. Choose therefore life, that both you and your seed [offspring] may live" (Deut 30:19). Jesus said: "I am come that they may have life, and may have it more abundantly" (John 10:10).

Life is the great gift of God. In this course, we will study the gift of life, and we will grow in our appreciation of God and His gift of life.

In Genesis, we read:

God said, "Let the Earth bring forth vegetation: every kind of plant that bears seed and every kind of fruit tree on Earth that bears fruit with its seed in it." And so it happened: the Earth brought forth every kind of plant that bears seed and every kind of fruit tree on Earth that bears fruit with its seed in it. God saw how good it was. Evening came, and morning followed - the third day. Then God said: "Let there be lights in the dome of the sky, to separate day from night. Let them mark the fixed times, the days and the years, and serve as luminaries in the dome of the sky, to shed light upon the Earth." And so it happened: God made the two great lights, the greater one to govern the day, and the lesser one to govern the night; and he made the stars. God set them in the dome of the sky, to shed light upon the Earth, to govern the day and the night, and to separate the light from the darkness. God saw how good it was. Evening came, and morning followed - the fourth day.

Then God said, "Let the water teem with an abundance of living creatures, and on the Earth let birds fly beneath the dome of the sky." And so it happened.

God created the great sea monsters and all kinds of swimming creatures with which the water teems, and all kinds of winged birds. God saw how good it was, and God blessed them, saying, "Be fertile, multiply, and fill the water of the seas; and let the birds multiply on the Earth." Evening came, and morning followed - the fifth day.

Then God said, "Let the Earth bring forth all kinds of living creatures: cattle, creeping things, and wild animals of all kinds." And so it happened: God made all kinds of wild animals, all kinds of cattle, and all kinds of creeping things of the Earth. God saw how good it was.

Then God said: "Let us make man in our image, after our likeness. Let them have dominion over the fish of the sea, the birds of the air, and the cattle, and over all the wild animals and all the creatures that crawl on the ground."

God created man in His image; in the divine image He created him; male and female He created them. God blessed them, saying: "Be fertile and multiply; fill the Earth and subdue it. Have dominion over the fish of the sea, the birds of the air, and all the living things that move on the Earth."

God also said: "See, I give you every seed-bearing plant all over the Earth and every tree that has seed-bearing fruit on it to be your food; and to all the animals of the land, all the birds of the air, and all the living creatures that crawl on the ground, I give all the green plants for food." And so it happened. God looked at everything He had made, and He found it very good. Evening came, and morning followed - the sixth day" (Genesis 1).

The Book of Genesis, in fact, all of Holy Scripture, teaches us the truths about God's work of creation. It tell us that God - the Father, the Son, and the Holy Spirit - is the Author of Life. God is the Creator of all life. Jesus, as the New Testament tells us, is the One for Whom and through Whom all things were created; and the Holy Spirit is "the Giver of Life."

The Book of Genesis tells us several other truths about creation. Genesis tells us that God **created** everything out of nothing. He did not simply form His creatures from materials that had already existed. Before God's creative act, no material things existed, none at all.

The Genesis account teaches that His physical creation was perfectly ordered. God created in an orderly fashion, in a perfect and purposeful manner. The order of His creation teaches a hierarchy of creatures from the least to the greatest, that is, to the summit of creation: man. God teaches us in Genesis that life is not the result of a series of random events or a result of chance. Holy Scripture teaches us the truths about God's creation that are necessary for our salvation. Scripture does not, however, provide us the details or a scientific account of creation and life.

This is our Faith. This is what we profess in the Creed, and it is not subject to scientific proof or to the Scientific Method, but our Faith does not exclude scientific understanding or exploration. The Bible is not a science book and was never meant to be. This, though, does not mean that there needs to be conflict between science and religion. In fact, the Catholic Church, through her saints, doctors, and popes, has recognized this throughout the centuries. St. Augustine, St. Thomas Aquinas, and many popes have taught that science is compatible with faith. Many scientists agree. Francis Collins, for example, a modern genetic scientist and convert to Christianity who was appointed to the Pontifical Academy of Sciences by Pope Benedict XVI, has written, "Science is not threatened by God; it is enhanced." Collins reminds us that it is God Who makes science, and all things, possible.

SCIENCE AND LIFE

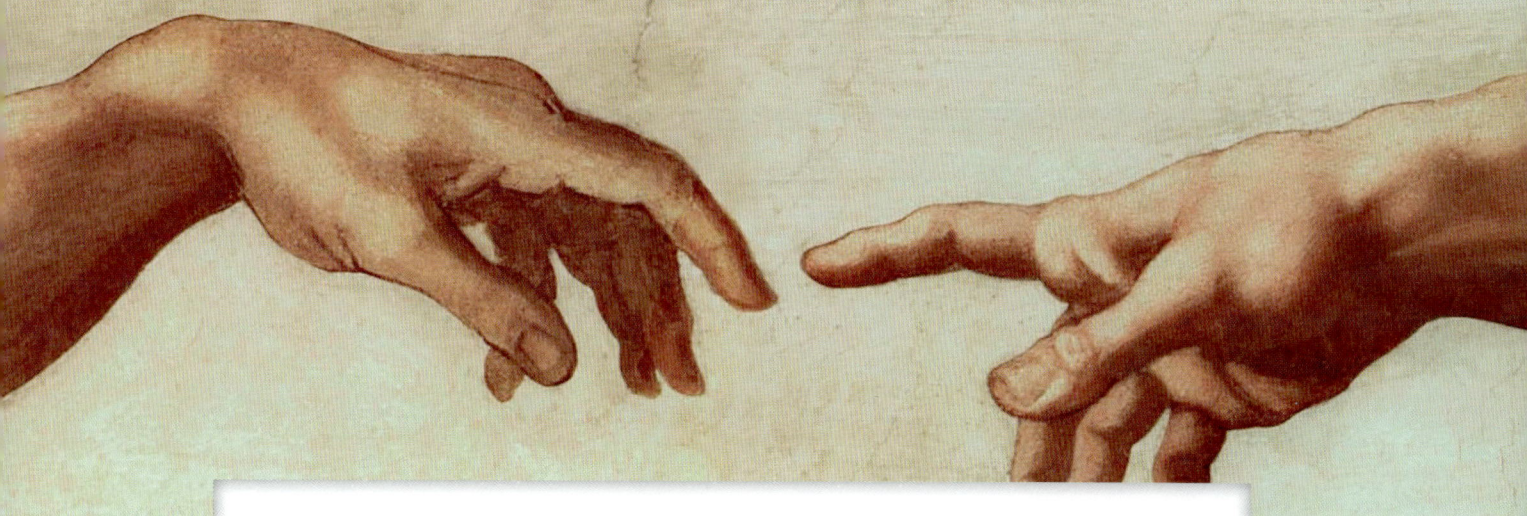

1.1 The Scientific Method

1.2 Living and Non-Living
    A. The Seven Processes of Life
        1. Movement
        2. Respiration
        3. Sensitivity
        4. Growth
        5. Reproduction
        6. Nutrition
        7. Excretion
    B. Viruses

1.3 Order of Creation

1.4 Purpose of Creation

Life Science for Young Catholics

Chapter 1
Science and Life

1.1 The Scientific Method

The **Scientific Method** consists of procedures involving systematic observation, measurement, and experiment of some object, event, or phenomena. The scientific method includes formulating an idea, called the hypothesis, and testing it. If the results agree with expectations, the hypothesis may be temporarily accepted, but it is not proved to be always true. If the results disagree with expectations, the hypothesis will need to be modified or rejected.

While our Faith is not subject to the Scientific Method, the study of science does utilize this procedure. St. Peter said in his first epistle that we should "Always be prepared to give an answer to everyone who asks you to give the reason for the hope that you have."

A scientific **hypothesis** (hi-**poth**-uh-sis) is the idea, or explanation, to be tested based on the currently known facts about something. The hypothesis tries to explain how those facts fit together and how the "something" works. The hypothesis, or explanation, can then be tested by a designed experiment. If the hypothesis was correct, the experiment should give the expected results. If the expected results do not happen, then a new explanation or hypothesis must be found to fit the updated set of facts.

The procedure for investigating something with the Scientific Method is to first ask a question, then research the topic and formulate a hypothesis or theory. After a theory is developed, test the hypothesis with an experiment; and lastly, analyze the results and draw conclusions. If the results support the hypothesis, you write a report. If the results do not support the hypothesis, rethink the question and develop a new hypothesis, and repeat the procedure.

Scientists have been using the Scientific Method since the 1600s.

With this in mind, we now begin our journey into Life Science - the study of God's living creation.

> **Section Review —**
> **1.1 The Scientific Method**
>
> 1. What is the Scientific Method?
> 2. What is the process used to implement the Scientific Method?

CHAPTER 1: SCIENCE AND LIFE

1.2 Living and Non-living

What does it mean to be alive? Look at the pictures below. It is not difficult to distinguish the living organisms in these photos from the non-living. Without much thought, we can quickly organize each photo into one of two groups, living or non-living.

The flowers, of course, are living as you are. Obviously, the dog and the eagle are living. The fossil, though an impression of a once-living creature, is not alive; nor are the rocks.

What are characteristics of the flowers, the dog, and the eagle that make them alive? What characteristics do all living things possess that non-living things do not? While even a young child can tell the difference, as we get older, we study the difference a little more closely.

A. The Seven Processes of Life

Scientists have discovered that all living things are composed of cells, the smallest units of life, and all living things share seven characteristics, or seven life processes. These life processes are: movement, respiration, sensitivity, growth, reproduction, nutrition, and excretion. It is these seven processes by which scientists identify living organisms. An organism **MUST** exhibit **ALL** seven of the life processes to be classified as living. As we study living things, we study these processes.

1. Movement. All living organisms move in some way and during some phase of development. Movement is sometimes obvious, such as in the dog running or the eagle flying. Plant movement may not be quite so obvious at first glance; however, plants do move. A growing seedling may turn to the right or to the left, and tendrils of a vine may wrap around nearby supports. Some plants, such as the Venus Fly Trap, have moveable parts that close like jaws around unsuspecting insects.

Some organisms can move only during certain stages of development. For example, adult sponges are stationary, attached at the base to the sea floor, while the immature sponge larvae are freely swimming. Non-living things do not have the capacity to move unless moved by some outside force.

2. Respiration (*res-puh-**rey**-shuhn*). All living organisms have the capacity to take in, transform, and use energy. In most living things, the process by which this occurs is known as cellular respiration. In

Some plants, such as the Venus Fly Trap, have moveable parts that close like jaws around unsuspecting insects.

WORDS TO REMEMBER

hypothesis (*hi-**poth**-uh-sis*): is an idea, or explanation, based on the currently known facts about something. The hypothesis tries to explain how those facts fit together and how the "something" works.

respiration (*res-puh-**rey**-shuhn*): All living organisms have the capacity to take in, transform, and use energy. The process by which all living organisms take in, transform, and use energy is known as cellular respiration. In cellular respiration, living organisms take in "food" for the energy needed to perform the processes of life, and carbon dioxide is produced.

Scientific Method: consists of procedures involving systematic observation, measurement, and experiment, of some object or event or phenomena. The scientific method includes formulating some ideas, testing them, and modifying the ideas, thus developing a hypothesis about that object or event or phenomena.

Flower

Fossil

Dog

Rocks

Eagle

Life Science for Young Catholics

cellular respiration, living organisms take in "food" for the energy needed to perform the processes of life, and carbon dioxide is produced. As you may already know, carbon dioxide is one of the three major gases in the air. The energy produced in respiration fuels growth and all other life processes.

Non-living objects may use energy but in an entirely different way. A car certainly needs gasoline to power its engine, but the car does not obtain its own gas or "food source," or produce its own gas or "food source," or transform the energy stored in the "food" to usable energy. The car's engine simply burns the fuel. A rock, likewise, may absorb energy, such as heat, when it is exposed to the sun. However, the rock has no capacity to transform the heat energy so that it can walk around or use it for other life processes.

3. Sensitivity. All living organisms can detect changes in their environment and can respond to stimuli, such as heat or cold; this is called sensitivity. We humans react to our environment and make adjustments continually. At times, we even think about our adjustments, such as when we feel cold and, as a result, put on more clothing. At times, though, our bodies are able to sense the need for changes and self-adjust without our conscious effort. This is the case when we feel cold and our bodies begin to shiver to produce heat and to maintain constant body temperature.

As humans, we perceive the environment around us with our five senses: taste, smell, sight, touch, and hearing. Plants also can react to external stimuli by growing toward the light. The fungal spores of mushrooms react to humidity and moisture; when conditions are just right, they grow into mushrooms. Plant a seed in moist dirt, and you will see a flower grow!

As for non-living objects, they have no such ability to sense or react to changes in the environment. Rocks do not internally regulate their temperature, run away from some perceived danger, or become hungry by smelling their favorite food.

4. Growth. All living things grow. Plants grow throughout their lifetime. Animals and humans grow until adulthood. After reaching maturity, though, individual cells in our bodies continue to grow and to be replaced throughout our lifetimes. Growth in living organisms is from within the organism. Growth is not simply an addition of external material, such as in "growing" crystals in the bottom of a solution.

5. Reproduction. All living organisms must be able to produce offspring similar to themselves. Reproduction may result from only one "parent," or it may be from the union of the genetic material from two parents. Some organisms, such as sponges and bacteria, can reproduce from either one or two "parents." Non-living things are not capable of reproducing themselves.

6. Nutrition. All living organisms need nutrition for life processes. Living organisms take in nutrients from their environment and use the energy from the nutrients for life processes. Plants absorb water and nutrients from the soil, and use energy from sunlight to make their own food, sugar, through photosynthesis. Most living organisms are not able to make their own food, but must acquire food or nutrition from other living organisms.

Plants can react to external stimuli by growing toward the light. The fungal spores of mushrooms react to humidity and moisture; when conditions are just right, they grow into mushrooms.

CHAPTER 1: SCIENCE AND LIFE

7. Excretion (*ex-**skree**-shuhn*). All living organisms produce byproducts from their **metabolic** (*met-uh-**bol**-ik*) **processes**, which are the processes necessary for life, such as the intake of nutrients and respiration. These byproducts are either useless or harmful to the organism. Excretion is the removal from the organism of these byproducts or wastes. Oxygen, for example, is produced as a byproduct of photosynthesis, and is released from plants. Animals release carbon dioxide waste when exhaling, and remove other substances in urine and sweat. Excretion is an active process, even for the simplest single-celled organisms.

Two of the above processes, excretion and sensitivity, allow the living organism to maintain homeostasis under changing conditions. **Homeostasis** (*hoh-mee-o-**stey**-sis*) is a stable internal environment which can be maintained despite changes in the external environment. For example, when we get hot from sitting in the sun, our bodies sense the temperature change externally. We then may decide to move out of the direct sunlight to cool ourselves. Our bodies react to the stimulus of the sun's heat by beginning to sweat. Sweating cools the body and helps the body to maintain a constant internal temperature. A constant internal temperature is necessary to keep our life processes, such as cellular respiration and growth, functioning properly.

WORDS TO REMEMBER

sensitivity: the ability of living organisms to detect changes in their environment and to respond to stimuli, such as heat or cold

growth: the gradual increase in size of an animal or vegetable body over time; the development of an organism, e.g., of a plant from a seed to full maturity.

reproduction: the ability of organisms to produce offspring similar to themselves. Non-living things are not capable of reproducing themselves.

nutrition: the process by which all living organisms take in nutrients from their environment and use the energy from the nutrients for life processes.

excretion: the active process through which living organisms remove by-products of metabolism from themselves.

metabolic processes: the processes necessary for life, such as the intake of nutrients and respiration, for the growth, repair, and reproduction of the organism.

homeostasis: a stable internal environment which can be maintained despite changes in the external environment.

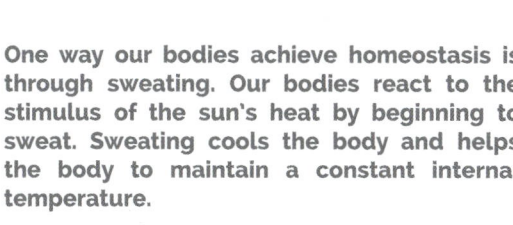

One way our bodies achieve homeostasis is through sweating. Our bodies react to the stimulus of the sun's heat by beginning to sweat. Sweating cools the body and helps the body to maintain a constant internal temperature.

QUICK REVIEW: The Seven Processes of Life

All living things share seven characteristics, or seven life processes. An organism MUST exhibit ALL seven of the life processes to be classified as living. These life processes are:

1. Movement
2. Respiration
3. Sensitivity
4. Growth
5. Reproduction
6. Nutrition
7. Excretion

Life Science for Young Catholics 7

CHAPTER 1: SCIENCE AND LIFE

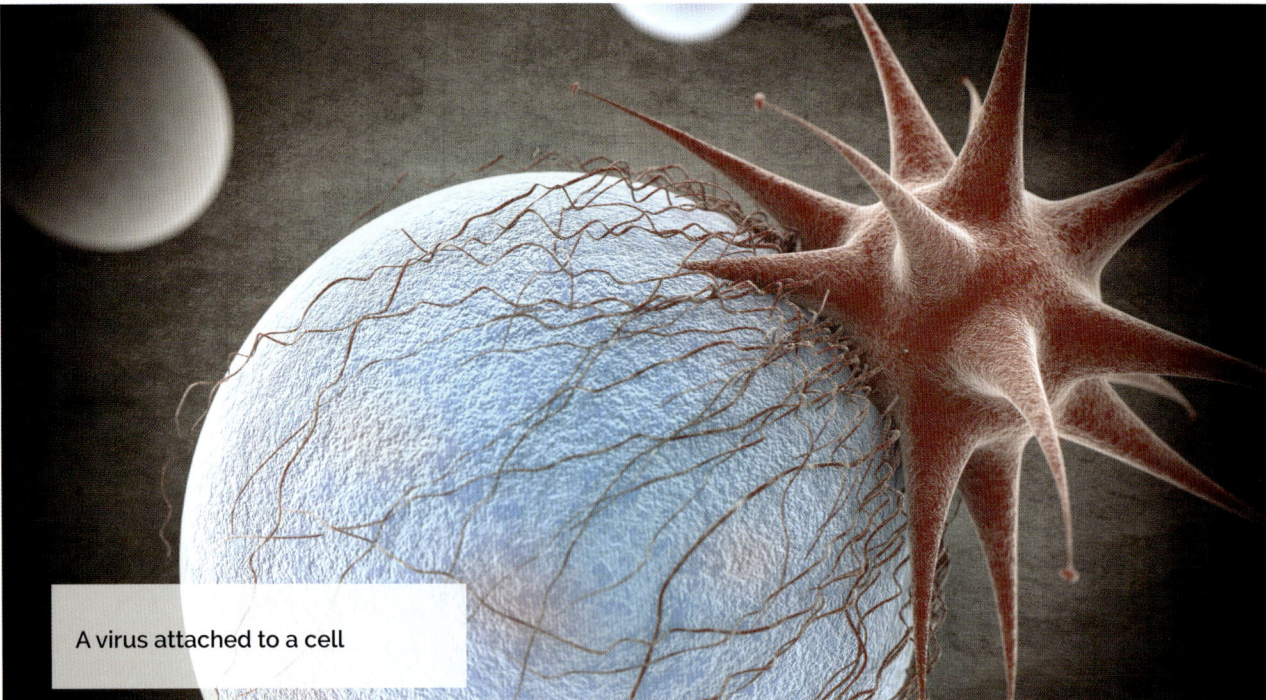

A virus attached to a cell

B. Viruses

The differences between the living organisms and the non-living objects on page 5 are obvious. The flowers, the dog, and the eagle clearly demonstrate all seven of the life processes, and are easily classified as living. The fossil and the rocks clearly lack all seven of the life processes and so are easily categorized as non-living. However, surprisingly, sometimes it is not so easy to be so clear about the seven processes, as is the case with the **virus**. Many scientists classify viruses as "between" living and non-living. Let's investigate.

A virus is a very tiny particle, which is made up of some of the same components, proteins and genetic material as living cells. Viruses can cause infection in all living organisms, from bacteria to man. However, viruses are not composed of cells; they are less than cells, of a category which we call subcellular particles.

Viruses do not move on their own. Virus particles can attach themselves to cells and move only with the cell's movement. Viruses do not have any means of cellular respiration, and therefore require no nutrition and produce no waste. Hence, viruses have no need for excretion.

Viruses do reproduce, but only through a cell. The virus, after attaching to a cell, takes over the cell's machinery and reprograms it to make more virus particles. Virus particles are formed, or grown, but by the hijacked cell. Some virus particles seem to have sensitivity and the ability to change themselves, making them more able to "survive" in the presence of certain medicines.

Because they reproduce, viruses seem to mimic life in some ways. However, they carry on only some life processes when in association with a true living cell, or host cell.

(Cells are the basic units of living things. Every living cell carries on all of the seven processes of life. Cell theory is discussed in Chapter 3.)

Alone, viruses are unable to maintain any life process and they lack any true cellular structure. Viruses, then, are non-living by strict definition.

Section Review — 1.2 Living and Non-living

1. What distinguishes created things as living as opposed to non-living?
2. List the seven processes that organisms must have to be considered alive.
3. Why is a virus considered to be non-living?
4. What is meant by homeostasis?

Life Science for Young Catholics

CHAPTER 1: SCIENCE AND LIFE

1.3 Order of Creation

We have begun to organize God's created world into the living and the non-living, but in this Life Science course, we will limit our study to the living creation. To do so, we must have an organized approach. If we do not have an organized approach, it would be impossible to learn about so many different organisms that have been identified. Scientists over the centuries have agreed to have an organized approach to study various organisms.

Aristotle devised a classification system for living things.

Scientifically classifying and naming God's living creatures for purposes of study and organization is called taxonomy (*tax-on-o-mee*). Such attempts to classify and name can be traced back to Aristotle, a student of many subjects, including biology. Aristotle, a Greek scientist, lived in the third century B.C., that is, Before Christ. Aristotle devised a classification system or scheme based on similarities between organisms and based on a hierarchy from "lowest to highest," with humans being the highest, of course! Some distinguishing characteristics in Aristotle's scheme included: animals with blood and animals without blood; animals that lived on the land and animals that lived in the water.

Over the centuries, many other scientists, mostly those studying plants, or botanists, devised many different systems of classification.

In the 1700s, Carolus Linnaeus (*kar-uh-luhs li-nee-uhs*), a Swedish botanist, devised a system of classification and naming of organisms that remains the basic framework of the modern system used today. His classification was based on the structures of organisms as he saw through direct observations. Linnaeus' framework included three kingdoms, which were further subdivided into Phylum (*fie-luhm*), Class, Order, **Genus**, and **Species**. This structure is still today the basis of taxonomy, the scientific organization of living things. Carolus Linnaeus is considered to be the modern "Father of Taxonomy."

Linnaeus also contributed to the naming of organisms. He was the first to adopt a **binomial nomenclature** (*bahy-noh-mee-uhl noh-muhn-kley-cher*), which means a two-part naming system. In this system, organisms are identified according to the genus and species. A genus is a group of organisms or species that are structurally similar. A species is a group of organisms

Carolus Linnaeus, a Swedish botanist, is the "Father of Taxonomy."

Aa WORDS TO REMEMBER

virus: a very tiny particle, which is made up of some of the same components, proteins and genetic material as living cells. Viruses are not composed of cells; they are less than cells, which we call subcellular particles. Viruses do not move on their own. Viruses do not reproduce on their own, but only through a cell. Viruses carry on only some life processes when in association with a true living cell, or host cell. Viruses, then, are non-living by strict definition.

host cell: the cell of a living organism in which a parasite or virus lives.

taxonomy: Scientific classification and naming of God's living creatures for purposes of study through an organized approach.

binomial nomenclature: a two-part naming system for living things. In this system, organisms are identified according to the genus and species.

botanist: a scientist who studies plants.

genus: a group of organisms or species that are structurally similar.

species: a group of organisms having common characteristics and capable of mating with one another to produce fertile offspring.

domain: classification of organisms based on the complexity of their cell structure. Modern scientists now consider this to be the broadest classification category of living things.

Life Science for Young Catholics

CHAPTER 1: SCIENCE AND LIFE

All organisms are now divided into three Domains and six Kingdoms.

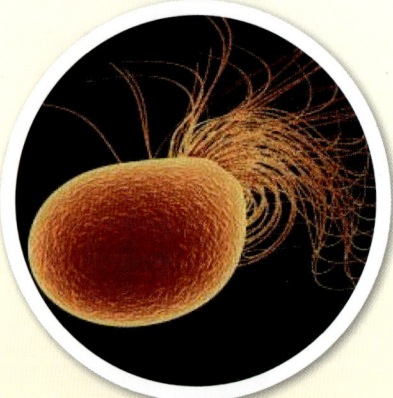

DOMAIN ARCHAE
Kingdom Archae

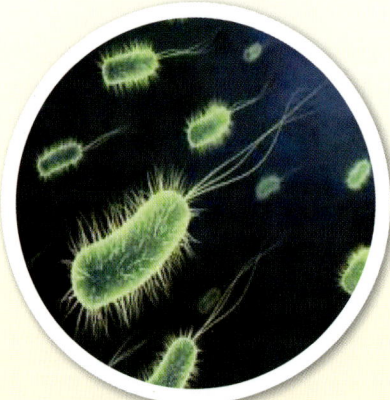

DOMAIN BACTERIA
Kingdom Bacteria

DOMAIN EUKARYA
Kingdom Protista
Kingdom Fungi
Kingdom Plantae
Kingdom Animalia

THE STRUCTURE OF TAXONOMY

Domain
Kingdom
Phylum
Class
Order
Family
Genus
Species

having common characteristics and capable of mating with one another to produce fertile offspring.

The binomial nomenclature becomes the scientific name and is always written italicized, in Latin, and with the genus capitalized and the species following in all lower case letters. Linnaeus was the first to designate human beings as **Homo sapiens**. *Homo sapiens* is Latin for "wise man."

In the early 1990s, the domain was added to the classification table. Domains classify organisms based on the complexity of their cell structure. Modern scientists now consider this to be the most widely accepted classification scheme:

Domain, Kingdom, Phylum, Class, Order, Family, Genus, Species. This is simply a way to break down and classify living organisms. A good way to remember these eight words would be by using a phrase made up of the first initial of each word: D-K-P-C-O-F-G-S. That phrase could be:

"Dear King Peter Cried Out 'For Goodness Sake.'"

Of course, you may wish to make up your own memory phrase!

Section Review – 1.3 Order of Creation.

1. What is taxonomy?
2. Who is considered to be the modern "Father of Taxonomy"?
3. What is binomial nomenclature?
4. What is the binomial nomenclature for humans?
5. What is the most widely used modern, classification scheme used today?
6. What are the three domains and which kingdoms belong to each?

10 Life Science for Young Catholics

1.4 Purpose of Creation

The Catholic Church teaches that God created the world and all its creatures out of His goodness, and, because of this, all creation shares in His goodness. The "goodness" of creation is repeated six times in the first chapter of Genesis alone. After all, what father would prepare a gift for his children that was not good? The Church teaches that all of creation is a "gift addressed to man." The purpose of this gift of creation is twofold.

First, God reveals Himself to us in and through His creation. As the Church teaches through Scripture and Tradition, "The world was created for the glory of God." This does not mean that God created the world and all of its creatures to increase His glory, but rather *to reveal His glory* to us through His creatures. By learning about the life forms that God has created, we can clearly understand the evidence of God's existence, and know of His goodness, truth, and beauty.

Second, God gives man the *gift of creation* with instructions to have "dominion" over all its creatures and to "fill the Earth and subdue it" (Genesis 1:26-28). This does not mean that we are to control the Earth for our own personal purposes, but that we are to be responsible caretakers of creation for all mankind to share.

It is important to know that the Church believes and teaches that God did not create the Earth and all of its creatures in the state of final perfection, but rather in a state of a continuing journey to an "ultimate perfection." Mankind was blessed to be fruitful and multiply, to fill God's creation with additional souls to know, love, and serve God, and to share "His everlasting happiness in Heaven," the ultimate, perfect perfection. In giving us the gift of creation, God also gives us the responsibility of cooperating with His plan. So, God's creation—Heaven and Earth, all things visible and invisible—is given to us as a means to know, love, and serve God in this life and in the next!

> ### DID YOU KNOW?
>
> **A 1999 Article in *National Geographic* Magazine listed the following numbers of species of each:**
>
> 963,000 insects & myriapods
> 270,000 plants
> 100,000 fungi & lichens
> 80,000 protozoans & algae
> 70,000 mollusks
> 40,000 crustaceans
> 25,000 nematodes
> 22,000 fish
> 20,000 flatworms
> 10,500 reptiles & amphibians
> 10,000 birds
> 10,000 sponges
> 45,000 mammals
> 4,000 bacteria & archae bacteria

Chapter 1 Review

A. List the seven life processes common to all living creatures and match each with the appropriate definition or description.

1. _____
2. _____
3. _____
4. _____
5. _____
6. _____
7. _____

a. the addition of new cells or substance to a living organism

b. expelling wastes from a cell or other living organism

c. producing an offspring

d. the ability of an organism to reposition itself

e. ingesting or absorbing nutrients

f. the ability of an organism to respond to changes in its environment

g. energy transformation within an organism

B. Categorize each of the following as living or non-living. Use "L" or "NL."

    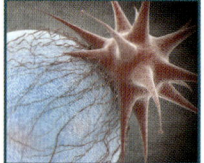 

_____ _____ _____ _____ _____ _____

C. Answer the following questions.

1. What is the Scientific Method?
2. Why is a virus considered to be non-living?
3. What is meant by homeostasis?
4. How do plants obtain nutrition?
5. What is taxonomy?
6. Who is considered to be the modern "Father of Taxonomy?"
7. What is binomial nomenclature?
8. What is the binomial nomenclature for humans?
9. What is the most widely used modern classification scheme used today?
10. Name two purposes that God had for creation.

Chapter 1: "Words to Remember" Crossword

ACROSS

5. a very tiny particle, which is made up of some of the same components, proteins and genetic material, as living cells
8. an active process through which living organisms remove by-products of metabolism from themselves
10. organisms take in nutrients from their environment and use the energy from the nutrients for life processes
12. a stable internal environment which can be maintained despite changes in the external environment
13. ___ nomenclature is a two-part naming system for living things.
15. scientific classification and naming of God's living creatures for purposes of study through an organized approach
16. a group of organisms or species that are structurally similar
17. the ability of organisms to produce offspring similar to themselves

DOWN

1. an idea, or explanation, based on the currently known facts about something
2. a Greek scientist and philosopher who developed a classification system for organisms
3. the gradual increase in size of an animal or vegetable body over time
4. a group of organisms having common characteristics and capable of mating with one another to produce fertile offspring
6. the ability of living organisms to detect changes in their environment and to respond to stimuli, such as heat or cold
7. The ___ Method consists of procedures involving systematic observation, measurement, and experiment, of some object or event or phenomena.
9. ___ processes are the processes necessary for life, such as the intake of nutrients and respiration, for the growth, repair, and reproduction of the organism.
11. scientists who study plants
14. classifies organisms based on the complexity of their cell structure

2 THE CHEMISTRY OF LIFE

2.1 Introduction

2.2 The Basics of Chemistry

2.3 Carbohydrates

2.4 Proteins

2.5 Lipids - Fats

2.6 Nucleic Acids

2.7 A Special Molecule: ATP

2.8 Conclusion: Order & Wisdom of Creation

Chapter 2
The Chemistry of Life

2.1 Introduction

Did you know that about 65% of your body is made up of water?

Approximately 93% of your body is made up of just three chemicals: oxygen, carbon, and hydrogen. Carbon, hydrogen, and oxygen are also the chemicals that make up most sugars, including table sugar. So maybe your mother knows what she is talking about when she says, "You're sweet."

The body is what makes us different from the angels. Angels, like God, are pure spirits. People have immortal souls, which are the spirit part of man. Our souls make us somewhat like the angels.

The body is so important that the Son of God chose to obtain a human body for Himself. The human body is the temple of the Holy Spirit. Therefore, your body should be treated with the utmost reverence and respect. God gave us our bodies and souls "on loan." As with the three servants who were given talents by their master, God expects us to return our bodies and souls to Him with a profit, through a life of obedience to His laws. If we do, He will reward us with eternal happiness in Heaven.

2.2 The Basics of Chemistry

Chemistry is the study of **matter**, its composition and properties. **Matter** is anything that has **mass** and takes up space. Matter is any substance that can exist in one of three phases: solid, liquid, or gas. Air is matter that is in the gas phase. Rocks, iron, and lead are matter in the solid phase. Water is matter in the liquid phase.

Living organisms are made of matter, too. We humans are composed of matter; dogs, monkeys, fish, and bacteria are all composed of matter. Matter can be classified as living or non-living. Similarly, chemistry, or the study of matter, can be divided into two basic branches: inorganic chemistry and organic chemistry. Inorganic chemistry is the study of non-living, non-carbon-based matter, while organic chemistry is the study of the carbon-based matter of organisms.

Carbon is the basic element of life; therefore, **organic chemistry** is the study of carbon-containing matter. The study of all the chemical reactions occurring in living organisms is called **biochemistry** (***bi·oh·kem·is·tree***).

From the Book of Genesis, we learn that God's creation is ordered in His wisdom. This means that there is logical order in all that God has created. It would follow, then, that all matter that exists has order. Scientists have discovered that the basic unit of all matter is the **atom**.

Life Science for Young Catholics 15

CHAPTER 2: THE CHEMISTRY OF LIFE

Simple Model of the Atom.

Red: protons.
Blue: neutrons.
Black: electrons.

Atoms vary in size, but all are approximately one million times smaller than the thickness of one human hair. This means that one million atoms lined up side by side would stretch across the width of one hair from your head! Scientists' knowledge of atoms took many centuries to discover. A scientist in ancient Greece proposed the idea of the atom, but it wasn't until the 1700s and after that modern scientists learned to unlock the secrets of the atom.

Scientists now know that an atom is the smallest unit of an **element**. An element is a pure substance, that is, a substance in its simplest form, which cannot be broken down further by normal chemical means.

Scientists have discovered many elements. Hydrogen is an element; helium is an element; carbon is the basic element of life. All known elements have been classified and organized by scientists into a table, or chart, known as the **Periodic Table of the Elements**.

Let's look at a typical atom. An atom is made of positively charged particles called **protons** and uncharged particles called **neutrons** (**noo·**trons) in the center, called the **nucleus**. The nucleus is surrounded by negatively charged **electrons**.

Protons and electrons have electric charges. These charges are of equal strength, but opposite direction, like the north and south poles of a magnet. In fact, scientists have learned that magnetic forces are strongly related to electric forces. In magnets, the north pole and the south pole attract each other, but two north poles will repel each other. It is the same with protons and electrons. Positively charged protons tend to repel each other, but will attract negatively charged electrons. Protons are kept together in the nucleus because of other forces that are stronger than the force of repulsion in the like charges.

The nucleus is the center of the atom. The nucleus is composed of protons and neutrons. Electrons orbit around the nucleus. The electrons orbit in paths that are different distances from the nucleus. These paths are called **shells**.

Each shell holds a specified number of electrons. For the purposes of this course, it is enough to know that the first shell holds up to two electrons, and the second shell holds a maximum of eight electrons. The number of electrons in the outermost shell determines how one atom will chemically combine with another.

The number of protons is the **atomic number** for that element. For example, all hydrogen atoms have one proton in the nucleus. All helium atoms have two protons in the nucleus. All carbon atoms have six protons in the nucleus. If a proton is added or subtracted from a nucleus, the element would be changed into a different element.

Generally, in an element, the number of electrons that orbit the nucleus of an atom equals the number of protons in the nucleus. The nucleus of an atom may also contain **neutrons**. Neutrons add only mass to the atom; they do not have any positive or negative charge. The sum of the number of protons plus the number of neutrons in an atom is called the **atomic mass number**.

On the Periodic Table of the Elements (usually abbreviated as just the Periodic Table), the elements are arranged in order of increasing atomic number. True to God's order of creation, all the elements on the Periodic Table in a vertical column

16 Life Science for Young Catholics

form a **family** or **group**, and they share certain characteristics. This did not happen by random chance alone. God created the elements and the laws that govern their behavior to uphold and sustain His creation.

A standard Periodic Table of Elements also provides the atomic mass number and the chemical abbreviation for each element.

View, explore, and study the Periodic Table of Elements. Find the following on the Periodic Table: carbon, hydrogen, oxygen, nitrogen, and phosphorus. These five elements are the most abundant elements in the human body. They make up about 95% of your weight. These five elements are so important that you should memorize them. To help you remember these, use the code **C-PHON**(e), for "cell phone." **C** for Carbon, **P** for Phosphorus, **H** for hydrogen, **O** for oxygen, and **N** for nitrogen, and **e** for end of the assignment.

The functional substance of most of creation is the **molecule** (*mol•e•kyool*). A molecule is a combination of two or more atoms, either of the same kind or of two or more kinds. For example, one molecule of hydrogen consists of two hydrogen atoms clinging together. One molecule of water consists of two hydrogen atoms attached to one oxygen atom. So a molecule is the smallest particle of a substance that retains all of the properties of that substance.

In summary, matter is composed of atoms, and atoms are composed of protons, electrons, and neutrons. Atoms are the smallest unit that determines an element. Atoms, then, are basic building blocks that combine with other atoms to form molecules.

When two or more elements combine, they form a new substance, or **compound**. The ratio of the elements in any compound is always the same for the molecules of that particular compound. For example, in water molecules, there are always two hydrogen atoms to one oxygen atom.

WORDS TO REMEMBER

chemistry: the study of matter, its composition and properties

organic chemistry: the study of matter of living organisms. Organic chemistry is the study of carbon-containing matter.

inorganic chemistry: the study of non-living matter

atom: the basic unit of all matter

nucleus: the center of an atom, made up of protons and neutrons. The large part of the mass of the atom is in the nucleus.

matter: anything that has mass and takes up space

mass: a property of a physical body which determines resistance to being accelerated by a force and the strength of its mutual gravitational attraction with other bodies

carbon: the basic element of life

biochemistry: the study of all the chemical reactions occurring in organisms

protons: positively charged sub-units within the nucleus of an atom

neutrons: uncharged, neutral sub-units within the nucleus of an atom

electrons: tiny, negatively charged sub-units of an atom that orbit about the nucleus

atomic number: is unique for each type of atom, or element. It is determined by the number of protons in that element.

compound: a combination of two or more elements. The ratio of the elements in any compound is always the same for the molecules of that particular compound.

molecule: the functional substance of most of creation. A molecule is a combination of two or more atoms, either of the same kind or of two or more kinds.

One molecule of water consists of two hydrogen atoms attached to one oxygen atom.

Life Science for Young Catholics

CHAPTER 2: THE CHEMISTRY OF LIFE

Molecules, atoms, and particles in motion.

SCIENCE TIPS

The Periodic Table of Elements summarizes the important information about each element.

In this figure:

C is the chemical abbreviation for Carbon.

6 is the atomic number, or number of protons, which is also the number of electrons.

12.011 is the atomic MASS number, or the number of protons PLUS the number of neutrons.

[Periodic table box: 6, C, Carbon, 12.011]

A **molecule** may be as simple as two atoms of the same element bonded together, or a molecule can be a large number of different atoms bonded together.

Molecules can be inorganic, such as table salt, or organic, such as sugar. Table salt is an inorganic compound formed by sodium and chlorine.

Organic molecules contain carbon and are usually made by organisms. Inorganic molecules do not contain carbon, and are not made by organisms.

Salt is non-organic; it is found in nature but it does not contain carbon, and it is not made by living organisms. Sugar is made of carbon, hydrogen, and oxygen, and it is made in plants. Carbon is the central element of life, because all organic molecules contain carbon.

Large organic molecules, called **macromolecules** (mak-roh-**mol**-uh-kyools), along with water, provide the basis for life in all living things.

Macromolecules:

1. provide and store energy needed for life processes,

2. help regulate and direct the chemical reactions necessary for all life,

3. store and pass on the genetic code of the organism.

These large molecules form the basic structural units of all living organisms. There are many, many unique macromolecules in living organisms.

However, only four basic groups of macromolecules provide the basis for all other macromolecules: **carbohydrates** (kahr-boh-**hahy**-dreyts), **proteins**, **lipids**, and **nucleic acids**.

Section Review – 2.2 The Basics of Chemistry

1. What is matter?
2. What are atoms?
3. What is an element?
4. What are organic compounds?
5. Explain what atomic number means.
6. Explain what atomic mass means.
7. Which elements make up 95% of the human body?
8. Table salt is made up of how many elements? What are they? Is table salt organic or inorganic?
9. Define macromolecule. What are the four basic groups of macromolecules?
10. Identify three functions of macromolecules.

Life Science for Young Catholics

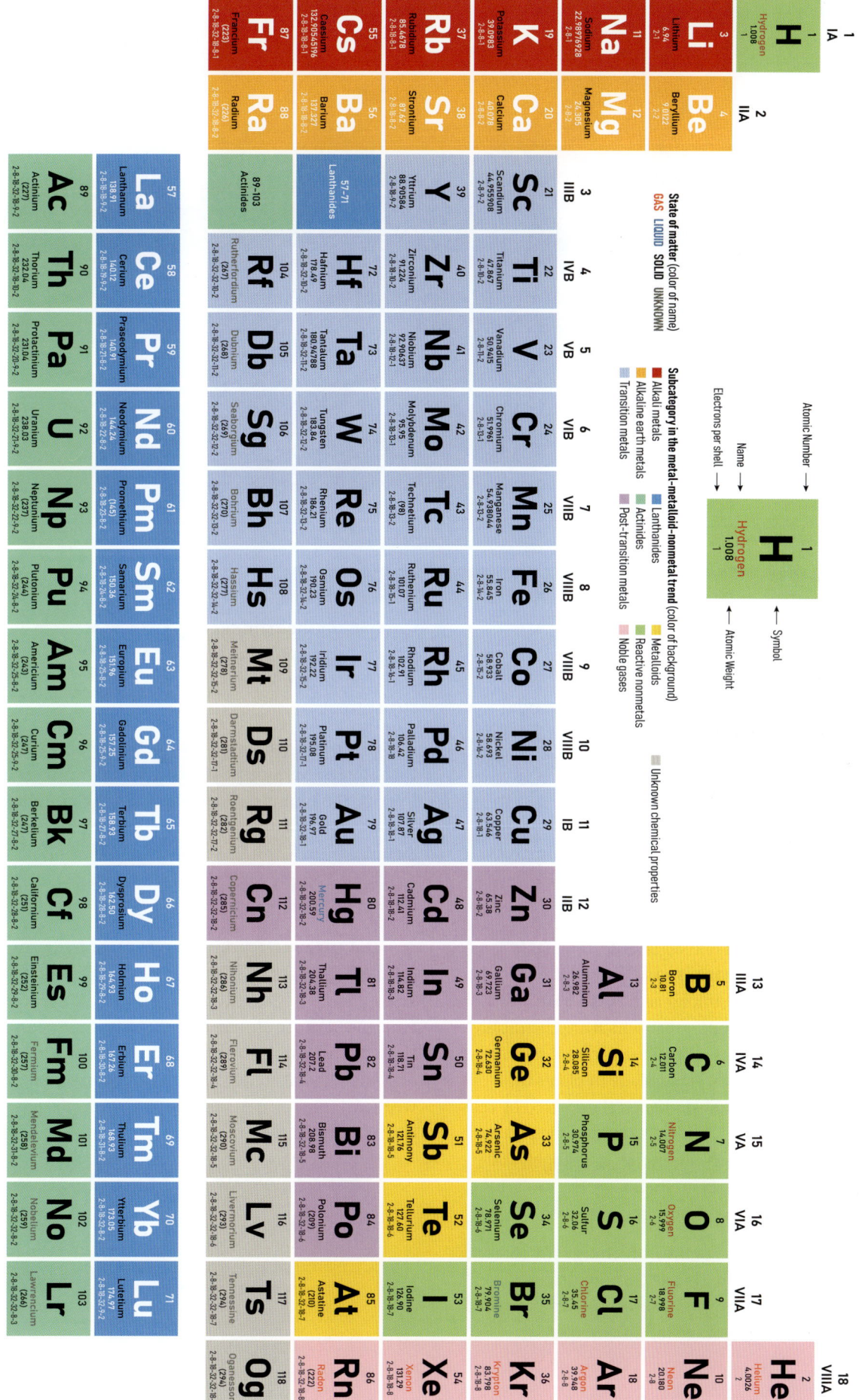

CHAPTER 2: THE CHEMISTRY OF LIFE

Periodic Table of the Elements

Life Science for Young Catholics

2.3 Carbohydrates

Carbohydrate is a familiar word in most vocabularies. When hearing the word "carbohydrate," we might think of pasta, bread, donuts, or table sugar. Actually, all **sugars** and **starches** are carbohydrates. The carbohydrates in the foods that we eat are the molecules that provide living organisms with most of their usable energy.

Along with sugars and starches, a third group of carbohydrates are the **fibers**. Fibers cannot be digested by human beings, but they are important for digestive health.

You probably use table sugar every day. Table sugar is known as **sucrose** (*soo*-*krohs*). Sucrose is made up of two other, simpler sugars, **glucose** (*gloo*-*kohs*) and **fructose** (*frook*-*tohs*), which are chemically bound together. Fructose is "fruit sugar," and has many uses. Glucose is the basic sugar made in plants by **photosynthesis** (*foh*-*tuh*-*sin*-*thuh*-*sis*) and used by cells in your body for energy. Photosynthesis is the process that plants use to convert the energy of sunlight, and the nutrients picked up from the soil by the roots, to make food in the forms of sugar and starches.

Sugars provide the plant with energy for current use. **Sugars** are usually simple carbohydrates. **Starches** are more complex carbohydrates produced in plants for energy storage for an emergency. Complex carbohydrates have more complicated chemical formulas and structures.

Glycogen (*glai*-*kuh*-*jen*) is a complex molecule that stores energy and is found in the muscles and liver of the human body. Glycogen is a complex carbohydrate with multiple strings of glucose. **Cellulose** (*sel*-*yuh*-*lohs*) and **chitin** (*kai*-*tin*) are other complex carbohydrates that give cells strength and support.

The energy stored in simple carbohydrates is released when the carbohydrate is digested. The energy from complex carbohydrates, like starches, is released more slowly and steadily over a longer time as compared to that from simple sugars. This explains why athletes, like marathon runners, will "carb up," or eat a diet high in complex carbohydrates, before a race.

> When hearing the word "carbohydrate," we might think of pasta, bread, donuts, or table sugar. Actually, all sugars and starches are carbohydrates.

> ### Section Review – 2.3 Carbohydrates
> 1. Define carbohydrate.
> 2. Name three groups of carbohydrates.
> 3. Name three specific carbohydrate sugars.

CHAPTER 2: **THE CHEMISTRY OF LIFE**

Proteins are a necessary component of our diet and are found in meat, chicken, turkey, fish, beans, nuts, eggs, cheese, and yogurt.

2.4 Proteins

Proteins are large molecules (atoms bonded together) composed of **amino** (*uh-mee-noh*) **acids**. Amino acids are organic molecules that are the building blocks of proteins. Proteins make up the muscles and other structural parts of the human body. There are twenty-two amino acids that occur naturally in nature.

Proteins serve multiple roles in living organisms. Proteins provide energy. Proteins are a necessary component of our diet and are found in meat, chicken, turkey, fish, beans, nuts, eggs, cheese, and yogurt. Along with providing energy, proteins also provide much of the structure of living things. Some proteins make up the fibers in muscle that allow the muscle to contract and relax. Protein is also the substance of hair and nails.

Proteins can store energy, as in the egg whites of birds. Proteins can act as carriers to transport materials through the bodies of organisms. For example, **hemoglobin** (*hee-muh-gloh-bin*) is a protein in the blood cells of humans that carries oxygen throughout the body.

Section Review – 2.4 Proteins

1. Define proteins.
2. Identify three functions of proteins.
3. Name one particular protein.

WORDS TO REMEMBER

carbohydrate: an organic macromolecule which is an important source of energy for your body. All sugars, starches, and fibers are carbohydrates.

proteins: large molecules composed of amino acids. Proteins make up the muscles and other structural parts of the human body.

sugars: usually simple carbohydrates.

starches: complex carbohydrates produced in plants for energy storage for an emergency

sucrose: common table sugar. It is a carbohydrate made up of two other, simpler sugars, glucose and fructose.

glucose: the basic sugar made in plants by photosynthesis

fructose: "fruit sugar"

photosynthesis: the process that plants use to convert the energy of sunlight, and the nutrients picked up from the soil by the roots, to make food in the forms of sugar and starches

glycogen: a complex molecule that stores energy and is found in the muscles of the human body

cellulose: a complex carbohydrate that gives cells strength and support

amino acids: organic molecules that are the building blocks of proteins. There are twenty-two amino acids that occur naturally in nature.

Life Science for Young Catholics

2.5 Lipids - Fats

The third group of large organic molecules is the lipid group. Lipids are made of **glycerol** (*glis•er•all*) and **fatty acids**.

Glycerol is a three-carbon molecule. A fatty acid is a very long chain of carbon and hydrogen molecules. Carbon can form long chains of carbon-to-carbon bonds. These bonds, like the links in a chain, are very strong, and provide great diversity to God's living creation.

The length of the carbon chain varies in different fatty acids. A **triglyceride** (*try•glis•er•ide*), or basic unit of fat, is formed when three fatty acids bond to one glycerol. Both fats and oils are triglycerides.

Fats and oils have different properties based on the types of fatty acids in their structure. Fats are solids at room temperature while oils are liquids at room temperature.

Waxes and **steroids** are also lipids. Waxes and steroids have structures which are different from those of fats and oils. This, of course, is according to God's plan and gives them different properties and different functions. Waxes form the protective covering over the leaves of plants and in the ears of animals; bees produce wax used to build honeycombs in which to store pollen and provide a place for young bees to develop and grow.

Steroids are lipids with the carbon atoms arranged in rings instead of chains. Steroids, like some small proteins, function as hormones. One steroid, **cholesterol** (*kol•es•ter•all*), is an important component of cell structure and a building block for other steroids.

Fats are also important in long-term energy storage in animals, and provide much nutritional energy. In fact, one gram of fat stores nine times as much energy as the same amount of carbohydrate.

Fats are solids at room temperature while oils are liquids at room temperature.

> ### Section Review – 2.5 Lipids - Fats
> 1. What are triglycerides?
> 2. Name one particular lipid or fat.
> 3. What is cholesterol?

CHAPTER 2: THE CHEMISTRY OF LIFE

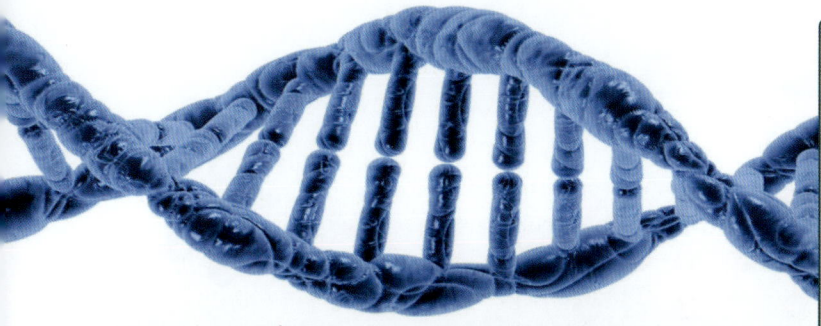

2.6 Nucleic Acids

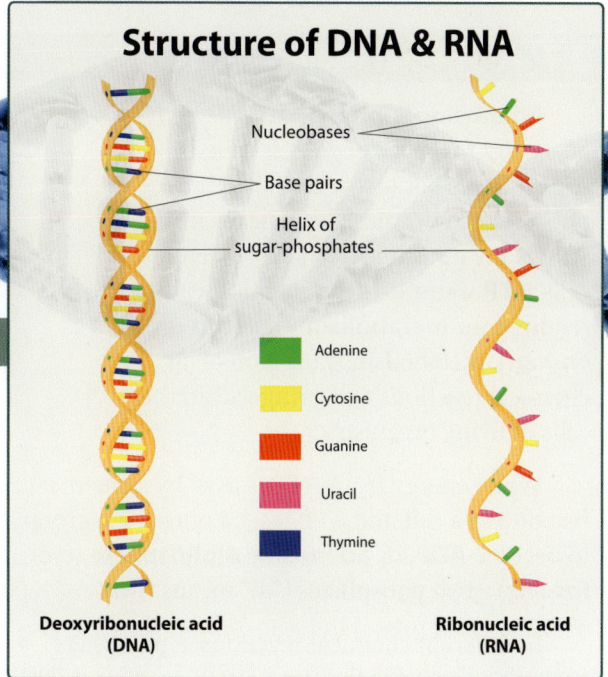

Nucleic (*noo-klee-ik*) **acids** are the large organic molecules which store the **genetic code**. The genetic code contains all information needed to build and maintain a complete organism, and to pass on traits from parents to offspring.

Nucleic acids are made up of **nucleotides** (*noo·klee·o·tides*). Each nucleotide is made up of three parts: a five-carbon sugar in the shape of a ring, a phosphate group of molecules, and a nitrogen **base**. This "base" is the opposite of an acid, with a Ph of over 7. You will learn more about this in a more complete chemistry course.

There are two different nucleic acids, **DNA** and **RNA**. DNA is **deoxyribonucleic** (*dee-ok-si-rahy-boh-noo-klee-ik*) **acid**, and RNA is **ribonucleic** (*rahy-boh-noo-klee-ik*) **acid**.

DNA is a **double-stranded** molecule built like a ladder with the nucleotide pairs made of **deoxyribose** (*dee-ok-si-rahy-bohs*), representing the steps, or rungs, of the ladder. The entire ladder of DNA twists to form the final structure of the molecule which is known as a **double helix** (**hee**-liks) as shown in the diagram above.

DNA carries the genetic code of the organism.

RNA, in contrast to DNA, is a **single-stranded** molecule, see the diagram above. There are several different types of RNA molecules, each of which has a different overall shape and function. RNA is the large nucleic molecule responsible for making proteins by coding and decoding the genetic information held in the DNA molecules. Unlike carbohydrates, proteins, and lipids, nucleic acids do not provide energy in the diet of organisms.

WORDS TO REMEMBER

glycerol: a three-carbon molecule

fatty acid: a very long chain of carbon and hydrogen molecules

tryglyceride: a basic unit of fat, it is formed when three fatty acids bond to one glycerol. Both fats and oils are triglycerides.

steroids: lipids with the carbon atoms arranged in rings instead of chains. Steroids, like some small proteins, function as hormones.

cholesterol: an important component of cell structure and a building block for other steroids.

nucleic acids: large organic molecules that store the genetic code

DNA: deoxyribonucleic acid. DNA carries the genetic code of the organism.

RNA: ribonucleic acid. RNA is a single-stranded molecule that is responsible for making proteins by coding and decoding the genetic information held in the DNA molecules.

Section Review – 2.6 Nucleic Acids

1. What are nucleic acids?
2. Describe DNA.
3. Describe RNA.
4. What are the differences in structure between DNA and RNA?

Life Science for Young Catholics

2.7 A Special Molecule: ATP

Adenosine triphosphate (*uh-den-uh-sin try-fos-feyt*), or **ATP**, is called triphosphate because it contains three phosphate molecules ("tri" means three). ATP is the molecule of energy in living cells. **ATP** transports the chemical energy required for **metabolism** (*muh-tab-uh-liz-uhm*). Metabolism is the sum of all chemical reactions occurring within the cells of living organisms.

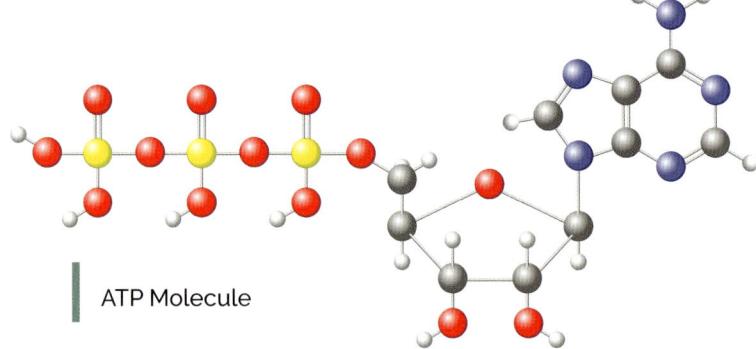

ATP Molecule

When energy from ATP is used by a chemical reaction in a cell, the ATP loses a phosphate group to become **ADP**, or **adenosine diphosphate** (*die-fos-feyt*) - two phosphates ("di" means two).

In different chemical reactions, a phosphate group is again added to the ADP to produce ATP. In this way, ATP is constantly recycled within the cells of an organism. Because ATP is the transporter of chemical energy, it is required in all life processes, including the production of other large organic molecules.

> **Section Review –**
> **2.7 Special Molecule: ATP**
> 1. Why is ATP so important?
> 2. What is metabolism?

2.8 Conclusion: Order & Wisdom of Creation

Think back to the truths of creation taught in the Book of Genesis. God created an ordered universe. He created the non-living, followed by the living; He created from the very simple to the very complex. This chapter illustrates some of these principles. The organization of matter increases from the simple atom, or element, to molecules, to compounds. Generally, most molecules in non-living things are relatively simple compared with the molecules in living things.

Living organisms require very specific conditions for the chemical reactions that support the life processes to occur. All chemical reactions needed for growth and cellular respiration in the human body require a specific temperature, 98.6° Fahrenheit. Even with the correct body temperature, some chemical reactions still require

WORDS TO REMEMBER

ATP: adenosine triphosphate. ATP is the molecule of energy in living cells. ATP transports the chemical energy required for metabolism. ATP has three phosphates.

ADP: adenosine diphosphate. ADP is involved in the synthesis and breakdown of ATP. ADP has only two phosphates.

metabolism: the sum of all chemical reactions occurring within the cells of living organisms.

CHAPTER 2: THE CHEMISTRY OF LIFE

the presence of enzymes to continue. Enzymes are organic catalysts that cause a bio-chemical reaction to proceed faster than normal. (A catalyst is something that causes a chemical reaction to proceed faster than normal, and is not used up in the reaction.) Enzymes are <u>created</u> in the body of an organism that requires them!

Think about DNA. Every bit of information that gives you your bodily characteristics is coded into a molecule made of only four different types of nitrogen bases. All of your genetic code, however, requires over 3 billion nitrogen bases!

The size and complexity of the universe, along with the diversity of God's creatures and the presence of the physical laws that govern and sustain all of creation, from the very simple to the very complex, clearly reveal God's existence, His omnipotence, and His wisdom. In Romans 1:19-20, it is written:

"For what can be known about God is evident to them, because God made it evident to them. Ever since the creation of the world, His invisible attributes of eternal power and divinity have been able to be understood and perceived in what He has made."

Life Science for Young Catholics

Chapter 2 Review

A. The figure for helium from the Periodic Table is given at right. Examine it and complete the following sentences:

1. The atomic mass number for helium is _____ .

2. The chemical abbreviation for helium is _____ .

3. The atomic number for helium is _____ .

B. Complete the following:

1. Sugars, starches, and fibers are all examples of _____ .

2. List the 6 functions of proteins:

a. _____

b. _____

c. _____

d. _____

e. _____

f. _____

C. Answer the following questions.

1. What is matter?
2. What are atoms?
3. What is an element?
4. What are organic compounds?
5. Which elements make up 95% of the human body?
6. Define carbohydrate. Name one.
7. Define proteins.
8. Name four types of food that provide protein.
9. What is cholesterol?
10. What are nucleic acids? What are the two main types of nucleic acids?
11. Why is ATP so important?
12. What are enzymes?

Life Science for Young Catholics

Chapter 2: "Words to Remember" Crossword

ACROSS

3 large molecules composed of amino acids
4 a combination of two or more elements
6 a complex molecule that stores energy and and is found in muscles of the human body
9 a three-carbon molecule
12 a basic unit of fat. It is formed when three fatty acids bond to one glycerol.
13 lipids with the carbon atoms arranged in rings instead of chains
14 the basic unit of all matter
15 the study of matter, its composition and properties
16 the functional substance of most of creation

DOWN

1 common table sugar
2 "fruit sugar"
5 anything that has mass and takes up space
7 tiny negatively charged sub-units of atom that orbit about the nucleus
8 positively charged sub-units within the nucleus of an atom
10 the basic element of life
11 the basic sugar made in plants by photosynthesis

Life Science for Young Catholics

3 THE CELL

3.1 Introduction

3.2 Cell Theory

3.3 Two Basic Types of Cell Structure: Simple and Complex
   A. Simple Cell Structure
   B. Complex Cell Structure
   C. Common Characteristics
   D. Cell Theory

3.4 The Cell Membrane
   A. Passive Transport
      1. Diffusion
      2. Osmosis
   B. Active Transport
      1. Endocytosis (entering the cell)
      2. Exocytosis (exiting the cell)

3.5 Cytoplasm and Cellular Organelles
   A. The Nucleus
   B. The Endoplasmic Reticulum and Ribosomes
   C. Golgi Bodies
   D. Lysosomes
   E. Mitochondria
   F. Centrioles
   G. Chloroplasts in Plant Cells
   H. Cell Differences

3.6 The Cell Cycle & Reproduction
   A. Simple Cell Reproduction
   B. Complex Cell Reproduction
      1. Interphase
      2. Cell Division

3.7 Levels of Cellular Organization

3.8 Many Parts, One Body

Chapter 3
The Cell

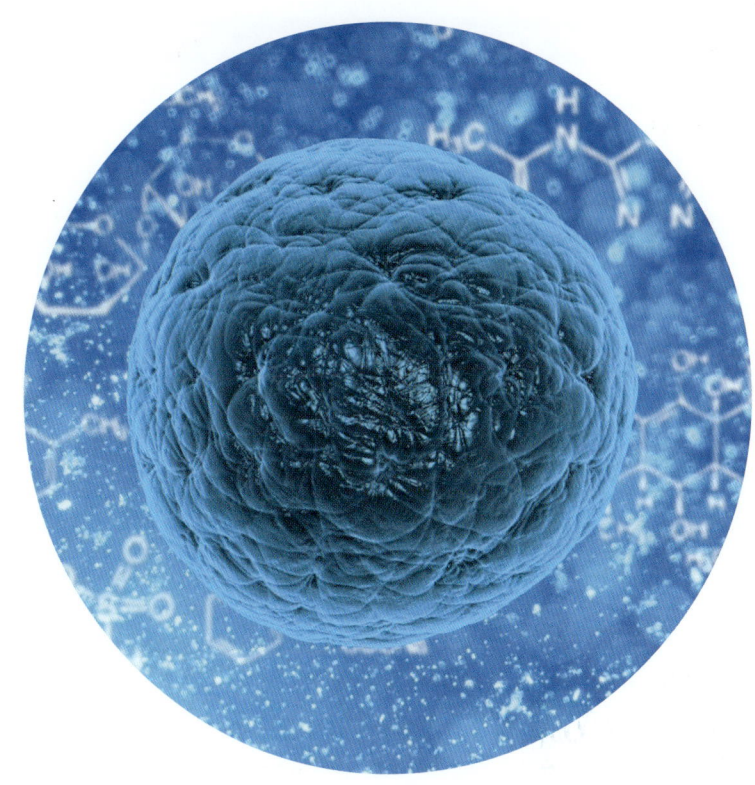

3.1 Introduction

Do you like to eat eggs for breakfast? Did you know that each chicken egg represents a single cell?

Cells are the basic structures of all living things. Most cells are very tiny, too small to see without a magnifying lens of some type. However, the eggs you may have had for breakfast are single cells. The ostrich egg is the largest cell known!

Your body is made up of ten trillion cells, according to the latest scientific count! Different cells perform different functions and make up different organs in your body.

St. Paul compared the Catholic Church to the human body. He said that all of the faithful together make up the Body of Christ. In his First Letter to the Corinthians, St. Paul said:

> For as the body is one, and hath many members; and all the members of the body, whereas they are many, yet are one body, so also is Christ. For in one Spirit were we all baptized into one body, whether Jews or Gentiles, whether bond or free; and in one Spirit we have all been made to drink. For the body also is not one member, but many. If the foot should say, because I am not the hand, I am not of the body; is it therefore not of the body? And if the ear should say, because I am not the eye, I am not of the body; is it therefore not of the body? If the whole body were the eye, where would be the hearing? If the whole were hearing, where would be the smelling? But now God hath set the members every one of them in the body as it hath pleased him.

The cell is like a very tiny miniature body. It has different parts that do different things. St. Paul might call the parts "members." Each part performs a necessary function, like the foot, hand, ear, and eye that St. Paul mentions in his comparison of the human body to the Catholic Church.

So let us now learn how the "little body" of the cell can be, in a way, like the full human body, and how the human body cannot get along without its tiny cells.

CHAPTER 3: THE CELL

3.2 Cell Theory

In 1665, a 26-year-old man by the name of Robert Hooke (1635-1703), working for the English king, Charles II, viewed a very thin slice of cork under a magnifying glass. Mr. Hooke discovered that the very thin slice of cork was made of very tiny empty spaces with each surrounded by wall-like structures. Hooke thought that the spaces looked like the little tiny rooms, called cells, that housed each monk in a monastery. So Mr. Hooke decided to call the tiny space in the cork **cells**, or *cellulae* in Latin.

More than 150 years later, a German botanist, Matthias Schleiden, observed some material of a plant under the microscope and, like Hooke, noticed many tiny organized spaces throughout the plant. Mr. Schleiden also noted a dark area within each tiny compartment of the plant material.

Around the same time, another German scientist, Theodore Schwann, described the very same pattern of compartments and darkened areas in animal tissue viewed under a microscope. In 1839, Schleiden speculated that the compartments in the plant material were living cells that were organized according to specific laws. Schwann agreed and proposed a conclusion: that the same organization as in the plant cells existed in animal cells. From these observations, the two men concluded that very tiny cells are the basic units of life.

In 1855, Rudolph Virchow, another German biologist, concluded from his research that cells can come only from pre-existing cells. They cannot come from nothing. These three scientists are credited for the basic principle of biology known as the **cell theory**, or **cell doctrine**.

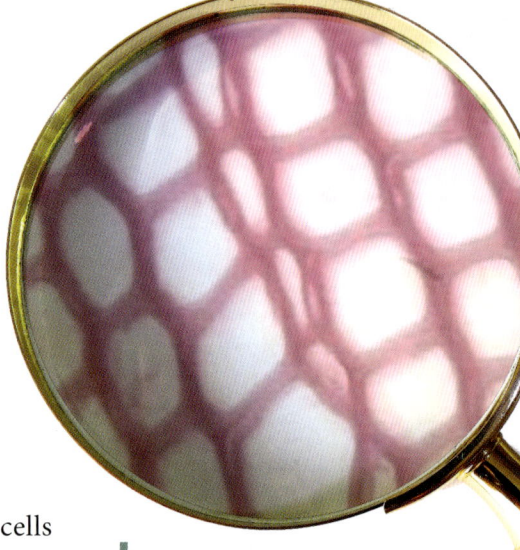

Cork "cells" viewed under a microscope

> ### Section Review – 3.2 Cell Theory
> 1. Who discovered cells? What was he studying at the time?
> 2. What are the six main points of Cell Theory?

The Outline of Cell Theory

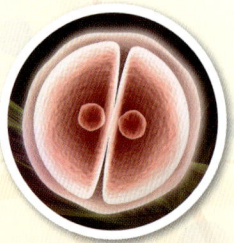

The original outline of the cell theory has three points:

1. All living organisms are composed of one or more cells.
2. The cell is the basic unit of life.
3. New cells are reproduced from pre-existing living cells.

Modern biologists have added details to the basic cell theory:

4. Energy flow, from the processes required for life, occurs within cells.
5. Heredity information is passed on from cell to cell through DNA.
6. All cells have the same basic chemical composition.

Life Science for Young Catholics

3.3 Two Basic Types of Cell Structure: Simple and Complex

As time went on, and more scientists looked under their microscopes at various organisms, certain conclusions were accepted by scientists. First, the structure of cells is determined by the organization of matter. Second, the matter of living organisms is organized from very tiny atoms, to tiny molecules, to large organic molecules, all according to the Laws of Nature set forth by God. Macromolecules, or large molecules, contribute to the next level of God's established order. These macromolecules, such as carbohydrates, proteins, lipids, and nucleic acids, contribute to the structures of the cell. The **cell** is the **basic unit of structure and function** of all living organisms.

A. Simple Cell Structure

The simplest cells are the **prokaryotic** (**pro**·*kar*·*ee*·*ot*·*ik*) cells. Prokaryotic comes from "pro" or before, and "karyon" or nut. The nut or "karyon" is the membrane-protected center, the nucleus of a living cell. Prokaryotes do not have a membrane-protected nucleus, so they are cells "before" a "nucleus." These are simple cells that lack an organized nucleus. They have cell walls, and are filled with cytoplasm.

Prokaryotic cells do not have membrane-enclosed organelles, the tiny organ-like structures in some cells that perform specific functions. However, prokaryotic cells do contain ribosomes, the cell structure that manufactures proteins for the cell. Prokaryotic cells contain DNA in unprotected clumps near the center of the cell. Prokaryotes are **single-celled** organisms in the Domains Archae and Bacteria.

B. Complex Cell Structure

The more complex cells are the **eukaryotic** (**you**·*kar*·*ee*·*ot*·*ik*) cells. Eukaryotic means "true nucleus." The "eu" in eukaryotic means "true," from both Latin and Greek.

Eukaryotic cells do have a true, organized nucleus, usually located near the center of the cell. This nucleus has a protective membrane around it to separate it from the cytoplasm within the cell. The nucleus contains the hereditary material in DNA, which controls the reproduction of the cell, but it also controls the normal processes of the cell.

TYPES OF CELL STRUCTURE

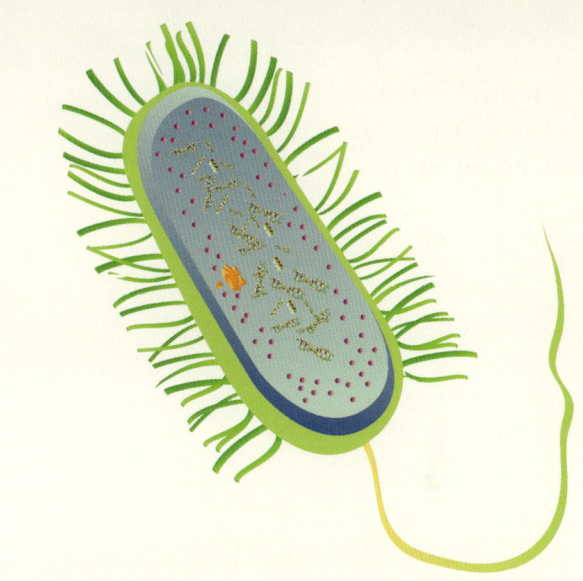

PROKARYOTIC CELL. Note that it is simple, with no complex internal structures. DNA in the center is not encased in a separate membrane.

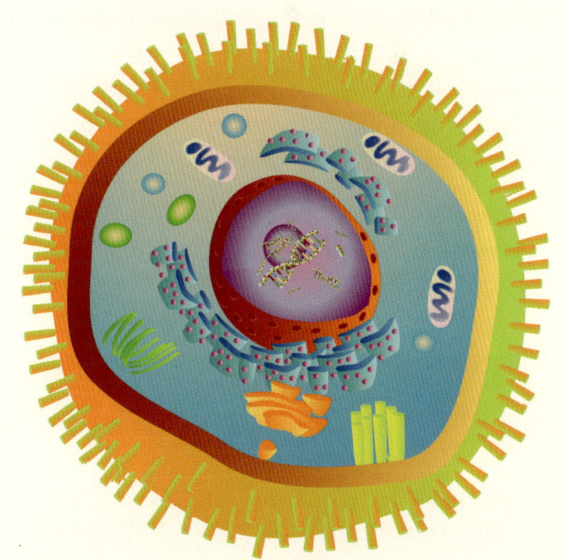

EUKARYOTIC CELL. Note that this cell is complex. There are different types of complex internal structures. The DNA near the center is protected by a separate membrane.

Life Science for Young Catholics

A prokaryotic cell

Eukaryotic cells also have membrane-enclosed organelles as well as ribosomes. Organelles function as the organs in larger creatures do. Ribosomes process information from the cell's DNA to make the proteins that the cell needs to maintain itself. Other organelles include mitochondria, Golgi bodies, centrioles, endoplasmic reticulum, vacuoles, and lysosomes.

See the illustrations on the previous page to compare a typical prokaryotic cell with a typical eukaryotic cell.

SCIENCE TIPS

It might help you to remember the difference between prokaryotic and eukaryotic with this memory rhyme:

Is there a nucleus in this cell?
Is there an easy way to tell?

"**Pro** is simply **no**" and
"**Eu** is complexly **true**."

C. Common Characteristics

All cells share some common characteristics. For example, both prokaryotic and eukaryotic cells are surrounded by a **cell membrane** and contain a jelly-like **cytoplasm** (*sigh·toe·plaz·m*) in which the chemical reactions necessary for life take place. Both also contain **genetic material**, and both contain **ribosomes** necessary for making protein. All cells carry on the basic processes of living organisms, such as respiration, excretion, and reproduction. The differences between prokaryotic and eukaryotic cells are based on the level of organization and complexity.

D. Cell Theory

According to cell theory, cells are the *basic units*, or *building blocks*, of all living organisms, from the most simple to the most complex. Cells, too, are the basic unit of *functioning* of all living organisms from the most simple to the most complex. The cells of all living organisms, both prokaryotic and eukaryotic, must carry out all seven functions, or processes, necessary for life.

CHAPTER 3: **THE CELL**

The seven life processes are: **movement**, **respiration**, **sensitivity**, **growth**, **reproduction**, **nutrition**, and **excretion**. Recall, in order to be classified as living, an organism - or a cell - must exhibit **ALL SEVEN** processes. To carry out these seven life processes, cells must be equipped with the proper "machinery." The chemical reactions of life do not occur haphazardly or randomly within a cell. The chemical reactions are consistent. From the surrounding cell membrane to each of the very tiny internal cellular organelles, God, in His wisdom, has created each tiny part of the cell to perform a specific function.

To help to understand the very tiny cell, first consider your house. Each room in your house has a specific function: the kitchen is for cooking, the bedrooms are for sleeping, the bathrooms are for cleaning up and eliminating waste. The cooking is never done in the bathroom! When all the rooms have all the proper equipment - refrigerators, stoves, sinks, showers, toilets, beds - the house functions properly. Such organization is in the cell. When each of the compartments of the cell, or the organelles, functions properly, the cell functions properly. As a single functional unit, then, the cell carries out the processes necessary for life. Learning the structure and function of cell membranes and each organelle gives a greater understanding and appreciation of God's creation and His love for all of us.

All of creation was made for us!

A eukaryotic cell

Section Review – 3.3 Two Basic Types of Cell Structure: Simple and Complex

1. Define prokaryotic cells.
2. Define eukaryotic cells.
3. Name four characteristics that prokaryotic cells and eukaryotic cells have in common.

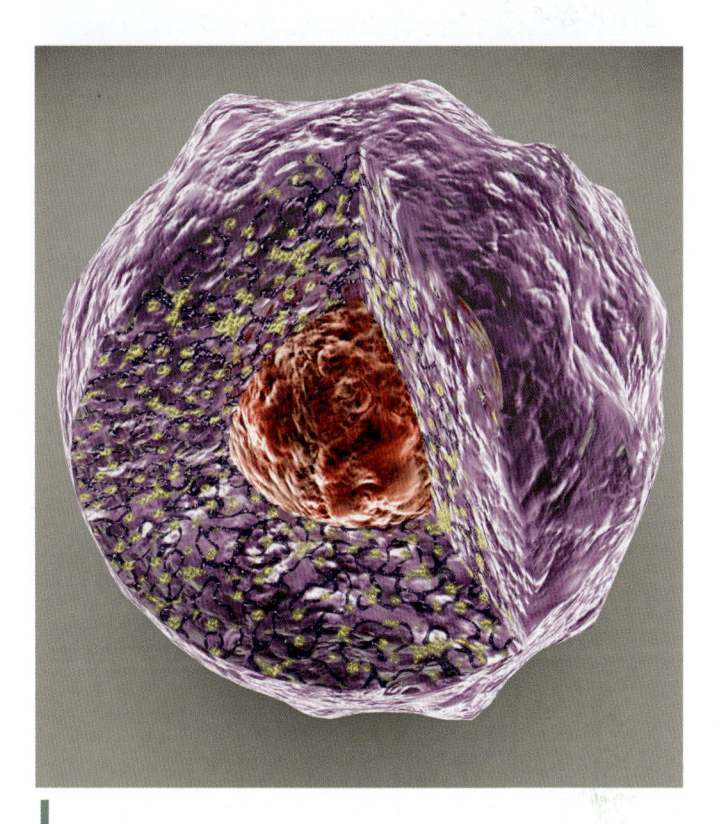

WORDS TO REMEMBER

cell: the basic unit of structure and function of all living organisms

prokaryotic cells: the simplest cells. Prokaryotic cells lack an organized nucleus. They have cell walls, and are filled with cytoplasm. Prokaryotic cells do not have membrane-enclosed organelles, the tiny organ-like structures in some cells that perform specific functions. Prokaryotic cells do contain ribosomes.

eukaryotic cells: complex cells. Eukaryotic cells have a true, organized nucleus, usually located near the center of the cell. This nucleus has a protective membrane around it to separate it from the cytoplasm within the cell. Eukaryotic cells also have membrane-enclosed organelles as well as ribosomes.

cell membrane: a biological membrane, made up of proteins and lipids, that separates the interior of all cells from the outside environment and protects the cell from its surroundings

cytoplasm: clear, gel-like substance outside the nucleus of the cell of plants and animals

Life Science for Young Catholics

CHAPTER 3: THE CELL

3.4 The Cell Membrane

All living cells, simple prokaryotic and more complex eukaryotic, are surrounded by a **cell membrane**.

The cell membrane provides a boundary between the contents of the cell and the surrounding environment. The cell membrane maintains homeostasis, which means a stable internal environment, by regulating which materials pass in and out of the cell. Cell membranes are **semi-permeable** (*sem·ee·per·mee·a·ble*); that is, they permit only certain substances to pass through.

A. Passive Transport

Passive transport is the movement of materials through the cell membrane without energy being used.

1. Diffusion

Some materials, such as oxygen and carbon dioxide, are small enough to move freely across the cell membrane by a process known as **diffusion** (*dih-fyoo-shun*). Diffusion is the movement of molecules across a membrane from an area of higher concentration to an area of lower concentration. Diffusion does not require the use of the cell's energy.

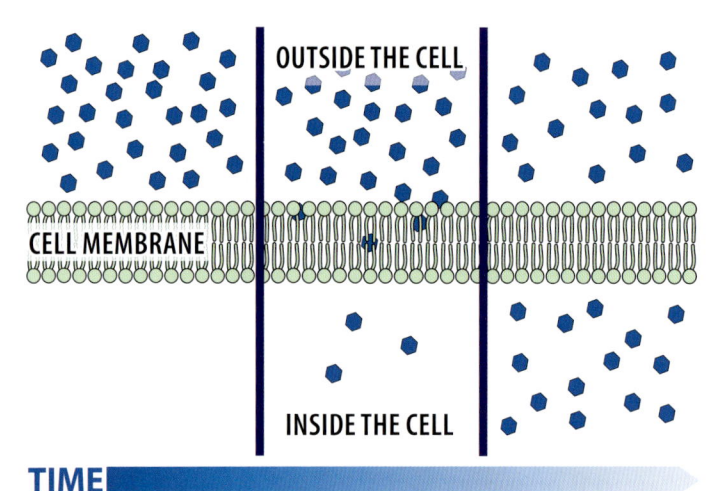

Diffusion of carbon dioxide (CO_2) across a cell membrane from an area of greater concentration to an area of lesser concentration

2. Osmosis

Osmosis (*os·mo·sis*) is a special form of diffusion.

Only very tiny substances are able to pass through the cell membrane by simple diffusion. Water and larger macromolecules, like proteins and carbohydrates, must also pass through cell membranes, but they cannot simply diffuse because of their size and other chemical properties.

God has added a special feature to cell membranes to allow larger materials to pass through. Embedded within the cell membrane are **pores** made of proteins that span the width of the membrane. These pores function like little tunnels to allow larger molecules passage into and out of the cell.

Water molecules pass through pores from an area of greater concentration of water, usually outside the cell, to an area of lesser concentration of water, usually inside the cell. The diffusion of water through the pores of a semipermeable membrane is known as **osmosis**.

Diffusion and osmosis are examples of **passive transport** because they do not require energy from the cell for the processes to occur.

B. Active Transport

Some substances require **active transport** to cross the cell membrane because they are too large, or their chemical properties do not permit diffusion, or they must be transported from an area of lesser concentration to an area of greater concentration. Active transport requires **energy from the cell** to move a substance into or out of the cell. Glucose, for example, requires energy from the cell in order to enter or leave the cell.

1. Endocytosis (entering the cell)

Endocytosis (*end·o·sigh·toe·sis*) is a type of active transport involving the proteins in cell membranes. Endocytosis brings materials **into the cell**. This involves a substance contacting a **receptor** protein on the surface of the cell membrane; this contact triggers the cell membrane to fold itself around the substance. Once the membrane entirely surrounds the

CHAPTER 3: **THE CELL**

ENDOCYTOSIS & EXOCYTOSIS

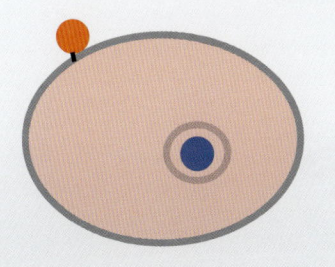

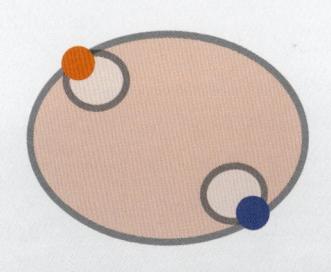

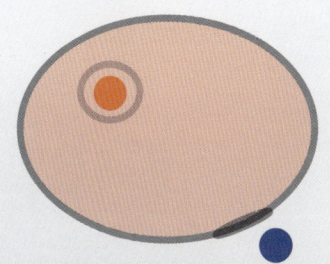

Endocytosis of the **orange particle** into a simplified cell, progressing from left to right; **exocytosis** of the **blue particle** out of the simplified cell, also progressing from left to right in the diagram.

substance, it pinches off from the original cell membrane to form a **vesicle**. The vesicle is then free to deliver the ingested substance to the proper location within the cell. Endocytosis is one process by which cells obtain nutrition.

2. **Exocytosis (exiting the cell)**

The reverse of endocytosis is **exocytosis** (**ex·o·sigh·toe·sis**). Exocytosis is **active transport** of materials **out of cells,** which also involves proteins. Exocytosis is the process by which waste is removed from cells; it is a means of excretion. The figure above illustrates both processes in a simplified cell; endocytosis is represented by the orange and exocytosis by the blue.

Keep in mind the "en" for endocytosis to "enter" the cell, and the "ex" in exocytosis for "exiting" the cell.

Section Review – 3.4 The Cell Membrane

1. Name four characteristics of the cell membrane.
2. What is passive transport?
3. Describe diffusion and osmosis.
4. What is active transport? Why is this important? What is required for active transport that is not needed for passive transport?
5. How does water move into and out of cells?

Aa WORDS TO REMEMBER

semi-permeable membrane: a membrane that protects a cell, or part of a cell, that only allows certain substances to pass through it

passive transport: the movement of materials through the cell membrane without energy being used.

diffusion: the movement of molecules across a membrane from an area of higher concentration to an area of lower concentration. Diffusion does not require the use of the cell's energy.

osmosis: a special form of diffusion. Water passes though the pores of semi-permeable membranes through osmosis.

pores (cell): portholes made of proteins that span the width of a membrane. These pores function like little tunnels to allow larger molecules passage into and out of the cell.

active transport: the movement of materials through the cell membrane that requires energy from the cell. Some substances require active transport to cross the cell membrane, either because their chemical properties do not permit diffusion, or because they must be transported from an area of lesser concentration to an area of greater concentration.

endocytosis: a type of active transport involving the proteins in cell membranes. Endocytosis brings materials into the cell.

vesicle: a capsule that has pinched off from a cell membrane after surrounding some substance

exocytosis: the active transport of materials out of cells, which also involves proteins. Exocytosis is the process by which waste is removed from cells; it is a means of excretion.

Life Science for Young Catholics

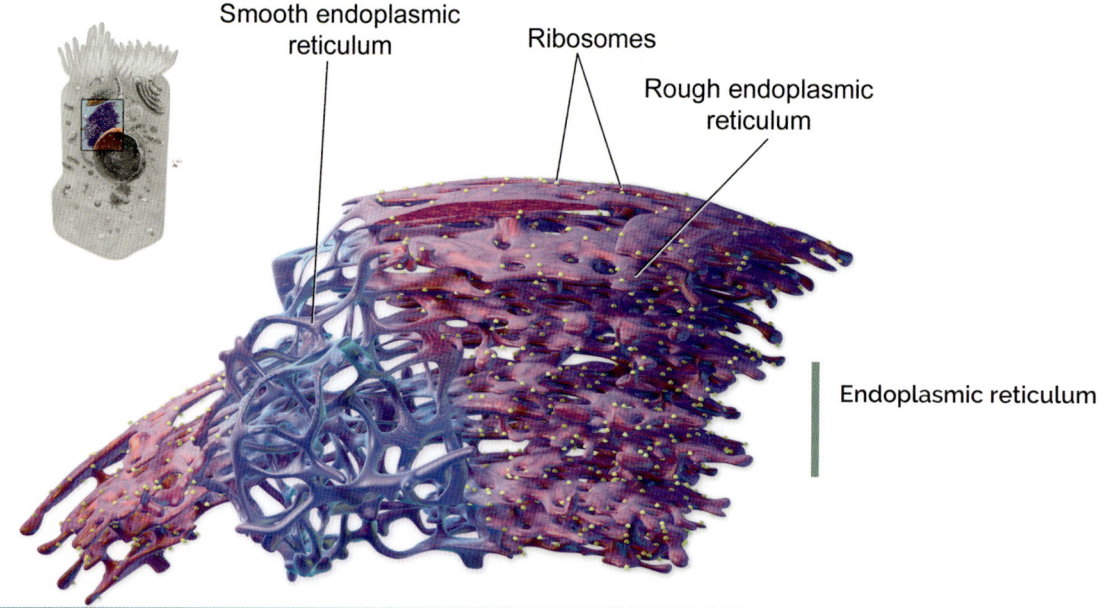

3.5 Cytoplasm and Cellular Organelles

The inside of a eukaryotic cell, a complex cell, is divided into two separate compartments: the **cytoplasm** and the **nucleus**. Inside the cell membrane, but outside of the nucleus, is the cytoplasm. The cytoplasm is the colorless, gel-like substance (stained purple-pink in the picture) that contains the very tiny organelles. **Organelles** are specialized structures found inside of cells, in the cytoplasm. They are called organelles because they are similar in function to the large organs found in multicellular creatures. Organs, such as the heart and the kidney, are groups of cells that together perform a specific task. While some necessary cellular functions occur in the cytoplasm itself, many important functions take place in organelles within the cytoplasm. Some of the major organelles in a cell are the nucleus, endoplasmic reticulum, ribosomes, Golgi bodies, lysosomes, mitochondria, and vacuoles.

A. The Nucleus

The nucleus, or control center of the cell, is separated from the cytoplasm by two membranes. The double membrane around the nucleus of a cell is called the **nuclear membrane**. The nuclear membrane contains large pores which allow the RNA to pass into the cytoplasm. The nucleus is called the control center of the cell because it contains the DNA with all the instructions for cell life. The nucleus also contains the **nucleolus** (*new·klee·o·lus*) which is involved in making proteins. The nucleus, because it controls the internal workings of the cell, is indirectly involved in all seven life processes.

B. The Endoplasmic Reticulum and Ribosomes

The outer layer of the double nuclear membrane forms a continuous network of membranes and pockets that extends and branches into the cytoplasm. This network is the organelle called the **endoplasmic reticulum** (*end·o·plaz·mik re·tick·you·lum*) and is involved in the production and movement of proteins. There are two types of endoplasmic reticulum as illustrated above, **rough** and **smooth**. The **rough endoplasmic reticulum** (RER) is studded with **ribosomes**. Ribosomes are small organelles made of RNA and proteins that are made in the nucleolus. Unlike many cellular organelles, ribosomes are not membrane-bound. Ribosomes are the site of protein synthesis, the process by which cells build protein. Ribosomes are present in both prokaryotic and eukaryotic cells. **Smooth endoplasmic reticulum** (SER) does not have ribosomes. Smooth endoplasmic reticulum is the site of lipid, or fat, and carbohydrate production.

C. Golgi Bodies

Golgi (*goal·jee*) **bodies** are organelles made of stacks of membrane pouches organized throughout the cytoplasm of a cell. Golgi bodies are the "post office" of the cell. Here, newly made proteins are sorted and packaged according to type. The packaged proteins are then either stored until needed, or released in packages known as **vacuoles** (*vak·you·oles*) from the Golgi bodies. Vacuoles pinch off of the Golgi bodies by exocytosis. See the illustration on page 35.

D. Lysosomes

Some vesicles or small sacs made from the Golgi bodies are known as **lysosomes** (*lice·o·somes*). Lysosomes contain enzymes (substances that cause a reaction) that help to digest and remove debris from the cell. Lysosomes are like the "stomachs" of the cell. After the enzymes within the lysosome break down the unwanted materials, the lysosomes move to the cell membrane and expel the waste by means of exocytosis, which means simply transporting a substance out of a cell.

E. Mitochondria

Much of the activity inside a cell requires energy, which comes from ATP. The ATP that fuels cell processes is made in specialized organelles called **mitochondria** (*might·o·con·dree·a*). Mitochondria are oblong sausage-shaped organelles made of a double layer of membrane. The inner membrane of the mitochondrion is folded into fingerlike projections called **cristae** (*kris·tay*); ATP is made here during cellular respiration.

Cellular respiration is the process by which a cell turns the energy stored in food into energy that is used by the cell. More specifically, cellular respiration is the process by which the sugar, which is glucose, is broken down to produce ATP. Oxygen is required for the breakdown of the sugar molecules; carbon dioxide and water are produced as the byproducts. Each individual molecule of glucose, when broken down, produces 36-38 molecules of ATP.

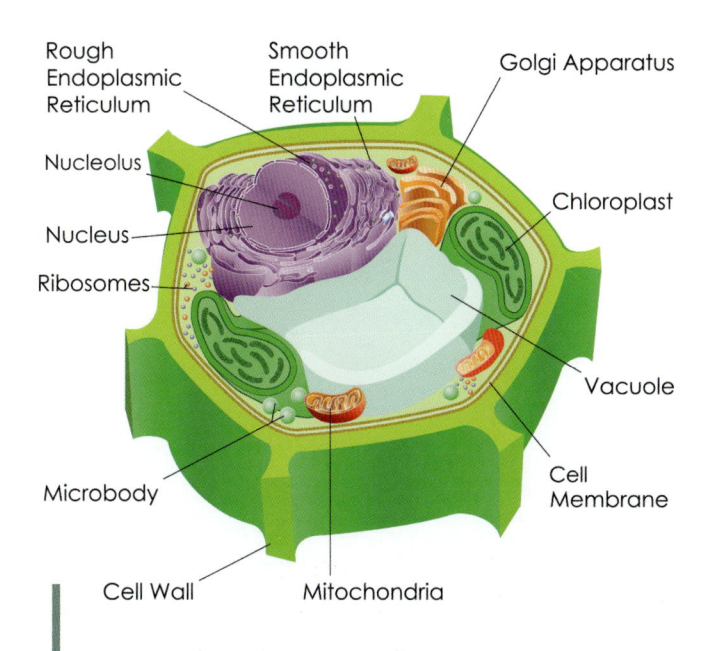

Diagram of a typical plant cell

F. Centrioles

The organelles discussed so far are found in all eukaryotic cells. Only animal cells, however, contain **centrioles**. Centrioles are small paired cylindrical structures that help to pull apart the two halves of a cell during cellular reproduction.

WORDS TO REMEMBER

nucleus (cell): the control center of the cell. It is separated from the cytoplasm by two membranes.

nuclear membrane: the double membrane around the nucleus of a cell. The nuclear membrane contains large pores which allow the RNA to pass into the cytoplasm.

nucleolus: a part of the nucleus of a cell which is involved in making proteins

endoplasmic reticulum: the network of membranes and pockets of the nuclear membrane that extends and branches into the cytoplasm. This network is involved in the production and movement of proteins. There are two types of endoplasmic reticulum, rough and smooth.

rough endoplasmic reticulum (RER): is studded with ribosomes. Ribosomes are the site of protein synthesis, the process by which cells build protein.

smooth endoplasmic reticulum (SER): does not have ribosomes. Smooth endoplasmic reticulum is the site of lipid, or fat, and carbohydrate production.

Golgi bodies: organelles made of stacks of membrane pouches organized throughout the cytoplasm of a cell. Golgi bodies are the "post office" of the cell. Here, newly made proteins are sorted and packaged according to type.

lysosomes: vesicles or small sacs made from the Golgi bodies that contain enzymes that help to digest and remove debris from the cell

mitochondria: the powerhouses of a cell. The ATP that fuels cell processes is made in mitochondria.

cristae: the folded, fingerlike projections of the inner wall of mitochondria. Cristae are important in the making of ATP during cellular respiration.

centrioles: small, paired cylindrical structures that help to pull apart the two halves of a cell during cellular reproduction

G. Chloroplasts in Plant Cells

Plant cells contain **chloroplasts** (**klor·o·plasts**). Chloroplasts are membrane-bound organelles that contain stacks of the green pigment **chlorophyll** (**klor·o·fill**). It is in these chloroplast organelles that light energy from the sun is transformed into glucose, sugar, during the process of **photosynthesis**.

The plant uses water and carbon dioxide to make sugar and oxygen. Sunlight provides the energy for this reaction. The cellular respiration of the animal uses sugar obtained from a plant, and oxygen that it breathed in, and produces energy and byproducts of water and carbon dioxide that it exhales or eliminates.

H. Cell Differences

Plants containing chlorophyll are **autotrophs** (**au-to-trofs**), or organisms that make their own food supply. Conversely, organisms that cannot make their own food supply are known as **heterotrophs**. In plant cells, photosynthesis provides the plant with its own source of nutrition for plant growth and function.

Plant cells differ from animal cells in that plant cells are surrounded by a rigid **cell wall**. The cell wall is what gives the plant its structure. It was the cell walls of the cork that Robert Hooke was viewing when he made his discovery of "cells."

Cells are the basic units of structure and function of all organisms. Cells carry out all seven life processes: **nutrition, respiration, sensitivity, growth, excretion, movement,** and **reproduction.**

In summary, organelles within the cell's structure are specialized units that carry out all of the seven processes. In plant cells, chloroplasts are the centers of **nutrition,** in which carbohydrates are made from carbon dioxide, water, and light energy from the sun. In animal

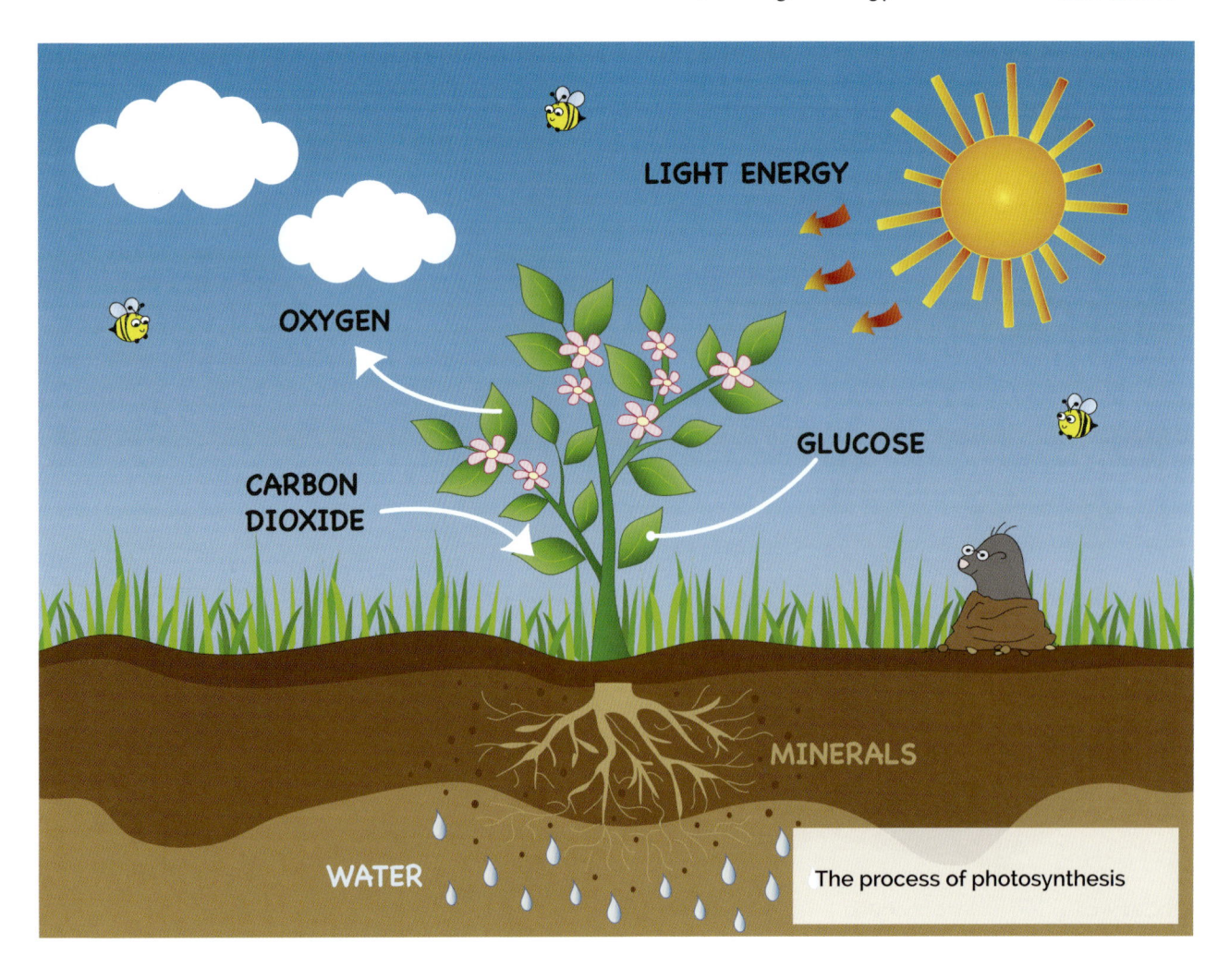

The process of photosynthesis

cells, the cell membrane is involved in acquiring nutrition through processes such as endocytosis.

Cellular respiration occurs within the mitochondria to transform the energy in food substances into ATP, the basic unit of energy within the cell. The cell membranes are responsible for maintaining homeostasis, the proper living environment, and cell membranes are involved in **excretion**. Lysosomes, which digest unwanted materials, are also involved in cellular excretion.

> **Section Review –
> 3.5 Cytoplasm and Cellular Organelles**
>
> 1. What is the nucleus of the cell?
> 2. Describe cytoplasm.
> 3. What are organelles?
> 4. Name and describe the major organelles.
> 5. What are ribosomes?

WORDS TO REMEMBER

chloroplasts: membrane-bound organelles that contain stacks of chlorophyll

chlorophyll: the green pigment in plant cells where photosynthesis takes place

photosynthesis: the process by which light energy from the sun is transformed into glucose

autotrophs: organisms that make their own food supply

heterotrophs: organisms that cannot make their own food supply

cell wall: the rigid structure on the outside of plant cells that provides their basic structure

3.6 The Cell Cycle & Reproduction

A. Simple Cell Reproduction

Prokaryotic cells, the simpler cells, reproduce by a process called **binary fission**. The chromosomes are replicated and move to opposite sides of the cell membrane. Then the cell membrane **grows inwardly** near the middle of the cell until it joins and forms two cells, each with its own set of chromosomes.

B. Complex Cell Reproduction

The more complex **Eukaryotic** cells multiply by **cell division**. This is not a mathematical problem, but a truth about cellular reproduction and the third tenet of cell theory. A single eukaryotic cell, the parent cell, undergoes the process of interphase followed by cell division to produce two identical and complete daughter cells.

1. Interphase

Interphase is the phase of the cell cycle in which the cell spends the majority of its time and performs the majority of its purposes, including preparation for cell division. During the interphase, the cell takes in nutrients, grows, and duplicates its chromosomes.

2. Cell Division

Cell division is the process by which a cell divides into two or more cells. Among eukaryotes, the cell nucleus divides first, and then a new cell membrane is formed between the nuclei to form the new cell. Cell division is the source or cause of tissue growth and repair in multicellular organisms.

During cell division, the nucleus divides in a process called **mitosis**, and then the divided nuclei are established in separate cells.

In order for a cell to produce two identical cells, some of the structures within the parent cell must first be duplicated. Otherwise, the daughter cells would be only half of what their parent cell was, and a cell cannot function with only half of the necessary equipment.

Life Science for Young Catholics

CHAPTER 3: THE CELL

Cell Division

parent cell → identical daughter cells

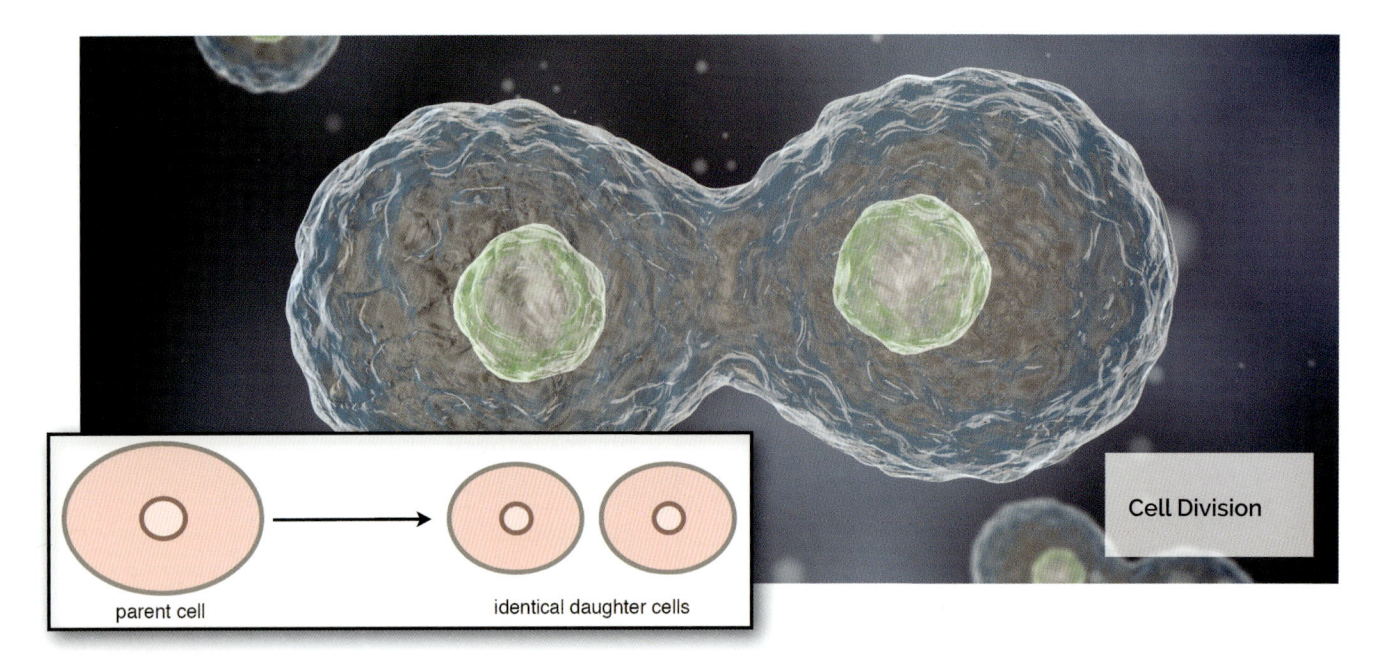

God, in His wisdom and order, created the process of eukaryotic cell division in such a way that each daughter cell has the same genetic material and cellular equipment as the parent cell. To understand how this happens, it is necessary to understand the **cell cycle**. The cell cycle is the life cycle of a cell that begins when the cell is first created and ends when it divides into two daughter cells. The cell cycle is an ordered series of events that can be divided into four phases.

Not all cells in an organism undergo cell division at the same time. Some cells continue to carry on their work while others divide. The time it takes for an animal cell to go through the cell cycle and complete division is typically about 24 hours.

Section Review – 3.6 The Cell Cycle & Reproduction

1. How do cells reproduce?
2. What is cell division?

3.7 Levels of Cellular Organization

So far, our study of life science has been based on God's order of increasing complexity. We began by distinguishing living from non-living. Next we studied the chemistry of life from simple molecules to complex macromolecules, such as carbohydrates, proteins, and lipids. In this chapter, we began with the cell, the basic unit of structure and function of all life. We discussed simple prokaryotic cells, and finally, more complex eukaryotic cells in which large and complex macromolecules are organized into functional structures, called organelles, which carry out the seven life processes.

Simple prokaryotic cells are **unicellular**, or **single-celled**, organisms that function wholly and independently from other prokaryotic cells.

The more complex eukaryotic cells may be unicellular or multicellular.

Multicellular, or **many-celled**, organisms have individual eukaryotic cells which perform unique and individual functions, but multicellular organisms also have groups of cells that work together. These groups of cells become interrelated and interdependent and work together to perform a specific job for the organism as a whole. There are five levels of organization in multicellular organisms, each with increasing complexity.

The five levels of organization in multicellular organisms are: **cells, tissues, organs, organ systems,** and **organisms**.

CHAPTER 3: **THE CELL**

Cells are the basic units of living organisms that we have been learning about.

Tissues are made of cells of similar structure and function that work together to perform a specific function, such as bone, muscle, and nerve tissue.

Organs are made of different tissues that work together to perform a specific function, such as the liver, brain, and heart.

Organ systems are made of two or more organs that work together to perform a specific function, such as the skeletal system, nervous system, and circulatory system.

Organisms are complex, multicellular living things composed of various levels of cellular organization, such as human beings, animals, and plants.

> **Section Review – 3.7 Levels of Cellular Organization**
>
> 1. Identify the differences in levels of organization between prokaryotic cells and eukaryotic cells.
> 2. Describe the five levels of organization in multicellular organisms.

WORDS TO REMEMBER

interphase: the phase of the cell cycle in which the cell spends the majority of its time and performs the majority of its purposes, including preparation for cell division During the interphase, the cell takes in nutrients, grows, and duplicates its chromosomes.

cell division: the process by which a cell divides into two or more cells. Cell division is the source or cause of tissue growth and repair in multicellular organisms.

mitosis: the process where the nucleus divides during the process of cell division.

unicellular: single-celled organisms that function wholly and independently from other organisms.

multicellular organisms: organisms that are made up of many cells. Some of these cells may be specialized, for example, bone cells or skin cells.

✓ QUICK REVIEW: Levels of Organization in Multicellular Organisms

The five levels of organization in multicellular organisms are:
cells, tissues, organs, organ systems, and organisms.

Level 1 **CELLS**	Basic unit of structure and function & may serve a unique function	**Example:** blood cells, nerve cells, skin (epithelial) cells
Level 2 **TISSUES**	Made of cells of similar structure and function that work together to perform a specific function	**Example:** muscle tissue made of all similar muscle cells that contract as a unit to move the body
Level 3 **ORGANS**	Made of different tissues that work together to perform a specific function	**Example:** liver made of liver cells, blood vessels, blood cells, connective tissue - all of which function together to remove toxins from the body
Level 4 **ORGAN SYSTEMS**	Made of two or more organs that work together to perform a specific function	**Example:** nervous system made of multiple organs - brain, spinal cord, nerves - that all function together to control all aspects of the organism
Level 5 **ORGANISMS**	Complex, multicellular living things composed of various levels of cellular organization	**Example:** human beings, animals, plants, fungi

Life Science for Young Catholics

3.8 Many Parts, One Body

We have just learned that the individual cell performs the same seven life functions that a large organism, like a human body, performs. In the cell, there are different parts that do different jobs, just as in people there are different organs, like the heart and lungs, that do special jobs to keep the person alive.

This basic format for the individual cell, and for the whole body, is similar to the format that God uses for His Church and His relationship with us. In fact, St. Paul uses the different functions of the body to teach how God views the Church.

In 1 Corinthians we read: "For as the body is one, and hath many members; and all the members of the body, whereas they are many, yet are one body, so also is Christ."

We, in Christ, can be likened to the cells of an organism. Each of us has been created by our loving Father to be unique, but also alike in His creation. We function independently but, like cells of a tissue, or tissues of an organ, or organs of an organ system, are all interdependent and must work together to fulfill a holy function: we must do God's will, and obey His laws. We are also to help each other to know, to love, and to serve God in this life, so that we may get to Heaven and help others get there as well.

All of us, like different cells, tissues, and organs of an individual organism, have been given different gifts in order that we may perform many different functions. However, we are to function wholly together, as the **Body of Christ**, *that is, as His Church*, with Christ as our Head. In the same way as the functioning of an organism depends on the total functioning of all its independent cells, the Body of Christ depends on the functioning of all of its individual human members.

CHAPTER 3: **THE CELL**

As in nature a body is not formed by any haphazard grouping of members but must be constituted of organs that have not the same function and are arranged in due order, so for this reason above all the Church is called a body. It is thus the Apostle describes the Church when he writes: "As in one body we have many members, but all the members have not the same office: so we, being many, are one body in Christ, and everyone members one of another."

Ven. Pope Pius XII, *On the Mystical Body of Christ*

Life Science for Young Catholics

Chapter 3 Review

A. Provide at least three tenets of cell theory.

_____

_____

_____

B. Complete the missing sections of the table. Provide at least one example for each category.

1. _____	Basic unit of structure and function & may serve a unique function	**Example:** _____
2. _____	Made of cells of similar structure and function that work together to perform a specific function	**Example:** _____
3. _____	Made of different tissues that work together to perform a specific function	**Example:** _____
4. _____	Made of two or more organs that work together to perform a specific function	**Example:** _____
5. _____	Complex, multicellular living things composed of various levels of cellular organization	**Example:** _____

C. Answer the following questions.

1. What is a cell?
2. Define prokaryotic cells.
3. Define eukaryotic cells.
4. Name four characteristics that prokaryotic cells and eukaryotic cells have in common.
5. Describe diffusion and osmosis.
6. What is active transport? Why is this important? What is required for active transport that is not needed for passive transport?
7. Explain endocytosis and exocytosis.
8. What is the nucleus of the cell? Why is it important?
9. Describe cytoplasm.
10. What are ribosomes?
11. Explain autotrophs and heterotrophs.
12. What is cell division?

Chapter 3: "Words to Remember" Crossword

ACROSS

1. clear, gel-like substance outside the nucleus of the cell of plants and animals.
5. organelles inside of cells that synthesize proteins
7. the folded, fingerlike projections of the inner wall of mitochondria
8. small paired cylindrical structures that help to pull apart the two halves of a cell during cellular reproduction
9. small sacs made from the Golgi bodies that contain enzymes that help to digest and remove debris from the cell
11. the movement of molecules across a membrane from an area of higher concentration to an area of lower concentration
12. the process by which light energy from the sun is transformed into glucose, sugar

DOWN

2. the simplest cells; they lack an organized nucleus.
3. the control center of the cell; it is separated from the cytoplasm by two membranes
4. complex cells that have a true, organized nucleus, usually located near the center of the cell
6. a part of the nucleus of a cell which is involved in making proteins
7. the basic unit of structure and function of all organisms
10. the process where the nucleus divides during the process of cell division

Life Science for Young Catholics

4 SINGLE-CELLED ORGANISMS

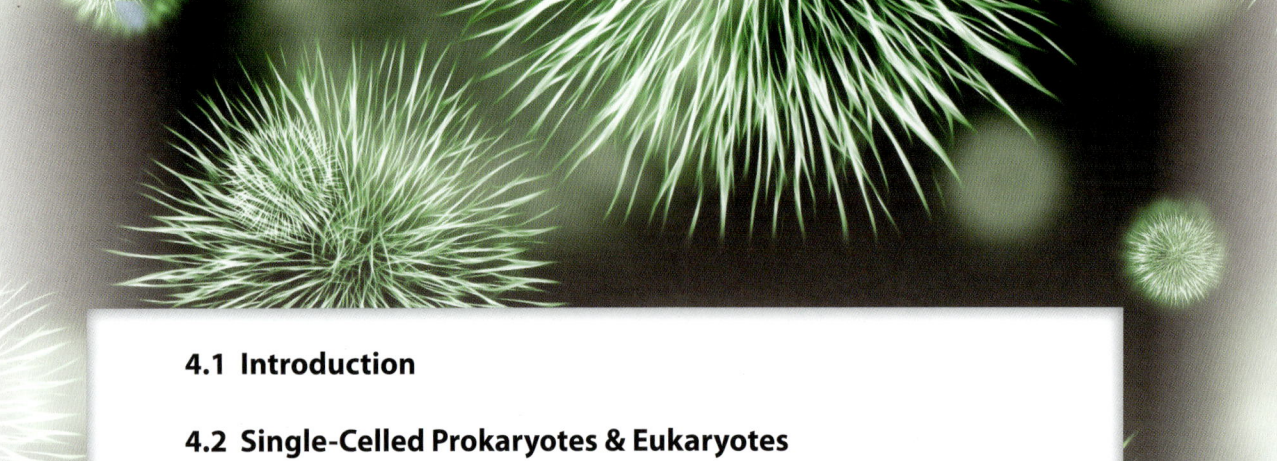

4.1 Introduction

4.2 Single-Celled Prokaryotes & Eukaryotes

4.3 Archaea – Extremophiles

4.4 Bacteria

4.5 The Roles of Archaea & Bacteria in the Environment
- A. Recyclers
- B. Decomposers
- C. Symbiotic Partners
    1. Mutualism Relationship – Example
    2. Commensal Relationship – Example
    3. Parasitic Relationship – Examples

4.6 Introduction to Protists

4.7 Single-celled Eukaryotes in Kingdom Protista

4.8 Plant-like Protists
- A. Algae
- B. Diatoms
- C. Euglena

4.9 Fungus-like Protists

4.10 Animal-like Protists

4.11 The Kingdom of Protists: Conclusion

4.12 Summary

Chapter 4
Single-Celled Organisms

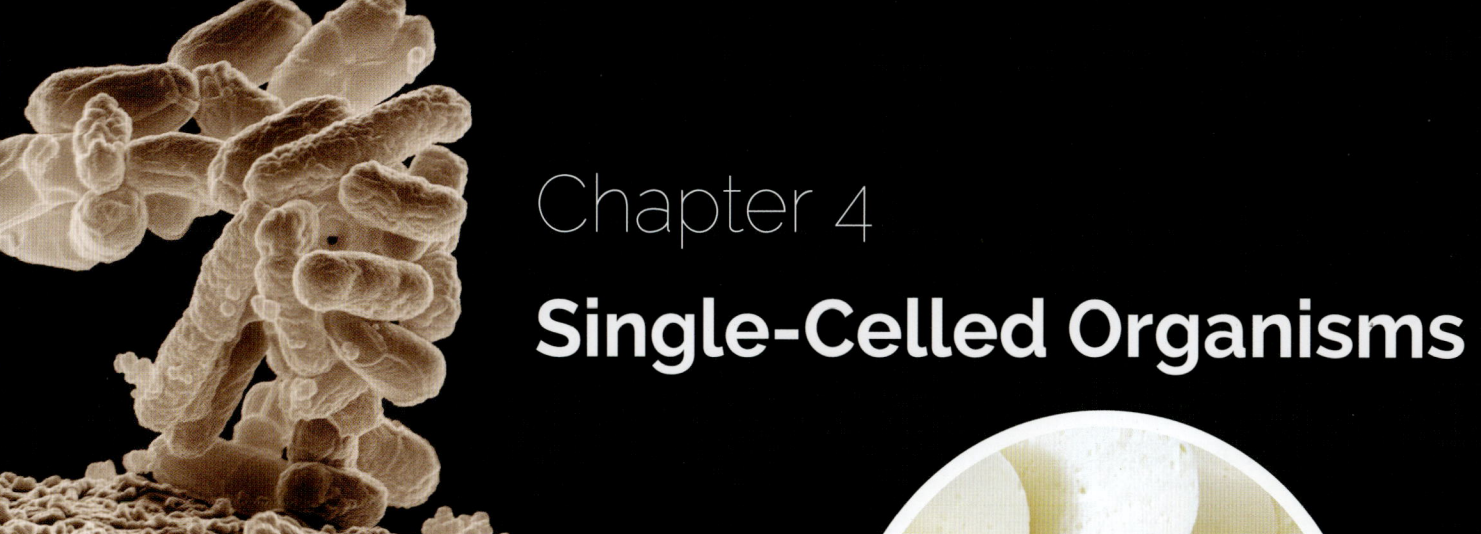

4.1 Introduction

Do you like to eat cheese? Suppose you have some in front of you, and you are so satisfied with that delicious cheese, you take a deep breath to appreciate the smell. Did you know that tiny bacteria are playing a vital process in your snack?

Did you know that single-celled organisms called bacteria are needed to process milk into cheese? Did you know that bacteria may produce up to 50% of the oxygen that we breathe? Did you know that bacteria cells in your intestinal tract help you to digest the food you eat? Believe it or not, scientists tell us that there are more tiny bacteria cells in your intestinal tract than there are people on Earth!

So for your satisfying afternoon snack, bacteria helped make the food, helped you enjoy the food with its taste and its smell, and then helped you to digest it. Bacteria probably provided the oxygen for your deep breath as you proclaimed, "I'm stuffed!"

4.2 Single-Celled Prokaryotes & Eukaryotes

We will learn about the simplest, single-celled creatures. They are similar in that they are single-celled, but they have significant differences, so they are classified differently. Many of the organisms discussed in this chapter are prokaryotic (*pro-kar-ee-o-tic*).

Recall from the previous chapter that the main classifying feature of simple prokaryotic cells is that they **do not have a membrane-protected, well defined nucleus**. Now we are going to think further about classifying the prokaryotic cells. Scientists have determined that the single-celled prokaryotic organisms are further divided into the **Archaea** (Ar-**kee**-uh) and **Bacteria**. Together these two groups, which are scientifically called **Domains**, make up approximately one half of the Earth's living mass. One teaspoon of sea water contains 5 million prokaryotic cells! That seems incredible, but scientific studies have proven it to be true.

We will also look at more complex eukaryotic organisms, but we will start with the very simplest of the eukaryotic organisms. As eukaryotes (*you-kar-ee-oats*), that is, cells with an organized

Life Science for Young Catholics

CHAPTER 4: SINGLE-CELLED ORGANISMS

nucleus, the organisms in Kingdom Protista have a membrane-protected nucleus, as well as tiny, specialized, membrane-protected organelles, which are specialized parts of a cell.

Prokaryotic organisms average only 2 micrometers in diameter. Eukaryotic cells are also tiny, but are somewhat larger, averaging 20 micrometers in diameter.

> **Section Review – 4.2 Single-Celled Prokaryotes & Eukaryotes**
>
> 1. What is the main classifying feature of simple prokaryotes?
> 2. What two domains make up the prokaryotes?
> 3. How many prokaryotic cells can be found in one teaspoon of sea water?

4.3 Archaea - Extremophiles

Archaea are single-celled organisms that lack a membrane-bound nucleus and membrane-bound organelles. Archaea are made of much stronger chemical bonds than are found in the membranes of bacteria and eukaryotes. The **unusual lipids in the cell membranes make the archaea more resistant to extremes of temperature, acidity, and the like, which allows them to live in extreme conditions.** Archaea have whip-like structures, similar to tails, called flagella (*fla·gel·uh*), that extend from the cell body and enable them to move through their environment.

Many archaea are called **extremophiles** (*ex·treem·o·files*) because they live and thrive in extreme conditions where other organisms could not. For example, some extremophiles live in volcanoes and hot springs, while others can thrive in the Dead Sea and the Great Salt Lake.

Thermophiles (*therm·o·files*) prefer extreme heat, often above 100° C, which is the boiling point of water. Think for a moment about how foods are preserved by heating them to a very hot temperature to kill unwanted microorganisms. Most organisms cannot survive such an extreme temperature. Thermophiles, however, actually inhabit volcanoes, hot springs, and very hot deep sea vents. At the other extreme, some archaea live in the frigid temperatures of the polar seas.

Halophiles (*hal·o·files*) live in extremely salty, or saline, environments, such as the Dead Sea and the Great Salt Lake.

The Grand Prismatic Spring surrounded by colorful layers of archaea bacteria.

CHAPTER 4: SINGLE-CELLED ORGANISMS

Acidophiles (*a·sid·o·files*) live in very acidic environments. Some archaea require oxygen-containing, or **aerobic** (*ay·row·bik*), environments, while some require oxygen-free, or **anaerobic** (*an·a·row·bik*), environments. **Methanogens** (*me·than·o·jens*) are archaea that require **anaerobic** conditions. These microorganisms live in the intestinal tracts of termites, cows, and humans, where they use the available carbon dioxide and hydrogen for energy and produce methane gas as a byproduct.

Section Review – 4.3 Archaea - Extremophiles

1. Explain what the term "extremophiles" means.
2. Name four locations where extremophiles can be found.
3. Explain why extremophiles can live in such difficult places.

4.4 Bacteria

The Domain Bacteria is the second of the prokaryotic domains. Bacteria are organisms that share many characteristics with the archaea, but also have some features that are unique.

Bacteria are single-celled organisms that lack a membrane-bound nucleus and membrane-bound organelles. Although bacteria are always single-celled, they do live in large groups called **colonies**. Within the colonies, which develop from a single cell, each bacteria organism, or bacterium, functions independently from the others.

Most bacteria move by means of flagella, a tail-like structure. Movement allows the bacteria to respond to changes in the surrounding environment and to acquire nutrition.

Interestingly, while bacteria have only one large chromosome, they also contain many smaller sections of DNA called **plasmids** (*plaz·mids*) in the cytoplasm. Plasmids help the bacteria to survive. There are different types of plasmids. Some help

WORDS TO REMEMBER

archaea: single-celled organisms that lack a membrane-bound nucleus and membrane-bound organelles, but have unusually strong cell membranes that allow them to survive in harsh environments.

bacteria: single-celled organisms that lack a membrane-bound nucleus and membrane-bound organelles, but have normal cell membranes that do not allow them to survive in harsh environments.

eukaryotes: cells with an organized nucleus as well as tiny, specialized, membrane-protected organelles

flagella: whip-like structures, similar to tails, that extend from the cell body and enable those cells to move through their environment

extremophiles: type of archaea that live and thrive in extreme conditions where other organisms could not

thermophiles: extremophiles that prefer extreme heat, often above 100° C, which is the boiling point of water

halophiles: extremophiles that live in extremely salty, or saline, environments such as the Dead Sea and the Great Salt Lake

acidophiles: extremophiles that live in very acidic environments

aerobic: organisms or processes that require oxygen

anaerobic: organisms or processes that do not require oxygen

methanogens: extremophile archaea that require anaerobic conditions, that is, conditions without oxygen. These microorganisms live in the intestinal tracts of termites, cows, and humans, where they use the available carbon dioxide and hydrogen for energy and produce methane gas as a byproduct.

Salmonella Bacteria

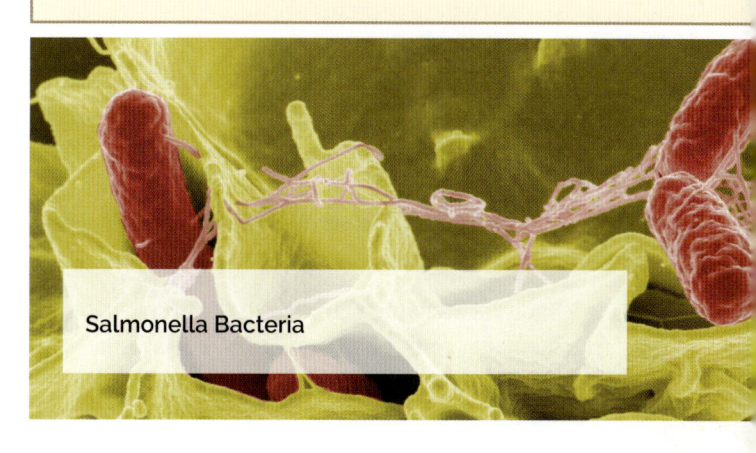

Life Science for Young Catholics 49

Structure and Shapes of Bacteria

Diagram labels: Capsule, Cell wall, Plasma membrane, Cytoplasm, Ribosomes, Plasmid, Pili, Flagellum, Nucleoid (circular DNA)

Shapes: Spiral-like, Rod-Shaped, Round

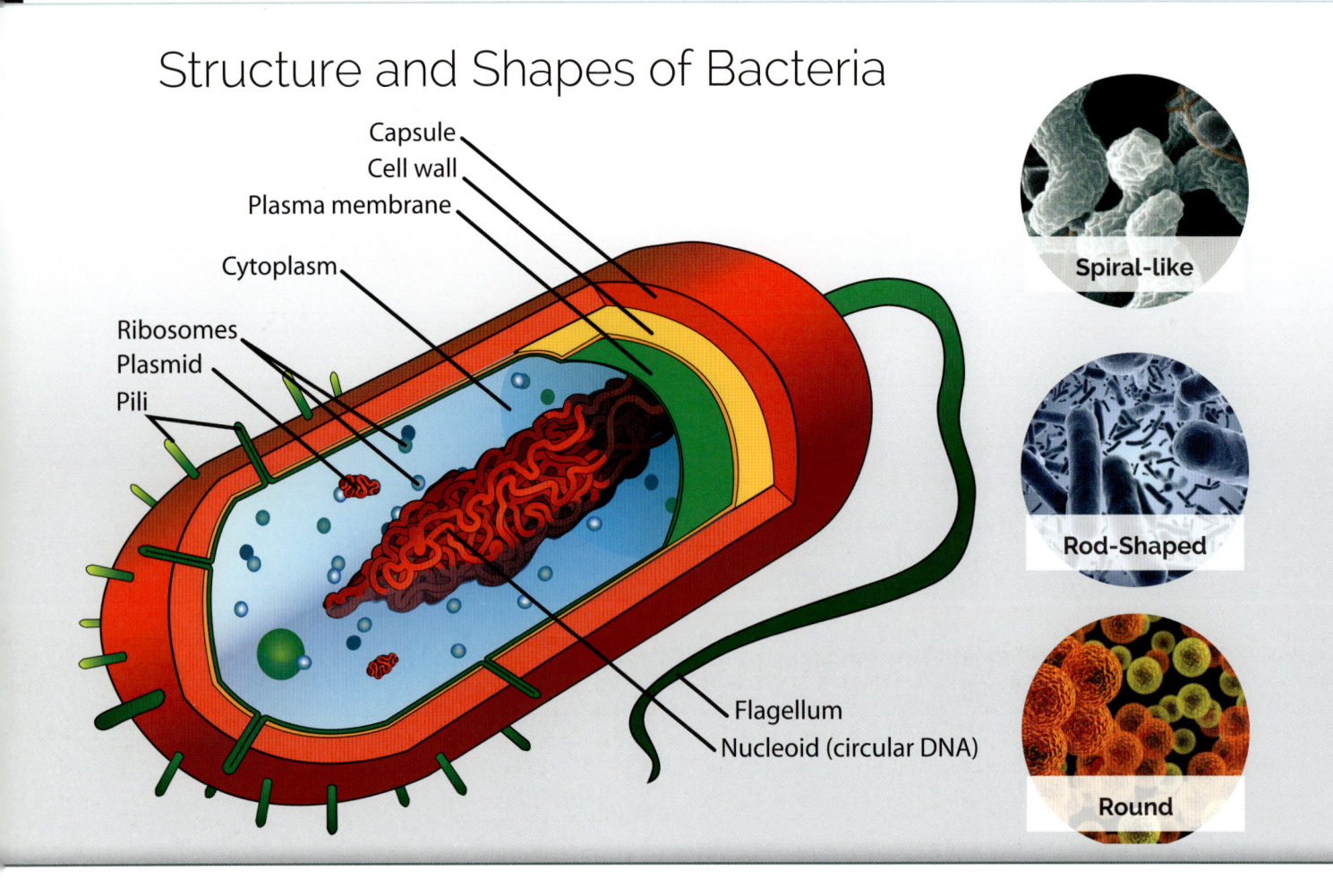

the bacteria resist poisons and antibiotics; other plasmids help the bacteria to digest unfamiliar substances. Other plasmids can help the bacteria defend itself from other bacteria.

Some bacteria are able to remove nitrogen gas from air and convert it into ammonia for use in the growth and metabolism of plants and animals. This process is called **nitrogen fixation**.

Along with the single chromosome and plasmids, the cytoplasm of bacteria contains ribosomes (where proteins are all synthesized, or made). **Synthesis** is the process where organic compounds are produced in a cell, often with the aid of enzymes. The ribosomes are in the cytoplasm because bacteria do not have an endoplasmic reticulum. Since bacteria do not have a nucleus, DNA is replicated, and RNA is transcribed in the cytoplasm of bacterial cells.

Bacteria are similar in size to the archaea, but much smaller than plant and animal cells. Like all cells, bacteria cells are surrounded by a cell membrane. Many of the bacteria's chemical reactions and metabolism occur in the cell membrane because there are no specialized organelles, small organ-like structures, as there are in eukaryotic cells.

The bacterial cell membrane is surrounded by a cell wall. The cell wall gives bacteria fixed shapes. The cell wall is covered by a tough capsule. The capsule helps defend the bacteria cell from viruses and white blood cells, but the capsule may also help the bacteria cell to cause diseases. Bacteria come in three main shapes as shown: spherical or round, rod-shaped like tiny hot dogs, and helical or spiral-like.

Section Review – 4.4 Bacteria

1. Draw and label the basic structure of bacteria.
2. Give one important purpose for each: for the bacteria's cell membrane, cell wall, and capsule.
3. What structure or structures permit movement in bacteria?
4. Describe nitrogen fixation.

4.5 The Roles of Archaea & Bacteria in the Environment

You may ask, "Why do we need to learn about these tiny creatures called archaea and bacteria?" The answer is that God, in His Wisdom, placed them on Earth for our benefit. We should be aware about bacteria which can affect us or our family and friends. While some are not so good for us, some bacteria are actually very good for us.

A. Recyclers

Prokaryotes (single-celled organisms without a defined nucleus) are essential to the recycling of carbon, nitrogen, phosphorus, iron, and other elements in the environment. It is the prokaryotes that are largely responsible for making these elements available and in a form that is usable to other organisms. Some archaea and bacteria take carbon dioxide from the atmosphere and make it into organic matter. Others, the nitrogen fixers, do the same with nitrogen from the air. Some bacteria even convert iron into a form that can be used by other organisms!

B. Decomposers

Prokaryotes are **decomposers** (*dee·com·pose·ers*). That is, prokaryotes break down dead organisms and organic matter into simpler organic compounds so they can release carbon and minerals back into the environment. Archaea also contribute to the carbon cycle by producing methane gas, the main component of natural gas, which is used as a fuel. Other prokaryotes actually consume methane gas to help maintain a balance in the atmosphere.

C. Symbiotic Relationships

Prokaryotes are often found to exist in **symbiotic** (*sim·bee·ot·ik*) **relationships** with other organisms. A symbiotic relationship is a close and long-term relationship between two different species that benefits one or both of the organisms. There are three basic types of symbiotic relationships: **mutualism** (*myoo·tyul·ism*), **commensalism** (*com·men·sal·ism*), and **parasitism** (*pair·a·site·ism*).

Mutualism relationships help both organisms. Commensal relationships help one organism but do not harm the other. One organism benefits, while the relationship is neutral for the other. Parasitic relationships help one species but harm the other.

1. Mutualism Relationship - Example

Some archaea live in a **mutualism** relationship with protozoa, small, single-celled eukaryotic organisms, that live in the digestive tracts of termites. The protozoa break down cellulose from the plants eaten by the termite. Hydrogen is released as a breakdown product from the cellulose. The hydrogen, if left to accumulate, decreases the energy of the protozoa.

Archaea (methanogens to be specific) remove the hydrogen from the local environment by converting it to methane gas. As a result, the protozoa have more energy. This relationship is beneficial to both the archaea and the protozoa.

WORDS TO REMEMBER

plasmids: small sections of DNA in the cytoplasm of bacteria

synthesis: the process in which organic compounds are produced in a cell, often with the aid of enzymes

recyclers: prokaryotes that recycle carbon, nitrogen, phosphorus, iron, and other elements in the environment

decomposers: prokaryotes that break down dead organisms and organic matter into simpler organic compounds so they can release carbon and minerals back into the environment

symbiotic relationships: close and long-term relationships between two different species that benefit one or both of the organisms

mutualism: a symbiotic relationship that helps both organisms

commensalism: a symbiotic relationship that benefits one organism, but neither helps nor harms the other organism

parasitism: a symbiotic relationship that helps one species and harms the other

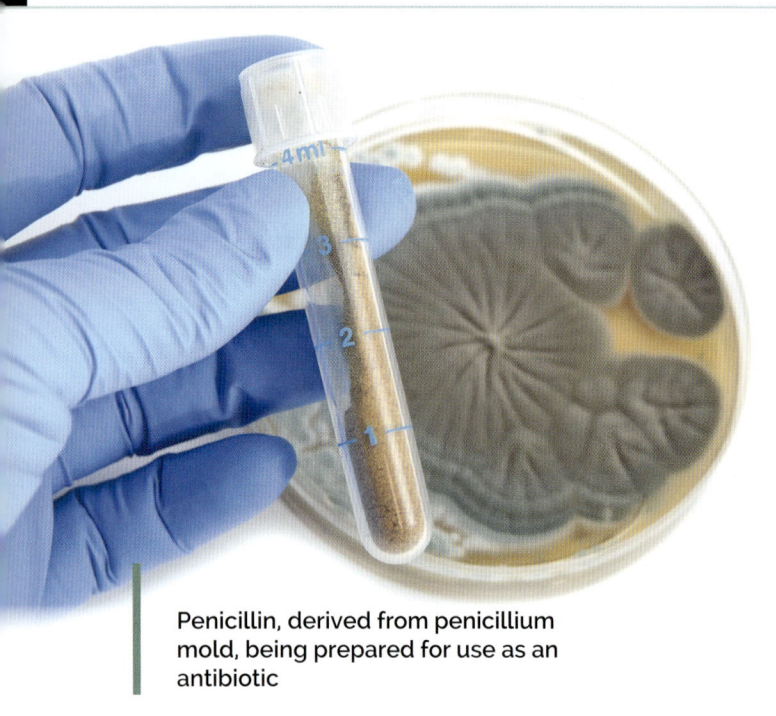

Penicillin, derived from penicillium mold, being prepared for use as an antibiotic

2. Commensal Relationship - Example

Likewise, in the same example, the archaea have a **commensal** relationship with the termite. By living in the intestinal tract of the termite, the archaea neither help nor harm the termite as they thrive on the hydrogen produced by the protozoa.

3. Parasitic Relationship - Examples

A parasitic relationship is the third type of symbiotic relationship. This is a relationship in which one organism benefits, but the other organism is harmed. The harmful organism is called a **parasite**; the organism being harmed is the **host**.

Bacteria are commonly known for their parasitic relationships. Bacterial parasites cause food to spoil and cause diseases in humans, animals, and plants.

A parasite bacterium which causes disease in a host is known as a **pathogen** (*path·o·jen*). Bacterial pathogens cause many diseases in human bodies. In fact, about one half of all human diseases are caused by bacterial pathogens, which we call germs.

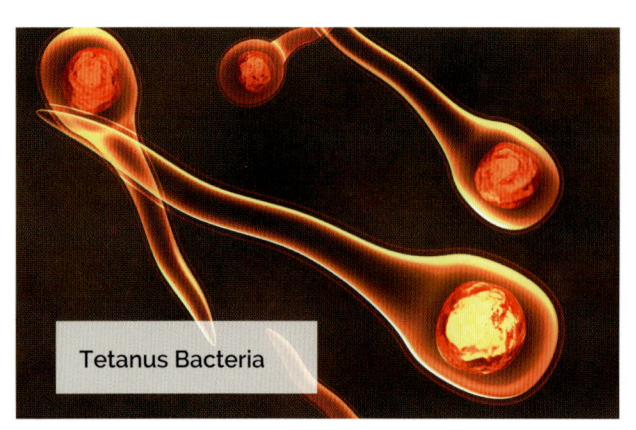

Tuberculosis, strep throat, pneumonia, whooping cough, Lyme disease, tetanus, and leprosy are among the many human diseases caused by different types of bacteria. Bacteria can also cause disease in plants. Blights, soft rot, and wilts are some of the bacterial diseases of plants.

Bacteria can cause disease by two different mechanisms: by directly invading the tissue, or by producing **toxins**, or poisons, that harm the host.

Leprosy and tuberculosis bacteria produce disease by directly damaging the host's tissues.

Tetanus, or "lock jaw," is a disease caused by a bacterial toxin. The bacterium that causes tetanus is found in the soil and usually enters the body through a cut or a puncture wound. As the bacteria grow and divide, they produce a strong toxin or poison that causes muscles to contract all over the human body. The jaw muscles are commonly affected so that the mouth cannot be opened, hence the name "lock jaw." Tetanus is a serious disease, and as many as one-third of all people who contract tetanus die from it.

Certain toxins are released only when certain bacteria are killed or injured, and the toxin enters the host at that time. These particular toxins usually do not produce serious diseases, but they do produce symptoms like fever and a runny nose.

Many bacterial diseases can be treated with the use of **antibiotics** (*ant·i·by·awe·tiks*). Antibiotics are powerful medicines that fight bacterial infections. Antibiotics either stop the growth of bacteria or directly kill bacteria. Penicillin is a familiar antibiotic used to treat strep throat and many other diseases.

Tetanus Bacteria

> ### Section Review – 4.5 The Roles of Archaea and Bacteria in the Environment
>
> 1. What are "symbiotic relationships"?
> 2. Explain "recyclers" and "decomposers."
> 3. Name 3 diseases caused in plants by bacteria.
> 4. What are antibiotics?

CHAPTER 4: **SINGLE-CELLED ORGANISMS**

✓ QUICK REVIEW: Symbiotic Relationships

Mutualism
A symbiotic relationship that benefits BOTH organisms involved.

The bee benefits by gathering nectar from the flower; the flower benefits because its pollen gets distributed by the bee.

Commensalism
A symbiotic relationship that benefits ONE organism, but neither helps nor harms the other organism.

The barnacles benefit by attaching themselves to the clam, but the clam neither benefits nor is harmed by the barnacles.

Parasitism
A symbiotic relationship that benefits ONE organism, but harms the other organism involved.

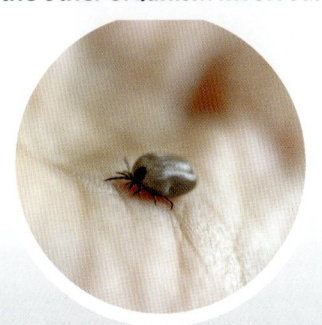

The tick benefits by obtaining blood from the human, but the human is harmed by the tick.

4.6 Introduction to Protists

If you have ever eaten ice cream, you may have algae (*al-jee*) to thank. Ice cream often contains carrageenan (*care-a-gee-nan*) to make it smoother and thicker. Carrageenan comes from red algae.

Have you ever flown on an airplane? Some airlines are now making jet fuel from algae. Fuel made from living things is called biofuel, as opposed to fossil fuel. Algae is fifty times as efficient in providing biofuel as ordinary plants.

Algae comes from the Kingdom of Protists. Very few of us ever think about how algae affects our normal activities. It is one more example of how God has planned for even the smallest creatures to provide us with such pleasant things, as ice cream and airplane rides!

Aa WORDS TO REMEMBER

pathogen: a bacteria that causes diseases. In fact, about one half of all human diseases are caused by bacterial pathogens, which we call germs.

antibiotics: powerful medicines that fight bacterial infections. Antibiotics either stop the growth of bacteria or directly kill bacteria.

penicillin: a familiar antibiotic used to treat strep throat and many other diseases.

protists: any eukaryotic organism that is not a fungus, a plant, or an animal but is fungus-like, or plant-like, or animal-like.

Life Science for Young Catholics

Algae, a plant-like protist, growing on the surface of water

4.7 Single-celled Eukaryotes in Kingdom Protista

You have studied the single-celled organisms of the two prokaryotic kingdoms, Archaea and Bacteria. Now we will look at more complex eukaryotic organisms, but we will look at the very simplest of the eukaryotic organisms. As **eukaryotes** (*you-**kar**-ee-oats*), that is cells with an organized nucleus, the organisms in **Kingdom Protista** have a **membrane-protected nucleus**, as well as tiny, **specialized, membrane-protected organelles, which are a specialized part of a cell.** Most protists are single-celled organisms, but some protists are multi-celled creatures.

A **protist** is any eukaryotic organism that is **not a fungus, nor a plant, nor an animal,** but is **fungus-like, or plant-like, or animal-like.** Because most protists are single-celled, they appear to be simple organisms. However, all the seven essential life processes occur in these microscopic single-celled organisms, with some processes, such as movement and reproduction, being much more complex than that of single-celled prokaryotes.

Most protists live in water, but some live on land, and some live in the human body.

Protists are divided into three groups, Plant-like, Fungus-like, and Animal-like, depending on how they obtain food.

Some protists make their own food supply through photosynthesis, like plants. These are described as **Plant-like Protists**. Some share characteristics with fungi and obtain nutrition from dead organic matter. These are known as **Fungus-like Protists**. Others take in their nutrition from the surrounding environment like animals; these are categorized as **Animal-like Protists**.

Protists may be free-living, independent organisms, or they may be found living in colonies with others of their own kind, or they may be living in symbiotic relationships with other organisms. While some organisms in symbiotic relationships are helpful to each other, some protists live in relationships with humans that are of no benefit to people, and other protists can be harmful to their human hosts.

> ### Section Review – 4.7 Single-celled Eukaryotes in Kingdom Protista
>
> 1. What makes the Kingdom of Protists separate from all others?
> 2. Identify the sub-groups of protists. How are these groups organized?
> 3. Where are protists usually found in the environment?
> 4. Are all protists single-celled, and do they all carry out all seven processes necessary for life?

Life Science for Young Catholics

CHAPTER 4: SINGLE-CELLED ORGANISMS

4.8 Plant-like Protists

You may wonder why plant-like protists are not considered to be plants. The answer to that good question is that protists don't have roots or leaves. Most plant-like protists are **single-celled**, and they **reproduce differently than plants**.

All plant-like protists have chloroplasts (**klor-o-plasts**), those special organelles that **allow plants to make sugar from the energy in sunlight**. Plant-like protists make their own food through photosynthesis like true plants. Many protists, also like plants, store starch and have cells surrounded by cell walls. Some plant-like protists have cell walls made of cellulose like those of true plants.

A. Algae

Algae (**al**·jee) are a diverse group of plant-like protists. Diverse means those in the group are different from each other. For instance, algae come in a variety of colors: gold, red, green, and brown. Despite their individual colors, all algae contain the green pigment chlorophyll. **Accessory** or additional **pigments** sometimes mask the basic green color of the chlorophyll, but the accessory colors are important in helping the algae capture light in varied depths of water.

All algae have cell walls. Many species of algae have more than one cell wall protecting each cell.

Diatoms

Algae are diverse in their shapes and sizes, as well as in their complexity of structures. Some algae are single-celled, but some are more than single cells. Some algae live in colonies, but some do not. Some algae are complex, multi-celled organisms, some even with specialized **tissues**. Recall from the previous chapter that tissues represent the second level of cellular organization. Tissues have cells of similar structure and work together to perform a specific function.

B. Diatoms

One group of plant-like algae is that of the **diatoms** (**die**·a·toms). Most diatoms are single-celled organisms that can be found in fresh water, salt water, moist soil, and on moist surfaces of some plants. Though single-celled organisms, some diatoms will

WORDS TO REMEMBER

protists: any eukaryotic organism that is not a fungus, a plant, or an animal but is fungus-like, or plant-like, or animal-like

protists (plant-like): a large and diverse group of protists that produce their own food. They perform photosynthesis to produce sugar by using carbon dioxide and water, and the energy from sunlight, just like plants. Unlike plants, however, plant-like protists do not have true stems, roots, or leaves.

protists (fungus-like): obtain food outside themselves. They also have cell walls and reproduce by forming spores, just like fungi. Fungus-like protists usually do not move on their own. Two major types of fungus-like protists are slime molds and water molds.

protists (animal-like): called protozoa. Protozoa are single-celled eukaryotes that share some traits with animals. Animal-like protists can move, and they obtain nutrition from outside of themselves instead of producing their own food.

algae: a plant-like protist that lives in water and contains chlorophyll

diatoms: single-celled organisms, a type of algae, that can be found in fresh water, salt water, moist soil, and on moist surfaces of some plants. Diatoms are a component or a part of plankton.

Life Science for Young Catholics

Fish feeding on plankton

live in colonies. Like snowflakes, diatoms have many different and intricate shapes. Each shape is unique to an individual species of diatom, and each shape is determined by the cell wall.

Like other algae, diatoms contain chloroplasts and produce their own food. Diatoms produce large amounts of the Earth's oxygen through photosynthesis. Many diatoms contain accessory pigments which give them their golden-brown color.

Diatoms form the basis of the food web (the interrelation of plants and animals) of oceans, ponds, and other aquatic environments. Diatoms are a component or a part of **plankton**. Plankton is a group of organisms, including diatoms and a variety of single-celled organisms, which live together in a body of water.

Plankton are not capable of swimming against the currents of water, so plankton are known as drifters. Perhaps most important, plankton are the basic source of nutrition for many aquatic organisms, ranging from newly hatched fish to large fish and whales.

Industry has important uses for diatoms. The hard outer layer of the outer cell wall of diatoms collects on the sea floors over many years, and produces **diatomaceous** (*di-at-o-**mah**-shus*) **earth**. Diatomaceous earth is very helpful for all of us. It is used in filtering systems, abrasives, cleansers, and paint. Modern scientists believe that the oil we discover in the ground is largely produced from fossilized diatom deposits.

C. Euglena

Another important group of plant-like algae are the euglena (*you-**glee**-na*). Euglena are found in fresh and salt water. Euglena are single-celled protists that contain chlorophyll and are capable of photosynthesis. At times when sunlight is not available for photosynthesis, the euglena engulfs food from the surrounding environment. This involves the cell membrane wrapping around the food particle, pinching off to form a vesicle, or a small sac, which moves into the cell and in which the food particle is eventually digested. Euglena do not have cell walls.

Diagram of Euglena

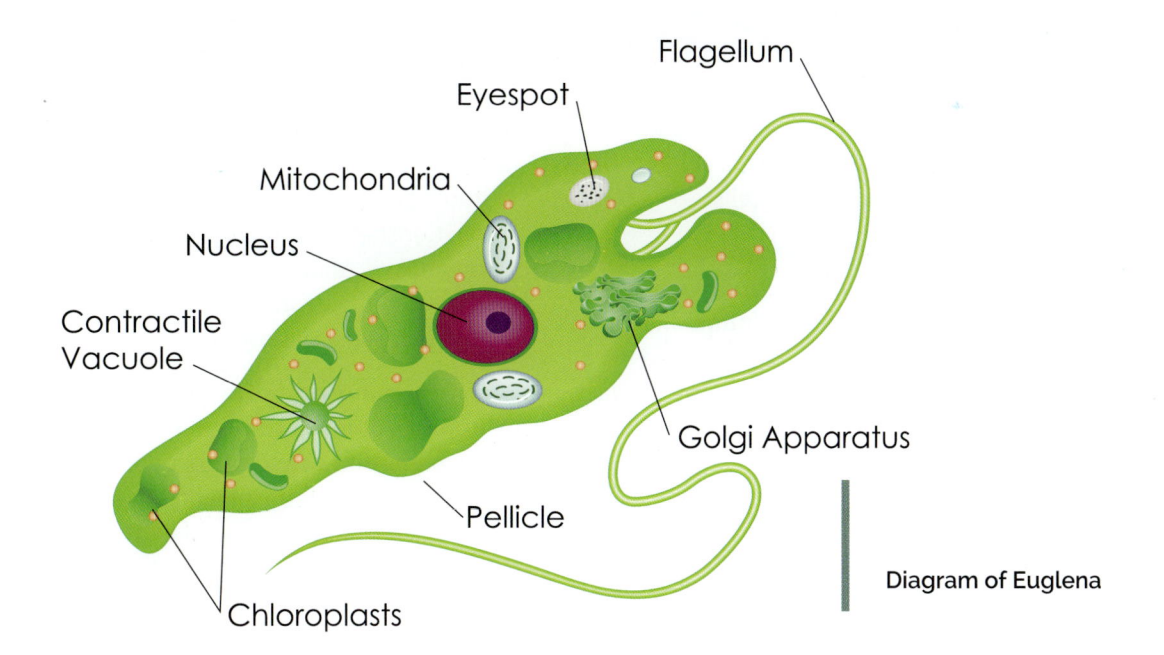

Labels: Flagellum, Eyespot, Mitochondria, Nucleus, Contractile Vacuole, Chloroplasts, Pellicle, Golgi Apparatus

One feature unique to some species of euglena is a **red eye spot**. This is a collection of pigment that helps the euglena detect light and move toward the light. This is an example of response to the environment, one of the seven life functions.

Euglena are very efficient oxygen producers. Euglena are able to convert carbon dioxide into sugars and oxygen much faster than plants. Euglena also help break down organic matter.

> **Section Review – 4.8 Plant-like Protists**
>
> 1. How are plant-like protists like true plants? How are they different?
> 2. Describe algae.
> 3. Describe diatoms.
> 4. Name four features of plankton.
> 5. Name four features of euglena.

4.9 Fungus-like Protists

You may not be as familiar with fungus-like protists as with plant-like or animal-like protists, but they are interesting to know about. You may ask, "Why are these creatures classified as fungus-like protists, and not as fungi?" The answer is the differences in the cell wall composition: fungus-like protist cell walls are made of cellulose; a true fungus has a cell wall with chitin, a harder and stronger molecule than cellulose.

There are three groups of fungus-like protists: **cellular slime molds**, **acellular slime molds**, and **water molds**.

Water molds are the cause of the potato **blight** of the Great Potato Famine in Ireland in the 1840s. Another disease, **downy mildew**, can be caused by water molds, and can damage the leaves of a wide variety of plants. Water molds, like fungi, are decomposers that break down dead organic material and help recycle the Earth's elements.

> **Section Review – 4.9 Fungus-like Protists**
>
> 1. Name the major types of fungus-like protists.
> 2. What are decomposers?

4.10 Animal-like Protists

The main difference between animal-like protists and true animals is in the cell count. Animal-like protists are single-celled, and creatures designated as animals have many cells.

Animal-like protists, or **protozoa** (**pro**·toe·**zoe**·a), are usually single-celled eukaryotic organisms, found in fresh water. Animal-like protists have cell membranes, but lack cell walls, and do not contain chlorophyll. Because the protozoa lack chlorophyll, they must obtain nutrition from an outside source.

All animal-like protists, or protozoa, can move, and are classified into four groups based on the way they move: **zooflagellates** (**zoe**·o·**flaj**·ell·ates), **sarcodines** (**sar**·ko·dines), **ciliates** (**seal**·ee·ates), and **sporozoans** (**spore**·o·**zoe**·ans).

A. Zooflagellates

The **zooflagellates** are all single-celled protozoa that move by means of flagella. The prefix "zoo" means animal, and "flagella" are small tail-like appendages that allow the organism to move. So a zooflagellate is an animal-like creature that moves by means of the flagella or whip-like tail.

There are many groups of zooflagellates and they exist in a great variety of shapes and sizes. The zooflagellates live in numerous habitats. Many zooflagellates live in mutualistic relationships, relationships of mutual benefit, with other organisms. Many zooflagellates, however, are parasites, organisms that feed on other organisms, and that cause diseases in animals and in humans.

Trypanosomes (tri·**pan**·o·somes) are an example of the harmful category of zooflagellates. Trypanosomes are protozoa with a single elongated flagellum attached to and extending from the cell membrane like the fin and tail of a fish. The arrangement of the flagellum causes the trypanosome to move in corkscrew-like motion.

Trypanosomes are parasites that live primarily in mammals, but require the **tsetse** (**tet**-see) **fly** to complete their life cycle. An infected tsetse fly carries and then transmits the trypanosome parasites to the human body through a bite when the fly feeds on human blood. The trypanosomes enter the human blood stream and multiply. Another tsetse fly may bite the infected human body and pick up the trypanosomes into its system. Once in

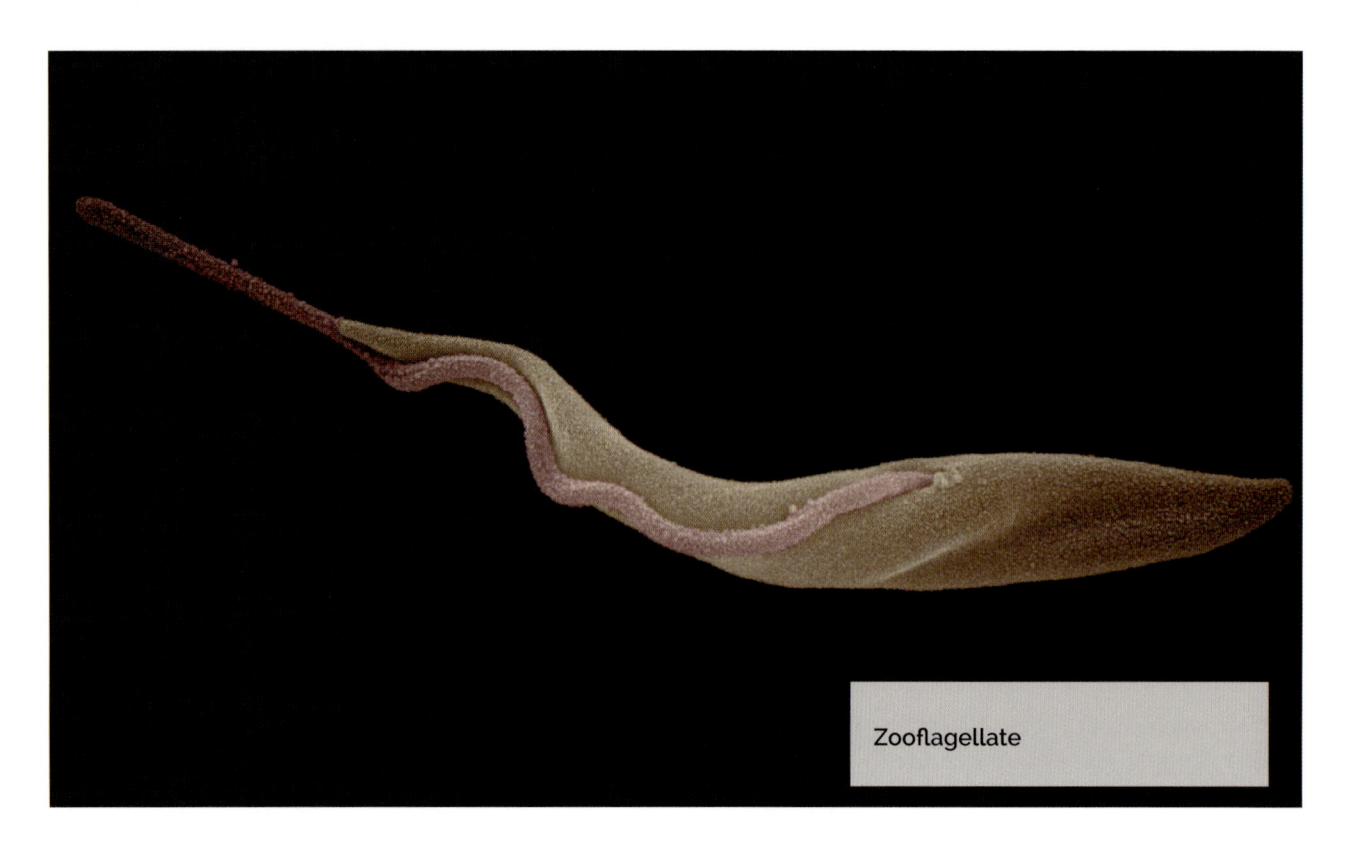

Zooflagellate

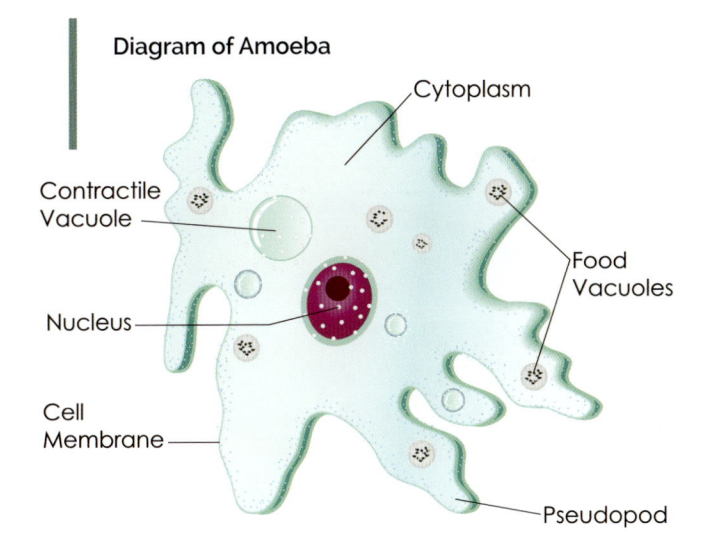

Diagram of Amoeba
- Cytoplasm
- Contractile Vacuole
- Food Vacuoles
- Nucleus
- Cell Membrane
- Pseudopod

the tsetse fly, the trypanosomes continue to grow, develop, and multiply to complete their life cycle, and then can be transmitted again to another human host.

The trypanosome can cause an illness known as **African sleeping sickness**. Once the human body is infected, the bite becomes painful and develops into a sore. Between one and three weeks after the bite, the person usually develops fever, severe headaches, irritability, extreme fatigue, body aches, and confusion. If the person is not quickly and properly treated, the infection will cause death within months.

B. Sarcodines – Amoeba

The **amoeba** are unicellular, or single-celled, protozoa that move by means of pseudopods. Pseudopods, also known as false feet, are extensions of cytoplasm that reach out and then retract to pull the organism along a surface. They live on land and in water environments.

Amoeba means change or changing. The name is descriptive because amoeba lack cell walls and have no definitive shape. Each amoeba is surrounded by a flexible cell membrane from which the pseudopods extend and retract. As a result, the amoeba cell is constantly changing in shape.

An amoeba takes in nutrition from the surrounding environment by using its pseudopods to engulf food particles. The pseudopod pinches off and then travels through the cytoplasm to fuse with a lysosome containing digestive enzymes. Diatoms and plankton make up the main food sources for the amoeba.

In the water environments, amoeba are a component of plankton. In the soil, amoeba are the largest consumers of bacteria and contribute to the recycling of elements. However, certain types of amoeba are harmful to the human body.

C. Ciliates – Paramecium

Ciliates are animal-like protists that are covered in short, **hair-like organelles** called **cilia**, which are used for movement, for attachment to surfaces and other organisms, for feeding, and for sensation. The ciliates are found in all water habitats and soils.

A **paramecium** (*pair·a·mee·see·um*) is a slipper-shaped, single-celled organism that has a flexible but well defined shape made by an elastic membrane that surrounds the cell. The paramecium is a somewhat complex organism with several specialized organelles that perform specific functions, like organs in multicellular animals.

WORDS TO REMEMBER

plankton: a group of organisms, including diatoms and a variety of single-celled organisms, which live together in a body of water. Plankton are known as drifters. Plankton are the basic source of nutrition for many aquatic organisms, ranging from newly hatched fish to large fish and whales.

euglena: single-celled protists that contain chlorophyll and are capable of photosynthesis. Euglena do not have cell walls. Some species of euglena have a red eye spot that helps the euglena detect and move toward light.

zooflagellates: single-celled protozoa that move by means of flagella. The prefix "zoo" means animal, and "flagella" are small, tail-like appendages that allow the organism to move.

trypanosomes: protozoa with a single elongated flagellum attached to and extending from the cell membrane like the fin and tail of a fish. The arrangement of the flagellum causes the trypanosome to move in a corkscrew-like motion. Trypanosomes are parasites that live primarily in mammals.

Life Science for Young Catholics

CHAPTER 4: SINGLE-CELLED ORGANISMS

A paramecium has complex behaviors in response to the environment. Paramecia have avoidance behaviors. That is, when a paramecium senses, or meets, an obstacle in its path, its cilia begin to beat in the opposite direction, causing the paramecium to back away from the obstacle. The paramecium turns around 180 degrees and begins again to move forward. A paramecium seems to prefer warm water because it tends to move away from cold water.

D. Sporozoans

Sporozoans are the fourth group of animal-like protists. Sporozoans get part of their name, "sporo," from the fact that they produce spores, like some plants. The other part of the name is from "zoo" which means "animal." So sporozoans are spore-producing, animal-like organisms.

Unlike the other animal-like protists, the sporozoans do not have flagella, pseudopods, or cilia. Throughout most of their life cycle, sporozoans cannot move on their own. Most sporozoa have complex life cycles that involve various forms of the sporozoa living in mosquito **vectors**. Vectors are organisms that do not cause disease but that carry disease. Vectors are animal hosts for disease-producing organisms, yet the disease does not harm the host animal.

It might interest you to learn about a representative type of sporozoan, the **plasmodium** (plas·**moe**·dee·um). There are over 200 species of plasmodia, with eleven species that cause disease in the human body, including **malaria** (ma·**lair**·ee·ah), which is caused by Plasmodium Malariae (ma·**lair**·ee·aye).

Malaria is a serious illness in humans that, if left untreated, can lead to death. People with malaria experience high fevers, shaking chills, and flu-like symptoms. Malaria is transmitted to humans through the bite of an **Anopheles** (an·**off**·ee·lees) mosquito

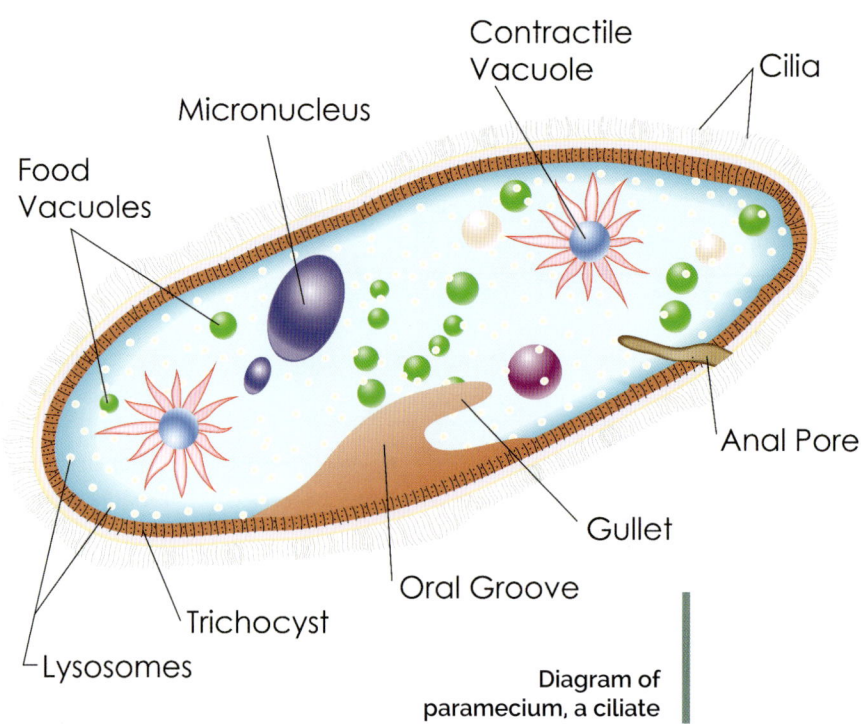

Diagram of paramecium, a ciliate — labels: Food Vacuoles, Micronucleus, Contractile Vacuole, Cilia, Anal Pore, Gullet, Oral Groove, Trichocyst, Lysosomes

and is common in tropical and subtropical areas where these mosquitoes are found.

**Section Review –
4.10 Animal-like Protists**

1. What is a flagellum? What is it used for?
2. Describe zooflagellates.
3. What major disease is caused by trypanosomes?
4. What are pseudopods?
5. What are cilia?
6. Name five characteristics of ciliates.
7. Draw and identify the parts of an amoeba.
8. Draw and identify the parts of a paramecium.
9. What major disease is caused by a plasmodium?

Life Science for Young Catholics

4.11 The Kingdom of Protists: Conclusion

St. Paul told us that "God hath chosen the weak things of the world to confound the things which are mighty" (I Corinthians 1:27). The tiny protists would certainly qualify as some of the weakest creatures in creation, yet they can cause diseases like malaria and African sleeping sickness that can seriously affect the lives of people.

However, God's Providence provides these tiny little beings for the benefit of mankind as well. Algae, diatoms, and plankton perform many useful purposes, including starting the food chain for larger creatures. Algae provide oxygen for the air we breathe and help to control the population of potentially harmful bacteria. The amoeba and paramecium feed on bacteria and algae, to help keep water supplies healthy.

We should thank God for the diversity He shows us, and for providing so many different creatures to make our planet perfect for human life.

> **Section Review – 4.11 The Kingdom of Protists: Conclusion**
>
> Give three reasons that we should thank God for protists.

4.12 Summary

On Ash Wednesday, the priest places ashes on our foreheads and prays, "Remember man, thou art dust, and to dust thou shall return." This is a reminder that due to Original Sin, death and decay entered the world.

This also reminds us that even the Temple of the Holy Spirit, the human body, is made of much smaller things, called cells.

In God's creation, there is a pattern of smaller things that are similar to larger things. The tiny, simple atom is the basic unit of all matter. The atom has a center with at least one electron orbiting it, just like the Earth with the Moon orbiting it. But it does not stop there! The Sun is a center with the Earth and other planets orbiting it. The Sun itself orbits the center of our Milky Way Galaxy. So the pattern is constantly being repeated in God's creation.

The tiny, simple cell is the basic unit of life. Each man is an independent living organism made up of trillions of cells. However, some organisms are complete living beings, but are made up of only one cell.

All of the organisms that we studied in this chapter are one-celled organisms, but are complete living organisms. They are very tiny creatures, but each in its own way presents the wonder and glory of God to us.

In the First Letter to the Corinthians, St. Paul taught that God chooses the weak things of the world to confound the strong and to teach the strong. This is why God chose a simple girl like Bernadette at Lourdes, or the three small children at Fatima, to deliver important messages to our modern world. These weak single-celled organisms also have important messages for us today. They make us realize that God has produced an incredible world of complexity and beauty to teach us about Himself and how much He loves us.

WORDS TO REMEMBER

amoeba: unicellular, or single-celled, protozoa that move by means of pseudopods. Pseudopods, also known as false feet, are extensions of cytoplasm that reach out and then retract to pull the organism along a surface. Amoeba live on land and in water environments.

ciliates: animal-like protists that are covered in short, hair-like organelles called cilia, which are used for movement, for attachment to surfaces and other organisms, for feeding, and for sensation. The ciliates are found in all water habitats and soils.

sporozoans: animal-like protists. Sporozoans get part of their name, "sporo," from the fact that they produce spores, like some plants. The other part of the name is from "zoo" which means "animal." So sporozoans are spore-producing, animal-like organisms.

Chapter 4 Review

A. Provide one example of each:

1. Mutualism: _____

2. Commensalism: _____

3. Parasitism: _____

B. Complete the missing labels.

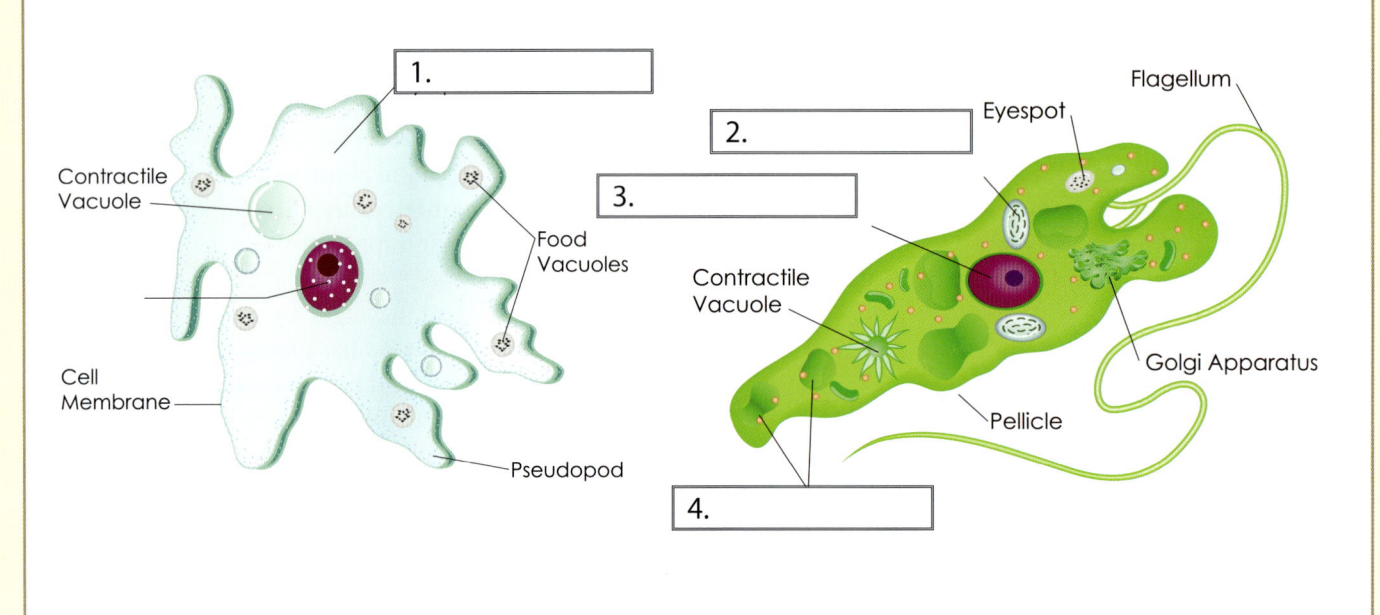

1. _____
2. _____
3. _____
4. _____

C. Answer the following questions.

1. What is the main classifying feature of simple prokaryotes?
2. What structure or structures permit movement in the archaea?
3. What are "symbiotic relationships"?
4. Explain "recyclers" and "decomposers."
5. Name 3 diseases caused in humans by bacteria.
6. What are antibiotics?
7. Where are protists usually found in the environment?
8. How are plant-like protists like true plants? How are they different?
9. Describe algae.
10. Describe diatoms.

Chapter 4: "Words to Remember" Crossword

ACROSS

1. single-celled protozoa that move by means of a flagella
3. organisms or processes that do not require oxygen
6. type of archaea that live and thrive in extreme conditions where other organisms could not
10. a symbiotic relationship that benefits one organism, but neither helps nor harms the other organism
12. a plant-like protist that lives in water, contains chlorophyll
13. any eukaryotic organism that is not a fungus, a plant, or an animal but is fungus-like, or plant-like, or animal-like
14. a symbiotic relationship that helps both organisms

DOWN

2. organisms or processes that require oxygen
4. a familiar antibiotic used to treat strep throat and many other diseases
5. single-celled organisms that lack a membrane-bound nucleus and membrane-bound organelles
7. a symbiotic relationship that helps one species and harms the other
8. unicellular, or single-celled, protozoa that move by means of pseudopods
9. small sections of DNA in the cytoplasm of bacteria
11. single-celled protists that contain chlorophyll, do not have cell walls, and are capable of photosynthesis

5 THE FUNGUS KINGDOM

5.1 Introduction

5.2 The Fungus Kingdom

5.3 The Life Processes in the Fungus Kingdom

5.4 The "Little Pots"

5.5 The Bread Molds

5.6 Root Fungus

5.7 The Sac Fungi
- A. Structure of Sac Fungi
- B. Benefits of Sac Fungi
- C. Lichen
- D. Yeast
- E. Disease-Causing Sac Fungi

5.8 The Club Fungi
- A. Structure of the Club Fungi
- B. Mushrooms

5.9 Micro Fungi and Anaerobic Fungi
- A. Micro Fungi
- B. Anaerobic Fungi

5.10 Summary

5.11 Precision of God's Creation

The Fungus Kingdom

5.1 Introduction

Have you ever read the book *Alice's Adventures in Wonderland*? If you have, you may recall that Alice met a caterpillar who sat on a mushroom. In the story, the mushroom had special properties. One side could make Alice grow taller, and the other side could make her shrink. Real mushrooms cannot do that, but mushrooms do possess chemicals that can affect you in ways that may surprise you! Mushrooms are a well-known kind of **fungus**.

At Mass, the priest uses unleavened bread to consecrate the Holy Eucharist. Unleavened bread is made without yeast. When yeast is added to dough, it makes the dough rise and get thicker. The unleavened bread used at Mass is very thin because it doesn't have yeast to make it rise. Yeast is another well-known kind of **fungus**.

5.2 The Fungus Kingdom

The Fungus Kingdom is classified under the Domain Eukarya (*you-**kar**-ee-a*). All members of the Fungus Kingdom are eukaryotes (*you-**kar**-ee-otes*), so their cells have membrane-bound nuclei and tiny organelles. The word **fungi** (plural of **fungus**) is pronounced like **fun**-jie, rhyming with the word lie. All fungi have similar RNA making up their ribosomes in their cells. Despite the similarities in RNA, however, the fungi are very diverse organisms that are classified according to the **shape** of the spore-producing structures. There are seven phyla within the Fungus Kingdom. They are: **micro fungi**, "**little pots**," **bread mold**, **root fungi**, **sac fungi**, **club fungi**, and **anaerobic fungi**.

This fungus kingdom includes tiny microscopic yeasts, chytrids (**kit**·*rids*) and molds, as well as the multicellular rusts, smuts, morels, truffles, and mushrooms.

All fungi share the following five characteristics:

1. Fungi have cell walls composed of chitin.

2. Fungi do not make their own food.

3. Fungi absorb their food.

4. Fungi have tubular filaments with rigid walls, called **hyphae** (**high**·*fee*).

5. Fungi reproduce by spores.

Life Science for Young Catholics

CHAPTER 5: THE FUNGUS KINGDOM

Fungi share some common characteristics with plants. Like plants, all fungi have cell walls. The cell walls of a fungus are made primarily of **chitin** (**ky**·tin). Chitin is a complex polysaccharide, or large sugar molecule, also found in the hard outer shell of insects and mollusks. The presence of a cell wall in fungi is similar to plants. However, the polysaccharides making up the fungus cell wall are like the polysaccharides found in the animal kingdom. Like plants, however, most fungi are relatively immobile.

Like animal cells, however, fungus cells do not contain chlorophyll. Therefore, fungi must obtain nutrition from outside sources. Most fungi obtain nutrition from dead and decaying organic matter. Many fungi are called decomposers because they break down or decompose dead and decaying organic matter. Some fungi are parasites, obtaining nourishment from living organisms, and consequently often cause diseases. Surprisingly, some fungi live in symbiotic, that is mutually helpful, relationships with other living organisms.

> **Section Review – 5.2 Fungus Kingdom**
>
> 1. The Fungus Kingdom is part of what Domain?
> 2. What is unique about the ribosomes of fungi?
> 3. Describe chitin in fungi. Where else is chitin found?
> 4. How are fungi classified? How many main classes are there?

5.3 The Life Processes in the Fungus Kingdom

Recall from previous chapters that all living organisms must carry out seven life functions, or processes: nutrition, cellular respiration, growth, reproduction, movement, and sensitivity, or response to the environment. Like all other living organisms, the fungi carry out all seven processes. In doing so, again, there are some **similarities between fungi and plants, but also some similarities between fungi and animals.**

Fungi **obtain nutrition** from their environment. Fungi do not ingest their food and then digest it internally. Instead, the fungi have specialized **hyphae** that grow into the organic matter of the surrounding environment to obtain nutrition. Hyphae are **long filaments of cytoplasm** surrounded by a cell membrane and cell wall. Some hyphae are divided into smaller compartments by **septa** (singular **septum**). The septa cross the width of the filament like walls in a building to make compartments, like rooms.

Septa perform three main functions within the hyphae. First, they give support to an otherwise long, thin tube, the hyphae. Second, the compartments they form provide a means of defense, like the water-tight doors in a submarine, should part of the hyphae get damaged. Finally, the compartments formed by the septa allow the hyphae to perform different life functions simultaneously. The compartments can become like tiny specialized organs for the fungus.

The hyphae cells secrete or discharge **exoenzymes** (**ex**-o-**en**-zimes). These are enzymes that are secreted out of the cell and work outside of the cell directly in the decaying matter. These enzymes digest the decaying matter outside of the fungal organism. The digested nutrients are then absorbed back into the fungus.

Fungi live and thrive in a wide variety of environments; thus, they are very diverse in the types of nutrients that they digest. Some fungi require **carbon compounds**, such as carbohydrates or alcohols, for cellular respiration and metabolism. Other fungi require **nitrogen compounds,** including nitrates and ammonia. Fungi, like all other living organisms, excrete their metabolic byproducts (waste) into the environment.

Most fungi live in the soil or on other decaying matter. In fact, most of the structure of the fungi is located under the surface of the soil. The underground structure of fungi is a network of hyphae called a **mycelium** (my·**see**·lee·um). The mycelium is very inconspicuous to us

CHAPTER 5: **THE FUNGUS KINGDOM**

Mycelium beneath the surface

because it is under the surface of the soil and the structures of the mycelium are very, very tiny.

The network of hyphae spread out under the soil, or under other decaying matter, but they can grow rapidly over large areas. Amazingly, some hyphae can grow at a rate of about half a mile each day! Watching that can keep young scientists busy!

By spreading out over a large area, the hyphae can absorb a large amount of nutrients from the surroundings. Most fungi become apparent to the human eye only when certain structures called **fruiting bodies** form on the surface of the soil. The fruiting bodies are made of tightly packed, specialized hyphae that fuse with other hyphae and finally grow up from the soil. See the illustration above.

The fruiting bodies are the structures most commonly recognized as fungi and are found in a wide variety of shapes, sizes, and colors. The part of the common mushroom that you can see on your lawn is a fruiting body. The fruiting bodies are specialized to produce and release **spores**, which are the reproductive cells of fungi.

Fungal spores are released into the environment by a variety of means. The spores may be released into the air and carried by the wind, or carried on water droplets, or transported by insects

WORDS TO REMEMBER

fungus: a large group of eukaryotic protists, including molds, mildews, mushrooms, rusts, and smuts, which are parasites on living organisms or feed upon dead organic material. Fungi lack chlorophyll, true roots, stems, and leaves, and they reproduce by means of spores.

chitin: a complex, large sugar molecule that makes up the cell walls of fungi. Chitin is also found in the hard outer shell of insects and mollusks.

hyphae: are long filaments of cytoplasm surrounded by a cell membrane and cell wall of fungi.

septa: are filaments within the hyphae that divide them into smaller compartments, like walls in a building to make rooms.

exoenzymes: enzymes that are secreted out of a fungus cell and work outside of the cell directly in decaying matter to digest it.

mycelium: the underground structure of fungi. It is a network of hyphae spread out under the soil.

fruiting bodies: are the part of a fungus that forms on the surface of the soil. The fruiting bodies are the structures most commonly recognized as fungi and are found in a wide variety of shapes, sizes, and colors. The part of the common mushroom that you can see on your lawn is a fruiting body. The fruiting bodies are specialized to produce and release spores, which are the reproductive cells of fungi.

Life Science for Young Catholics

CHAPTER 5: THE FUNGUS KINGDOM

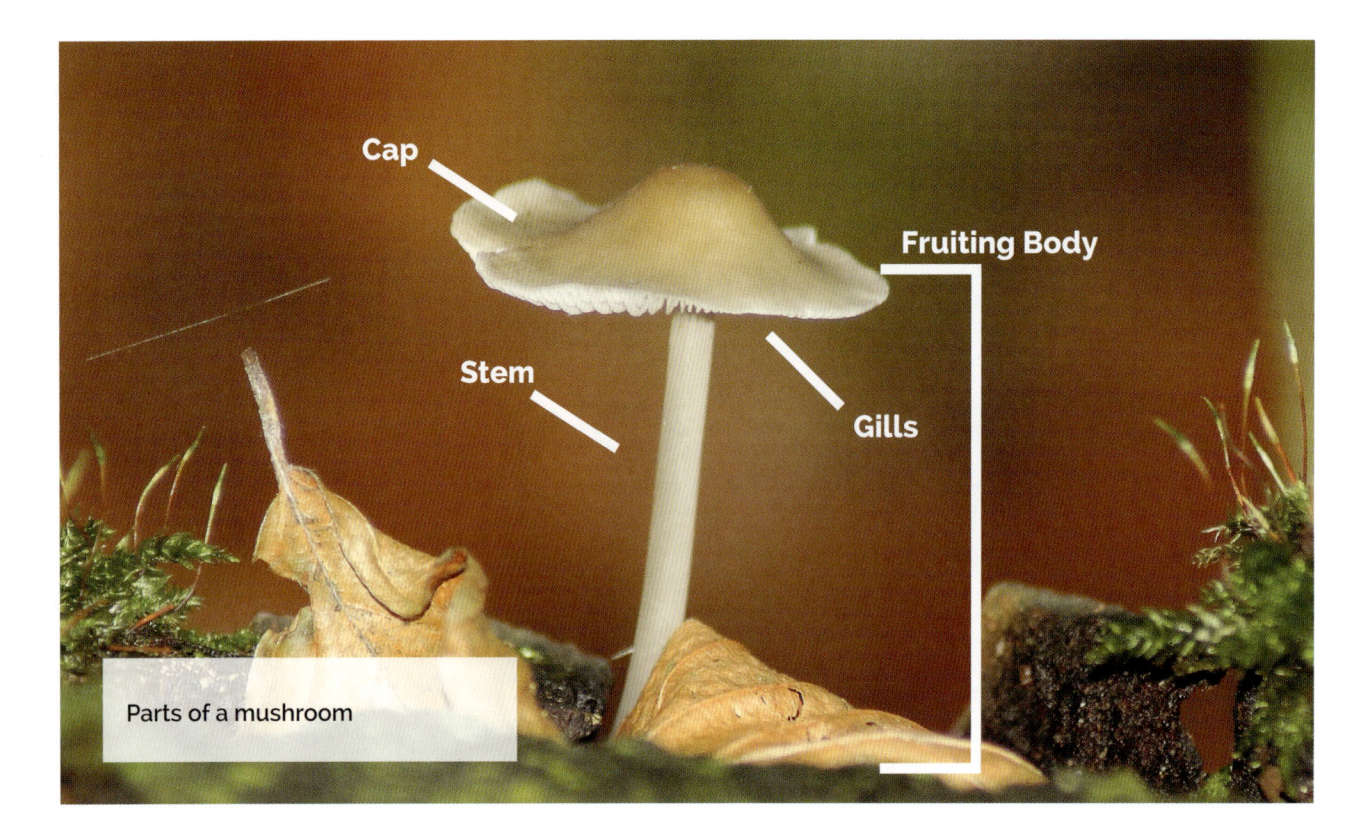

Parts of a mushroom
- Cap
- Stem
- Fruiting Body
- Gills

and other animals. Once the spores come to rest in a favorable location, they begin to grow new hyphae and develop into new mycelium. Hence, the life cycle of the fungus continues. See the illustration of the mycelium.

In summary, all fungi, just as all living creatures, carry out the seven life processes. The processes may differ slightly in specifics among the many diverse members of the Kingdom Fungi. Strangely enough, the members of the Kingdom Fungi are classified according to the shape of the spore-producing structures.

> **Section Review – 5.3 The Life Processes in the Fungus Kingdom**
>
> 1. Describe eight characteristics of fungi.
> 2. Provide three characteristics of hyphae in fungi.
> 3. What are septa in fungi? What do they do?
> 4. Describe fruiting bodies. Include what they are made of and their main functions.

5.4 The "Little Pots"

The **chytrids** (**ky**·trids) get their name from the Greek word that means "little pot." This describes the shape of the structures in which the spores are made. Chytrids are the simplest of the fungi. They exist mainly in aquatic environments, including both fresh water and salt water, but chytrids have been found also in moist soil. Most chytrids are simple spherical cells, some of which are able to grow hyphae; some chytrids, however, are branched hyphae without septa.

Among the fungi, the chytrids are unique because they are the only group of fungi that produce mobile or movable spores known as zoospores (**zoh**·oh·spores). The zoospores each contain a single flagellum, a long thread-like or whip-like organ extending from one end of the cell, that enables the spores to disperse by swimming, a distribution method appropriate for an aquatic fungus.

Life Science for Young Catholics

CHAPTER 5: **THE FUNGUS KINGDOM**

Many chytrids are decomposers (can break down dead plants or animal matter) which help recycle the Earth's elements. However, many chytrids are parasites, organisms that live at the expense or off of other organisms; and some chytrids are pathogens, disease-causing, to algae and to animals, like frogs.

> **Section Review – 5.4 The "Little Pots"**
> 1. Describe chytrids.
> 2. To what do chytrids cause diseases?

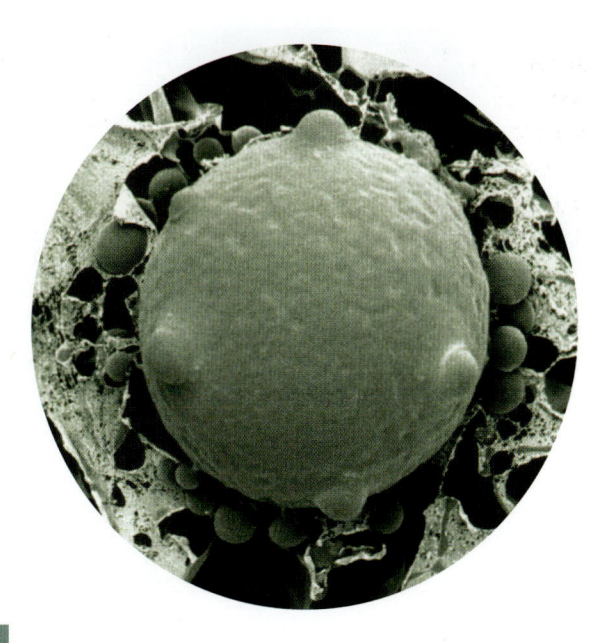

5.5 The Bread Molds

The molds on bread and fruit consist of this kind of fungus, called bread molds. Bread molds can exist in places that are not considered to be food to humans. The bread molds live on land, in soil, and on decaying organic matter. Bread molds are a major cause of spoiling fruits and vegetables.

> **Section Review – 5.5 The Bread Molds**
> 1. Describe bread molds.
> 2. What are they known for spoiling?

Magnification of bread mold

Life Science for Young Catholics

Root fungus

5.6 Root Fungus

The root fungi have a unique relationship with plants. These fungi are found only in symbiotic relationships, that is, mutually beneficial relationships, with plants. It is estimated that over 80% of all land plants have root fungi living in and among their roots!

The root fungi secrete, or send out, enzymes into their surroundings and, at the same time, they absorb nutrients. In the mutually beneficial symbiotic relationship of root fungi and plants, the fungi absorb sugars made by the plants during photosynthesis. These fungi also absorb from the soil minerals that the plants are not able to absorb. The root fungi process the minerals and excrete them into the root cells, or into the immediate surrounding environment, in a form the plants can use. Root fungi are especially important in providing plants with a source of nitrogen and phosphorus. These root fungi need to be considered friendly for the plants!

Section Review – 5.6 Root Fungus

1. Describe root fungus.
2. What do root fungi provide to plants?

5.7 The Sac Fungi

There are more **sac fungi** than any other type of fungi, with over 64,000 varieties! They are named sac fungi because of the bag-like shape of their spore-forming structures.

A. Structure of Sac Fungi

The hyphae, or tubular filaments of the sac fungi, have **septa** which are smaller filaments within the hyphae. The smaller filaments go across the hyphae and divide individual cells into smaller compartments. In the center of each septa is a small, simple pore which allows materials to move between compartments within the filament. The hyphae of the sac fungi form a dense network, or mycelium, within the soil or other decaying material.

Under certain conditions, the hyphae grow up and out of the soil to form the fruiting body, as in the picture below. Fruiting bodies grow in a wide variety of colors, shapes, and textures. Truffles and morels, similar to mushrooms and prized as gourmet foods, are two more examples of sac fungi fruiting bodies. Each fruiting body produces a large number of spores.

CHAPTER 5: THE FUNGUS KINGDOM

The purpose of the fruiting body is to provide a safe structure in which spore formation can occur. The shape of the fruiting body is important, not only for protecting developing spores, but to make sure that the mature spores are dispersed efficiently. This is an example of God's care for even the tiniest creatures.

B. Benefits of Sac Fungi

Most sac fungi live on land and are decomposers that break down dead and decaying organisms. Sac fungi contribute to the recycling of the Earth's elements. Some sac fungi, such as truffles and morel mushrooms, not only provide food for humans, but also live in symbiotic, or mutually beneficial, relationships with plants and algae.

C. Lichen

The combination of fungus with algae is known as **lichen** (*lie·kin*). In this particular relationship, the fungus grows around the algae cells. The algae provide carbohydrates for the fungus, and the fungus protects the algae and helps to collect and retain minerals and water from the surroundings that are needed by the algae for growth and development.

Lichens, combining fungus and algae, grow on many unusual surfaces such as rocks, trees, and rooftops. Lichens are found in many unexpected environments, including the extreme cold of the Arctic tundra, where they are an important source of food for reindeer!

Aa WORDS TO REMEMBER

chytrids: are fungi shaped like "little pots." Chytrids are the simplest of the fungi. They exist mainly in aquatic environments, including both fresh water and salt water.

zoospores: are chytrid spores that contain a single flagellum, a long thread-like or whip-like organ, extending from one end of the cell, that enables the spores to disperse by swimming, a distribution method appropriate for an aquatic fungus.

bread molds: are a type of fungus that live on land, in soil, and on decaying organic matter. Bread molds are a major cause of spoiling fruits and vegetables.

root fungi: live only in mutualistic relationships, that is mutually beneficial relationships, with plants. It is estimated that over 80% of all land plants have root fungi living in and among their roots!

sac fungi: bag-like shape of their spore-forming structures. There are over 64,000 varieties!

lichen: is a symbiotic combination of fungus with algae. The algae provide carbohydrates for the fungus, and the fungus protects the algae and helps to collect and retain minerals and water from the surroundings that are needed by the algae for growth and development.

Sac fungi

Life Science for Young Catholics

D. Yeast

Some other sac fungi, called yeasts, are extremely important in the food industry. Baker's yeast is an important type of organism. Yeasts are typically single-celled fungi that reproduce by budding and metabolize sugars, producing both alcohols and carbon dioxide by the process of **fermentation** (fur·men·**tay**·shun). Yeasts are necessary in making wine and brewing beer. Yeasts are the agent that makes bread dough rise.

E. Disease-Causing Sac Fungi

Some species of sac fungi are pathogens, that is, disease-causing organisms, to plants. Plant pathogens from sac fungi include those that cause chestnut blight, Dutch elm disease, and apple scab. Dutch elm disease is one of the most destructive tree diseases in America.

> **Section Review – 5.7 The Sac Fungi**
> 1. Why are sac fungi named the way they are?
> 2. How many kinds of sac fungi have scientists discovered?
> 3. What are the benefits of sac fungi?
> 4. Name three diseases caused by sac fungi.
> 5. What is lichen?
> 6. What is fermentation?
> 7. Name two sac-like fungi that are foods for humans.

5.8 The Club Fungi

Club fungi are important decomposers of decaying materials in the soil. Club fungi are also symbiotic partners, providing mutual benefits for many plants.

A. Structure of the Club Fungi

Club fungi are named according to the club shape of their spore-producing structures. Their spores are formed by the fusion of two compatible hyphae or filaments.

The fruiting bodies of club fungi are networks of hyphae with septa filaments that grow up from the mycelium, or underground hyphae. The hyphae of the club fungi have pores that allow the movement of cytoplasm and other cellular materials from cell to cell. The club fungi have great variety in their appearance. Mushrooms, toadstools, and puffballs are well-known kinds of club fungi.

B. Mushrooms

You are probably familiar with mushrooms. You may have found them in your backyard at one time or another. Mushrooms are made of collections of **hyphae** which are organized into various structures.

Club fungi

Gills are the feather-like structures under the **cap**. The spore-bearing or spore-producing organ called basidia form on the gills. A large number of gills provide the mushroom with a large surface area to produce a large number of spores. The cap provides protection for the developing spores, and the **stem** raises the spores off of the ground for more efficient scattering of the mature spores.

God gave mushrooms the role of recycling the Earth's elements, and many other uses. Many mushrooms are edible and can be bought in the supermarket. Most of these mushrooms are farmed, and include White mushrooms, Oyster mushrooms, and Portobello mushrooms.

Some edible mushrooms grow in the wild, but are not easily distinguished from the poisonous varieties. There is not one feature of any mushroom that dependably identifies a mushroom as poisonous or not poisonous. Therefore, one should NEVER eat mushrooms picked in the wild. Poisonous mushrooms can cause death even if eaten in small amounts. The toxins or poisons produced by the mushrooms protect the fruiting bodies from being eaten!

Mushrooms are very interesting to many people. Some are beautiful, some are ugly. They grow like wildflowers almost anyplace. Perhaps most interesting is that some mushrooms are used to make medicines. If you ever visit a natural foods store or a farmers' market, look for the many different kinds of mushrooms.

WORDS TO REMEMBER

yeast: a variety of sac fungi that is extremely important in the food industry. Yeasts are typically single-celled fungi that reproduce by budding and metabolize sugars, producing both alcohols and carbon dioxide by the process of fermentation.

fermentation: the process by which yeasts turn sugars into alcohols

club fungi: a type of fungi that have club-shaped, spore-producing structures and are important decomposers of decaying materials in the soil. Club fungi are also symbiotic partners, providing mutual benefits for many plants. Club fungi include mushrooms, toadstools, and puffballs.

mushrooms: club fungi that have fruiting bodies shaped like umbrellas

Section Review – 5.8 The Club Fungi

1. Describe the parts of a mushroom.
2. What is the purpose of the gills?
3. What is the function of the cap?
4. What is the function of the stem?

5.9 Micro Fungi and Anaerobic Fungi

A. Micro Fungi

The micro fungi were once considered to be protists, but they are true fungi. They are also the smallest and the simplest in organization. The micro fungi are parasites in larger animals.

B. Anaerobic Fungi

The anaerobic (*an-a-**ro**-bik*) fungi are found only in the digestive tracts of certain plant-eating animals. These fungi do not require oxygen, hence the name anaerobic, meaning without oxygen. These fungi are necessary for the larger animals to break down plant materials in the digestive process.

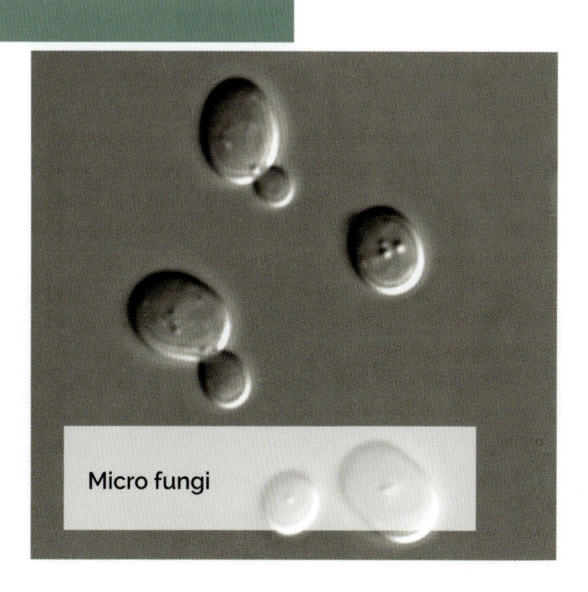

Micro fungi

5.10 Summary

The Kingdom Fungi is a diverse kingdom of eukaryotic organisms that inhabit a great variety of environments and climates. As a group, the fungi are important decomposers that break down and recycle carbon and other elements from decaying organisms, putting those elements back into the environment for use by other organisms.

All fungi have cell walls made of chitin and are heterotrophs, that is, they must obtain nutrition from the environment because they cannot make their own. The fungi are unique in that they secrete digestive enzymes which digest materials **outside their cells** and then absorb the nutrients.

All fungi reproduce by spores. There are five groups of fungi which are classified according to the shape of their spore-forming structures, and two types classified by size, Micro Fungi, or respiration type, Anaerobic Fungi.

Fungi are diverse in their appearance, color, and functions. Most are decomposers, but some are pathogens, causing disease, and some live in mutually beneficial relationships with plants and algae. Fungi provide a food source for many organisms, including humans, and can be used in medicine.

Mushrooms

5.11 Precision of God's Creation

Recall Chapter 1 of the Book of Genesis. It teaches us several truths about God's Creation: God created all out of nothing; God created all in a precise, purposeful, and orderly fashion; God created a hierarchy of organisms, with man as the summit of creation on planet Earth; and God's creation is good.

We have witnessed, through study, the precision and purpose of God's creation. Every element has a purpose. Every molecule serves a function. Macromolecules make up the components of cells; cells are the building blocks of all living organisms. Some organisms function completely as single cells! Other organisms are multicellular, with all cells working together for the life of the organism.

With perfect knowledge and precision, God created each organism to fulfill a specific role in creation as a whole. For example, we have studied single-celled archaea, bacteria, and protists, which are relatively simple in structure. These provide the basis of the global food chain, and without these tiny creatures, the world as we know it would cease to exist.

We have studied the algae, again, simple in structure, but perhaps the largest producers of oxygen on the planet.

We have now learned of the fungi. Fungi are mostly multicellular organisms that decompose organic matter and are important in recycling the Earth's elements and in supplying nutrients to other organisms.

God's creation is an amazing gift to mankind. Through His creation, we are able to come to know, to love, and to serve God in this life, so that we can be happy with Him forever in heaven. To study His creation is to appreciate the complexity and the interrelatedness of all organisms on our planet. Most importantly, we come to know the majesty and perfection of God. As stated in Romans 1:20:

Ever since the creation of the world, His invisible attributes of eternal power and divinity have been able to be understood and perceived in what He has made.

Chapter 5 Review

A. Identify the four marked sections of the mushroom.

1.
2.
3.
4.

B. Answer the following questions.

1. Identify the seven phyla within the Fungus Kingdom.
2. Describe five characteristics of fungi.
3. Describe fruiting bodies. Include what they are made of and their main functions.
4. Describe chytrids.
5. Describe bread molds.
6. What are bread molds known for spoiling?
7. Describe root fungus.
8. What do root fungi provide to plants?
9. Name three diseases caused by sac fungi.
10. What is lichen?
11. What is fermentation?
12. Name two sac-like fungi that are foods for humans.
13. What is the purpose of the gills?
14. What is the function of the cap?
15. What is the function of the stem?

Chapter 5: "Words to Remember" Crossword

ACROSS

3 a symbiotic combination of fungus with algae

4 a variety of sac fungi that are extremely important in the food industry

5 __ Fungi are noted for the bag-like shape of their spore-forming structures

7 fungi that have fruiting bodies shaped like an umbrella

9 __ molds are a type of fungus that live on land, in soil, and on decaying organic matter. They are a major cause of spoiled fruits and vegetables.

10 __ fungi are the smallest, and the simplest fungi in organization

11 the process by which yeasts turn sugars into alcohols

DOWN

1 the feather-like structures under the cap of a mushroom

2 The spore-producing structures of these fungi are shaped like little pots

6 __ fungi have club-shaped spore-producing structures, and are important decomposers of decaying materials in the soil

7 the underground structure of fungi. It is a network of hyphae spread out under the soil

8 a complex, large sugar molecule that makes up the cell walls of fungi

Life Science for Young Catholics

6 THE PLANT KINGDOM

6.1 Introduction

6.2 Psalm 104 and a Review of the Truths of Creation

6.3 Characteristics & Life Processes of the Plant Kingdom
  A. Nutrition
  B. Movement
  C. Growth
  D. Reproduction

6.4 Specialized Plant Tissues and Organs: Roots, Stems, and Leaves
  A. Roots
  B. Stems
  C. Leaves
  D. Summary of Specialized Plant Tissues and Organs

6.5 Classification within the Plant Kingdom

6.6 Non-Vascular Plants

6.7 Vascular Plants
  A. Spore-Bearing Plants
  B. Seed-Bearing Plants
    1. Gymnosperms
    2. Angiosperms
      a. Flowers
      b. Fruit
      c. Monocots and Dicots
      d. Vegetables
      e. Use in Medicine
      f. Other Uses

6.8 God's Perfection: Structure & Function

Chapter 6

The Plant Kingdom

6.1 Introduction

Did you ever roast chestnuts over an open fire on a yule log? While you did so, were you near an evergreen Christmas tree as you sipped a cup of hot chocolate?

If you answered yes to any of these questions, you were using parts of the Plant Kingdom to honor the birth of the King of kings.

The wood that burned, the chestnuts, the Christmas tree, and the chocolate all came from the wonderful world of plants that God gave us to use while on this Earth.

6.2 Psalm 104 and a Review of the Truths of Creation

Psalm 104 begins with praise to the Lord for the goodness of His creation:

Bless the LORD, my soul. LORD, my God, you are great indeed! You are clothed with majesty and splendor, robed in light as with a cloak.

The psalmist continues to marvel at the works of God:

You make the grass grow for the cattle and plants for people's work to bring forth food from the Earth, wine to gladden their hearts, oil to make their faces shine, and bread to sustain the human heart. The trees of the Lord drink their fill, the cedars of Lebanon, which you planted.

There the birds build their nests; the stork in the junipers, its home. How varied are your works, Lord. In wisdom, You have made them all; the Earth is full of your creatures (Psalm 104: 1, 14-17).

One of the most popular and beloved phrases from the Bible is "In wisdom, Lord, You have made them all."

Recall in Chapter 1, we began with the story of creation from the Book of Genesis. From Genesis, we learn the truths of creation: God created all out of nothing; He created in a perfect fashion and in a perfect order; and all of His creation is good.

To say that God created in a perfect order is to say that each of God's creatures is perfectly created to fulfill a role in the Earth's creation as a whole. In His perfection, God created each organism in such a manner that each possesses all the qualities and characteristics needed to fulfill its role for the good of all creation on planet Earth.

Psalm 104 above speaks of the plants that God created and the purpose of each. The grass, the author writes, is for cattle, and the bread, or grains, to sustain the human heart. These words echo those in the Genesis account of creation: "God also said: 'See, I give you every seed-bearing plant all over the Earth and every tree that has seed-bearing fruit on it to be your food; and to all the animals of the land, all the birds of the air, and all the living creatures that crawl on the ground, I give all the green plants for food.' And so it happened."

In His perfection and order, God created the plants in all their diversity, from the tiny mosses to the giant redwood trees. God created each with a purpose, and He designed each accordingly. God designed the moss to survive and reproduce in the shadows of other larger plants in areas of moist soil. God designed the giant redwood so that nutrients and water are transported some 370 feet straight up against gravity to supply the lofty leaves!

As we learn about the Plant Kingdom, keep in mind the diversity in structure of the many plants. Remember, we come to know God in His glory through His works. Imagine the wonder and awe that the psalmist might have expressed at the complexity and perfection of God's creation had he had the knowledge that we have today!

6.3 Characteristics & Life Processes of the Plant Kingdom

The members of the Plant Kingdom, or plants, are multicellular organisms classified in the Domain Eukarya (*yu-**kar**-ee-a*). Plants are distinct in their classification from fungi and animals. Despite the great diversity in the Plant Kingdom, all plants share many characteristics.

Typical Plant Cell

In Chapter 3, we learned the features of plant cells that distinguish them from animal cells: the presence of chloroplasts (part of a plant cell containing chlorophyll), a single large vacuole (a membrane-bound organelle), a rigid cell wall made of cellulose, and the lack of centrioles (found in animal cells).

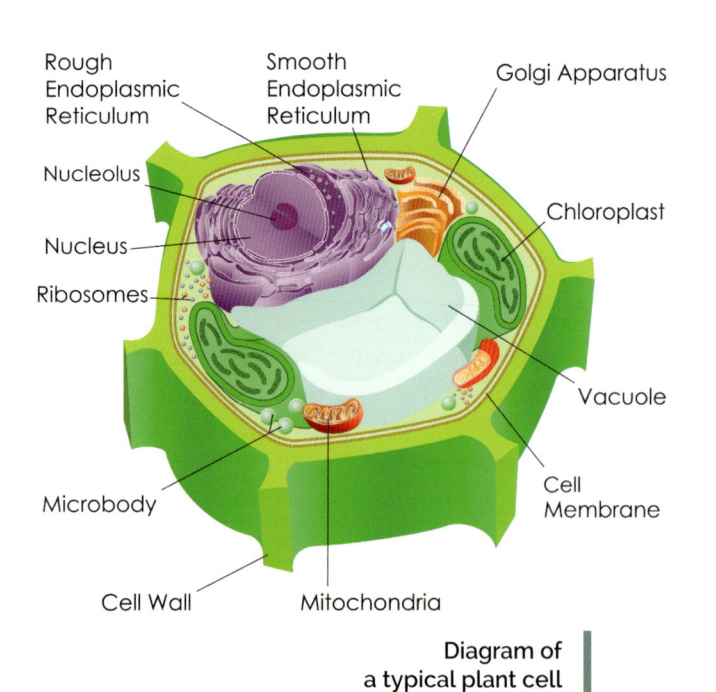

A. Nutrition

All plants contain chlorophyll because God has endowed all plants with the ability to produce their own nutrition, **glucose** or sugar, through the process of photosynthesis, which requires chlorophyll. Remember that **photosynthesis** is the process whereby plants and other organisms **convert energy from the sun into chemical energy** that the plant or other organism can use. Plants, therefore, are known as photosynthetic **autotrophs**, that is, they make their own food. The glucose produced from photosynthesis is used for the plants' own metabolism.

The glucose which is converted to **starch** will eventually provide a food source for other organisms. Plants provide the basis for the food chain for all land-dwelling animals, and for all the people on Earth! Though plants use some of the oxygen produced through photosynthesis for their own cellular respiration, much of the oxygen is released into the atmosphere. Through photosynthesis, plants are a major **source of oxygen production** and **carbon dioxide absorption** on planet Earth.

B. Movement

Plants may appear to be immobile, but all living creatures exhibit movement in at least some degree in some stage of their life cycles. Plants exhibit movement in several different ways.

Some plants, such as mosses, produce **motile** (capable of moving) male gametes that independently move through water by means of flagella.

Diagram of a typical plant cell

Moss

Plants also "move" in response to certain stimuli in their environment. The general term for this type of movement is "tropism." For example, plants will grow toward a light source. This growth, or movement, toward light is known as phototropism (fo·**tot**·rope·ism).

Some plants grow directionally in response to gravity, a response called **geotropism** (**gee**·o·trope·ism). For example, roots grow down towards gravity and stems grow up away from gravity.

Some plants grow directionally in response to touch. This is called **thigmotropism** (**thig**·moe·trope·ism). The tendrils (thin, often winding stems) of climbing plants grow around the main stem, trunk, or trellis they touch. While roots grow down towards gravity, they will move around buried rocks that may get in their way due to thigmotropism! Thus, in many plants, movement and growth are modified or redirected as a response to the environment.

C. Growth

All plants grow, but not all plants grow in the same manner. All plants exhibit **primary growth**, which is the increase in the length or height of a plant by cell division. Primary growth occurs as a plant grows upward toward the sun and extends roots downward into the soil.

WORDS TO REMEMBER

autotrophs: organisms that make their own food

glucose: the sugar produced from photosynthesis in plants, and used for the plants' own metabolism

motile: capable of moving on its own

phototropism: the growth or movement of a plant towards light

geotropism: the growth of parts of a plant towards or away from the source of gravity: for example, roots grow down towards gravity, and stems grow up away from gravity.

thigmotropism: the growth of parts of a plant in response to touch

primary growth: the increase in the length or height of all plants by cell division; primary growth occurs as a plant grows upward toward the sun and extends roots downward into the soil.

Life Science for Young Catholics

Some plants also exhibit **lateral growth**. This type of growth results in increasing girth, or thickness, of the plant stem. Lateral growth is evident in the rings which can be seen on the cross section of a fallen tree trunk.

D. Reproduction

Like all organisms, plants reproduce. All plants share a defining characteristic in their reproductive life cycles, known as **alternation of generations**. Alternation of generations is the name given to a life cycle that includes both a sexual stage and an asexual stage (without sexual reproduction).

> **Section Review –
> 6.3 Characteristics & Life Processes of the Plant Kingdom**
>
> 1. Name four features of plant cells that distinguish them from animal cells.
> 2. List ten significant facts about plants.
> 3. Name and describe three forms of plant movement.

6.4 Specialized Plant Tissues and Organs: Roots, Stems, and Leaves

The structure of all plants involves specialized organs that, first, ensure or guarantee the **delivery of water and carbon dioxide**; and second, guarantee the maximum exposure to **sunlight** of the structures necessary for photosynthesis. Specialized organs are one of the characteristics that distinguishes plants from other organisms.

Since plants are the producers on planet Earth, and must supply all the animals and all the people of the Earth with nutrition, plants are perfectly created to accomplish the huge task. In other words, the structure of plants must maximize the function of plants. In His wisdom, God designed and created plants with specialized tissues and organs to maximize the production of glucose and its storage as starch. Recall that a **tissue** is a group of similar cells working together to perform a specific function, and an **organ** is a group of tissues working together to perform a specific function.

The three organs that are common to all plants are: **roots**, **stems**, and **leaves**.

A. Roots

Roots are the organs that anchor the plants in the soil, and that absorb water and minerals from the soil. In some plants, roots store food produced by the plant. Primary and secondary roots make up most of a plant's **root system**.

In addition to anchoring a plant, the root system is designed to maximize the absorption of water and minerals from the soil, through both **osmosis** (oz-**moh**-sis) and active transport. Osmosis is the movement of liquid, usually water, through a porous membrane, such as the root of a plant. Root systems are underground, and some can be quite large. Have you ever tried to pull up a big weed in your yard? They hold on pretty well underground! Roots play an important role in breaking up the ground and in holding soil in place to prevent erosion. While you may not like to mow the lawn and trim the bushes, the roots keep the soil in place during rain storms, and thus keep your house safe in place!

A **primary root**, or **taproot**, is the structure that grows downward directly from the seed. Taproots are single structures that grow straight down into the soil. From the primary roots, **secondary**, or **lateral**, **roots** develop. As their name suggests, lateral roots grow out from the taproots in a sideways direction. Primary and secondary roots may develop root hairs, which are fine hair-like projections that grow near the root tip.

Both lateral roots and root hairs are important structures that increase the surface area of the root system to allow greater absorption of water and minerals from the soil. Taproots that enlarge and store sugars and starches are known as fleshy roots. Carrots and beets are two common examples of **fleshy roots**.

While taproots are single structures that grow straight down, a second type of root system is known as a **fibrous root system**. In the development of a fibrous root system, a single taproot grows from the plant embryo, but this dies quickly and

CHAPTER 6: **THE PLANT KINGDOM**

WORDS TO REMEMBER

lateral growth: the increasing girth, or thickness, of some plant stems. Lateral growth is evident in the rings which can be seen on the cross section of a fallen tree trunk.

roots: the organs that anchor the plants in the soil, and that absorb water and minerals from the soil. In some plants, roots store food produced by the plant.

taproot (or primary root): the structure that grows downward directly from the seed. Taproots are single structures that grow straight down into the soil. From the primary roots, secondary, or lateral, roots develop.

fleshy roots: taproots that enlarge and store sugars and starches. Carrots and beets are two common examples of fleshy roots.

Zone of Maturation

Primary Root

Lateral Root

Zone of Elongation

Root Tip

Meristematic Zone

Root Cap

83

is replaced by a great number of smaller roots. These smaller roots grow into a highly intertwined network that spreads throughout the soil. This type of fibrous root system is seen in grasses and in plants used to prevent surface erosion to hold the soil so it does not wash away in a rain storm.

Because roots are organs, they are made up of various tissues that function together to absorb water and minerals necessary for plant metabolism, that is, the functions necessary to sustain life for the plant. The outermost tissue is the **epidermis** (*ep·uh·der-mis*), which protects the root and helps prevent water loss. It is from these epidermis cells that the **root hairs** grow.

The epidermis covers the **cortex**, the outermost layer of a stem. The cortex allows the diffusion of materials into the center of the root. The central cylinder of a root, which contains **vascular tissue**, transports water and minerals throughout the remainder of the plant.

There are two types of vascular tissue: **xylem** (*zy·lem*) and **phloem** (*flo-em*). The xylem tissues carry water and minerals to the plant from the root; phloem tissues carry sugars back to the root from the remainder of the plant.

B. Stems

Stems are the organs through which the water and minerals are transported to other parts of a plant. Stems also allow plants to grow upward toward the sun to better capture the sun's energy for photosynthesis.

The **stem** is a part of the **shoot system**. Stems vary in shapes and sizes, but all stems function similarly. The stem is typically an elongated organ composed of various tissues designed to support the plant in an upright position. Stems hold the leaves in a position to maximize exposure to the sun's rays. Stems also serve as a conduit or tube for water, minerals, and sugars to move between the roots and the leaves. Some stems, such as those of the asparagus plant, even serve as storage of food made by the plant. Potatoes are actually specialized stems called **tubers** (*too·bers*) that grow underground.

Some stems may be the site of photosynthesis, the process to convert light energy from the sun into chemical energy which can be used by the plant.

C. Leaves

Leaves are the organs in which photosynthesis occurs. The leaves are involved also in **excretion** and in homeostasis, that is, maintaining healthy functioning, particularly in water balance. Together, the stems and leaves make up the **shoot system**.

Leaves are typically the organs in which most of the plant's photosynthesis occurs. Leaves are generally made of flat, thin structures called **blades** that catch the sun's rays. Blades vary greatly in size and shape throughout the plant kingdom. A leaf may be made of only a single blade, or it can be divided into smaller units called **leaflets**. Leaves that contain many leaflets are known as **compound leaves**. Leaves with a single blade are known as **simple leaves**. Despite their outward differences, however, most leaves have similar internal tissues and external structures that maximize photosynthesis and contribute to water homeostasis, that is, keeping enough water in the plant for healthy stability and proper functioning.

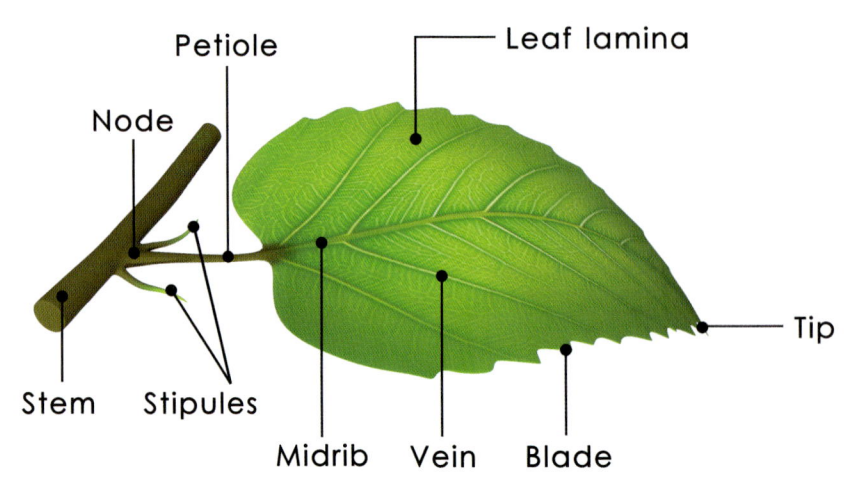

Leaf tissue

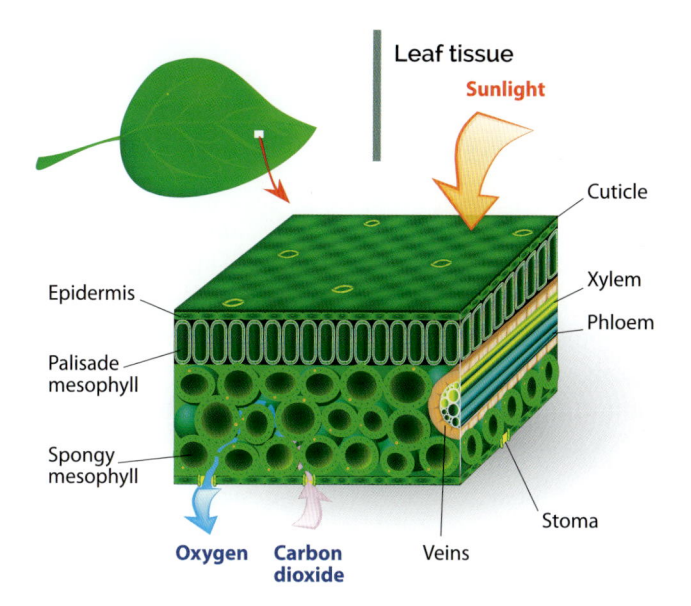

- Sunlight
- Cuticle
- Epidermis
- Palisade mesophyll
- Spongy mesophyll
- Xylem
- Phloem
- Stoma
- Veins
- Oxygen
- Carbon dioxide

region of the stem known as the **node**. The leaves are attached to the stem by a part of the leaf known as the **petiole** (**pet**-tee-ole). The broad, flat portion of the leaf is the blade. Each leaf has vascular tissue as well, tissue to conduct liquid, as seen in the figure: the **primary**, or **mid-vein**, also called the **midrib**, and smaller secondary veins. The pattern of veins in a leaf varies throughout the Plant Kingdom.

Leaves are made of layers of tissues which together function as a unit. The top outermost layer of leaf tissue is the **upper epidermis**. The cells of this top layer of epidermis are tightly packed together. These top layer cells secrete a tough waxy substance that protects the leaf from outside injury and excessive water loss. The waxy layer is known as the **cuticle** (**kyoo**·tik·al).

The middle layer of leaf tissue is where most of photosynthesis occurs. Therefore, the **mesophyll** is a layer that is packed full of chloroplasts, small cells containing chlorophyll. This middle layer is divided into two regions, a layer of **palisade cells** and a layer of **spongy cells**.

Palisade cells are long, relatively narrow cells that have the highest content of chlorophyll and are responsible for most of the plant's photosynthesis.

The **spongy cells** are packed loosely and are separated by large air spaces. The air spaces allow the diffusion of carbon dioxide into each individual cell so that it is readily available for photosynthesis. The air spaces also allow for the diffusion of oxygen, a byproduct of photosynthesis, out of the cells.

CHAPTER 6: THE PLANT KINGDOM

WORDS TO REMEMBER

fibrous root system: the network of secondary roots that develops by replacing an embryonic taproot with a great number of smaller roots. These smaller roots grow into a highly intertwined network that spreads throughout the soil. This type of fibrous root system is seen in grasses and in plants used to prevent surface erosion by holding the soil so it does not wash away in a rain storm.

epidermis: the outermost tissue of a root which protects the root and helps prevent water loss

vascular tissue: specialized tissue in the central cylinder of a root or stem that transports water and minerals throughout the remainder of the plant

xylem: carries water and minerals to the plant from the root

phloem: carries sugars back to the root from the remainder of the plant

stems: the organs through which the water and minerals are transported to other parts of a plant. Stems also allow plants to grow upward toward the sun to better capture the sun's energy for photosynthesis.

leaves: the organs in which photosynthesis occurs. The leaves are also involved in excretion and in homeostasis, that is, maintaining healthy functioning, particularly in water balance.

tubers: specialized stems that grow underground. Potatoes are actually tubers.

cuticle: the waxy layer on a leaf that protects the leaf from outside injury and excessive water loss

palisade cells: long, relatively narrow cells that have the highest content of chlorophyll and are responsible for most of the plant's photosynthesis

spongy cells: cells packed loosely and separated by large air spaces. The air spaces allow the diffusion of carbon dioxide into each individual cell so that it is readily available for photosynthesis. The air spaces also allow for the diffusion of oxygen, a byproduct of photosynthesis, out of the cells.

Life Science for Young Catholics

The veins of the leaf are found within the middle layer. Leaf veins are composed of two types of vascular tissue: **xylem** and **phloem**. As in roots and stems, the xylem brings water and minerals to the leaves, and the phloem carries manufactured sugars from the leaves to the remainder of the plant.

The outermost layer on the underside of a leaf is a layer of lower epidermis. The lower epidermis has many tiny openings, or **pores**. These pores open and close in response to conditions inside and outside of the leaf. At the opening of each pore are two special cells called **guard cells**. The guard cells open and close the pore. This allows the movement of air in and out of the leaf. The pores also help regulate the movement of evaporated water from the leaf.

D. Summary of Specialized Plant Tissues and Organs

In summary, roots, stems, and leaves are the basic organs of all plants. All roots anchor the plants into the soil and absorb water and nutrients necessary for growth and photosynthesis. All stems support the plants and provide a conduit or tube for the water and minerals between the root system and the remainder of the plant's structure. All leaves serve as the site of photosynthesis and help maintain water homeostasis, that is, help to maintain stability and health within the plants.

God designed each plant with the characteristics necessary to live and thrive in the environment in which He placed it. God used a basic design for all plants with some special "gifts" or characteristics given to each plant based on the role each is supposed to fulfill in all of creation. As an example, consider the cactus. The cactus was designed to live and thrive in hot, dry desert climates. The basic structure of a cactus demonstrates how structure serves function, and also demonstrates the wisdom of the Creator.

The stem of the cactus not only supports the rest of the plant, but is designed to store large amounts of water. The stem is also the main site of photosynthesis for these plants. Cactus stems are large flattened stems with a sturdy structure to support the plant, but also a large flat surface area on which to absorb the sun's light for photosynthesis.

The root systems of cacti are designed to maximize water absorption in a typically dry environment. For this reason, the roots of many cacti remain underground, but very near the surface, and they branch out for large distances, up to 15 feet, around the base of the stem. Roots that remain close to the surface can quickly absorb water from brief rain showers before it evaporates from the surface in the desert heat. The waxy layer over the epidermis of cacti is also an enhanced feature to help prevent water loss. The spines of the cactus are modified leaves that are not important in photosynthesis, but are important in protection from predators. How perfectly designed are all of God's creatures!

> ### Section Review – 6.4 Specialized Plant Tissues & Organs: Roots, Stems, and Leaves
>
> 1. Name and briefly describe the three basic organs of plants.
> 2. Briefly describe three functions of roots.
> 3. Identify taproots, fibrous roots, and fleshy roots.
> 4. Name three characteristics of fibrous root systems.
> 5. Identify xylem and phloem.
> 6. Briefly describe three functions of stems.
> 7. Briefly describe three functions of leaves.
> 8. What makes a potato unusual?

CHAPTER 6: THE PLANT KINGDOM

6.5 Classification within the Plant Kingdom

This chapter thus far has focused on the similarities in structure and in function of the members of the plant kingdom, but with over 375,000 species, there is enormous diversity within the plant kingdom. Scientists have broadly classified this large number of plants into two major groups based on the presence or absence of vascular tissue, that is, fluid-bearing tissues. These are **non-vascular plants** and **vascular plants**.

Vascular plants are further divided into those plants that do not produce seeds and those that do produce seeds. Seed-bearing vascular tissue plants are further divided into two groups, the **gymnosperms** (*jim·no·sperms*) and the **angiosperms** (*an·jee·o·sperms*), based on the type of seed produced. Gymnosperms produce "naked" seeds, seeds without a cover. Angiosperms are flowering plants which produce seeds protected by a cover.

Angiosperms are further classified into two smaller groups, **monocots** and **dicots**, based on the number of embryonic leaves found within the seed. Monocots have one embryonic leaf, and dicots have two.

Angiosperms comprise the largest group of plants with approximately 350,000 different species. There are approximately 20,000 species of non-vascular plants, approximately 13,000 species of non-seed-bearing vascular plants, and approximately 1,000 species of gymnosperms.

> ### WORDS TO REMEMBER
>
> **non-vascular plants**: the group of plants which does not have vessels that carry fluid. Non-vascular plants include mosses, liverworts, and hornworts. Non-vascular plants have cell walls containing cellulose chlorophyll. These plants also produce sugars through photosynthesis.
>
> **vascular plants**: plants that have vascular tissues like pipes or blood vessels, which conduct water and nutrients throughout the plant
>
> **rhizoids**: root-like structures that anchor non-vascular plants to the ground, but do not absorb water or other nutrients

> ### Section Review – 6.5 Classification within the Plant Kingdom
>
> 1. Identify three facts about gymnosperms.
> 2. Identify three facts about angiosperms.

6.6 Non-Vascular Plants

The non-vascular plant group, the group of plants which **does not have vessels that carry fluid**, includes **mosses**, **liverworts**, and **hornworts**. Non-vascular plants, like all plants, have cell walls containing cellulose and chlorophyll. These plants also produce sugars through photosynthesis. Most of the non-vascular plants have simple leaves and stems, although some grow in a flat, sheet-like structure called a thallus. The internal structure of the thallus is different than that of true leaves and stems.

Non-vascular plants differ from vascular plants in several other ways. As their name implies, non-vascular plants **do not contain true vascular tissues** such as xylem. Non-vascular plants have root-like structures, called **rhizoids** (*rye·zoyds*), which anchor

Moss

Liverwort

Hornwort

Life Science for Young Catholics

the plant to the ground, but they do not absorb water or other nutrients. In non-vascular plants, the **leaves and stems absorb water and minerals directly from their surroundings**, including from the air.

Non-vascular plants are able to **absorb water vapor** from the air, and are able to survive in many different habitats or kinds of environments, from the tropical rain forests to the arctic tundra! Non-vascular plants, by their structure and function, fill many ecological roles, that is, interaction with their environment, in all of the different locations that they inhabit. Importantly, non-vascular plants **capture and recycle minerals** and other nutrients that fall to the ground from plants above. They also capture and recycle nutrients from the decay of animals and plants on the ground around them. Their rhizoids and low, flat structures help hold the soil together, and prevent erosion wherever they grow.

Because non-vascular plants have the remarkable ability to absorb large amounts of water and then to slowly release it back into the environment, these plants help maintain a moist environment for other plants in drier climates.

Peat moss is a non-vascular plant that can absorb up to twenty times its weight in water! As a result, peat moss reserves water and can grow in drier areas. Because the peat absorbs and retains large amounts of water, it eventually provides a bed of nutrient-rich soil on which other plants may grow. Additionally, dried peat moss is used to condition soil that is poor in nutrients and to increase the water-retaining ability of sandy soil.

> **Section Review – 6.6 Non-Vascular Plants**
>
> 1. How are non-vascular plants unique in absorbing water?
> 2. Provide four facts about peat moss.

6.7 Vascular Plants

Vascular plants are identified by their vascular tissues, which are like pipes or blood vessels, which conduct water and nutrients throughout the plant.

Vascular plants are divided into spore-bearing and seed-bearing.

A. Spore-Bearing Plants

The spore-bearing plant group includes **ferns**, **horsetails**, and **club-mosses**. The members of this group are vascular plants that have leaves, stems, and roots, complete with xylem and phloem. Like all plants, the spore-bearing plants have a life cycle of alternations of generations. These plants do not produce seeds, but reproduce by spores.

The fern is the representative organism for spore-bearing plants. Ferns have a unique structure in which the leaves, or **fronds**, arise from an underground stem called a **rhizome** (**rye**·zome). Spores are formed in structures on the underside of the fronds. The spores are dispersed by the wind and germinate, that is, start to grow into new plants, under appropriate conditions.

Spore-bearing plants grow in a wide variety of environments. In addition, the spores provide a food source for mice and other small animals.

Ferns are popular with home owners who grow them in gardens. Ferns are the answer for those looking for pretty landscaping. People like to put ferns in baskets and hang them around their porches, patios, and decks.

The **fiddleheads**, or young developing fronds of a fern, are full of nutritional iron and fiber. Though it is said that some people eat fiddleheads as vegetables, recipes are hard to find! Fiddleheads are probably hard to find, too, except perhaps at a farmer's market.

B. Seed-Bearing Plants

1. Gymnosperms

A seed is a plant **embryo** (**em**·bree·o), which is a complete miniature young plant in a dormant state, a period of time before a seed starts to grow. The plant embryo is complete with a food supply and a protective covering. Under appropriate conditions, the seed will germinate, that is, start growing, and eventually grow into the mature plant.

CHAPTER 6: THE PLANT KINGDOM

Ferns

Horsetails

Club-moss

Seed-producing plants are divided into two groups: gymnosperms and angiosperms. Gymnosperms are vascular plants that produce "naked" or exposed seeds, while angiosperms are flowering plants that produce a seed protected within a fruit.

Gymnosperms have seeds that develop on the surface of the reproductive structures, or **cones**. The gymnosperm group includes the **ginkgo** (*gink·o*) trees and the **conifers** (*con·uh·furs*), among others.

Ginkgo trees are the oldest of all known living trees. They produce unprotected seeds at the tips of short branches of the female trees. Ginkgo trees do not produce cones as other gymnosperms do. They have distinct fan-shaped leaves that are shed yearly. These trees produce a substance that is used in health supplements and is believed to enhance a person's memory and concentration. However, it is wise for students to have their parents investigate whether or not to use a substance from a ginkgo tree!

The **conifers** are cone-bearing woody gymnosperms that are found in a wide variety of climates on all continents except Antarctica. As all gymnosperms, the conifers are vascular plants that produce "naked" seeds not enclosed by fruit. Most conifers are trees, but a few are shrubs. The conifers include: cedars, cypresses, firs, pines, hemlocks, redwoods, junipers, and spruces, among others. Most conifers are evergreens and have specialized leaves, or needles, which carry out photosynthesis throughout the entire year.

Conifers form vast forests throughout the world. In forests, these conifer trees convert large amounts of carbon dioxide from the atmosphere into organic

WORDS TO REMEMBER

peat moss: a non-vascular plant that can absorb up to twenty times its weight in water

spore-bearing plants: vascular plants that reproduce by spores, not seeds

fronds: the leaves of ferns

conifers: cone-bearing, woody gymnosperms, or trees; found in a wide variety of climates on all continents except Antarctica

gymnosperms: vascular plants that produce "naked" or exposed seeds

Life Science for Young Catholics

CHAPTER 6: THE PLANT KINGDOM

A conifer: Note the shape of the leaves and the cones.

carbon compounds. Conifers are used for timber, paper, turpentine, and materials such as rayon.

Conifers are used in gardening, but more as decoration in yards and along highways. Many conifers have edible seeds that provide a great deal of food for wildlife, such as birds and squirrels. Of course, conifers are the trees of choice to help us celebrate our Savior's birth and under which we spread gifts for the family.

As Psalm 104 reminds us, the juniper and other conifers serve as home for many of God's beautiful creatures, the great variety of birds.

2. Angiosperms

The angiosperms are the largest and the most diverse group of the seed-bearing plants. They are commonly known as the flowering plants, and all have seeds enclosed within some type of fruit.

The basic structure of angiosperms is similar to all plants: (1) **roots**, generally underground, to anchor the plant into the soil and absorb water and minerals; (2) **stems** of various types to support the plant, and to serve as a conduit for materials, such as water, to pass from leaves to roots and back; and (3) **leaves** of various configurations to serve as sites of photosynthesis and water homeostasis.

a. Flowers

In addition to the basic organs, all angiosperms have **flowers**. Flowers house the reproductive structures.

The male reproductive structure of a flower is called the **stamen** (**stay**·men). The stamen is made of the **filament**, or stalk, and the **anther**, where the pollen is formed. The female reproductive structure is called the **pistil**. The pistil consists of the **stigma**, or outer sticky tip which collects the pollen, and the **style**, or tube-like structure that leads the pollen to the ovule. The **ovary** is the organ that contains the ovule, in which fertilization occurs and the seed is produced. The ovary matures around the seed to form the **fruit**.

b. Fruit

A **fruit** acts as a means of protection and dispersal for the seeds. Fruits may be **simple**, **aggregate**, or **multiple**.

A **simple fruit** develops from one ovary of one flower. Cucumbers, tomatoes, walnuts, apples, cherries, and oranges are examples of simple fruits.

Aggregate fruits, such as strawberries and raspberries, are formed from several ovaries in one plant.

Anatomy of a flower

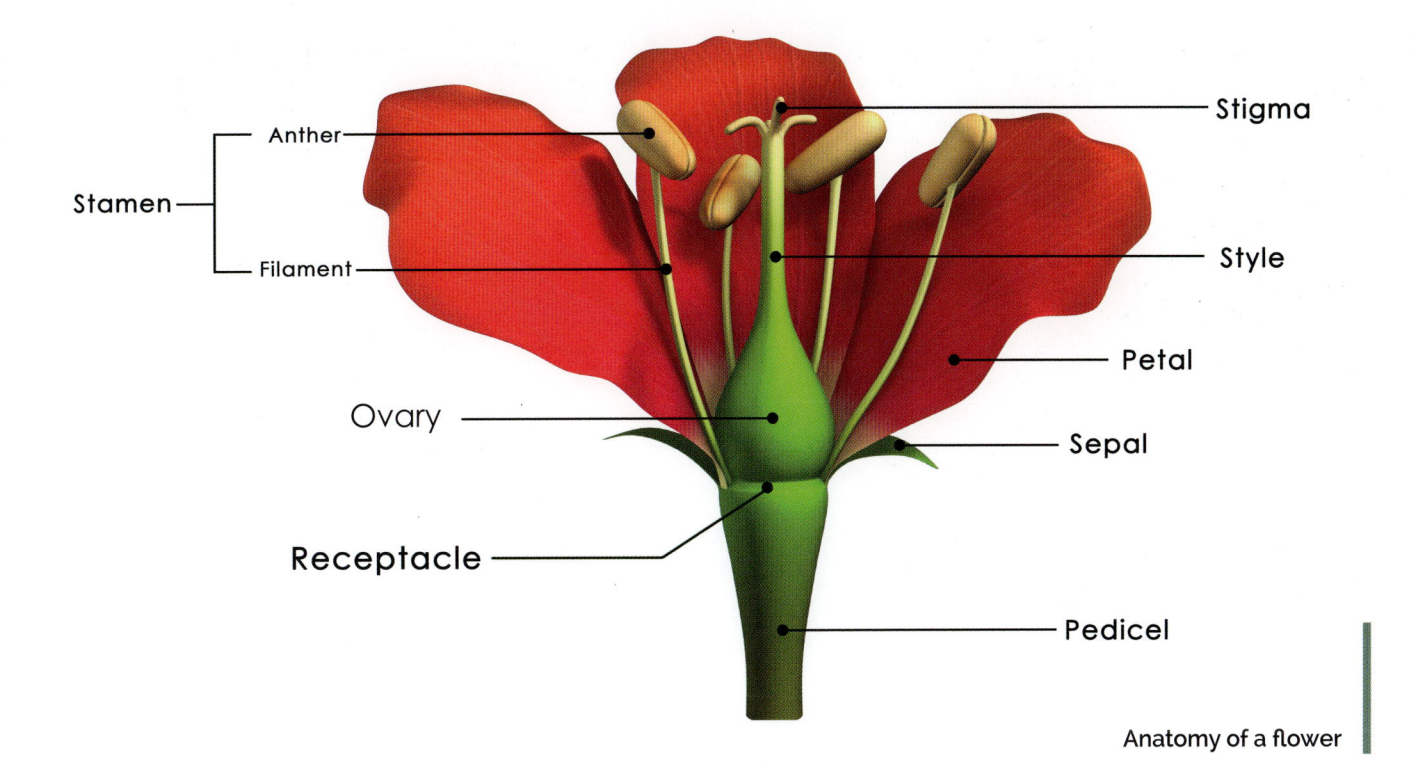

Multiple fruits arise from many ovaries of many flowers clustered closely together to form one fruit. Pineapples and mulberries are multiple fruits.

The pistil and the stamens are surrounded by **petals**. Petals are brightly colored so as to attract insect pollinators, such as bees. Collectively, the petals are known as the **corolla** (*co·rol·la*). At the base of each flower are small modified leaves, or **sepals** (*see·pulls*) that cover and protect the flower as it develops.

Some angiosperms produce only one flower per plant, while other angiosperms produce many flowers per plant in a wide variety of arrangements.

c. Monocots and Dicots

Angiosperms are divided into two groups, **monocots** and **dicots**, based on the number of seed leaves, or **cotyledons** (*kot-uhl-eed-uns*), that develop within the seed. As the names suggest, seeds with **one embryonic seed leaf** are known as **monocots**; those with **two embryonic seed leaves** are known as **dicots**. Each group has several distinguishing characteristics.

Monocots produce flowers with petals in multiples of three; dicots produce flowers with petals in multiples of four and five.

Monocot leaves have veins that are parallel to each other and run the length of each leaf. Dicot leaves have veins that form a branching, or netted, pattern from a central mid-vein.

The stems of both groups contain vascular tissue, xylem and phloem, that is grouped into

Aa WORDS TO REMEMBER

angiosperms: flowering plants which produce seeds protected by a cover

flowers: house reproductive structures of angiosperms.

stamen: the male reproductive structure of a flower, containing pollen. The stamen is made of the filament, or stalk, and the anther where the pollen is formed.

pistil: the female reproductive structure of an angiosperm

ovary: the organ that contains the ovule, and in which fertilization occurs and the seed is produced. The ovary matures around the seed to form the fruit.

fruit: forms from a mature fertilized ovary in an angiosperm plant. A fruit acts as a means of protection and dispersal for the seeds.

vascular bundles. However, the arrangement of these bundles differs between the two groups. The vascular bundles in the stems of monocots are somewhat scattered throughout the stem. The vascular bundles in dicots are arranged in definite order around the perimeter of the stem.

Monocots have fibrous root systems, while dicots have taproot systems.

As the largest and most diverse group of plants on Earth, and the principal plants found in nearly all habitats, the angiosperms have immeasurable value for the environment, and also economic value.

Angiosperms provide over 80% of the world's food supply for humans and livestock. All grains, seeds, fruits, and vegetables come from angiosperms. Recall that fruits are the seed-containing mature ovaries of plants. Apples, oranges, strawberries, and watermelons are commonly recognized as fruits. Tomatoes, cucumbers, pumpkins, peppers, eggplants, okra, squash, corn, zucchini, and any seed-containing vegetable are actually fruits, by definition, but called vegetables in the grocery store.

d. Vegetables

A **vegetable** is any edible part of a plant. Vegetables may be the leaves of the plants, such as lettuce, kale, spinach, collard greens, and chard. Specialized leaves called bulbs form the vegetables known as onions, garlic, and shallots.

Vegetables may be stems or modified stems, such as asparagus, ginger, potatoes, sweet potatoes, and yams. Vegetables may be stems of leaves, such as celery and rhubarb. Carrots, turnips, beets, and radishes are root vegetables. Broccoli and cauliflower are actually flower buds.

e. Use in Medicine

Many medicines come from angiosperms. In fact, other than antibiotics, at least 25% of medications either are directly derived from angiosperms or were first discovered as a chemical made by an angiosperm. Digitalis, a medication used to treat heart disease, comes from the foxglove plant. Vitamin C was originally extracted from citrus fruits. Aspirin was originally derived from the bark of a tree.

f. Other Uses

Angiosperms are used extensively in landscaping and gardening, textiles or cloth, lumber, cosmetics, and spices.

Angiosperms provide food and homes for many living organisms. Angiosperms contribute significantly to the absorption of carbon dioxide from the atmosphere and the production of oxygen.

Many angiosperms live in symbiotic relationships with fungus, lichens, and other plant life.

Certainly, God created the angiosperms to fulfill the diverse functions necessary to sustain life for all of His creation.

Section Review – 6.7 Vascular Plants

1. Name four facts about seeds.
2. Provide two facts about conifers.
3. Name six major species of conifers.
4. Identify and describe four facts about flowers.
5. Describe the importance of fruit.
6. Identify four distinguishing features of monocots.
7. Identify four distinguishing features of dicots.
8. Name five parts of plants that are considered to be "vegetables" in terms of being edible, and provide two examples of each that are common human foods.

A foxglove plant, from which is derived the medication digitalis

6.8 God's Perfection: Structure & Function

This chapter began with Psalm 104, in which the psalmist praised God for the perfection of His creation. The members of the Plant Kingdom provide wonderful and awe-inspiring examples of His wisdom, the order of His creation, and His gifts to mankind. God created the plants mainly to provide food for us. He gave plants the ability to produce food for all of His creation.

God structured some plants, trees, to provide a means of shelter for His creatures, especially for us whom He created to attain eternal life with Him in Heaven. God created the plants in such a way that they would produce oxygen to sustain our lives. He even gave plants the ability to produce medicines that heal our illnesses and wounds.

Plants are still dependent on God and on the rest of His creation. They need water, wind, insects, and animals to live, thrive, and reproduce. Plants cooperate with creation not only to obtain the nutrients that they need for their own growth, but to supply nutrients that people need to live and thrive. Each of God's creatures, whether it be bacteria, plant, animal, or human, has a God-given purpose. As illustrated by the marvels of the plants, each has been given the gifts necessary to accomplish what God, in His great wisdom, has intended. We have been given the gifts of our planet to maintain our physical lives, and the gifts of the Church to maintain our spiritual lives.

WORDS TO REMEMBER

monocots: seed-bearing plants that contain one embryonic seed leaf. Monocots produce flowers with petals in multiples of three. Monocot leaves have veins that are parallel to each other and run the length of each leaf.

cotyledons: seed leaves that develop within the seed

dicots: seed-bearing plants that contain two embryonic seed leaves. Dicots produce flowers with petals in multiples of four and five. Dicot leaves have veins that form a branching, or netted, pattern from a central midvein.

vegetable: any edible part of a plant

Chapter 6 Review

A. Identify the various parts of a typical leaf.

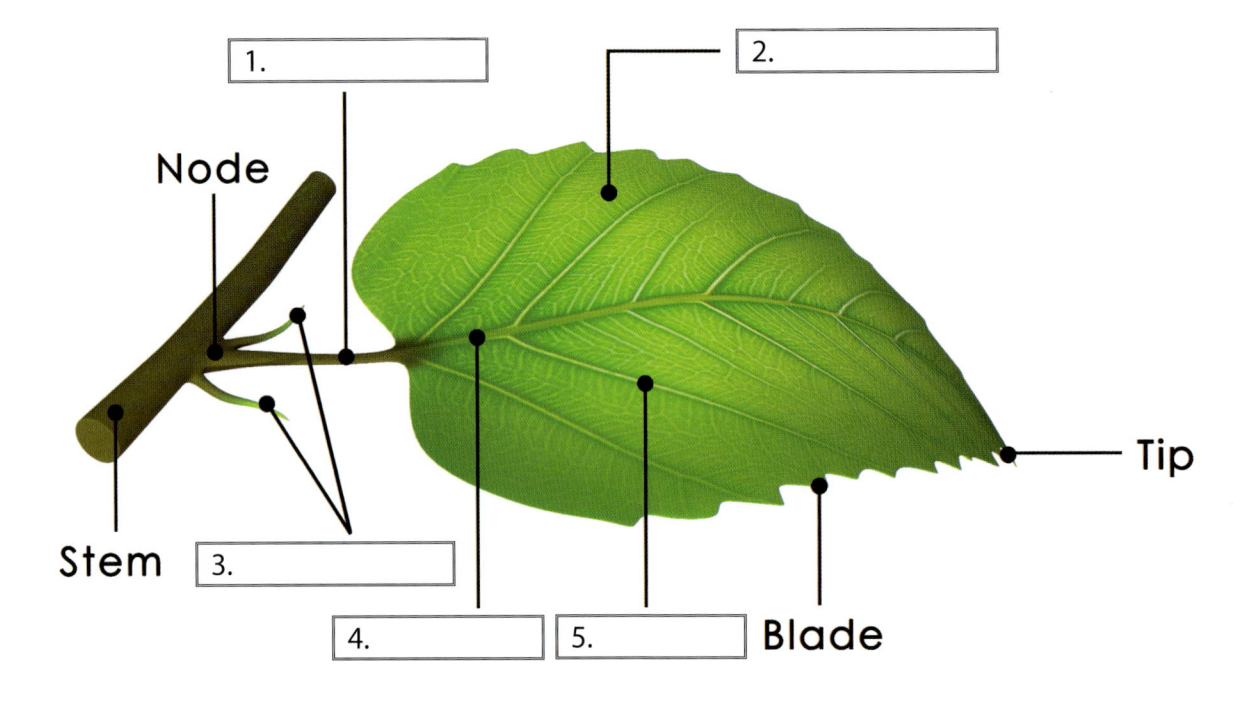

1.
2.
3.
4.
5.

Node
Stem
Tip
Blade

B. Answer the following questions.

1. Name and describe three forms of plant movement.
2. Name and briefly describe the three basic organs of plants.
3. Identify xylem and phloem.
4. Briefly describe three functions of stems.
5. Name four facts about seeds.
6. Provide two facts about conifers.
7. Name six major species of conifers.
8. Identify and describe four facts about flowers.
9. Identify four distinguishing features of monocots.
10. Identify four distinguishing features of dicots.

Chapter 6: "Words to Remember" Crossword

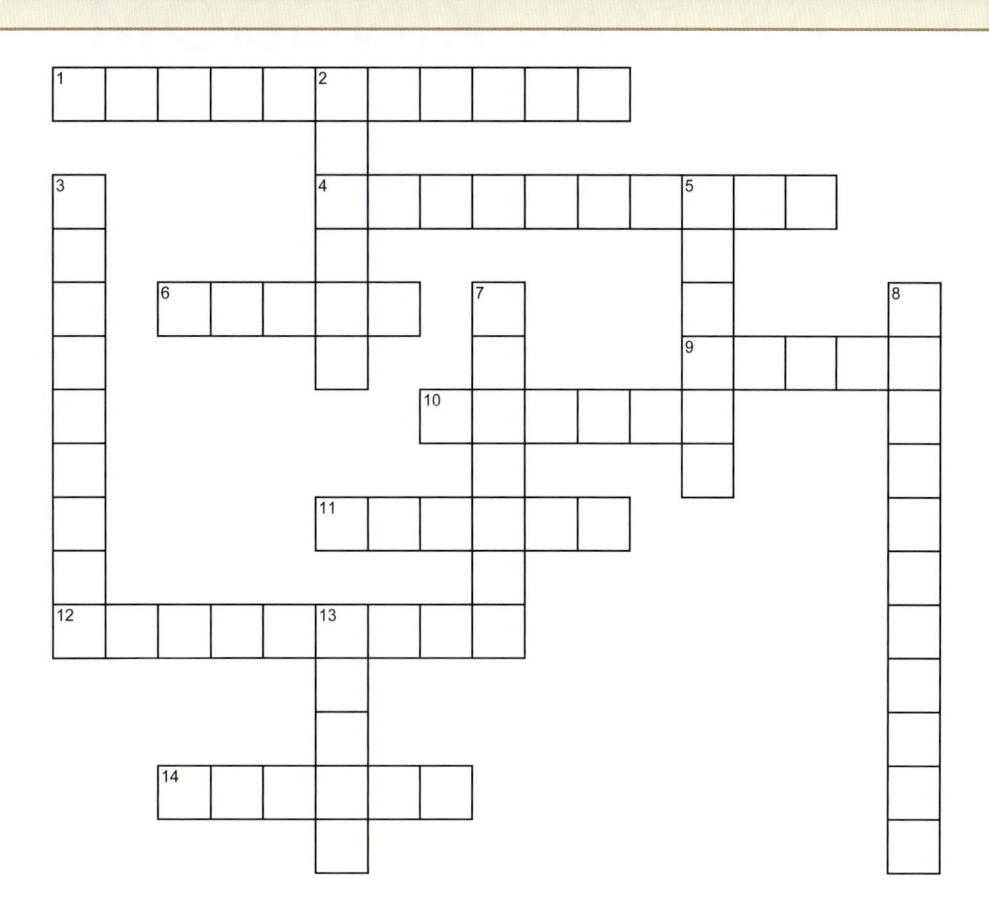

ACROSS

1. flowering plants which produce seeds protected by a cover
4. organisms that make their own food
6. vascular tissue that carries water and minerals to the plant from the root
9. the organ that contains the ovule, and in which fertilization occurs and the seed is produced
10. capable of moving on its own
11. specialized stems that grow underground
12. the outermost tissue of a root which protects the root and helps prevent water loss
14. the female reproductive structure of an angiosperm

DOWN

2. the male reproductive structure of a flower, containing pollen
3. any edible part of a plant
5. vascular tissue that carries sugars back to the root from the remainder of the plant
7. house the reproductive structures of angiosperms
8. vascular plants that produce "naked" or exposed seeds
13. the organs that anchor the plants in the soil, and which absorb water and minerals from the soil

Life Science for Young Catholics

7 THE ANIMAL KINGDOM

7.1 Introduction

7.2 Characteristics and Life Processes of the Kingdom Animalia
   A. Epithelial Tissue
   B. Connective Tissue
   C. Muscle Tissue
   D. Nerve Tissue

7.3 Classification of Animals
   A. Symmetry
   B. Segmentation
   C. Backbones

7.4 The Stingers: Jellyfish, Corals, and Others

7.5 The Soft Bodies: Mollusks
   A. Body
   B. Benefits of Mollusks

7.6 The Jointed Appendages: Arthropods
   A. Centipedes and Millipedes
   B. Insects
   C. Arachnids
   D. Crustaceans

7.7 Chordates

7.8 Invertebrate Chordates

7.9 Vertebrates

7.10 The Jawless Fish

7.11 Cartilaginous Fish

7.12 Bony Fish

7.13 Amphibians

7.14 Reptiles

7.15 Birds

7.16 Mammals

7.17 Classification of Mammals
   A. Monotremes
   B. Marsupials
   C. Placental Mammals

7.18 Mammals in the Bible

Chapter 7
The Animal Kingdom

7.1 Introduction

Do you know the Bible story of Balaam's donkey? Balaam was a false prophet who was asked to speak evil about the Israelites to stop their conquest of the Holy Land after leaving Egypt. God became angry with Balaam and sent an angel to stop him. The angel had a sword and was visible only to the donkey. Three times the donkey changed direction to avoid the angel, and three times, Balaam hit the donkey and tried to change his direction.

After the third time that Balaam struck the donkey, God gave the donkey the power to talk, and the donkey asked Balaam why he hit her. After Balaam and the donkey finished their conversation, Balaam's eyes were opened to the presence of the angel. The angel then told Balaam that the donkey had saved his life, because the angel would have killed Balaam for his evil plan to hurt God's people. Balaam repented and did not help the devil's plan to destroy Israel.

This story emphasizes God's concern for mankind by providing not only food but other kinds of help from animals. He gave the donkey the ability to see the angel and the ability to talk to save the donkey's owner. In His Providence, God arranged for the angel and the donkey to save Balaam.

While God does not normally give animals the ability to talk, He does give animals to the people on Earth to provide various things for people. Animals provide fun as pets and entertainment as they do tricks. Animals provide transportation sometimes, such as by horses and camels, and animals provide food, such as cows for milk. Isn't God wonderful in His plan for animals, and for all His creation, but especially for us people whom He plans to join Him in eternal life in Heaven?

CHAPTER 7: THE ANIMAL KINGDOM

7.2 Characteristics and Life Processes of the Kingdom Animalia

The Animal Kingdom is the fourth kingdom in the Domain Eukarya. This domain includes creatures with a membrane-organized nucleus.

Animal cells contain a membrane-bound nucleus and organelles, which are tiny structures inside a cell. Animal cells are enclosed by a flexible cell membrane, not a rigid cell wall like those of plants. Animal cells contain **centrioles** (*sent*-ree-oles), which are organelles that aid in cell division. Animals do not produce their own nutrition, but must obtain their nutrition from outside sources. Animals must ingest their food and digest it internally.

Obviously, all animals are multicellular. Furthermore, all animals except sponges have **tissues** and **organs**. Tissues are groups of cells that work together to serve a specific function. Organs are groups of tissues that work together to perform a specific function. There are four basic types of tissues found in animals: **epithelial tissue**, **connective tissue**, **muscle tissue**, and **nerve tissue**.

A. Epithelial Tissue

Epithelial (*ep-i-thee-li-al*) **tissue** is made of groups of cells tightly packed together in sheets or clusters and assembled on a **membrane**. Some epithelial tissues line body cavities and the surfaces of structures and organs throughout the body. Some form the structure of **glands**, or organs that secrete hormones and other substances, such as mucus. Epithelial tissue is important in protection, secretion, absorption, and transportation of materials between cells.

B. Connective Tissue

Connective tissue is made up of cells and fibers distributed throughout a fluid environment. Some connective tissue supports and connects other tissue types within organs. Some connective tissue serves as a barrier between different layers of tissues within organs, and some provide structure to organisms. Some connective tissues serve to transport materials from one part of the organism to another.

C. Muscle Tissue

Muscle tissue is made of interconnected, elongated cells that have the ability to contract and relax. Muscle tissues are responsible for movement in almost all animals. The movement in animals is often much more complex than that seen in other living organisms.

Some muscle tissue adds support to the organism, some keeps the heart beating, and some produces heat in a variety of animals. There are three basic types of muscle tissue: **skeletal** (or voluntary), **smooth** (or involuntary), and **cardiac** muscle tissue.

D. Nerve Tissue

Nerve tissue is composed of **neurons**, or impulse-conducting cells, and **glial** (*glee*-all) **cells**, or supporting cells. Nerve tissues make up the nervous system. Nerves and **ganglia** (*gang*-lee-ah), which are collections of neurons, transmit electrical impulses to control and regulate all bodily functions, both voluntary and involuntary. The complexity of the nervous system varies among the members of the animal kingdom. However, all animals respond to stimuli in their environments, and most do so by means of specialized nerve tissue.

Diagram of a typical animal cell

- cell membrane
- nuclear membrane
- nucleoplasm
- nucleus
- nucleolus
- vacuole (vessicle)
- lysosome
- cytoplasm
- mitochondrion
- endoplasmic reticulum
- golgi complex

Life Science for Young Catholics

Types of Muscle

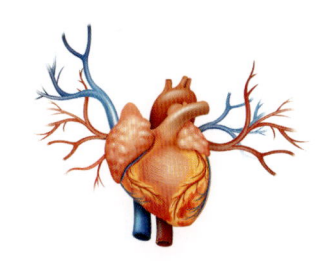

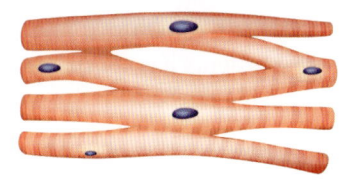

Cardiac muscle **Skeletal muscle** **Smooth muscle**

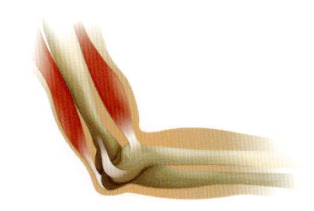

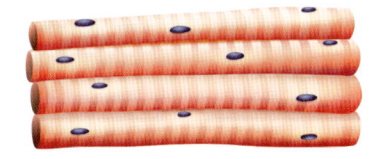

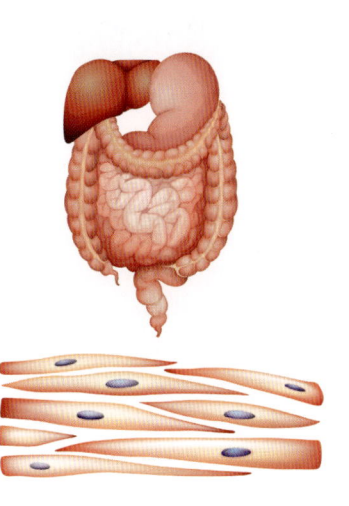

Section Review –
7.2 Characteristics and Life Processes of the Kingdom Animalia

1. Give six characteristics of the Kingdom Animalia.
2. What type of animal is an exception to the rule that all animals have tissues and organs?
3. Name and briefly describe the four basic types of tissues found in animals.
4. Describe muscle tissue.
5. Describe nerve tissue.
6. Identify ganglia.
7. Identify the system by which most animals react to stimuli in the environment.
8. Draw and label a typical animal cell.

WORDS TO REMEMBER

centrioles: organelles in animal cells that aid in cell division

tissues: groups of cells that work together to serve a specific function. There are four basic types of tissues found in animals: epithelial tissue, connective tissue, muscle tissue, and nerve tissue.

organs: groups of tissues that work together to perform a specific function

epithelial tissue: groups of cells tightly packed together in sheets or clusters and assembled on a membrane

connective tissue: cells and fibers distributed throughout a fluid environment; supports and connects other tissue types within organs; serves as a barrier between different layers of tissues within organs; provides structure to organisms; serves to transport materials from one part of the organism to another

muscle tissue: made of interconnected, elongated cells that have the ability to contract and relax. Muscle tissues are responsible for movement in almost all animals.

nerve tissue: responsible for brain activity, sensory input, integration, control of muscles and glands, and homeostasis. Nerve tissue is composed of neurons, or impulse-conducting cells, and glial cells, or supporting cells.

CHAPTER 7: THE ANIMAL KINGDOM

7.3 Classification of Animals

The classification of animals meets with the same difficulties as classification of organisms in other kingdoms. Classification schemes are constantly changing as new information about God's creation is discovered. Recall that all classification systems are men's imperfect attempts to classify God's perfect creation. Man's knowledge of creation is growing, but it is still insufficient to understand all of God's works, both spiritual and physical.

Most animals can be classified into one of eleven groups based on the characteristics of a basic body plan. Some of these characteristics are body symmetry, segmentation, and the presence of a backbone.

A. Symmetry

Symmetry is the characteristic of having exactly similar parts facing each other, or similar parts around an axis. **Body symmetry** in animals is characterized by exactly similar body parts organized facing each other. Some animals may have an **asymmetrical** body, or an irregular body with no orderly repeating parts. Other animals may have bodies with either **radial** or **bilateral** symmetry. **Radially symmetrical** animals have bodies that are symmetrical in several directions about a central point, like a spoked bicycle wheel. **Bilaterally symmetrical** animals have bodies that can be divided into two identical halves.

B. Segmentation

The second characteristic of a body plan that helps to classify animals is **segmentation**. A segment is a small piece or portion of a larger whole. In terms of animals, segmentation describes a body plan in which an animal has distinct body segments. Some animals, such as earthworms, have small, similar segments that are repeated throughout the entire length of the body. Some animals, however, have only two or three segments and each segment is specialized. For example, insects are animals with three body segments: the **head**, the **thorax**, and the **abdomen**; each of these segments has special organs and systems to serve a specific purpose in the overall functioning of the animal.

C. Backbones

In addition to body plan characteristics, the presence or absence of a backbone helps to further classify and study animals. Those animals that do not have a backbone are called **invertebrates**. Invertebrates make up over 95% of all species of animals. The invertebrates include: sponges, flatworms, mollusks, roundworms, and many other groups. Animals that do have backbones are called **vertebrates**.

Section Review –
7.3 Classification of Animals

1. Identify the three main characteristics that scientists use to classify animals.

2. What characteristic is present in 95% of all species of animals?

Animal Body Symmetry Types

Radial Symmetry Asymmetry Bilateral Symmetry

Life Science for Young Catholics

7.4 The Stingers: Jellyfish, Corals, and Others

The Stingers are a diverse group of aquatic animals that include jellyfish, corals, anemones (*a-**nem**-o-nees*), and hydras. Stingers have special stingers they use for defense. Their stingers are also used like harpoons, sending out poison to immobilize little creatures in the water, which are then captured and eaten by the Stingers.

The muscle cells around the mouths of Stingers are involved in locomotion as well as digestion and excretion. The muscle tissue draws in and expels water. Expelling water results in a type of jet propulsion. The expelled currents propel the Stingers through the water like jet engines propel a plane through the air.

Stingers are able to **regenerate** missing parts. Regeneration is the ability of an injured or fragmented organism to grow back into a full, intact organism. If a stinger loses part of its body, it automatically regrows that missing part!

Many Stingers live in **mutualistic relationships** with other organisms. **Mutualistic relationships** are relationships in which two dissimilar organisms live together for mutual benefit. The clownfish, for example, is immune to the stings of a Stinger called a sea anemone (*a-**nem**-o-nee*). The clownfish lives without harm among the tentacles of the sea anemone. The poison tentacles of the anemone actually protect the clownfish from larger predators, and the clownfish chases away fish that eat anemones.

You may have seen anemones and clownfish in a mutualistic relationship in the movie *Finding Nemo*. The sea anemone was a Stinger that lived in a mutualistic relationship with the clownfish, Nemo's father.

A jellyfish

Aa WORDS TO REMEMBER

symmetry: the characteristic of having exactly similar parts facing each other, or similar parts around an axis

asymmetrical body symmetry: describes bodies with no orderly repeating parts

radial symmetry: describes animals that have bodies that are symmetrical in several directions about a central point, like a spoked bicycle wheel

bilateral symmetry: describes animals that have bodies that can be divided into two identical halves

segmentation: describes a body plan in which an animal has distinct body segments

invertebrates: animals that do not have a backbone. Invertebrates make up over 95% of all species of animals.

stingers: a diverse group of aquatic animals that include jellyfish, corals, anemones, and hydras. Stingers have special stinging cells they use for defense and for killing prey.

regeneration: the ability of an injured or fragmented organism to grow back into a full, intact organism

mutualistic relationships: relationships in which two dissimilar organisms live together for mutual benefit

Section Review – 7.4 The Stingers: Jellyfish, Corals, and Others

1. Identify three characteristics of Stingers.
2. Name four types of Stingers.

Life Science for Young Catholics

CHAPTER 7: THE ANIMAL KINGDOM

7.5 The Soft Bodies: Mollusks

A. Body

All mollusks have a soft body without a backbone and usually live in a shell. Snails and clams are mollusks. Mollusks are a large group of invertebrate animals that inhabit a wide variety of habitats; most are marine animals - that is, they live in ocean waters - but some mollusks live in fresh water and some even live on land. The mollusk group includes over 80,000 different species of snails, squids, oysters, and octopuses!

B. Benefits of Mollusks

Mollusks are important members of many ecosystems. Remember that ecosystems are locations where plants and animals depend on each other for survival. Snails and slugs, while they can be pests in gardens, provide a good food source for many animals. Similarly, freshwater snails provide a food source for fish and other aquatic animals.

Many mollusks provide food for humans. Mussels, clams, squid, conch, and oysters are common seafood dishes in many parts of the world. The shells of mollusks have been used by people throughout history for jewelry and even as a form of currency. Oysters produce valuable pearls used in jewelry. Some mollusks produce chemicals that are used to make medications to treat cancer and reduce pain!

> **Section Review –**
> **7.5 The Soft Bodies: Mollusks**
>
> 1. Where do mollusks live?
> 2. Name three features of mollusks.
> 3. Name three types of mollusks.

A snail is a type of mollusk.

CHAPTER 7: THE ANIMAL KINGDOM

A spider is an arthropod.

7.6 The Jointed Appendages: Arthropods

The arthropods (**arth**-ro-pods) are the largest group of the whole animal kingdom; this group includes **myriapods** (**meer**·ee·uh·pods) or multi-foots, **insects**, **arachnids** (a·**rack**·nids), and **crustaceans** (crus·**tay**·shuns). As the largest group of animals, arthropods exhibit a large amount of diversity in appearance, but all share a basic body plan. All arthropods are bilaterally symmetric, with similar parts on each side of their bodies. Arthropods also have jointed appendages, or jointed limbs.

A. Centipedes and Millipedes

Centipedes and millipedes are known as **myriapods**, so named because they have "myriads," or a great number, of legs! The myriapods have multiple body segments that bear the legs. Centipedes have one pair of legs per body segment, while millipedes have two pairs of legs per body segment.

B. Insects

Insects are the largest and most diverse group of arthropods. It is believed that insects alone make up over half of all of the animals known to man; there are over one million known species! Insects have three body parts: head, thorax, and abdomen with legs.

C. Arachnids

Arachnids are arthropods that have bodies comprised of two segments and eight legs. Those eight legs help them to move very quickly! Arachnids, including **spiders**, **mites**, **scorpions**, and **ticks**, have an **abdomen** and a **cephalothorax** (**seff**·ah·low·**thor**·ax). A cephalothorax means the head and the thorax are joined. Thus the arachnids have only two body segments.

Arachnids kill their prey with venom or poison, and then bathe their prey in digestive juices from their stomach. The digestive juices turn the prey into liquid which is then consumed by the arachnid.

D. Crustaceans

Crustaceans include **lobsters**, **crabs**, **crayfish**, **shrimp**, **krill**, **barnacles**, and **pill bugs**. All crustaceans are aquatic and live in salt water, except crayfish, which live in fresh water, and pill bugs, which live on land. They have exoskeletons.

> **WORDS TO REMEMBER**
>
> **mollusks:** have a soft body without a backbone and usually live in a shell
>
> **arthropods:** the largest group of the whole animal kingdom; includes myriapods or multi-foots, insects, arachnids, and crustaceans
>
> **myriapods:** have "myriads," or a great number, of legs. They have multiple body segments that bear the legs.
>
> **insects:** the largest and most diverse group of arthropods
>
> **arachnids:** arthropods that have bodies comprised of two segments and eight legs
>
> **crustaceans:** mostly aquatic arthropods that typically have a body covered with a hard shell or crust

> **Section Review – 7.6 The Jointed Appendages: Arthropods**
>
> 1. Name four types of arthropods.
> 2. How many legs per segment do centipedes have?
> 3. How many legs per segment do millipedes have?
> 4. Identify four kinds of arachnids.
> 5. Identify five kinds of crustaceans.

Life Science for Young Catholics

CHAPTER 7: THE ANIMAL KINGDOM

These household pets are chordates (having bilateral symmetry) and vertebrates (having backbones).

7.7 Chordates

Chordates (**kor**-dates) are the animals most familiar to most people. Dogs, cats, horses, fish, frogs, and birds are all chordates. What makes an animal a chordate? All chordates have a notochord, a flexible rod-like structure, during some part of their life cycle. Most adult chordates have a backbone which replaced the notochord during embryonic development. All chordates share a similar body plan with bilateral symmetry or duplicate body parts on both sides, a body cavity, and segmented bodies. All chordates are animals with a digestive tract that has an intake opening, or mouth, and an exit opening, or anus.

Section Review – 7.7 Chordates

Describe what all chordates have in common.

7.8 Invertebrate Chordates

There are two groups of invertebrate chordates, that is, chordates lacking a backbone. The two groups are the **lancelets** (**lance**·uh·lets), and the **tunicates** (**tune**·i·kates). The **lancelets** are shaped like a knife blade. They are salt water, or marine, animals that are only a few centimeters long with elongated, segmented bodies. The **tunicates** are immobile animals (they don't move) with a tunic-like covering that gives the animal its name.

The lancelets and tunicates are important members of the plankton food chain. They consume plankton and, as a result, help to control the overgrowth of algae and other microscopic sea organisms.

Section Review – 7.8 Invertebrate Chordates

1. Name two groups of invertebrate chordates.
2. Why are invertebrate chordates important to the environment or ecosystem?

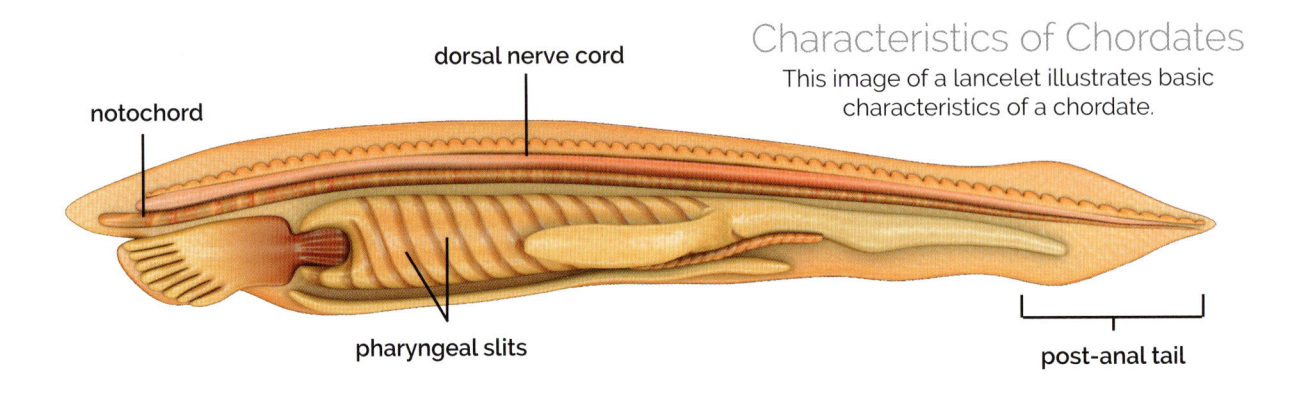

Characteristics of Chordates

This image of a lancelet illustrates basic characteristics of a chordate.

- notochord
- dorsal nerve cord
- pharyngeal slits
- post-anal tail

Life Science for Young Catholics

CHAPTER 7: THE ANIMAL KINGDOM

7.9 Vertebrates

The **vertebrates** are perhaps the most familiar group of animals. This group has backbones, and includes most of the animals of our daily lives: cats, dogs, birds, fish, and frogs. All vertebrates are chordates, that is, they have backbones. Most vertebrates have a basic bilateral body plan of a head, trunk, and two pairs of appendages, or limbs.

What characteristics make a vertebrate a vertebrate? First, vertebrates are animals of the chordate group which have backbones, or **vertebrae** columns. The backbone is also known as the spine, and is made of individual bony units called **vertebrae** (singular, **vertebra**).

A well-developed brain and a dorsally located, (dorsal means on the back), hollow nerve cord (spinal cord) comprise the **central nervous system** of the vertebrate group. Two well-developed eyes are a part of the vertebrate nervous system.

Section Review – 7.9 Vertebrates

1. Name four features that all vertebrates have in common.
2. Describe the central nervous system of chordates.

7.10 The Jawless Fish

The jawless fish are represented by **lampreys** (**lam**·prays). Lampreys are long, eel-like fish with smooth skin and no scales. They are distinguished by having a round, sucker-like mouth without jaws. The mouth is supported by a ring of cartilage and has multiple rows of hard teeth and a rasping tongue. Lampreys are parasites that live off other living organisms. Lampreys attach to the bodies of other fish with the suction created by their mouths and feed off the flesh and blood of fish.

Section Review – 7.10 The Jawless Fish

1. Describe lampreys.
2. Briefly describe the parasitic nature of a lamprey.

A lamprey

WORDS TO REMEMBER

chordates: have a notochord or replacement vertebral spine, bilateral symmetry or duplicate body parts on both sides, a body cavity, and segmented bodies. All chordates are animals with a digestive track that has an intake opening or mouth, and an exit opening or anus.

lancelets: invertebrate chordates shaped like a knife blade. They are salt water, or marine, animals that are only a few centimeters long with elongated, segmented bodies.

tunicates: immobile, invertebrate chordates with a tunic-like covering that gives the animal its name

vertebrates: animals of the chordate group that have backbones, or vertebrae columns. The backbone is also known as the spine, and is made of individual bony units called vertebrae (singular, vertebra). Vertebrates have a well-developed brain and a dorsally located hollow nerve cord (spinal cord), comprising a central nervous system.

lampreys: long, eel-like, jawless fish with smooth skin and no scales. They are distinguished by having a round, sucker-like mouth without jaws.

Life Science for Young Catholics

7.11 Cartilaginous Fish

The cartilaginous fish are fish whose internal structure is not bone but cartilage, which is like a tough elastic tissue, and they do not have ribs to protect internal organs. All cartilaginous fish have two pairs of limbs.

These cartilaginous fish include sharks, rays, and chimaeras (*kim·eer-as*). There are many shapes and sizes of sharks and rays, from the enormous whale shark, to the sleek torpedo-shaped reef shark, to the flat, bottom-dwelling rays, skates, and angel sharks.

The **lateral line** system of sensory organs unique to fish detects vibrations in the water, and even helps the fish determine the position of their own bodies. An important sensory organ helps the fish locate prey for food and navigate through the vast oceans. Lateral line tissues are arranged in a long line along the sides of fish from the head to the tip of the tail.

Scientists have discovered that sharks have a seventh sense: the ability to detect **electric fields** in the water created by the movements of other sea animals and by changes in the Earth's magnetic field. This unique seventh sense helps sharks locate and catch prey, and helps them to migrate through the vast oceans.

Section Review – 7.11 Cartilaginous Fish

1. Name three types of cartilaginous fish.
2. What does cartilaginous mean?
3. Identify the lateral line of sharks.

A school of sharks circling in open water

7.12 Bony Fish

Unlike cartilaginous fish, **bony fish**, as their name implies, have an internal structure made up of bones. The **bony fish** comprise the largest group of vertebrates, with approximately 30,000 different species of fish divided into two major subgroups: the **ray-finned fish** and the **lobe-finned fish**. Over 99% of all bony fish are ray-finned; there are only eight living species of lobe-finned fish.

The ray-finned fish come in a tremendous variety of shapes, sizes, and colors, but all have bony rays, or spines, that support their fins. The lobe-finned fish also have fins supported by rays, but the fins are more fleshy, and attached to the body with a single bone. These rounded fins of the lobe-finned fish somewhat resemble the limbs of animals. Compare the fins of the fish represented in the pictures to the right.

A lobe-finned fish

A ray-finned fish

Section Review – 7.12 Bony Fish

1. How do bony fish differ from cartilaginous fish?
2. How do ray-finned fish differ from lobe-finned fish?

7.13 Amphibians

The **amphibian** (am-**fib**-ee-an) group includes **frogs**, **toads**, **salamanders**, and **caecilians** (see·**sill**·ee·ans). The amphibians are part of the larger group known as the **tetrapods** (*tetra* meaning four, *pod* meaning feet) because all amphibians, except the caecilians, have four limbs. These vertebrate animals, with backbones, are unique in that their life cycle is spent partly in the water and partly on the land.

Amphibians are cold-blooded animals which take on the temperature of their surroundings. Amphibians' body temperature is regulated by the outside environment. Their own metabolism or body functions contribute nothing to body heat, or keeping them warm. Cold-blooded animals are sluggish in cold weather and more active in warm weather.

Section Review – 7.13 Amphibians

1. Name three types of amphibians.
2. Describe the meaning of *cold-blooded*.

WORDS TO REMEMBER

cartilaginous fish: fish whose internal structure is not bone but cartilage and do not have ribs to protect internal organs; these fish include sharks, rays, and chimaeras

lateral line: a system of sensory organs unique to fish that detects vibrations in the water; helps the fish determine the position of their bodies

bony fish: comprise the largest group of vertebrates with approximately 30,000 different species of fish divided into two major subgroups: the ray-finned fish and the lobe-finned fish. Over 99% of all bony fish are ray-finned; there are only eight living species of lobe-finned fish.

ray-finned fish: have bony rays or spines that support their fins.

lobe-finned fish: have fins supported by more fleshy rays that are attached to the body with a single bone

amphibians: cold-blooded, vertebrate animals that live part of their life cycle in the water and part on the land. Amphibians include frogs, toads, salamanders, and caecilians.

tetrapods: animals having four limbs

Life Science for Young Catholics

7.14 Reptiles

Snakes, **turtles**, **crocodiles**, and **lizards** are the main animals comprising the reptiles. These four kinds of reptiles are vertebrates that primarily live on land. Some of us have seen turtles and snakes in our gardens, and some of these reptiles even wander onto a street or sidewalk. Some of us may have seen a lizard, but most of us have never seen a crocodile except in a zoo or in a movie.

Reptiles, except for the snakes, have two pairs of limbs. Each limb typically has toes with **claws**. The reptiles have complete and complex organ systems, including a closed circulatory system with a three-chambered heart.

Reptiles have water-tight skin that is covered by scales; its main function is to preserve total body water.

Most reptiles lay eggs on land, but the eggs have special features to prevent them from drying. Reptile eggs contain embryos that are surrounded by a series of membranes.

> **Section Review – 7.14 Reptiles**
>
> 1. Name four types of reptiles.
> 2. Describe the type of skin found on most reptiles.
> 3. Which reptiles are legless?

7.15 Birds

The group of animals known as **aves** (**ay**·vees), or **birds**, comprises between 9,000 and 10,000 different types of feathered vertebrates. God's artistry is revealed in the incredible multitude of sizes, shapes, and colors of the many, many birds.

The **skeleton** of birds is unique in the animal kingdom with special features to facilitate flight, that is, to make flight easier. The bird's breastbone is relatively large to provide a large surface area for the attachment of the flying, pectoral muscles. All birds that fly have fewer bones than other animals, and fewer bones that contain bone **marrow**. Bone marrow lines only a few of the long bones of the limbs of birds and some of the vertebrae, which is the location of blood cell production. All the other bones in a bird's skeleton are very lightweight. Most are hollow and contain **air cavities**.

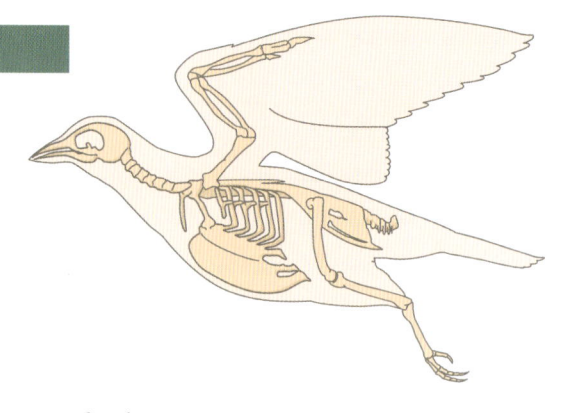

Amazingly, the air cavities inside the bones of birds are connected to the respiratory system.

> **Section Review – 7.15 Birds**
>
> What is unique about the skeletons of birds?

7.16 Mammals

Mammals have complex and well-developed organ systems, multilayered skin with appendages, and an endoskeleton composed of a cranium, or head bones; shoulder and hip girdles; back bone; and paired appendages, their arms and legs.

Mammals are warm-blooded animals that live on the land or in the sea. Mammals have a closed circulatory system with a four-chambered heart. Mammals breathe exclusively with lungs. Mammals are recognized as a distinct group within the animal kingdom based on several unique characteristics. Unlike all other animals, mammals have **hair**. What is significantly different from other creatures is that mammals nourish their young with milk produced in **mammary glands**.

Mammary Glands

Mammals are named after the **mammary glands**. Mammary glands are a unique trait found in both male and female mammals. However, they develop fully only in females. Mammary glands differ somewhat among the various species of mammals.

Mammary glands are composed of a system of **ducts**, or tubes, surrounded by **gland** tissue that produces **milk**. The ducts lead to a common reservoir, which then opens to the outside by way of a single opening, or of multiple ducts that open separately, onto an area of fleshy skin called a **nipple**.

Mammary glands are found in various mammals anywhere from the abdomen to the pectoral area, and vary in number from two in many species of mammals, to twenty in other mammals. The milk produced also varies greatly in its composition from mammal to mammal. All mammalian milk is very rich in fats, proteins, and sugars, especially lactose, and provides the nutrition needed for a rapidly growing baby mammal.

Baby pigs receiving milk from the mother pig.

WORDS TO REMEMBER

reptiles: cold-blooded vertebrates that have dry scaly skin and usually lay soft-shelled eggs on land. Snakes, turtles, crocodiles, and lizards are reptiles.

birds: warm-blooded, egg-laying vertebrates with feathers, wings, and a beak. Most birds have the ability to fly.

mammals: warm-blooded vertebrates that have a four-chambered heart, breathe exclusively with lungs, have hair, and nourish their young with milk produced in mammary glands. Mammals may be divided into three large groups based on the development of their offspring: monotremes, marsupials, and placental mammals.

mammary glands: a unique trait found in both male and female mammals. However, they develop fully only in females to produce milk to feed the young.

ducts: tubes surrounded by tissue to conduct liquids

nipple: an area of fleshy skin on mammals that allows milk to exit when feeding the young

---

Section Review – 7.16 Mammals

1. What feature is responsible for the name mammals?
2. Briefly describe mammary glands. Why are they significant?

Life Science for Young Catholics

7.17 Classification of Mammals

Most scientists agree that mammals may be divided into three large groups based on the development of their offspring. The three designations include: **monotremes**, **marsupials** (mar·**soup**·ee·als), and **placental mammals**.

A. Monotremes

Monotremes are the mammals that lay eggs. This is the smallest group of mammals, with only about five living species. The monotremes include the **duckbilled platypus** (**plat**-i-puss) and the **spiny anteaters**.

B. Marsupials

Marsupials are mammals that give birth to very undeveloped young, called **joeys**. Immediately after birth, the immature joeys climb into a pouch usually located on the mother's abdomen. The joeys attach to a nipple for nourishment from the mother and stay attached until their development is complete.

There are approximately 270 species of marsupials, which include **opossums** (o-**poss**·ums), **kangaroos**, **wallabies** (**wall**·a·bees), **wombats**, **koalas** (kuh·**wall**·uhs), and some others.

C. Placental Mammals

The placental mammals all bear live young which develop in the mother's **uterus**, nourished by a special organ known as the **placenta**, which is connected to the developing offspring by an **umbilical** (um·**bill**·i·cull) **cord**. The placenta transfers nutrients and oxygen to the developing offspring from the mother's digestive and circulatory systems. The placenta also transfers waste products, including carbon dioxide, from the developing offspring to the mother for removal. The placenta is expelled from the mother's body after the offspring is born. The **placental mammals** make up the largest and most diverse group of mammals, with well over 4,000 known species.

> **Section Review – 7.17 Classification of Mammals**
>
> 1. Describe the three major groups of mammals, including how they are differentiated.
> 2. Which group of mammals is the largest?
> 3. Which mammals do not bear live young?
> 4. Name two kinds of monotremes.
> 5. Name four kinds of marsupials.
> 6. Describe how marsupials are unique in bearing and raising their young.
> 7. Describe the purpose of the placenta.

7.18 Mammals in the Bible

The diversity in God's creation can be seen throughout the pages of the Bible. Over 100 different types of animals are mentioned in the pages of Holy Scripture, beginning with the story of creation in Genesis, and continuing through the pages of the New Testament. Many mammals, including donkeys, horses, dogs, oxen, camels, cows, goats, sheep, pigs, bears, deer, lions, whales, and wolves, are mentioned in different books of the Bible. Horses alone are mentioned more than 150 times throughout Scripture; donkeys appear more than 120 times.

CHAPTER 7: **THE ANIMAL KINGDOM**

The story of creation in Genesis introduces all animals as created by God and named by Adam, but classifies all animals only according to the order in which they were created. Leviticus distinguishes between clean and unclean animals; Deuteronomy lists those that can be consumed by man and those that should not be, and distinguishes between different hoofed animals and ruminants:

> You shall not eat any abominable thing. These are the animals you may eat: the ox, the sheep, the goat, the deer, the gazelle, the roebuck, the wild goat, the ibex, the antelope, and the mountain sheep. Any among the animals that has divided hooves, with the foot cloven in two, and that chews the cud you may eat. But you shall not eat any of the following that chew the cud or have cloven hooves: the camel, the hare, and the rock badger, which indeed chew the cud, but do not have divided hooves; they are unclean for you. And the pig, which indeed has divided hooves, with cloven foot, but does not chew the cud, is unclean for you. Their flesh you shall not eat, and their dead bodies you shall not touch. (Deuteronomy 14:3-8)

Animals are used throughout the Bible as signs and symbols; they are used to describe many things. In this psalm, evildoers are compared to three different mammals:

WORDS TO REMEMBER

monotremes: mammals that lay eggs

marsupials: mammals that give birth to very undeveloped young, called joeys, that develop in a pouch usually located on the mother's abdomen. The marsupials include opossums, kangaroos, wallabies, wombats, koalas, and some others.

placental mammals: bear live young which develop in the mother's uterus, nourished by a special organ known as the placenta which is connected to the developing offspring by an umbilical cord.

> Dogs surround me; a pack of evildoers closes in on me. They have pierced my hands and my feet. I can count all my bones. They stare at me and gloat; they divide my garments among them; for my clothing they cast lots. But you, LORD, do not stay far off; my strength, come quickly to help me. Deliver my soul from the sword, my life from the grip of the dog. Save me from the lion's mouth, my poor life from the horns of wild bulls. (Psalm 22:17-22)

Life Science for Young Catholics

Chapter 7 Review

A. Identify these types of muscle.

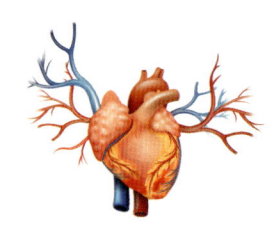

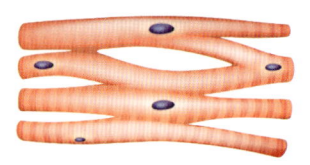

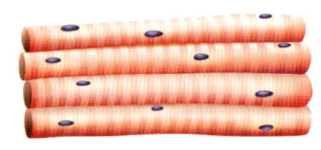

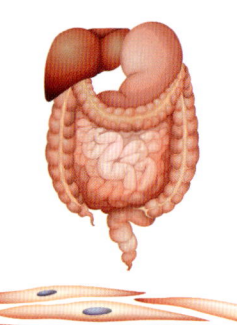

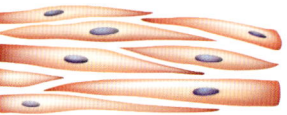

_____   _____   _____

B. Are the following mammals? Write true or false.

___ ___ ___ ___ ___ ___

C. Answer the following questions.

1. Identify the three main characteristics that scientists use to classify animals.
2. Name three features of mollusks.
3. Name four types of arthropods.
4. Identify four kinds of arachnids.
5. Identify five kinds of crustaceans.
6. Name the two groups of invertebrate chordates.
7. Why are invertebrate chordates important to the environment or ecosystem?
8. Name four features that all vertebrates have in common.
9. Name three types of cartilaginous fish.
10. How do bony fish differ from cartilaginous fish?
11. How do ray-finned fish differ from lobe-finned fish?
12. Name four types of reptiles.
13. What is unique about the skeleton of birds?
14. What feature is responsible for the name mammals?
15. Describe the three major groups of mammals, including how they are differentiated.

112 Life Science for Young Catholics

Chapter 7: "Words to Remember" Crossword

ACROSS

1. have bilateral symmetry or duplicate body parts on both sides, a body cavity, and segmented bodies
5. warm-blooded vertebrates with a four-chambered heart, that breathe exclusively with lungs, have hair, and nourish their young with milk produced in mammary glands
7. the characteristic of having exactly similar parts facing each other, or similar parts around an axis.
9. animals of the chordate group which have backbones, or vertebrae columns
10. These have four limbs.
11. animals that do not have a backbone
12. have a soft body without a backbone and usually live in a shell

DOWN

2. groups of tissues that work together to perform a specific function
3. mammals that give birth to very undeveloped young, called joeys, that develop in a pouch usually located on the mother's abdomen
4. mostly aquatic arthropods that typically have the body covered with a hard shell or crust
5. these have "myriads," or a great number, of legs
6. organelles in animal cells that aid in cell division
8. a diverse group of aquatic animals that include jellyfish, corals, anemones, and hydras

Life Science for Young Catholics

8 THE HUMAN INTEGUMENTARY SYSTEM

Chapter 8 Outline

8.1 Introduction

8.2 Man: Body and Soul

8.3 The Human Body: Organization and Interdependence

8.4 The Integumentary System: The Skin

8.5 Summary

Chapter 8
The Human Integumentary System

8.1 Introduction

Do you know the story of Samson? Samson was one of the judges of Israel, before they had a king to rule them. God gave Samson super strength to defend the people of Israel. However, God told Samson that he would lose his strength if he let his hair be cut.

A woman named Delilah tricked Samson into telling her the secret of his strength, and she had his hair cut while he slept. Then the Philistines captured him and blinded him in his weakened state. Samson prayed for forgiveness and asked that his strength be returned to him. Then his hair started to grow again. Samson used his newfound strength to destroy the temple and leadership of the enemy.

Our Lord Jesus Christ proclaimed that God knows the number of hairs on our heads! Imagine that! God loves us so much that He even keeps track of that! God is telling us that He knows every little thing about us.

In this chapter, we will study about our largest organ, the skin. Hair is a part of the skin and not just on our heads.

8.2 Man: Body and Soul

Chapter 1 began with the Genesis account of creation, which teaches the truths of creation. God created all from nothing. God created in a perfect and orderly fashion. He began with the planet Earth: the light, the sky, the waters, the land, the vegetation. He then created the creatures of the waters, the birds of the sky, and the animals of the land; and, as the summit of His creation, God created man, the first man Adam.

Then God said: Let Us make human beings in Our dignity, after Our likeness. Let them have dominion over the fish of the sea, the birds of the air, the tame animals, all the wild animals, and all the creatures that crawl on the earth. God created mankind in His image; in the image of God He created them; male and female He created them.

God blessed them and God said to them: Be fertile and multiply; fill the earth and subdue it. Have dominion over the fish of the sea, the birds of the air, and all the living things that crawl on the earth. (Genesis 1:26-28)

These few lines from Genesis contain several truths about the creation of man. First, God planned for man to be distinct from the other creatures. Just as He willed the plants, the aquatic animals, the birds of the sky, and the animals of the land as separate entities, He created man to be unique. He did not create man in the likeness of the other living things, but in His own likeness. God set man apart from all of the previous creation, from the beginning of man's existence, to be in the image of Himself.

Life Science for Young Catholics

CHAPTER 8: THE HUMAN INTEGUMENTARY SYSTEM

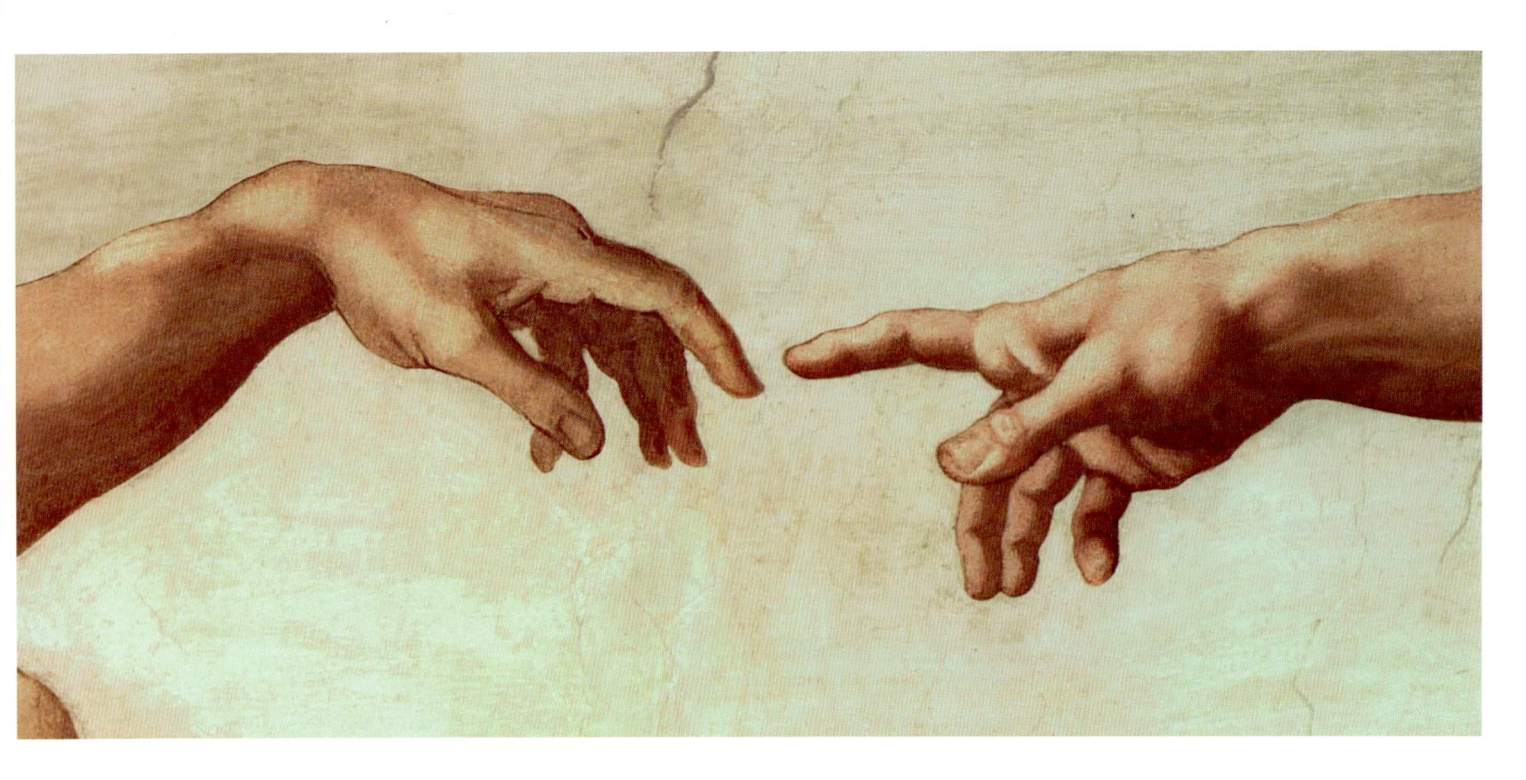

God, in His wisdom, created creatures with the same building materials, but fashioned His many creatures with almost endless diversity. The basic macromolecules - proteins, carbohydrates, lipids, nucleic acids - are found throughout all of creation with unique additions and deletions and modifications among the various species and organisms. The basic structure of the cell is unchanged throughout the animal kingdom.

All of God's 9-to-10 million animals, with all the diversity discussed in chapter 7, are built on one of only eleven basic body plans. Humans, scientifically speaking, share the mammalian characteristics and have much of the same genetic material. Despite these similarities, however, Holy Scripture teaches that God created man **apart** from the animals, not from the animals, not in the likeness of the animals, but as a unique creation in God's own image.

God created man with a body and a **soul**. According to the *Catechism of the Catholic Church*, the body and soul are unified into **one nature**, and the soul is that which "animates the matter of the body." In other words, the spiritual soul is precisely what makes man human, in the image of God, and thus dramatically different from the rest of God's creation. Furthermore, the Catholic Church teaches:

[E]very spiritual soul is created immediately by God—it is not "produced" by the parents—and also...it is immortal: it does not perish when it separates from the body at death, and it will be reunited with the body at the final Resurrection."

The human soul is, therefore, willed into existence by God at the second of physical conception. In fact, it is the soul that gives life or existence. There is not a second of physical human life without a soul. There is no physical body at all, dead or alive, which can precede the human soul because God gives both physical and spiritual life, the body and soul, at the very same instant.

The very dignity of the human being comes from His creation in the image and likeness of God Himself and, for this reason, man is the summit, or the greatest part, of God's creation.

<u>The study of the summit of creation, the human body and soul</u>, as well as the study of all of creation, reveals the greatness of God, the Creator. The incredible complexity and the marvelous organization, the amazing interdependence of organs and organ systems, the awe-inspiring design, the magnificent structure related to function—every fantastic detail of the human body gives testimony to the awesome wisdom and perfection of God. It also gives testimony to the incredible love that God has

CHAPTER 8: THE HUMAN INTEGUMENTARY SYSTEM

for each one of us. His incredible love inspires us to love Him to such an extent that we should be willing and determined to be obedient to His commands, to His laws. What God wants to see is that we love and care for those whom He has put into our lives, such as our parents and others in our family.

8.3 The Human Body: Organization and Interdependence

The human body is made of a countless number of individual cells that are organized into four basic types of tissues: muscle tissue, nerve tissue, connective tissue, and epithelial tissue, which is the special tissue that covers the surfaces and linings of many organs, such as the skin.

The tissues are organized into organs: the brain, the liver, the spleen, the heart, the lungs, and others. The organs are grouped into systems. There are ten or eleven organ systems comprising the human body, depending on how the systems are grouped.

Each organ system has a specialized function to perform to keep the entire body functioning properly as a whole. However, none of the organ systems is fully independent of the others. For example, the endocrine system produces hormones that regulate many other systems, including the cardiovascular and the reproductive systems. The endocrine system is itself dependent on the blood of the cardiovascular system for the delivery of its hormones to other body parts.

In the lessons that follow, it is important to keep in mind the interdependence of organs and organ systems. The remainder of this course will focus on each system of the human body in some detail, beginning with the skin, which holds it all together.

> **Section Review –
> 8.3 The Human Body: Organization and Interdependence**
>
> 1. How many organ systems comprise the human body?
> 2. Briefly explain how the organ systems are interdependent, yet also independent.

8.4 The Integumentary System: The Skin

As the skeletal system affords protection to the underlying organs, the integumentary (*in-te-gu-**men**-tar-ee*) system, the skin, protects the body from the outside. The integumentary system, the skin, is the largest organ of the body; it includes the **epidermis**, **dermis**, **subcutaneous** (*sub-cue-**tane**-ee-us*) **tissue**, **hair**, **nails**, **sweat glands**, **sebaceous** (*see·**bay**·shus*) **glands**, and **specialized sensory nerves**, along with related muscles and blood vessels. When you add up all the parts of the skin, you can see why it is the largest organ of the body!

The skin has many functions. First, it protects the internal organs of the body from physical damage. Second, the skin protects the body from harmful ultraviolet radiation from the sun. Third, it prevents excessive water loss, or **dehydration** (*dee-hi-**dray**-shun*). Fourth, it stores fat, which provides energy as well as insulation from heat and cold. Fifth, it produces vitamins and hormones. Sixth, it helps maintain a constant body temperature. Seventh, it acts as a defense against bacteria and viruses, which can cause disease.

We don't think too much about the importance of our skin, but now we should realize how important it is to take good care of our skin!

Did you know that the skin of the human body consists of three layers? The three layers are the epidermis, the dermis, and the subcutaneous layer.

The outer layer is called the **epidermis** (*ep-uh-**der**-miss*) and is made of **epithelial** (*ep-uh-**thee**-lee-al*) cells. These are flat, scale-like cells. Vitamin D is produced in these cells. Vitamin D helps the body to absorb calcium to keep bones strong, and is also an important factor in fighting some diseases.

Life Science for Young Catholics

CHAPTER 8: THE HUMAN INTEGUMENTARY SYSTEM

The **dermis**, the middle layer of skin, contains the base of the hair follicles and that of the sweat glands. These are important in regulating the body for comfort in very hot or very cold weather!

The lowest layer of skin, the **subcutaneous layer**, contains mostly fat and support tissues. These tissues are important for good health and need to be protected and treated carefully in case of an accident.

The human skin is an amazing gift from God. We don't think of it too much, but it is important in our daily life because it is a sensory organ that can detect four important things: temperature, touch, pressure, and pain.

One of the specialized cells in the epidermis, in the outer layer, produces the brown pigment **melanin** (**mel**·uh·nin), which gives the skin its color and also protects it from the ultraviolet radiation from the sun. On sunny days, near the beach or any body of water, be sure to use sunscreen so as not to get a burn. Most people don't even realize their skin is being burned until they start having pain at night! So use the sunscreen even if you don't feel you are getting burned. Better safe than sorry! Your parents can purchase the best sunscreen for your type of skin.

As you know, your skin includes hair. Your hair is made of thin filaments consisting predominantly of keratin. Hair grows from a follicle, a small depression, that is situated below the epidermis layer of skin.

Sebaceous (see-**bay**-shus) glands in the skin produce a waxy substance called **sebum** (**see**-bum) that lubricates and waterproofs the hair in your skin. Hair gets its color from the pigment melanin.

Hair serves to protect the body in different ways. Eyelashes and eyebrows protect the eyes from dust and other irritants. Hairs in the nose trap foreign materials and bacteria to prevent them from entering the respiratory tract to cause injury or infection. Hair on the body and on the scalp insulates and helps the body stay warm in cooler temperatures. Nails, a modified form of hair, protect the sensitive fingers and toes from injury.

Hair is important for maintaining the proper body temperature. When the body is cold, body hair tends to "stand on end" to trap warm air near the skin to keep it warm. When the body is too warm, hair tends to lie flat, and allows excess heat to escape through the skin.

Campers know that a large portion of body heat can escape through the head, so when sleeping in the open, they are careful to keep their heads covered. The hair on the head is a natural barrier to keep the heat inside.

Hair is also connected to special nerves that detect touch. The hair of eyelashes is especially sensitive to touch. If dust or other things contact the eyelashes, a reflex will cause the eye to close to prevent possible injury.

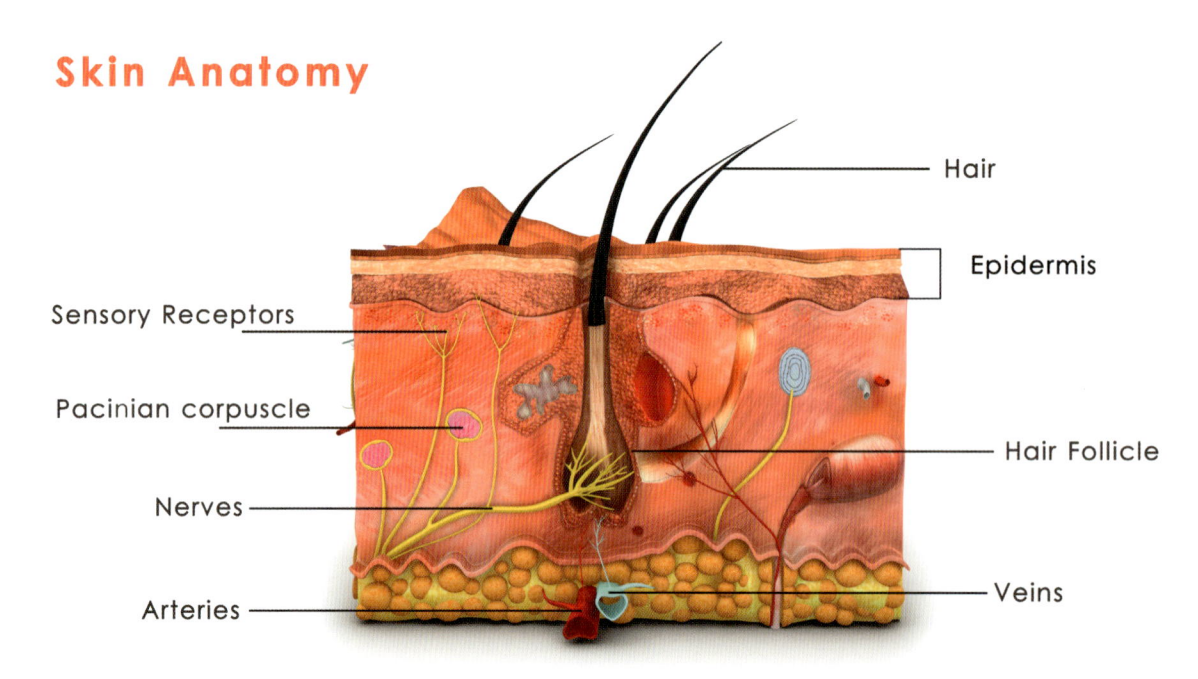

Skin Anatomy

- Sensory Receptors
- Pacinian corpuscle
- Nerves
- Arteries
- Hair
- Epidermis
- Hair Follicle
- Veins

Life Science for Young Catholics

CHAPTER 8: THE HUMAN INTEGUMENTARY SYSTEM

The skin is interdependent on every other organ system of the human body. Other parts of the body help the skin, and the skin helps other parts! The skin receives its blood supply from the circulatory system. In addition, the skin has special nerve endings to send sensory information back to the brain and spinal cord. These nerve endings protect the body against large temperature fluctuations and help maintain a stable body temperature.

Fat and sweat glands in the skin contribute to temperature balance. The skin participates as part of the immune system by acting as a barrier to bacteria and other germs so they never enter the body! Vitamin D is produced in the skin to help absorb calcium to keep the bones strong. The skin is also connected to the endocrine system, which works to produce and activate different hormones or chemical messengers that regulate growth and help in chemical reactions necessary for good health.

Section Review – 8.4 The Integumentary System: The Skin

1. Provide three ways the skin protects the body.
2. What is the function of sebaceous glands?
3. Identify melanin and its basic functions.
4. Name the parts of the skin.
5. Identify three functions of hair.
6. What vitamin is produced in the skin? What is its function?

WORDS TO REMEMBER

Integumentary system: the skin, which protects the body from the outside. The skin is the largest organ of the body and includes the epidermis, dermis, subcutaneous tissue, hair, nails, sweat glands, sebaceous glands, and specialized sensory nerves, along with related muscles and blood vessels.

dehydration: excessive loss of water from the body

subcutaneous layer (skin): the third and deepest layer of the skin. It lies below the middle layer, or the dermis. The subcutaneous layer contains mostly fat and support tissues.

epidermis layer (skin): the outer layer, or top layer of the skin. It is made up of epithelial cells.

epithelial cells: flat, scale-like cells on the outermost layer of the skin. Vitamin D is produced in these cells.

vitamin D: made in the skin with help from sunlight. Vitamin D helps the body to absorb calcium to keep bones strong, and is an important factor in fighting some diseases.

dermis layer (skin): the middle layer of skin that contains the base of the hair follicles and that of the sweat glands

melanin: a brown pigment produced in the epidermis, which gives the skin its color and gives the skin protection from the ultraviolet radiation from the sun.

keratin: a protein; hair, nails, and part of the skin is made up of keratin

sebum: a thick substance secreted by sebaceous glands. Sebum consists of fat and cell fragments that lubricate and waterproof the hair in your skin.

8.5 Summary

God has revealed Himself to us through His prophets, and through His only begotten Son, Jesus Christ. The revelations show that God made the whole universe for mankind, and that He gave man dominion over all of creation. God gave man a body, but also an immortal soul, destined to an eternal life with God in His home in Heaven.

The most visible aspect of man is his skin. The beauty of the skin is not just skin deep, so to speak. The skin provides structure and protection from various hazards to life, regulates our temperatures, and gives a vehicle for our sense of touch. God showed His love for us with the gift of skin, and all that lies beneath it.

Life Science for Young Catholics

CHAPTER 8: THE HUMAN INTEGUMENTARY SYSTEM

Chapter 8 Review

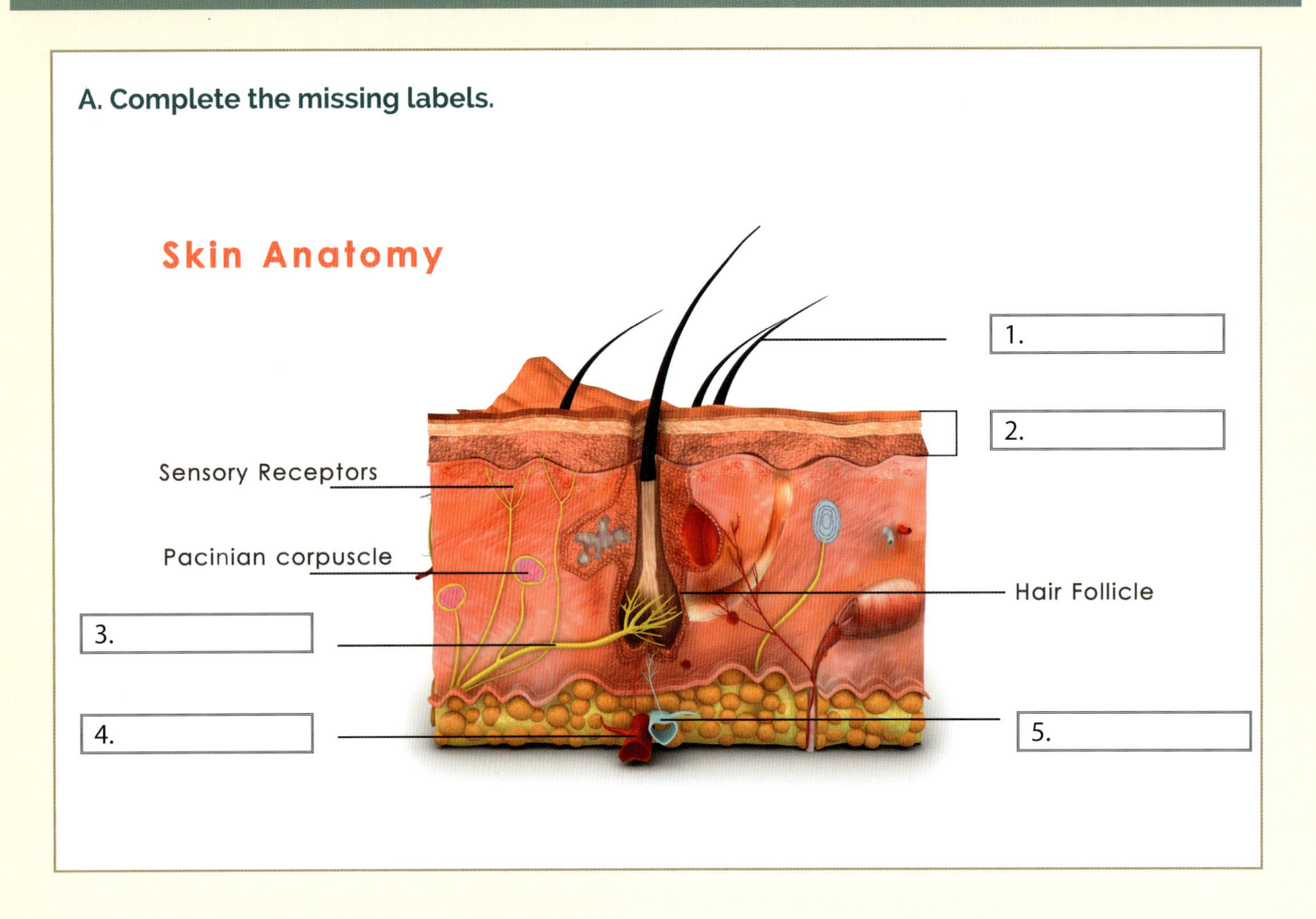

A. Complete the missing labels.

Skin Anatomy

- Sensory Receptors
- Pacinian corpuscle
- Hair Follicle
- 1.
- 2.
- 3.
- 4.
- 5.

B. Answer the following questions.

1. How many organ systems comprise the human body?
2. Briefly explain how these are interdependent, yet also independent.
3. Provide three ways the skin protects the body.
4. What is the function of sebaceous glands?
5. Identify melanin and its basic functions.
6. Identify three functions of hair.
7. What vitamin is produced in the skin? What is its function?
8. Identify three layers of the skin.
9. What is significant about the top layer?
10. What is significant about the middle layer?
11. What is significant about the lowest layer?

Chapter 8: "Words to Remember" Crossword

ACROSS

1. __ layer of the skin is the outer layer or top layer of the skin. It is made up of epithelial cells.
6. __ cells are flat, scale-like cells on the outermost layer of the skin.
7. a protein; hair, nails, and part of the skin consists of this protein.
8. __ system, is the skin, which protects the body from the outside.
9. __ layer of the skin is the third and deepest layer of the skin.

DOWN

2. __ layer of the skin is the middle layer of skin that contains the base of the hair follicles and contains the base of the sweat glands.
3. a brown pigment produced in the epidermis that gives the skin its color and also gives the skin protection from the ultraviolet radiation from the sun
4. excessive loss of water from the body
5. a thick substance secreted by sebaceous glands

THE HUMAN MUSCULOSKELETAL SYSTEM

Chapter 9 Outline

9.1 Introduction

9.2 The Musculoskeletal System

9.3 Bones

9.4 Joints

9.5 Muscles

9.6 Summary

Chapter 9
The Human Musculoskeletal System

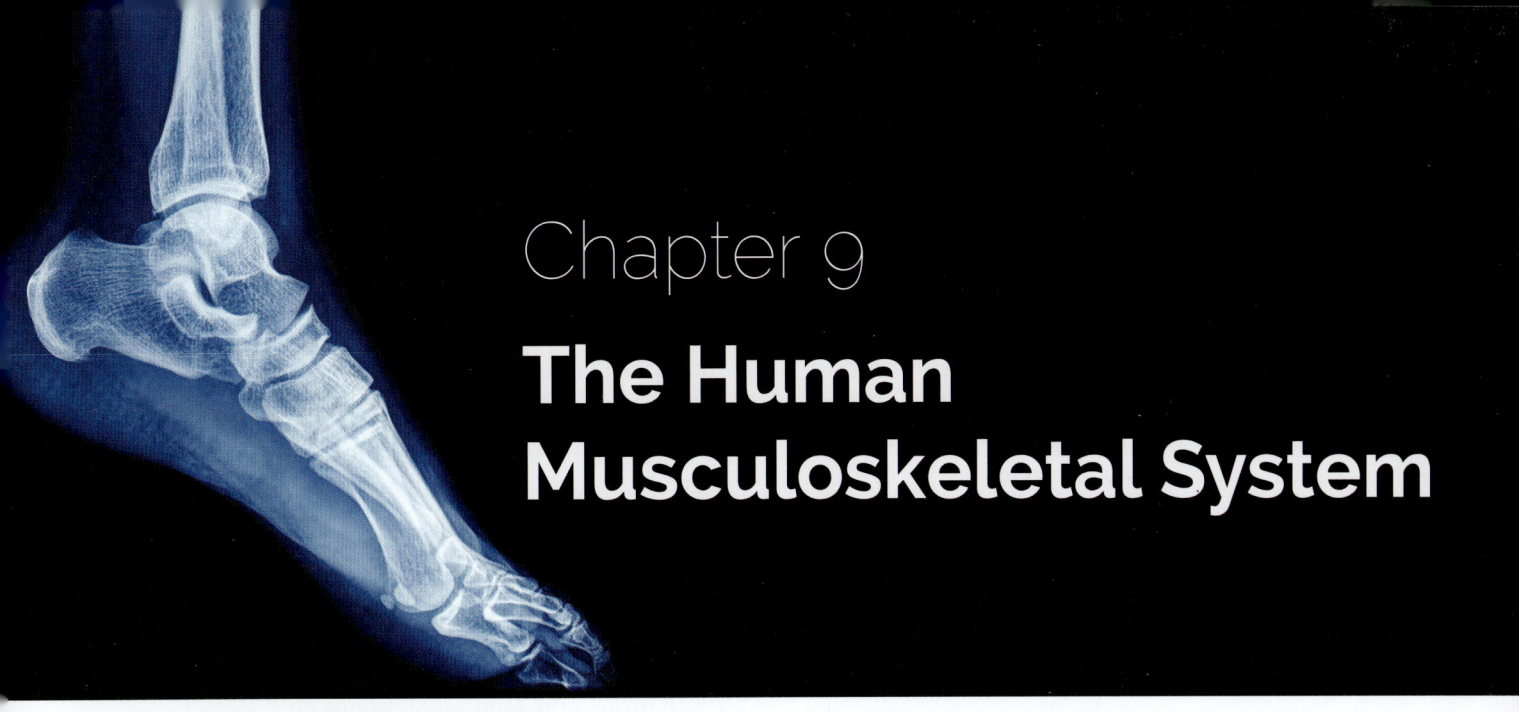

9.1 Introduction

Do you know the story of the prophet Ezekiel and the valley of dry bones? God brought Ezekiel to a plain full of dry bones and told the prophet to command the bones to "hear the word of the Lord." Ezekiel did as he was ordered and the bones started to reassemble.

And I prophesied as He had commanded me: and as I prophesied, there was a noise, and behold a commotion: and the bones came together, each one to its joint. And I saw, and beheld the sinews, and the flesh came up upon them: and the skin was stretched out over them, but there was no spirit in them. And He said to me: Prophesy to the Spirit, prophesy, O son of man, and say to the Spirit: Thus says the Lord God: Come, Spirit, from the four winds, and blow upon these slain, and let them live again. And I prophesied as He had commanded me: and the Spirit came into them, and they lived: and they stood up upon their feet, an exceeding great army.

Notice that the bones came together at joints, then sinews came to hold the bones together, then flesh, and finally skin developed to enclose everything. However, there was still no life in these creatures until God sent the Spirit to give life to them.

In Genesis, God created man from the dust of the ground, but there was no life in that first man until God "breathed into his nostrils the breath of life, and the man became a living being."

In God's plan, through the Sacrament of Marriage, mothers and fathers form the body of a new human being, but God cooperates each time and forms the immortal soul and this gives the body life.

Let's learn about the human body that God has created for each one of us!

9.2 The Musculoskeletal System

There are three types of human muscle tissues: **skeletal**, **cardiac**, and **smooth**. Because this chapter deals with the musculoskeletal system, cardiac and smooth muscle will not be discussed here.

The musculoskeletal system of the human body includes all the **skeletal muscles** and **bones** of the human body as well as all the **joints**, **ligaments**, **tendons**, and **cartilage** that hold the bones and muscles together.

Section Review — 9.2 The Musculoskeletal System

1. Identify the number and types of human muscle tissues.
2. Name the types of structures included in the musculoskeletal system.

Life Science for Young Catholics

CHAPTER 9: THE MUSCULOSKELETAL SYSTEM

9.3 Bones

Bone is a rigid connective tissue that gives the body shape, support, and protection. Bones manufacture both red and white blood cells and store minerals for the body. There are three types of cells found throughout the bone structure. These cells restore the bones after injuries, and strengthen bones as a result of work or exercise.

There are **206** bones in the human body, which is amazing. We don't realize or even think about the many bones we have. There are five different types of bones: **long** bones, **short** bones, **flat** bones, **irregular** bones, and **sesamoid** (**sess**·a·moyd) bones.

Long bones are longer than they are wide, with a center called the medullary cavity which contains red and yellow bone marrow. Bone marrow is a jelly-like substance that contains red blood cells. Long bones are the bones of the arms and the legs. The long bones have two major parts, the ends and the shaft. Growth takes place between the two parts in an area known as the **growth plate**.

Short bones are as wide as they are long, and often cube-shaped or round; short bones are found in the wrists and feet.

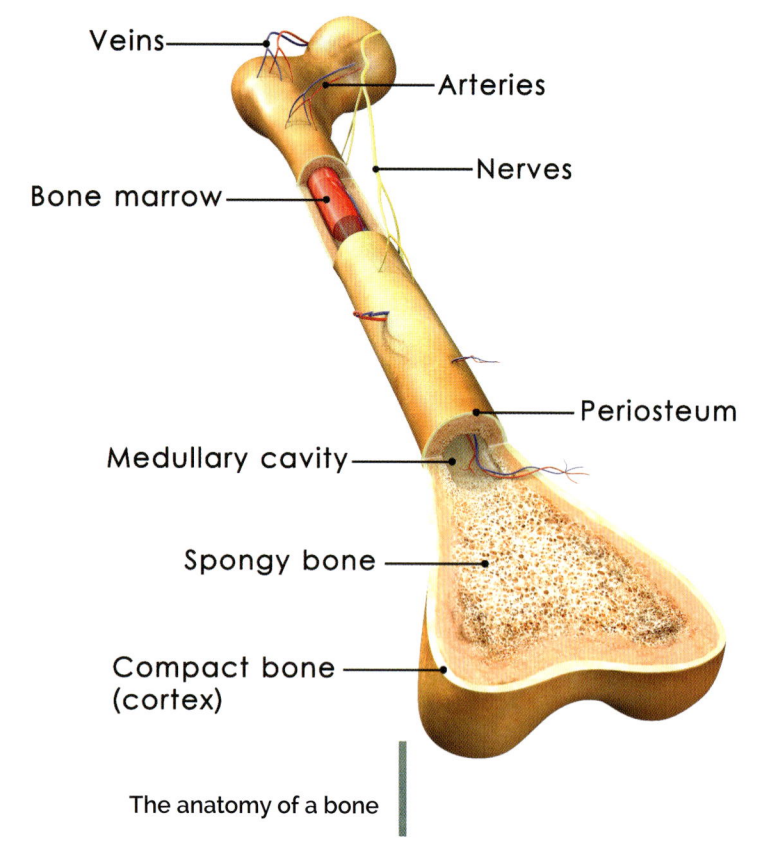

Flat bones are, as their name suggests, thin, flat bones, without a medullary cavity. Flat bones vary in shape and size and include the large bones of the skull, as well as the ribs and the hip bones.

Irregular bones are bones of a variety of shapes and sizes that do not fit into the other categories of bones. Irregular bones include the middle ear bones, the vertebrae, the jaw bone, and some facial bones.

The skull is made up of flat bones and irregular bones.

Sesamoid bones are bones that develop after birth to protect the tendons. Tendons are cords of tissue that attach muscles to bones. Sesamoid bones protect the tendons from the stress placed on them from movement around a **joint**. Sesamoid bones are commonly found in the hands and the feet; the kneecap also is a sesamoid bone.

All bones have an inner layer of **spongy bone**, an outer layer of **compact bone**, and a membrane covering the bone called the **periosteum** (*pear·ee·**ost**·ee·um*). The periosteum is a thick, fibrous, two-layered covering of bone containing blood vessels and nerves.

Collectively, the bones of the human body together form the skeleton, or support system, of the entire human body. The human skeleton is divided into the **axial** (**ax**·ee·ahl) skeleton and the **appendicular** (app·en·**dik**·you·lar) skeleton.

The axial skeleton is made of 80 bones and includes all the bones of the body's axis: the spinal column, head, and ribs.

The appendicular skeleton consists of the 126 bones that attach from the central axis, that is, the spinal column, and includes all the bones of the shoulder and hip girdles, that is, the arms, legs, hands, fingers, feet, and toes.

Besides providing support for the body and protection for the internal organs, the bones of the human

The anatomy of a bone

skeleton serve several other major functions. Bone serves as a reservoir or storage place for the minerals calcium and phosphorus. Calcium and phosphorus are released from the bone or taken up into the bone as needed to maintain homeostasis, the stable internal environment, in the blood, or as needed for the production of new bone.

Many bones, long bones in particular, also store fat. In addition, the central cavity of long bones is filled with **bone marrow**. Bone marrow is the site of new blood cell formation. Both red blood cells and white blood cells, and platelets which form blood clots, are made within the bone marrow.

In summary, bones store minerals, fat, and bone marrow in which blood cells and platelets are made. It is really incredible how much the body depends on healthy bones, inside as well as outside!

The anatomy of a human skull

Section Review – 9.3 Bones

1. Identify bone and its purpose.
2. How many bones are in the human body?
3. Name five types of bones.
4. Explain the difference between the axial skeleton and the appendicular skeleton. Include the number of bones in each and the major structures these bones form.
5. Describe the bones of the skull.
6. Where is bone marrow found? What is its function?

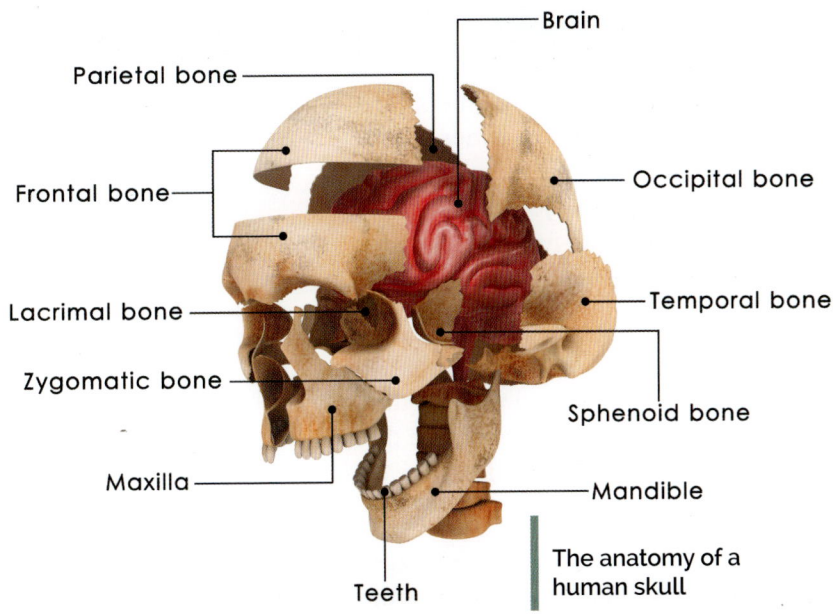

Aa WORDS TO REMEMBER

skeletal muscles: the striated muscles that move the bones in the skeleton

cardiac muscles: the specialized muscles of the heart that pump blood throughout the body

smooth muscles: the specialized muscles inside arteries and other organs; performs involuntary functions, such as opening and closing valves in blood vessels and moving food through the digestive system

tendon: a very strong band of fibrous tissue that connects a muscle to a bone

cartilage: firm but rubbery tissue that serves as a cushion at the joints

growth plate: zones of cartilage at each end of the long bones. New bone forms at the growth plate.

spongy bone: the tissue that makes up the interior of bones. Spongy bone has air pockets and may look like a kitchen sponge.

compact bone: the hard, smooth bone tissue that forms the surface of bones

periosteum: a thick, fibrous, two-layered covering of bone containing blood vessels and nerves

bone marrow: a jelly-like substance that contains red blood cells.

Life Science for Young Catholics

CHAPTER 9: THE MUSCULOSKELETAL SYSTEM

9.4 Joints

The bones are joined to other bones by thick connective tissue bands called **ligaments**, and the space between two bones is known as the **joint**. Many of the bones of the skull are fused together to form immoveable joints.

Moveable joints have a complex structure. The ends of the bones that meet in the joint are lined with **cartilage**. Cartilage is firm but rubbery tissue that serves as a cushion at the joints. The ears are examples of cartilage.

The smooth surface of the cartilage acts as a shock absorber and reduces the friction that occurs in the joint when the bones move. There is also a thick fluid that lubricates joints to further reduce friction. This thick fluid is called **synovial** (*syn-no-vee-al*) **fluid**, and the joints that this fluid lubricates are called **synovial joints**. Synovial joints are the joints that move in the body; for example, the joints that move the elbow, wrist and fingers are synovial joints.

There are several different types of synovial joints throughout the human body.

A **hinge joint** allows movement back and forth in only one plane; the elbow is a hinge joint.

A **ball and socket joint**, like that of the shoulder or of the hip, is the only type of joint that allows movement in a full circle around a fixed point. A ball and socket joint is formed when the rounded surface of one bone fits into the cup-like surface of another.

A **pivot joint**, like that between the two bones of the forearm, allows the forearm to rotate so that the palm can face up or down. A pivot joint in the neck allows turning of the head from left to right.

Other synovial joints include **gliding joints**, as between the carpal bones of the wrist, **biaxial joints**, as in the knuckles of the hand, and **saddle joints**, as at the base of the thumb.

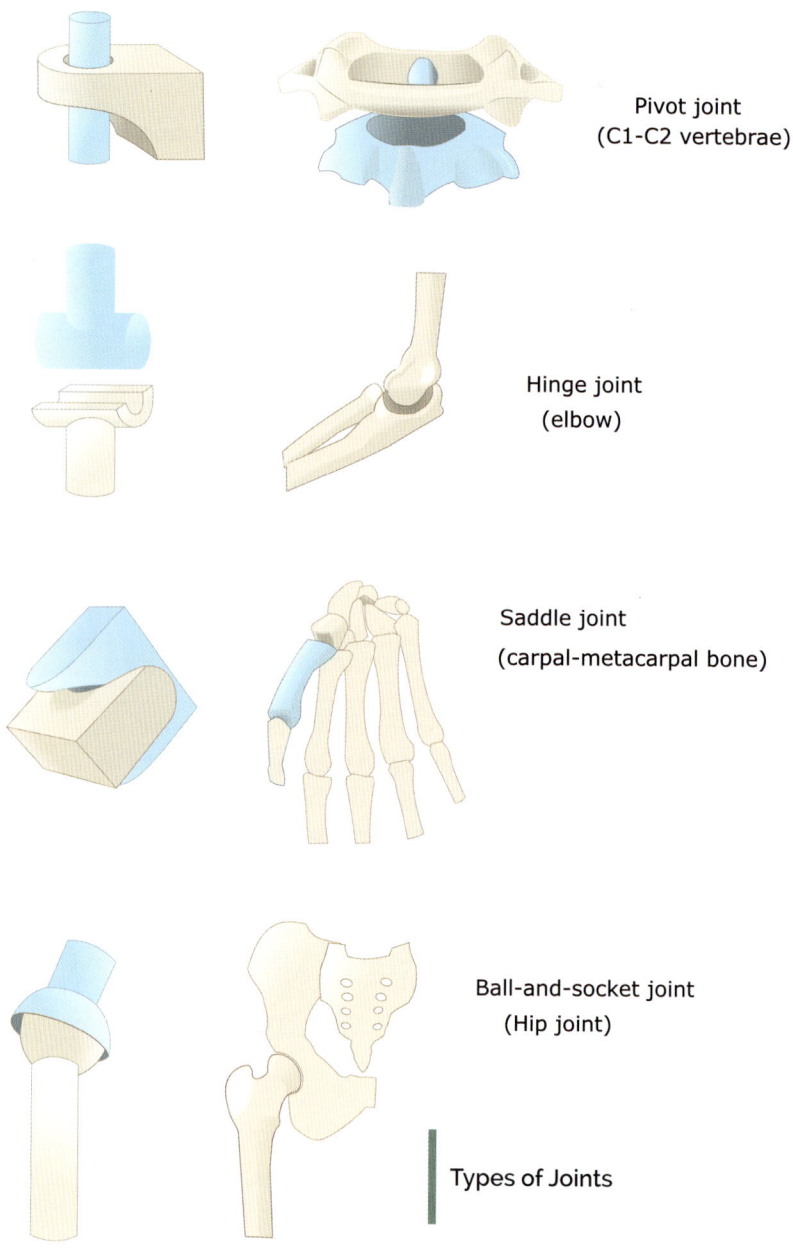

Pivot joint (C1-C2 vertebrae)

Hinge joint (elbow)

Saddle joint (carpal-metacarpal bone)

Ball-and-socket joint (Hip joint)

Types of Joints

Section Review – 9.4 Joints

1. What are synovial joints? Name six types of synovial joints.
2. Where are most joints found that are not synovial joints?

Life Science for Young Catholics

CHAPTER 9: THE MUSCULOSKELETAL SYSTEM

The structure of a skeletal muscle

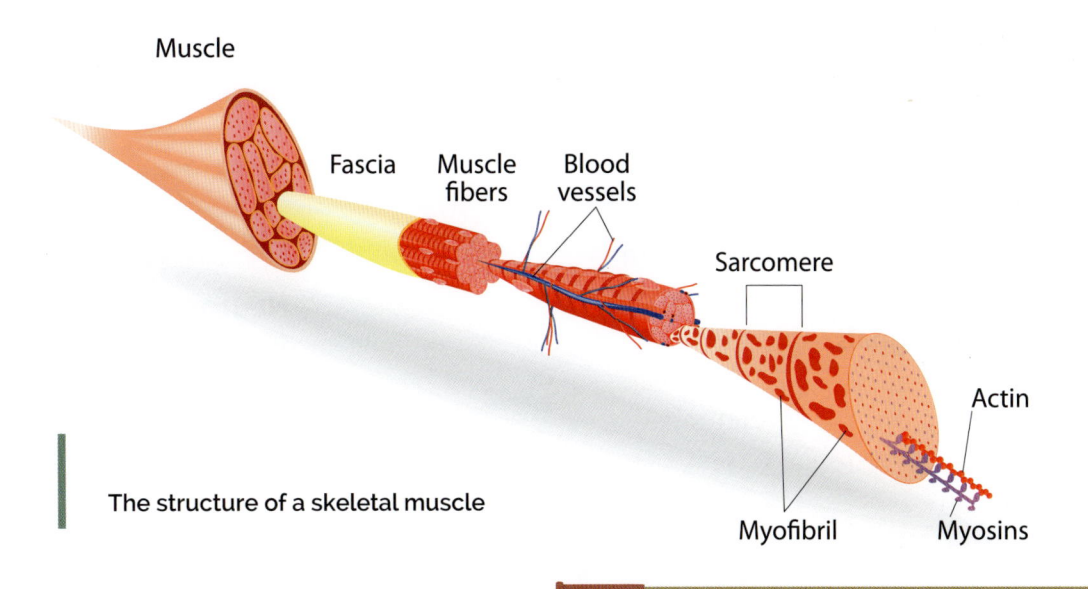

Labels: Muscle, Fascia, Muscle fibers, Blood vessels, Sarcomere, Actin, Myofibril, Myosins

9.5 Muscles

The human musculoskeletal system, composed of muscles and bones, contains over 650 muscles! The musculoskeletal system contributes to approximately 50% of the body's weight. Like the bones of the skeleton, the muscles support and protect other body organs, but most importantly, muscles are the agents or the cause of movement for the body.

Muscles are soft tissues composed of hundreds of thousands of **striated** (*stry-ay-ted*) **muscle cells**. These muscle cells are sometimes called muscle fibers. Muscle fibers are called "striated" because they look like long bands or stripes. Muscle fibers are long, thin cells bundled together, and each fiber, or cell, looks like an individual stripe.

The individual muscle fibers are grouped to form a bundle. The bundles form the **belly** of the muscle. The muscle is attached to bone by means of a very strong band of fibrous tissue called a **tendon**. Each muscle is separated from another by **fascia** (*fash·ah*), which is a layer of loose connective tissue. Skeletal muscles vary in size and shape, as well as in number and in arrangement of muscle fibers.

WORDS TO REMEMBER

joint: the location at which bones connect. Most joints allow movement and provide mechanical support.

ligaments: thick bands of connective tissue that join two bones together

synovial fluid: a thick fluid that lubricates joints to further reduce friction. The joints that this fluid lubricates are called synovial joints.

hinge joint: allows movement back and forth in only one plane. The elbow is a hinge joint.

ball and socket joint: like that of the shoulder or of the hip, is the only type of joint that allows movement in a full circle around a fixed point.

pivot joint: like that between the two bones of the forearm, allows the forearm to rotate so that the palm can face up or down. A pivot joint in the neck allows turning of the head from left to right.

gliding joint: two bone plates that glide against one another. The joints in ankles and wrists are gliding joints.

biaxial joints: allow movements in two planes, as in the knuckles of the hand.

saddle joints: joints where one of the bones forming the joint is shaped like a saddle, with the other bone resting on it like a rider on a horse. Saddle joints provide stability to the bones while providing more flexibility than a hinge or gliding joint. The best example of a saddle joint in the body is at the base of the thumb.

The structure of a motor unit.

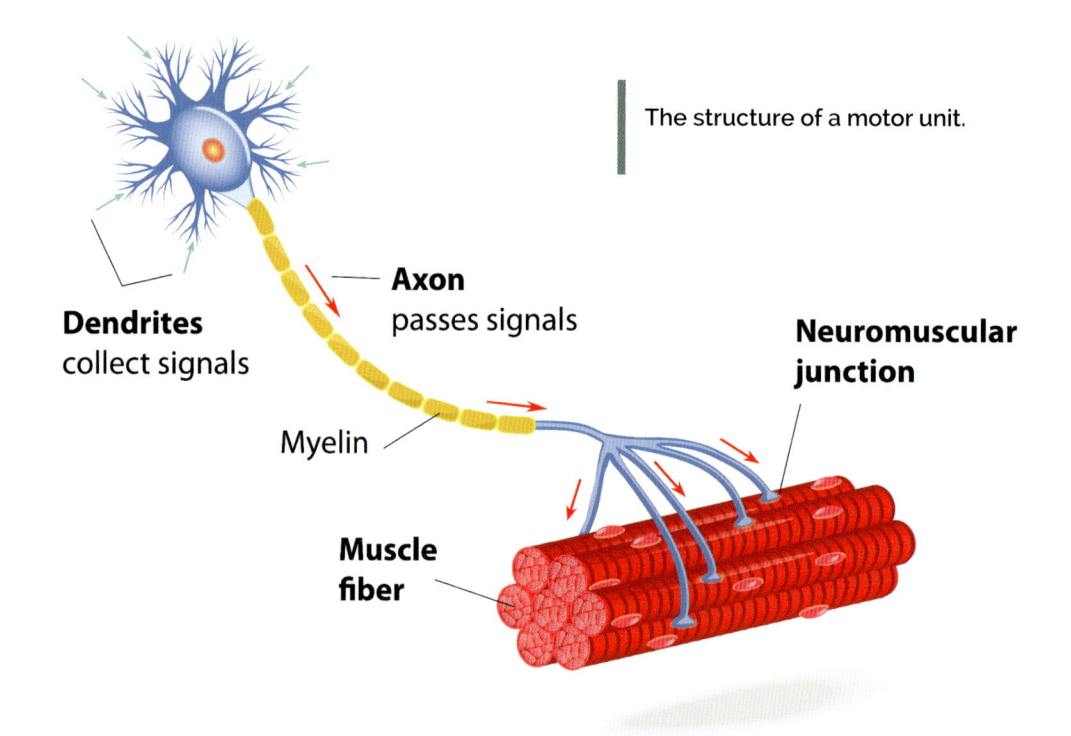

Dendrites collect signals
Axon passes signals
Myelin
Muscle fiber
Neuromuscular junction

Skeletal muscles are under voluntary control by the person. Skeletal muscles contract only when they receive an impulse from the nervous system. Muscles contract in **motor units**, which consist of a nerve and all the muscle fibers that the nerve activates.

Muscles are attached to two or more bones across a joint. The point of muscle attachment to the bone that does **not** move is called the **origin**; the point of attachment to the bone that moves is called the **insertion**.

Contraction of the muscle fibers shortens or pulls the muscle, causing movement of the attached bones. Skeletal muscles operate in opposite pairs, or **complementary muscles**, so that when one muscle of the pair contracts, the other relaxes.

The biceps (**bye**·seps) and the triceps (**try**·seps) muscles of the upper arm are an example of paired muscles. When the biceps contracts, the triceps relaxes, and the forearm flexes upward at the elbow toward the shoulder. However, when the triceps contracts, it shortens, and extends the forearm, causing the biceps to lengthen and relax.

The musculoskeletal system illustrates the interdependence of all organ systems in the human body. The bones support and protect all other organs, and provide sites of attachments for muscles. Muscles support bones and give them movement.

Bones and muscles are nourished by blood provided by the circulatory system. Muscles help the blood and other body fluid move back to the heart with the fluid's metabolic waste products. Blood cells are produced in the marrow cavities of the bones.

The healthy functioning of the musculoskeletal system is required for the healthy functioning of the entire human body.

Section Review – 9.5 Muscles

1. Describe skeletal muscles.
2. What are complementary muscles? Provide an example.
3. Explain the term "motor unit."
4. Identify tendons.
5. Draw and label the structure of a skeletal muscle.
6. Draw and label a typical motor unit.

CHAPTER 9: THE MUSCULOSKELETAL SYSTEM

Anatomy of the Elbow

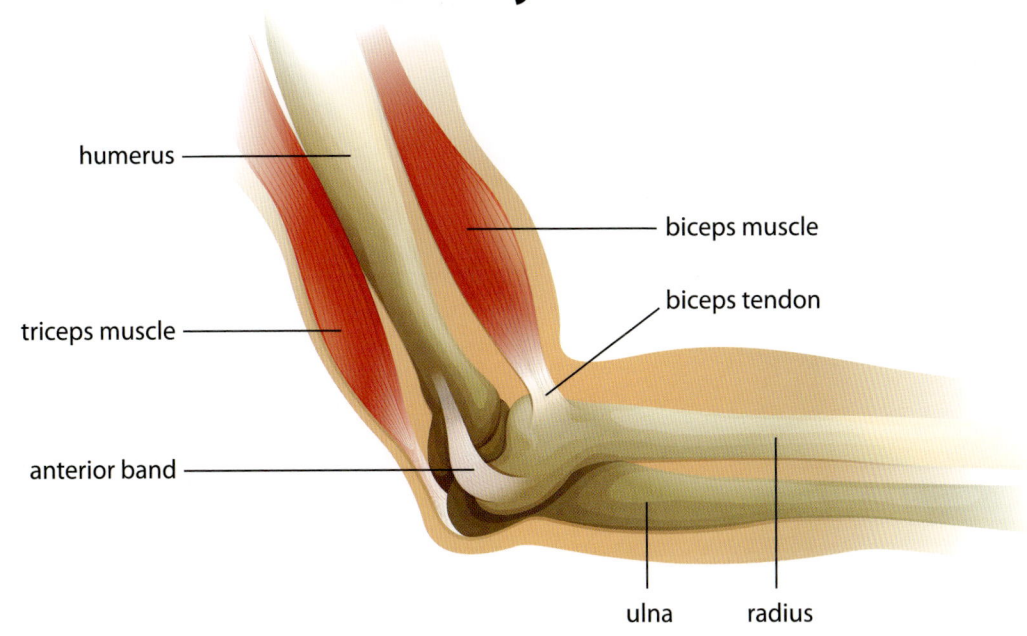

- humerus
- biceps muscle
- biceps tendon
- triceps muscle
- anterior band
- ulna
- radius

9.6 Summary

The love and care that God has for mankind can be found within our bodies. We do not need to look out to the faraway stars to realize the wonder of God our Creator. We can simply look at the care that He took in creating our specialized muscles, bones, joints, and skin. We can look at how the muscles and bones, as well as the joints and skin, work together for our body's good health. The study of the way the body works teaches us about His loving care towards each one of us. Let's remember to thank God for all He has given us for good health. In addition, we can pray to our patron saints to help us stay in good health by taking good care of our bodies.

WORDS TO REMEMBER

striated muscle cells: "striated" muscles receive that name because they look like long bands or stripes

motor units: consist of a nerve and all the muscle fibers that the nerve activates

origin: the point of muscle attachment to the bone that does not move

insertion: the point of attachment to the bone that moves

complementary muscles: muscles that operate in pairs, but in opposite directions. When one muscle contracts, the other muscle of the pair relaxes.

CHAPTER 9: THE MUSCULOSKELETAL SYSTEM

Chapter 9 Review

A. Indicate what type of joint is shown below.

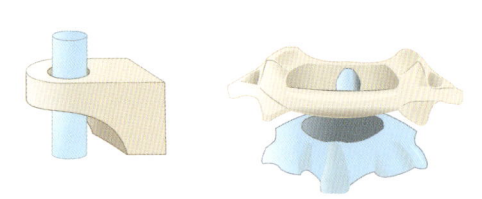

1. _____

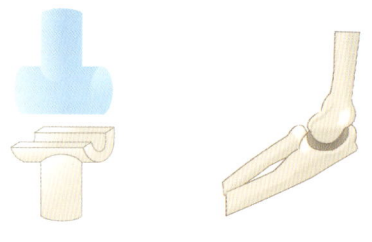

2. _____

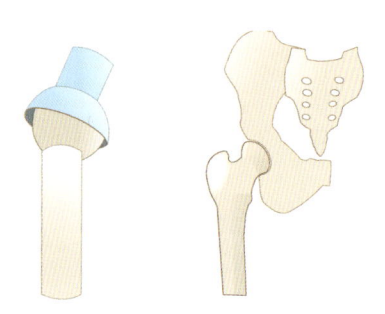

3. _____

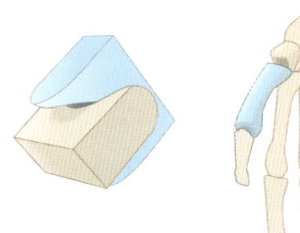

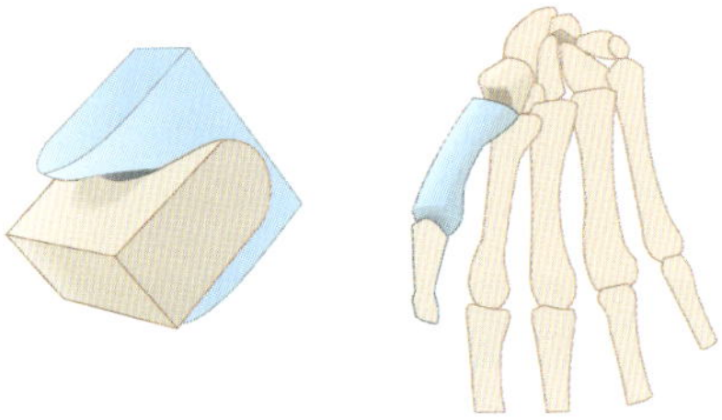

4. _____

B. Answer the following questions.

1. Identify the number and types of human muscle tissues.
2. Name the types of structures included in the musculoskeletal system.
3. Identify bone and its purpose.
4. Name the types of bones.
5. Explain the difference between the axial skeleton and the appendicular skeleton.
6. Where is bone marrow found? What is its function?
7. What is the purpose of cartilage in joints?
8. What are ligaments?
9. What are synovial joints? Name six types of synovial joints.
10. What are complementary muscles? Provide an example.
11. Explain the term "motor unit."
12. Identify tendons.

Chapter 9: "Words to Remember" Crossword

ACROSS

1. bone is the tissue that makes up the interior of bones.
3. bones are bones that develop after birth to protect the tendons.
6. a thick, fibrous, two-layered covering of bone containing blood vessels and nerves
8. firm but rubbery tissue that serves as a cushion at the joints
10. units consist of a nerve and all the muscle fibers that the nerve activates.
11. a very strong band of fibrous tissue that connects a muscle to a bone
12. the location at which bones connect

DOWN

1. muscles are the striated muscles that move the bones in the skeleton.
2. thick bands of connective tissue that join two bones together
3. fluid is a thick fluid that lubricates joints to further reduce friction
4. support and protect other body organs, but most importantly, they are the agents or the cause of movement for the body.
5. the point of muscle attachment to the bone that does not move
7. Bone ___ is a jelly-like substance that contains red blood cells.
9. plates are zones of cartilage at each end of the long bones.

10 THE HUMAN RESPIRATORY SYSTEM

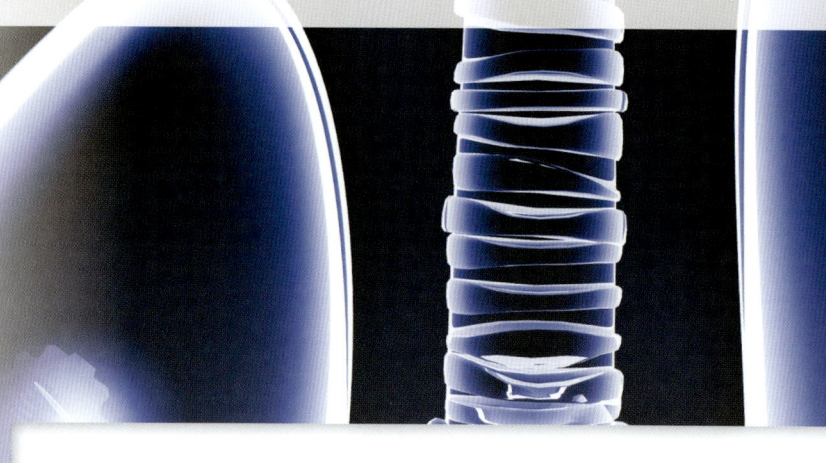

10.1 Introduction

10.2 The Respiratory System

10.3 The Airways

10.4 Cilia and Bronchi

10.5 The Lungs

10.6 The Diaphragm and Intercostal Muscles

10.7 Summary

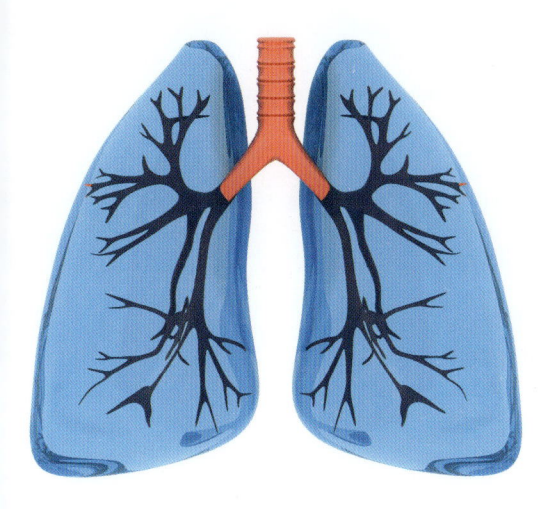

Chapter 10

The Human Respiratory System

10.1 Introduction

In Genesis 2, the second account of creation in the Bible, God creates the human body out of the dust from the Earth. However, the body of itself was not alive until it was given the **breath of life** from the Lord God, our Creator.

> This is the story of the heavens and the earth at their creation. When the LORD God made the earth and the heavens—there was no field shrub on earth and no grass of the field had sprouted, for the LORD God had sent no rain upon the earth and there was no man to till the ground, but a stream was welling up out of the earth and watering all the surface of the ground. Then the LORD God formed the man out of the dust of the ground and blew into his nostrils the **breath of life**, and the man became a living being. (Genesis 2:4-7, emphasis added)

In the Gospel of John, after the Resurrection, Jesus appeared to the Apostles and breathed on them, giving them **spiritual life**. This breath is likened to both God's breath of life given to Adam at the time of creation, and God's breath into the dry bones in Ezekiel's vision. All these Bible references illustrate clearly that life, in body and spirit, is from God.

> The disciples rejoiced when they saw the Lord. [Jesus] said to them again, "Peace be with you. As the Father has sent me, so I send you." And when he had said this, he **breathed** on them and said to them, "Receive the Holy Spirit." (John 20:20-22, emphasis added)

Just as the breath of God, the Father, the Son and the Holy Spirit, gives life to every man, in the beginning and for all times, breathing is vital to the life of the human body. There are many organs and structures of the body that humans can live without, but no one can live without the ability to breathe. Breath is truly life-giving. The process of breathing is known as **respiration**. The term **respiration** is both for the whole body when it breathes in the air, and for the process within individual cells, **cellular respiration**, which provides energy for the cell to use.

The oxygen required for cellular respiration is supplied by the **respiratory system** when we inhale the air around us. Carbon dioxide and water vapor are the byproducts of cellular respiration, and must be removed from the body. Carbon dioxide and water vapor are what we exhale through the **respiratory system**. Every inhalation brings oxygen into the body, and every exhalation removes carbon dioxide.

Section Review – 10.1 Introduction

1. What is the primary gas moved into the body tissues by the respiratory system?
2. What are the primary substances removed from the body tissues by the respiratory system?

CHAPTER 10: THE HUMAN RESPIRATORY SYSTEM

The human respiratory system

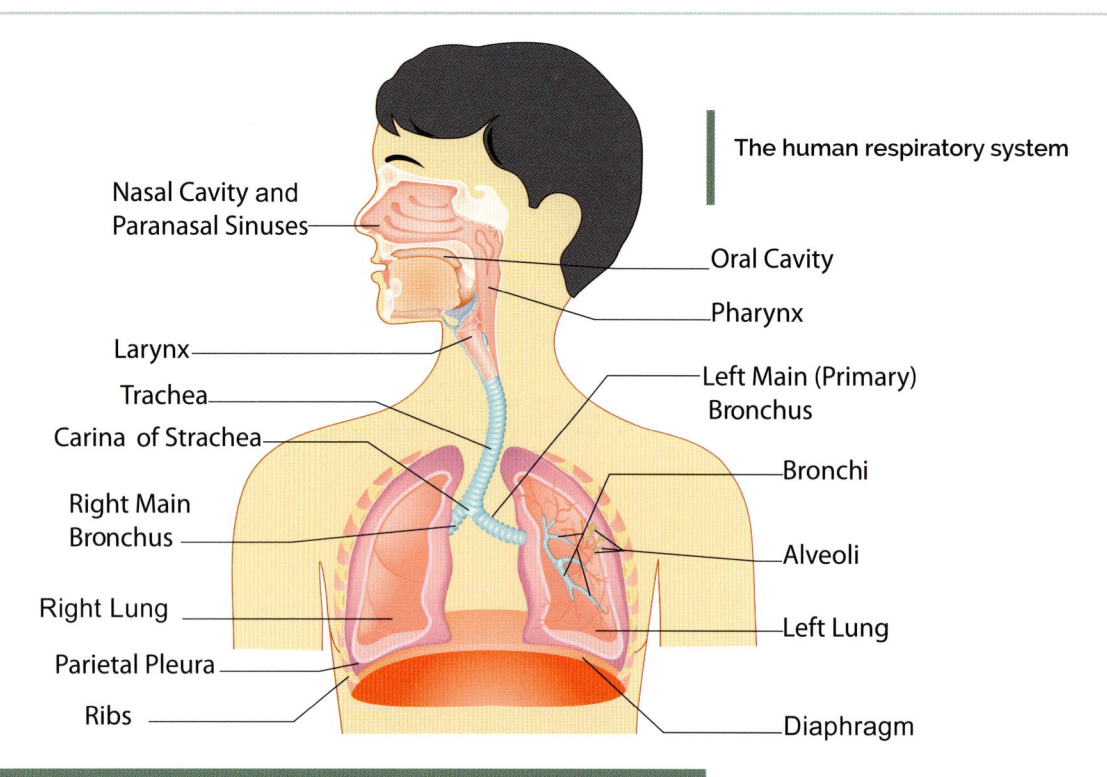

- Nasal Cavity and Paranasal Sinuses
- Oral Cavity
- Pharynx
- Larynx
- Left Main (Primary) Bronchus
- Trachea
- Carina of Strachea
- Bronchi
- Right Main Bronchus
- Alveoli
- Right Lung
- Left Lung
- Parietal Pleura
- Ribs
- Diaphragm

10.2 The Respiratory System

The **respiratory system** is composed of every organ and structure that is involved in bringing oxygen into the blood. These organs and structures have special features that protect the respiratory tract from debris and other foreign matter, such as bacteria. Many of the structures were created with mechanisms for removing any such foreign particles that do find their way into the system. The purpose of the respiratory system is to provide the oxygen necessary for cellular respiration and to eliminate waste gases from the body. The respiratory system can be divided into several areas: the **airways**, the **lungs**, and the **muscles used for breathing**. See the diagram above for the major organs and tissues of the respiratory system.

> **Section Review –
> 10.2 The Respiratory System**
>
> 1. Name the major organs and tissues of the respiratory system.
>
> 2. What is the primary purpose of the respiratory system?

10.3 The Airways

The airways are tube-like structures that carry oxygen-containing air into the respiratory system and carry carbon dioxide out of the system. Air is typically inhaled through the nostrils, into the nasal cavity. Air can also be taken in through the mouth. The nose, mouth, and throat warm and moisten the air as it passes through them. The nose is lined with many bristle-like hairs and mucus produced in glands that line the nasal cavity. The hairs and mucus trap dirt, bacteria, and other debris from the air to prevent the particles from passing deeper into the respiratory tract where they could possibly do harm.

Once the air is warmed, it passes through the **pharynx** (*fair*·inx), or throat, and through the **larynx** (*lair*·inx), or voice box. At the base of the throat is a small flap of tissue known as the **epiglottis** (*ep·uh·glott*·iss). The epiglottis is another protective feature of the respiratory system. Since food also passes through the mouth and throat on its way through the digestive tract, it has the potential to slip into the airway. This is what happens when a person chokes.

To prevent the swallowed food from entering the respiratory tract, the epiglottis automatically closes over the voice box, that is, the opening of the windpipe, when a person swallows. After the food passes into the food tube, the epiglottis automatically opens so that air is again channeled through the voice box to the windpipe.

From the voice box, the warm, moist air passes into the windpipe, also known as the **trachea** (**tray**·key·ah). The trachea is a tube-like pipe supported by rings of cartilage and lined with **cilia** (**sill**·ee·ah). Cartilage is a tough elastic tissue, and cilia are tiny hair-like projections. The cartilage keeps the trachea from being compressed by other organs to ensure an open airway at all times.

> **Section Review – 10.3 The Airways**
> 1. What is the role of the nose in respiration?
> 2. Describe the trachea.

10.4 Cilia and Bronchi

Cilia are short hair-like structures that extend from the surface of some cells. Cilia move together in a wavelike fashion. In the human trachea, the cilia are covered with mucus. The mucus traps debris from the air that has reached the trachea. The cilia, beating in an organized wavelike fashion, move the mucus up the trachea to the nose or the mouth where they are coughed or sneezed out of the respiratory tract, or swallowed.

The trachea divides into a left main-stem **bronchus** (**bronk**·us) and a right main-stem bronchus. Like the trachea, the two bronchi are supported by cartilage in their walls and contain mucous glands and cilia for removal of foreign materials.

As the bronchi branch out into smaller and smaller tubes, the amount of cartilage in their walls decreases. The smallest of these tubes, the **bronchioles** (**bronk**·ee·oles), have no cartilage to give support. Each bronchiole ends in tiny air sacs, or **alveoli** (al·vee·**oh**·lee), that make up the inside of the lungs.

The alveoli are tiny balloon- or sac-like structures made of endothelial cells that are only one cell-layer thick. The alveoli are the location of gas exchange in the lungs. Each alveolus (a single alveoli) is surrounded by a network of tiny blood vessels called **capillaries** (**cap**·ill·air·ees). The tiny capillaries have walls that are only one cell-layer thick. Because of the thinness of the walls of each alveolus and capillary, oxygen and carbon dioxide are able to freely move in and out between the alveoli air sacs and the blood in the capillaries by diffusion.

When the oxygen is picked up by the blood, it is then distributed throughout the body tissues by the blood, while the carbon dioxide is exhaled through the respiratory system and out into the surrounding air.

> **Section Review – 10.4 Cilia and Bronchi**
> 1. Briefly explain the bronchioles. Include where they begin, where they terminate, and how their structure differs from the structure of the bronchus.
> 2. Briefly explain alveoli. Include what they are made of and their purpose.

WORDS TO REMEMBER

respiration: breathing in air for oxygen and breathing out carbon dioxide, a waste product

respiratory system: every organ and structure that is involved in bringing oxygen into the blood

airways: tube-like structures that carry oxygen-containing air into the respiratory system and carry carbon dioxide out of the system

pharynx: or throat, a hollow section of the body that connects the oral cavity to the esophagus

larynx: a tube-shaped organ in the neck that contains the vocal cords; also called the voice box

epiglottis: a small flap of tissue at the base of the throat; a protective feature of the respiratory system; automatically closes over the voice box, that is, the opening of the windpipe, when a person swallows, to prevent choking

CHAPTER 10: THE HUMAN RESPIRATORY SYSTEM

10.5 The Lungs

The lungs are two air-filled, spongy internal organs located on either side of the chest. Each lung is protected by a thin tissue layer called the pleura. Pleura also protects the inside of the thoracic (thor-*as*-ic), or chest, cavity. There is also a thin layer of pleural fluid that lubricates the lungs, permitting them to slip smoothly as they expand and contract with each breath.

The human body has two lungs, a right lung and a left lung. The left lung has two lobes or rounded projections. The left lung is slightly smaller than the right lung, which has three lobes. Together with the heart, the lungs fill the entire thoracic cavity.

The lungs are protected by the chest wall, which includes the ribs and sternum, or breastbone, the thoracic vertebrae of the spine, and the intercostal muscles. The lungs are made up of millions of very tiny alveoli or air sacs, and are surrounded by a double-layered protective membrane.

> **Section Review – 10.5 The Lungs**
> 1. Give a brief overview of the lungs. Include their position in the body and their construction.
> 2. How are they protected?

10.6 The Diaphragm and Intercostal Muscles

The **diaphragm** (*die*·uh·*fram*) and the **intercostal muscles**, those muscles between the ribs, are the primary muscles involved in normal respiration or breathing. The diaphragm is a large, thin muscle that makes up the bottom of the chest or thoracic cavity. The diaphragm separates the contents of the thorax, where the heart and lungs are located, from the contents of the abdominal or lower cavity area.

When the diaphragm contracts, the muscle moves downward and closer to the abdomen. In doing so, the size of the thoracic cavity is increased and air is drawn into the lungs; this is inhalation. Conversely, as the diaphragm relaxes, it returns to its original position, which makes the thoracic cavity smaller and forces the air out of the lungs; this is exhalation. The illustration shows the inspiration and the expiration of incoming and outgoing air.

The intercostal muscles are two sets of muscles between the ribs that help the diaphragm by lifting the ribs during inhalation and compressing the ribs during exhalation. The abdominal and neck muscles also can help with breathing when the demand for oxygen is increased, during exercise, for instance. Exercise, or if the normal respiratory muscles are not working well, are causes of increased demand on the respiratory system.

The muscles of the respiratory system are under both voluntary control and involuntary control.

The Diaphragm and Respiration

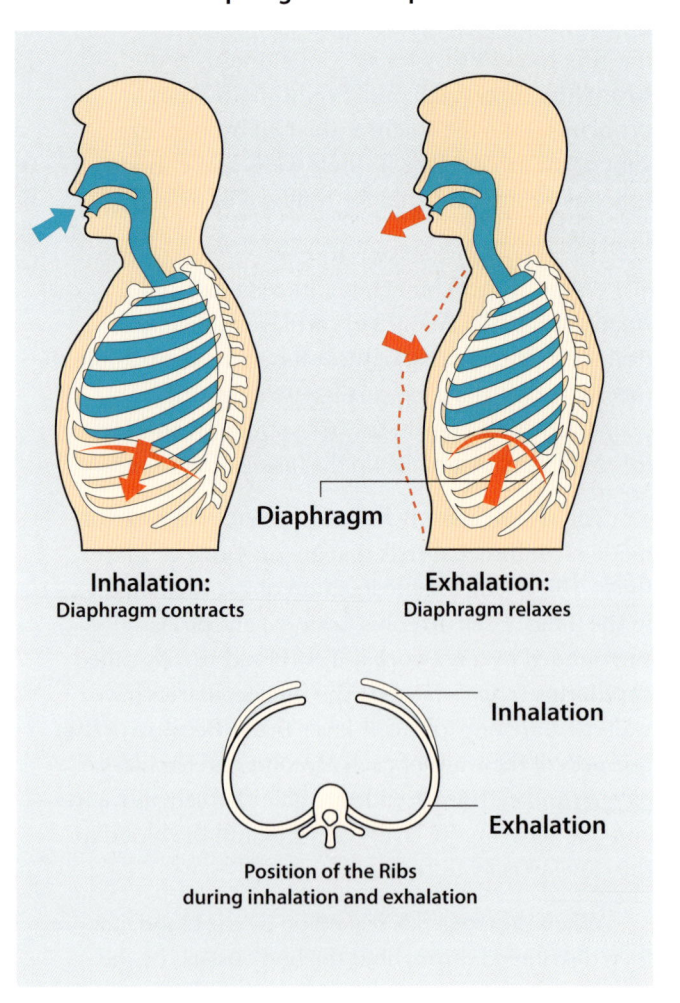

Inhalation: Diaphragm contracts

Exhalation: Diaphragm relaxes

Diaphragm

Position of the Ribs during inhalation and exhalation

Inhalation

Exhalation

Life Science for Young Catholics

Breathing is typically involuntary; the average adult at rest breathes 12-20 times per minute. Special receptors throughout the body monitor the concentrations of oxygen and carbon dioxide in the blood and send the information to the respiratory center in the brain. The brain automatically adjusts the respiratory rate, to make it faster or slower, to keep healthy levels of oxygen and carbon dioxide in the body.

For example, the respiratory rate increases automatically as the body needs more oxygen. Think how the rate of breathing automatically increases with strenuous exercise. Respiration can also slow down without conscious effort; this happens regularly with speaking and swallowing. It is not possible to speak and breathe in, or to swallow and breathe, at the same time.

The respiratory rate can, however, be controlled by voluntary means. Think of how a musician breathing into an instrument can control the amount of air taken in, the times at which breaths are taken in, and the amount and rate of air exhaled through the instrument. Think of a swimmer holding his breath for periods of time while under water, and controlling the number of breaths he takes while swimming.

> **Section Review – 10.6**
> **The Diaphragm and Intercostal Muscles**
>
> 1. Explain the diaphragm and the intercostal muscles.
> 2. How are the diaphragm and intercostal muscles controlled by the body to maintain breathing?
> 3. Describe how the movement of the diaphragm and intercostal muscles allows the body to breathe.

10.7 Summary

St. Paul used the example of the human body to describe the Church as the Body of Christ. St. Paul pointed out that the body needs all of the different parts. The eyes, without the feet, cannot escape some danger they see, but the feet would not know to run if the eyes did not spy the danger to run from. For the Church, St. Paul said, all are not teachers, all are not healers, and so on; but the Church needs all members to contribute to the life of the Church.

In the same way, the respiratory system is necessary for the whole body, but it, too, depends on the rest of the body to work properly. The respiratory system needs the circulatory system to bring its oxygen to the body, and to bring carbon dioxide to be exhaled. It also needs the digestive system to provide the energy for the diaphragm, and intercostal muscles to move the air in and out. The brain and nervous system are needed to control the rate of breathing. So we can see both the importance and the interdependence of all of the systems of the wondrous body God gave us.

WORDS TO REMEMBER

lungs: two air-filled, spongy internal organs located on either side of the chest

bronchi: tubes at the end of the trachea that bring air into the lungs. The bottom of the trachea divides into two main bronchi; these divide again into smaller and smaller tubes.

bronchioles: smallest tubes of the bronchi

alveoli: tiny balloon- or sac-like structures made of endothelial cells that are only one cell-layer thick. The alveoli are the location of gas exchange in the lungs.

capillaries: smallest of blood vessels, with walls only one cell-layer thick. In the capillaries, oxygen and carbon dioxide are able to freely move in and out of the blood by diffusion.

diaphragm: a large muscle at the bottom of the chest cavity. The contraction and relaxation of this muscle controls the movement of air into and out of the lungs.

intercostal muscles: muscles between the ribs that aid the diaphragm in controlling normal respiration, or breathing

Chapter 10 Review

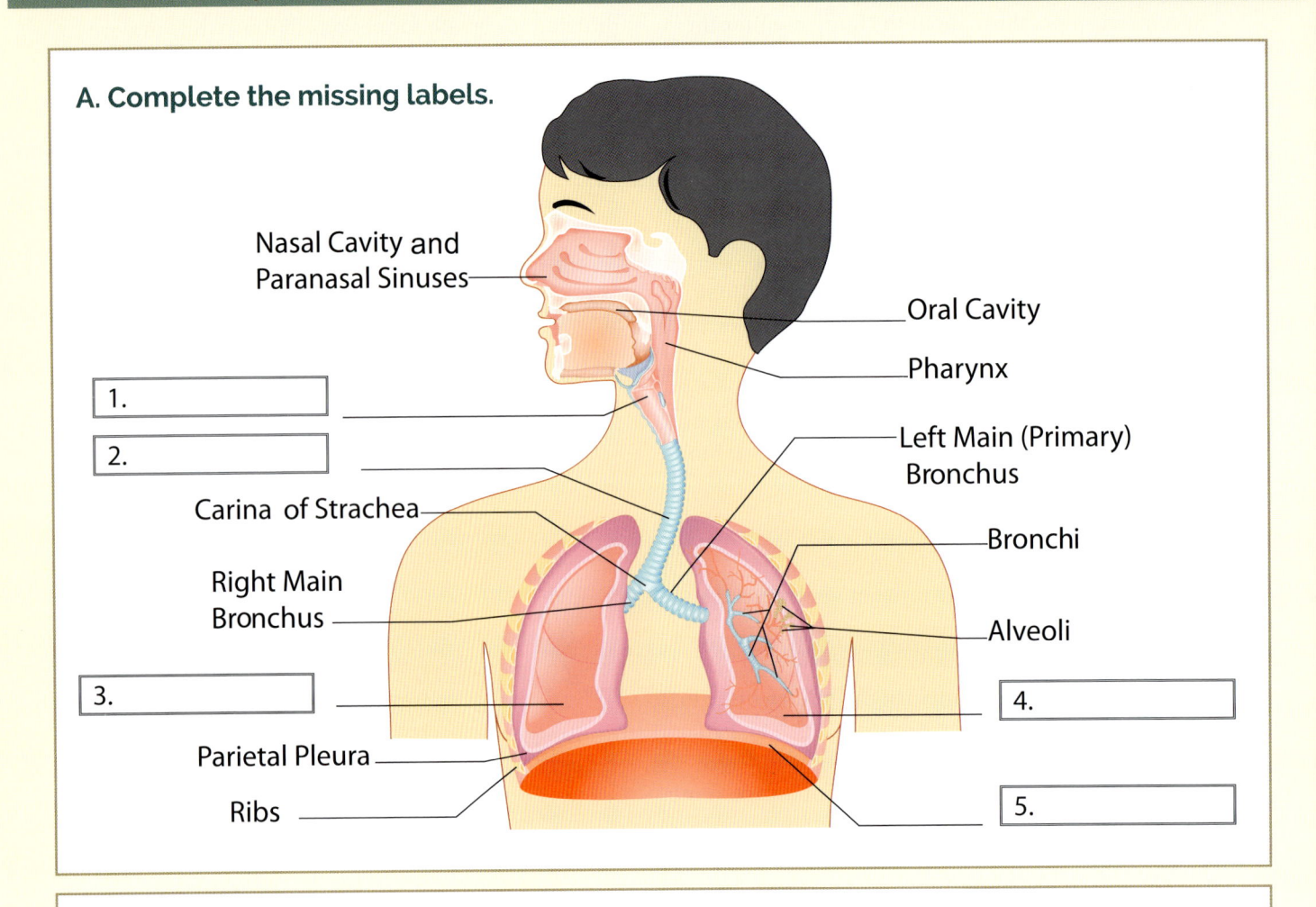

A. Complete the missing labels.

- Nasal Cavity and Paranasal Sinuses
- Oral Cavity
- Pharynx
- Left Main (Primary) Bronchus
- Carina of Strachea
- Bronchi
- Right Main Bronchus
- Alveoli
- Parietal Pleura
- Ribs

1. ___
2. ___
3. ___
4. ___
5. ___

B. Answer the following questions.

1. What is the primary gas moved into the body tissues by the respiratory system?
2. What are the primary substances removed from the body tissues by the respiratory system?
3. The respiratory system can be divided into what areas?
4. Describe the function of the epiglottis.
5. Identify the pharynx and larynx.
6. What is the role of cartilage in the respiratory system?
7. What is the role of the nose in respiration?
8. Describe the trachea.
9. Briefly explain alveoli. Include what they are made of and their purpose.
10. What process allows oxygen and carbon dioxide to move in and out of the alveoli?
11. How are the lungs protected?
12. What is the role of the pleural fluid?
13. Explain the diaphragm and the intercostal muscles.
14. Describe how the movement of the diaphragm and intercostal muscles allows the body to breathe.

Chapter 10: "Words to Remember" Crossword

ACROSS

6 a hollow section of the body that connects the oral cavity to the esophagus

7 a large muscle at the bottom of the chest cavity. The contraction and relaxation of this muscle controls the movement of air into and out of the lungs.

9 tube-like structures that carry oxygen-containing air into the respiratory system and carry carbon dioxide out of the system

10 breathing

11 a tube-shaped organ in the neck that contains the vocal cords; is also called the voice box.

DOWN

1 the tubes at the end of the trachea that bring air into the lungs

2 the smallest of blood vessels that have walls that are only one cell-layer thick

3 The ___ system is composed of every organ and structure that is involved in bringing oxygen into the blood.

4 two air-filled, spongy internal organs located on either side of the chest

5 a small flap of tissue at the base of the throat

8 tiny balloon, or sac-like, structures made of endothelial cells that are only one cell-layer thick

Life Science for Young Catholics

11 THE HUMAN CIRCULATORY SYSTEM

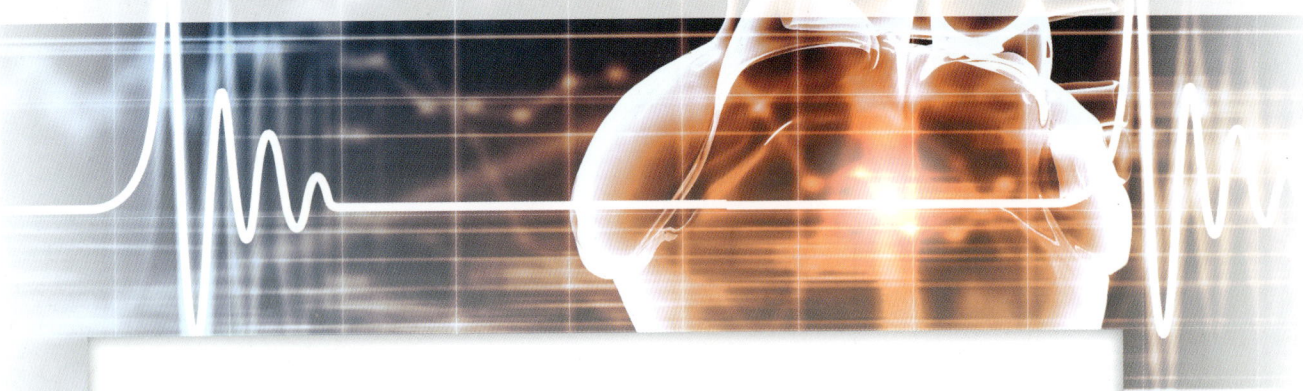

11.1 Introduction
11.2 The Circulatory System
11.3 Blood
- A. Plasma
- B. Red Blood Cells
- C. White Blood Cells
- D. Platelets

11.4 Blood Vessels
- A. Arteries
- B. Veins
- C. Capillaries

11.5 The Human Heart
- A. Cardiac Muscle
- B. Pacemakers
- C. Heart Chambers & Valves
- D. The Pericardium

11.6 Circulation
- A. Pulmonary Circulation
- B. Systemic Circulation
- C. Coronary Circulation

11.7 Other Functions of the Circulatory System
- A. Prevent Blood Loss
- B. Protect Against Infection
- C. Maintain Body Temperature
- D. Maintain Blood Pressure

11.8 The Heart, Holy Scripture, and Devotion

Chapter 11

The Human Circulatory System

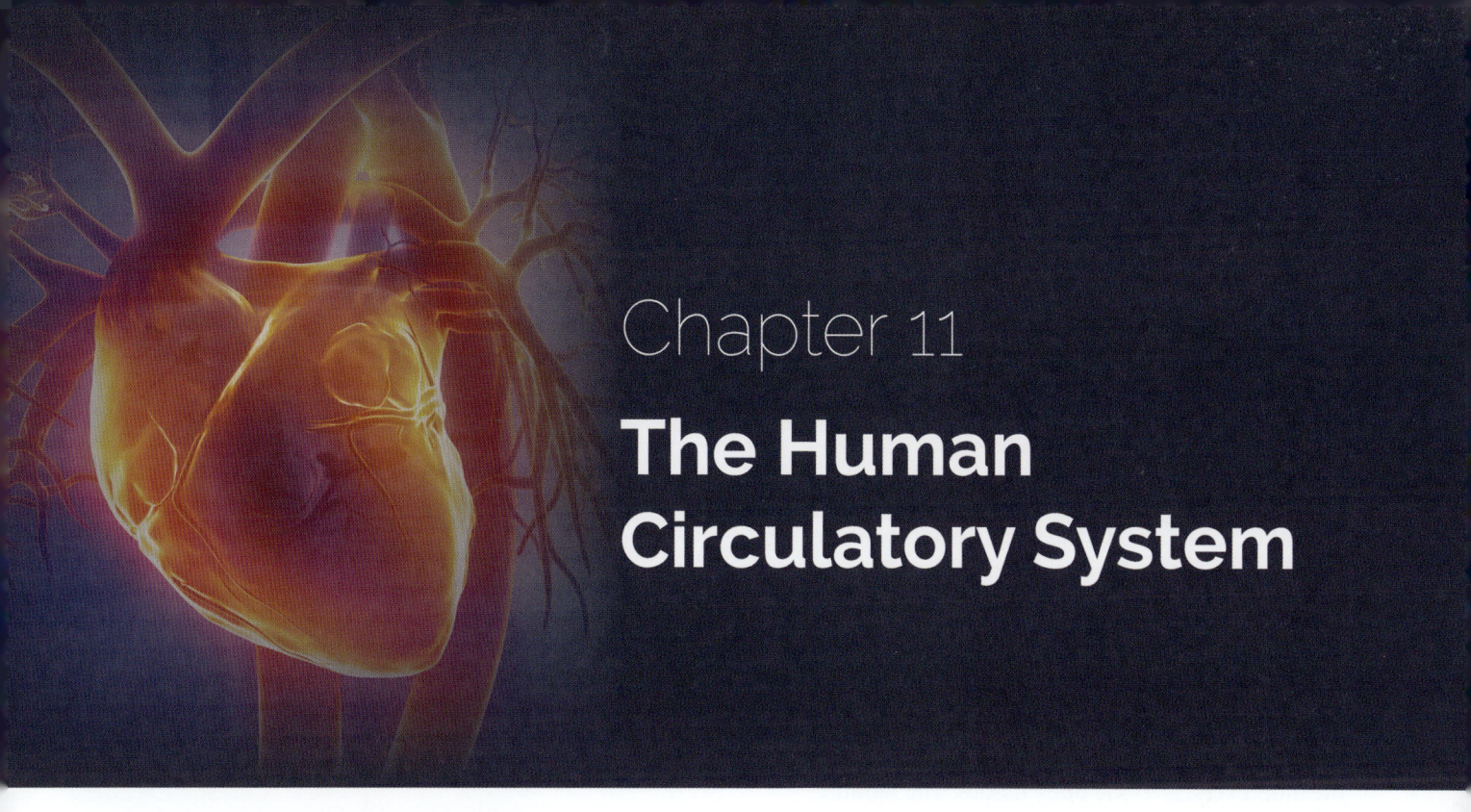

11.1 Introduction

Have you heard the saying, "The blood of martyrs is the seed of the Church"? A priest from North Africa, Tertullian, had this phrase in his famous letter to the governors of the Roman Empire in about the year 200 A.D. Tertullian is one of the Fathers of the Church.

You may ask, "How is the blood of martyrs the seed of the Church?" God taught mankind that blood gives life. In the Book of Leviticus, the Bible states that "the life of the flesh is in the blood." In his first epistle, St. John taught, "This is He Who came by water and blood, Jesus Christ, not by the water only but by the water and the blood. And the Spirit is the One Who testifies, because the Spirit is the Truth."

Remember that Jesus is Life, and He came to give us life, so that we might have it more abundantly. He poured out His Most Precious Blood to redeem us from our sins and thus to open the gates of Heaven so that we may all go to Heaven if we love Him and obey His Commandments. Jesus gave us the Holy Spirit as His ongoing gift to us. The Holy Spirit breathes life into all things.

In this chapter, we will study the human circulatory system, where we have life in the blood.

The **circulatory system**, or **cardiovascular system**, is primarily responsible for distributing oxygen to the body. The circulatory system also distributes nutrients, minerals, and other substances to the tissues and organs throughout the body.

Likewise, it is the circulatory system that collects the carbon dioxide and other metabolic wastes from the body tissues and transports them to the proper organ of excretion, either to the lungs or to the kidneys.

Life Science for Young Catholics

CHAPTER 11: THE HUMAN CIRCULATORY SYSTEM

11.2 The Circulatory System

The **cardiovascular system**, or the **circulatory system**, receives oxygen from the alveoli or air sacs in the lungs of the respiratory system. Then the blood transports the oxygen to the rest of the body tissues. The circulatory system includes the **blood**, the **blood vessels**, and the **heart**.

Along with oxygen, the circulatory system transports nutrients, as well as hormones, chemicals, and other substances **to** the body tissues. The circulatory system also transports carbon dioxide and other metabolic waste products **from** all the body tissues to various organs where they are processed and excreted.

The heart is the muscular organ at the center of the circulatory system that pumps the blood through the blood vessels to the body tissues. The blood vessels are the "pipes" and the blood is the "river" by which substances are transported.

> **Section Review – 11.2 The Circulatory System**
>
> 1. Name the major organs and tissues of the circulatory, or cardiovascular, system.
> 2. Describe the primary purpose of the circulatory system.
> 3. What are the major items moved to the body tissues by the circulatory system?
> 4. Name the major items removed from the body tissues by the circulatory system.

11.3 Blood

The typical human body contains about five liters of blood to transport the many substances that it carries throughout the body. (A liter is a little less liquid than a quart.) Blood is a specialized tissue composed of living cells in a liquid environment. Blood includes **plasma**, **red blood cells**, **white blood cells**, and **platelets**.

A. Plasma

Plasma is the liquid part of blood, and makes up over half of the volume of blood. Plasma is composed of water, as well as many different proteins, dissolved nutrients, and **electrolytes** (*ee·lek·tro·lites*).

Electrolytes include sodium, potassium, chloride, and other substances. Electrolytes are chemicals that allow cells to maintain the correct electrical voltage to work properly. Nerve impulses have an electric component that signals cells what to do. Without a proper balance of the electrolytes, cells would not respond properly.

B. Red Blood Cells

The most numerous of the blood cells are the **red blood cells**. These make up about 45% of the blood volume. Red blood cells are tiny, flexible cells, without a nucleus, that contain **hemoglobin** (*heem·oh·globe·in*). Hemoglobin is the very important molecule that carries oxygen throughout the body. The size and flexibility of the red blood cells allows them to fit through very tiny capillaries.

C. White Blood Cells

White blood cells are responsible for fighting infection and will be discussed as a part of the immune system.

D. Platelets

Platelets are small cell fragments responsible for blood clotting to protect the body from excessive blood loss.

> **Section Review – 11.3 Blood**
>
> 1. Describe red blood cells.
> 2. What do white blood cells do?
> 3. What is the importance of hemoglobin?
> 4. What are platelets and what is their main contribution to the body?

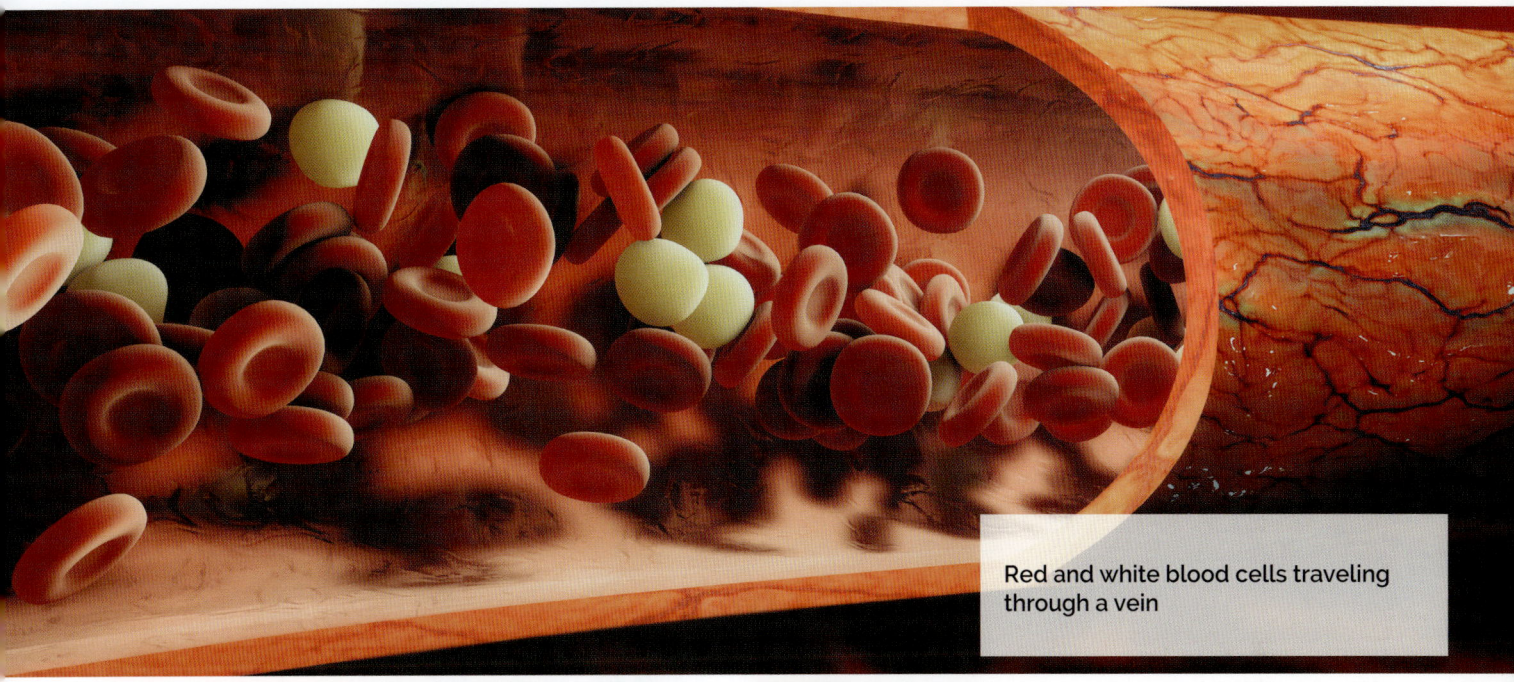

Red and white blood cells traveling through a vein

11.4 Blood Vessels

Blood circulates through the body in a closed system of blood vessels. All blood vessels have walls made of smooth muscle cells, elastic connective tissue, and are lined with endothelial cells.

Endothelial cells are specialized cells that line the inside of the blood vessels. These cells prevent the blood from clotting within the blood vessels.

The amount of smooth muscle and connective tissue in the vessel walls varies with the type and size of the blood vessel.

There are three major types of blood vessels: **arteries**, **veins**, and **capillaries**.

A. Arteries

Arteries are vessels that carry blood away from the heart. Arteries have thick muscular walls with much elastic connective tissue and a smaller central cavity because they carry blood pumped under high pressure from the heart. Arteries branch and become smaller as they move farther from the heart. The smallest arteries are called **arterioles** (*are·teer·ee·oles*). Arterioles downsize the blood flow so that it can be handled by the tiny capillaries that interact with individual body cells.

WORDS TO REMEMBER

circulatory system (or cardiovascular system): includes the heart, blood vessels, and blood. This system brings oxygen and nutrients to the cells in the body, and brings waste products, like carbon dioxide, to the lungs and other organs of waste disposal for elimination from the body.

blood: a specialized tissue composed of living cells in a liquid environment

heart: the muscular organ at the center of the circulatory system that pumps the blood through the blood vessels to the body tissues

red blood cells: tiny flexible cells without a nucleus that contain hemoglobin; make up about 45% of the blood volume; carry oxygen throughout the body

hemoglobin: important molecule that carries oxygen throughout the body

white blood cells: responsible for fighting infection; a part of the immune system

platelets: small cell fragments responsible for blood clotting to protect the body from excessive blood loss

electrolytes: include sodium, potassium, chloride, and other substances; chemicals that allow cells to maintain the correct electrical voltage to work properly

Life Science for Young Catholics

B. Veins

Veins are vessels that carry blood from the body tissues back to the heart. Veins have thinner walls with less elastic and smooth muscle and a larger lumen, or hole in the tube, because they receive blood from the tissues that is not under pressure. Veins rely on muscle contractions throughout the body and rely on gravity to move the blood from the tissues back to the heart. Larger veins have valves to prevent backward flow of blood. Like arteries, veins are smaller at greater distances from the heart; the smallest veins are called **venules** (**ven ·yulls**). Venules bring deoxygenated blood from the capillaries to larger veins, which eventually return the blood to the heart.

C. Capillaries

Capillaries are the smallest blood vessels, with walls only one cell layer thick. Capillaries are found throughout every tissue in the body. The capillaries are the blood vessels through which the exchange of oxygen, carbon dioxide, nutrients, electrolytes, and wastes occurs.

The tiny arterioles bring oxygen-rich blood to the capillary. In the capillary, oxygen and other nutrients pass through the capillary wall to the surrounding body cells. From the body cells, carbon dioxide and other waste products pass through the capillary cell wall and into the blood. The blood leaves the capillary and moves into the connected venule, which leads to larger veins that bring the deoxygenated blood back to the heart.

> ### Section Review – 11.4 Blood Vessels
> 1. Identify the following: arteries, arterioles, capillaries, venules, veins.
> 2. Describe the importance of capillaries.

Diagram of the major arteries (red) and veins (blue) of the human body

Life Science for Young Catholics

11.5 The Human Heart

The **human heart** is responsible for continuously pumping blood throughout the body. The heart is a muscular organ located under the rib cage and sternum between the two lungs. It is made primarily of **cardiac muscle**.

A. Cardiac Muscle

Cardiac muscle is specialized muscle that contracts without stimulation from nerves. Although cardiac muscle does not require nerves for contracting, it does respond to nervous stimuli which can increase or decrease the rate of contraction, or the heartbeat.

Cardiac muscle fibers are branched cells joined end to end to form a large network of cardiac tissue. Special connections between the individual cells allow the entire network of cells to contract at the same time. This simultaneous contraction of large groups of muscle fibers creates the pumping action of the heart. The rate of contractions is controlled by two special areas within the heart muscle, known as **pacemakers**.

B. Pacemakers

The heart is controlled by an electrical system that has two **pacemakers** and other specialized cells. The two pacemakers are the sinoatrial node (SA node), and the atrioventricular node (AV node). The SA node is the primary pacemaker and is located at the top of the right atrium. The SA node generates the electrical signal for the heart to beat about 70-80 times per minute in a healthy adult heart. The electrical impulse from the SA node travels to the two atria and to the AV node, located in the floor of the right atrium.

The impulse from the SA node causes the two upper chambers, the atria, to contract, pumping blood to the ventricles. The AV node delays the signal from the SA node to the ventricle by about 1/10 of a second. This permits the atria to empty into the ventricles, and thus gives the ventricles time to fill. Then the AV node signals both ventricles to pump the blood to the lungs and the rest of the body.

C. Heart Chambers and Valves

The human heart is a **four-chambered** structure. With four chambers, the heart is very efficient. A four-chambered heart prevents mixing of the oxygen-rich blood coming from the lungs with deoxygenated blood from body tissues. If the oxygenated blood could mix with the deoxygenated blood, then some deoxygenated blood would be sent to the tissues where it would do no good, and some oxygenated blood would be sent back to the lungs where it would not give up carbon dioxide or capture more oxygen. The heart would need to pump harder and faster to make up for these inefficiencies. The four-chambered heart saves energy. It is a marvel of God's design.

The heart is made of two smaller atria (*ay-tree·uh*), and two larger ventricles. Fibrous valves separate each atrium from its corresponding ventricle. The **tricuspid** (*tri-cus-pid*) **valve** separates the right atrium from the right ventricle to prevent blood from flowing backwards when the heart is beating. The **mitral** (*my-trill*) **valve** separates the left atrium from the left ventricle for the same purpose, to prevent blood from flowing backwards.

WORDS TO REMEMBER

arteries: vessels that carry blood away from the heart; have thick muscular walls with much elastic connective tissue and a smaller central cavity because they carry blood pumped under high pressure from the heart.

veins: vessels that carry blood from the body tissues back to the heart; have thinner walls with less elastic and smooth muscle and a larger lumen, or hole in the tube, because they receive blood from the tissues that is not under pressure.

venules: small veins that connect to capillaries; bring deoxygenated blood from the capillaries to larger veins, which eventually return the blood to the heart

cardiac muscle: specialized muscle that contracts without stimulation from nerves

pacemakers: specialized cells in the heart that control the electrical system of the heart to cause it to beat

tricuspid valve: separates the right atrium from the right ventricle to prevent blood from flowing backwards when the heart is beating

CHAPTER 11: THE HUMAN CIRCULATORY SYSTEM

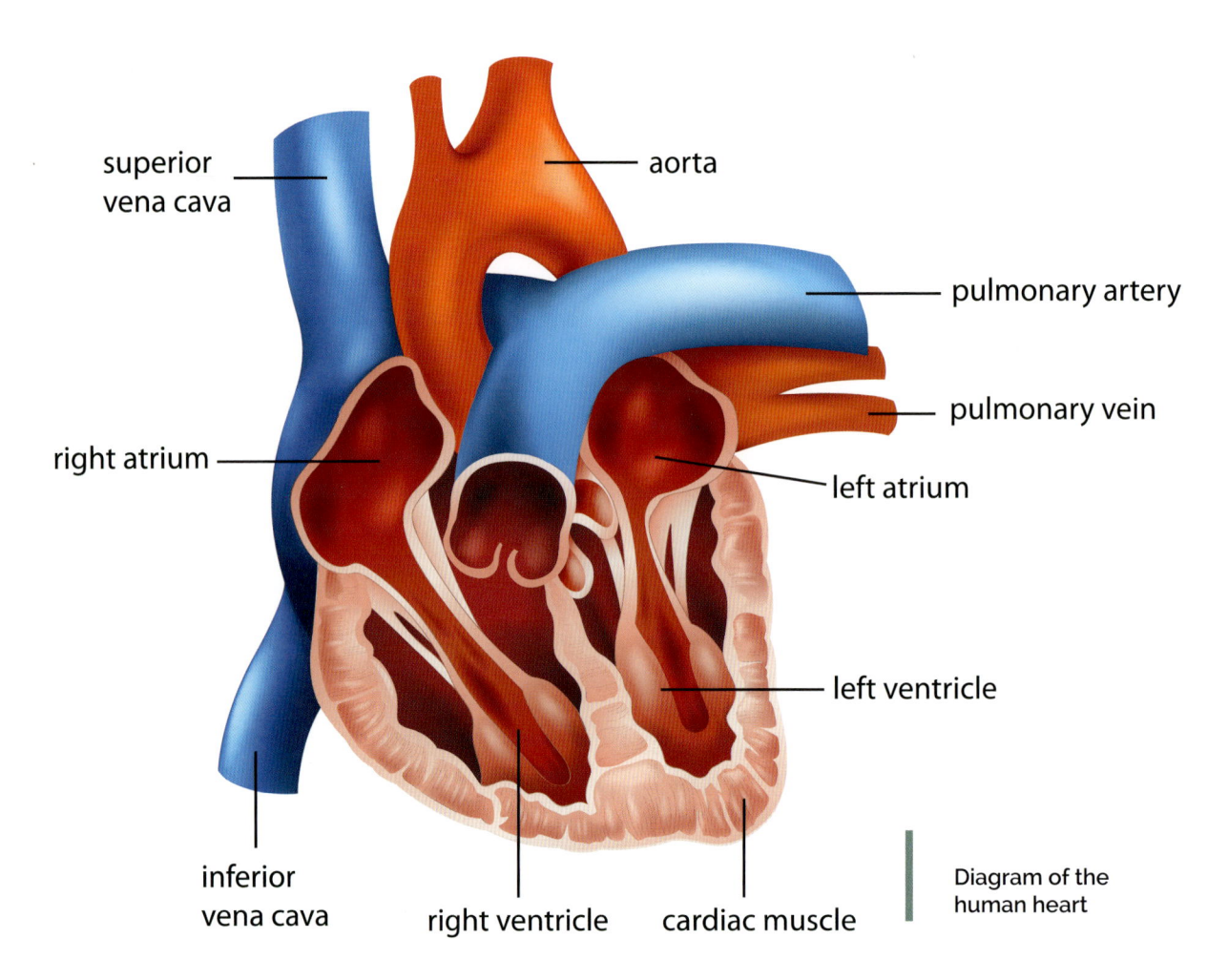

Diagram of the human heart — labels: superior vena cava, aorta, pulmonary artery, pulmonary vein, right atrium, left atrium, left ventricle, inferior vena cava, right ventricle, cardiac muscle.

Two other valves separate the ventricles from the major arteries leaving the heart. The **aortic valve** allows blood pumped by the left ventricle to pass into the aorta and to the rest of the body, but does not permit blood to flow back from the aorta into the left ventricle. The **pulmonary valve** regulates the blood flow from the right ventricle into the pulmonary artery for the lungs in the same way.

D. The Pericardium

The heart is protected by the structures of the chest wall. It is also protected by a tough, fibrous sac called the **pericardium** (*per·ih-**kar**-dee-um*). The pericardium keeps the heart positioned correctly in the chest, prevents the heart from over-expanding when filling with blood, and limits the motion of the heart when the person is breathing.

The pericardium is actually a double-walled sac with a fluid in between. When the Heart of Jesus was pierced by a lance, and blood and water came out, the water was the fluid of the pericardium.

Section Review – 11.5. The Human Heart

1. Describe the advantages of a four-chambered heart.
2. Draw and label the major structures of the human heart.

Life Science for Young Catholics

11.6 Circulation

There are, in effect, two circulatory loops surrounding the four-chambered heart. One loop is responsible for transporting deoxygenated blood from the heart to the lungs, to collect oxygen, and bring this oxygenated blood back to the heart. This is called **pulmonary circulation**. The right side of the heart is responsible for pulmonary circulation.

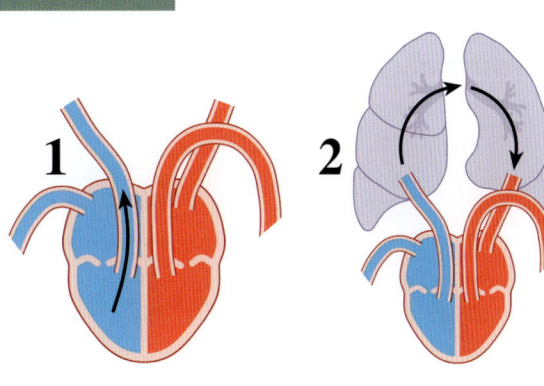

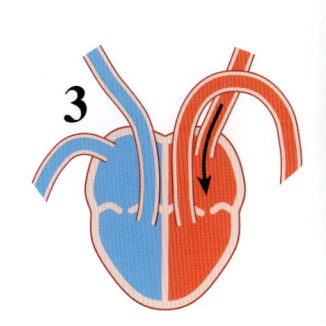

The second loop delivers the oxygenated blood to the body and returns the deoxygenated blood to the heart. This is the process of circulating blood through the body called **systemic circulation**. The left side of the heart is responsible for systemic circulation.

A. Pulmonary Circulation

Pulmonary circulation starts when deoxygenated blood returns to the right side of the heart by way of two large veins. Blood from the head, neck, and arms returns to the heart through the higher, **superior vena cava** (*vee·nuh cave-uh*), while blood from the rest of the body returns to the heart through the lower, **inferior vena cava**. Both large veins empty into the **right atrium**. As the right atrium contracts, the blood passes through the tricuspid valve into the **right ventricle**.

Deoxygenated blood (blue in picture above) moves from the body to the right side of the heart, and from there to the lungs to pick up oxygen. Oxygenated blood (red in picture above) from the lungs moves to the left side of the heart, to go to the body.

The right ventricle contracts and pumps the blood through the **pulmonary valve** into the **pulmonary artery**. Remember, arteries carry blood away from the heart. The pulmonary artery carries deoxygenated blood away from the heart to the lungs, where it picks up oxygen. The oxygenated blood returns to the heart through the pulmonary vein into the left atrium.

B. Systemic Circulation

From the left atrium, the oxygenated blood passes through the mitral valve and into the most muscular chamber of the heart, the left ventricle. The left ventricle has the thickest and most muscular wall of all the chambers in the heart because it must have enough force to pump the blood throughout the body. As the left ventricle contracts, the oxygenated blood is forced into the **aorta**. The aorta is the largest artery in the body, with highly elastic and muscular walls to withstand the high pressure flow of blood from the left ventricle.

WORDS TO REMEMBER

mitral valve: separates the left atrium from the left ventricle to prevent blood from flowing backwards

aortic valve: allows blood pumped by the left ventricle to pass into the aorta and to the rest of the body, but does not permit blood to flow back from the aorta into the left ventricle.

pulmonary valve: regulates the blood flow from the right ventricle into the pulmonary artery for the lungs and prevents blood from flowing backward to the heart

pericardium: a tough, fibrous sac that protects the heart.

pulmonary circulation: brings deoxygenated blood to the lungs to discard carbon dioxide and pick up oxygen. The right side of the heart is responsible for pulmonary circulation.

systemic circulation: brings oxygenated blood from the heart to the rest of the body. The left side of the heart is responsible for systemic circulation.

oxygenated blood from heart

venous capillary

Systemic circulation

arteriole

venule

arterial capillary

deoxygenated blood to heart

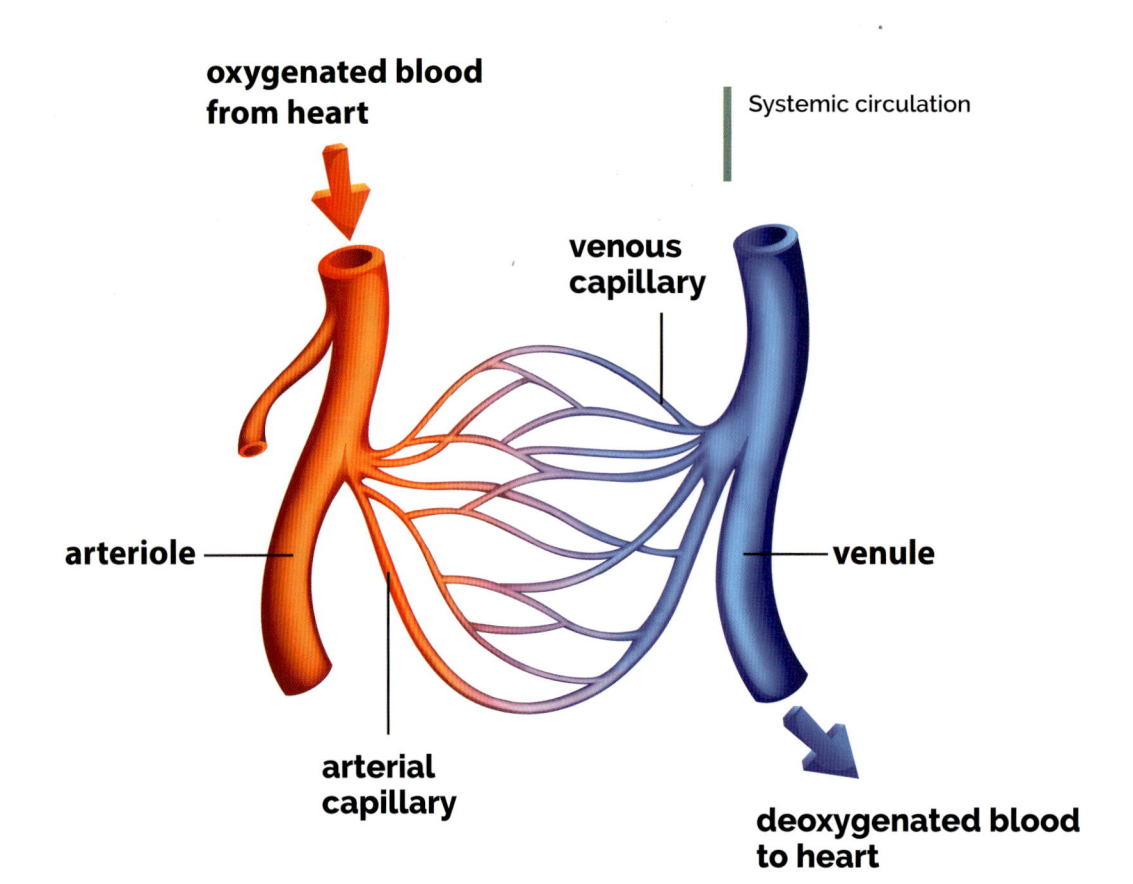

Oxygenated blood (red in picture above) moves from the lungs, to the left side of the heart, to all body tissues. Deoxygenated blood (blue in picture above) moves from the body tissues to the right side of the heart.

From the aorta, blood flows into all other arteries, arterioles, and eventually into the capillaries at the tissue level. Gas exchange takes place at the capillary level with the oxygen diffusing into the tissues; deoxygenated blood passes to the venules, then veins, and is eventually returned to the heart to repeat the cycle.

C. Coronary Circulation

Along with pulmonary circulation and systemic circulation, the heart has a third system that provides oxygen and nutrients to the cardiac muscle itself. This third circulation is known as **coronary** (*core·uh·nair·ee*) **circulation**.

Two main **coronary arteries**, the left and the right coronary artery, branch directly from the aorta to supply the heart with oxygenated blood. These two arteries run down the sides of the outside of the heart, and divide into branches to supply all areas of the heart with oxygen.

When a person has a heart attack, it is because the blood supply to the heart muscle from one or more of the coronary arteries has been blocked and the **heart does not receive the oxygen it needs to function**.

Section Review – 11.6 - Circulation

1. Briefly describe the pulmonary and systemic circulatory systems.
2. What is the purpose of coronary circulation?
3. What is the importance of the aorta?

11.7 Other Functions of the Circulatory System

Along with transporting oxygen, nutrients, and wastes throughout the body, the circulatory system performs several other important functions. The components of the blood also protect the body against blood loss, protect the body from infection, help to maintain the correct body temperature, and maintain a constant blood pressure.

A. Prevent Blood Loss

When a blood vessel is damaged, bleeding ensues. Platelets in blood collect at the site of injury as a first line of defense and form a **blood clot**, or a patch, to cover the damaged site. After the platelet plug is formed, a protein called **fibrin** (**fie**·brin) solidifies the clot.

B. Protect Against Infection

The white blood cells protect against and fight off infection. White blood cells will find and destroy cells that are foreign to the body, for example, bacteria and viruses.

C. Maintain Body Temperature

In cooperation with several other organ systems, the circulatory system provides the maintenance of a constant internal body temperature. The normal human body temperature is 98.6° Fahrenheit, or 37° Celsius. In healthy individuals, this temperature fluctuates in either direction by less than one degree.

D. Maintain Blood Pressure

The circulatory system also helps to maintain a constant **blood pressure**. The blood being pumped from the left ventricle through the aorta and through the entire arterial system of the body requires enough pressure to reach all the tissues in all parts of the body. Blood pressure must be high enough so that all the tissues are adequately supplied, but also low enough so that the tissues are not damaged.

There are two components to blood pressure, **systolic** (*sis·taul·ik*) **pressure** and **diastolic** (*die·as·taul·ik*) **pressure**.

The **systolic** pressure is the pressure generated through the circulatory system by the contraction of the left ventricle of the heart. The **diastolic** pressure is the pressure that remains throughout the circulatory system when the left ventricle is relaxing and not pumping blood.

A normal blood pressure is less than or equal to **120/80**. We read it "120 over 80." The top number is the systolic pressure, or the pressure as the left ventricle contracts. The bottom number is the diastolic pressure, or the pressure as the left ventricle relaxes and is filled with blood. Blood pressure measures the pressure in the arteries or arterial system, not in the veins or venous system.

Section Review – 11.7 Other Functions of the Circulatory System

1. What causes blood pressure?
2. Identify systolic and diastolic blood pressure.

WORDS TO REMEMBER

ventricles: two large chambers that pump blood out of the heart to the lungs and to the body

aorta: the largest artery of the circulatory system, located on the top of the heart

coronary circulation: provides oxygen and nutrients to the cardiac muscle (heart muscle) itself

fibrin: a protein that solidifies a clot

blood pressure: the force needed to keep blood flowing through the vessels to the whole body. Blood pressure must be high enough so that all the tissues are adequately supplied, but also low enough so that the tissues are not damaged.

systolic pressure: the pressure generated through the circulatory system by the contraction of the left ventricle of the heart

diastolic pressure: the pressure that remains throughout the circulatory system when the left ventricle is relaxing and not pumping blood

CHAPTER 11: THE HUMAN CIRCULATORY SYSTEM

11.8 The Heart, Holy Scripture, and Devotion

All organ systems of the human body are interdependent; that is, no organ functions solely on its own. The respiratory and circulatory systems are, in fact, completely dependent on one another. The heart requires oxygen from the respiratory system to function; the lungs require the heart, blood, and vessels to supply oxygen to the body. Both are vital systems without which all other organs and organ systems would cease to live. The heart is the most central and vital organ in the human body.

The word "heart" is mentioned more than a thousand times in the Old and New Testaments collectively. Most often in Scripture, "heart" is used to mean the inner, true, and spiritual person. The condition of the inner person is said to be the "condition of the heart," and all that a person thinks, says, and does comes first from the inner self, or "from the heart." The "heart," the inner self, of the person, is what matters most to God, not the outward appearance of the body.

> But the LORD said to Samuel: Do not judge from his appearance or from his lofty stature, because I have rejected him. God does not see as a mortal, who sees the appearance. The LORD looks into the heart. (1 Samuel 16:7)

The Catechism of the Catholic Church teaches:

> The heart is our hidden center, beyond the grasp of our reason and of others; only the Spirit of God can fathom [understand] the human heart and know it fully. (CCC 2563)

> The desire for God is written in the human heart, because man is created by God and for God; and God never ceases to draw man to Himself. Only in God will he find the truth and happiness he never stops searching for. (CCC 27)

> The Beatitudes respond to the natural desire for happiness. This desire is of divine origin: God has placed it in the human heart in order to draw man to the One who alone can fulfill it. (CCC 1718)

> Since they express man's fundamental duties towards God and towards his neighbor, the Ten Commandments reveal ... grave obligations. They are fundamentally immutable [unchangeable], and they oblige [command] always and everywhere. No one can dispense from them. The Ten Commandments are engraved by God in the human heart. (CCC 2072)

Just as the human heart can be damaged by illness or lack of proper care and respect for the body, the "condition of the heart," or the inner, true person, can be damaged by lack of spiritual care and by the dangers and temptations of the world.

The Bible instructs in Proverbs 4:23, "With all vigilance, guard your heart, for in it are the sources of life." Jesus Christ, through His example and His Holy Church, provides everything necessary to guard, protect, and purify the heart: Holy Mass, the Sacraments, the help of the Communion of Saints, prayer, and Holy Scripture. By embracing the Catholic Faith and seeking God above all things, the heart can be purified and eventually share in God's eternal joy. For, as Jesus teaches in His Sermon on the Mount, "Blessed are the clean of heart, for they will see God" (Matthew 5:8).

For centuries, the heart has been associated with love. The heart symbol is recognized as an abbreviation of sorts for the word *love*, and, second to the cross, is one of the most utilized and recognized symbols of all times. The heart symbolizes love. A perfect heart would, as it follows, symbolize perfect love. The Sacred Heart of Jesus is the Perfect Heart, the Heart of God.

Devotion to the Sacred Heart of Jesus is a particular devotion to Jesus Christ, which became universal in the late 1600s after Jesus appeared to St. Margaret Mary Alacoque and instructed her on devotion to His Heart. Jesus asked that devotion be made to His Heart which, according to Pope Leo XIII, is "the symbol and express image of the infinite love of Jesus Christ which moves us to love in return." Devotion to the Sacred Heart of Jesus involves consecrating oneself to His service, and making reparations for man's indifference to His love.

CHAPTER 11: THE HUMAN CIRCULATORY SYSTEM

Chapter 11 Review

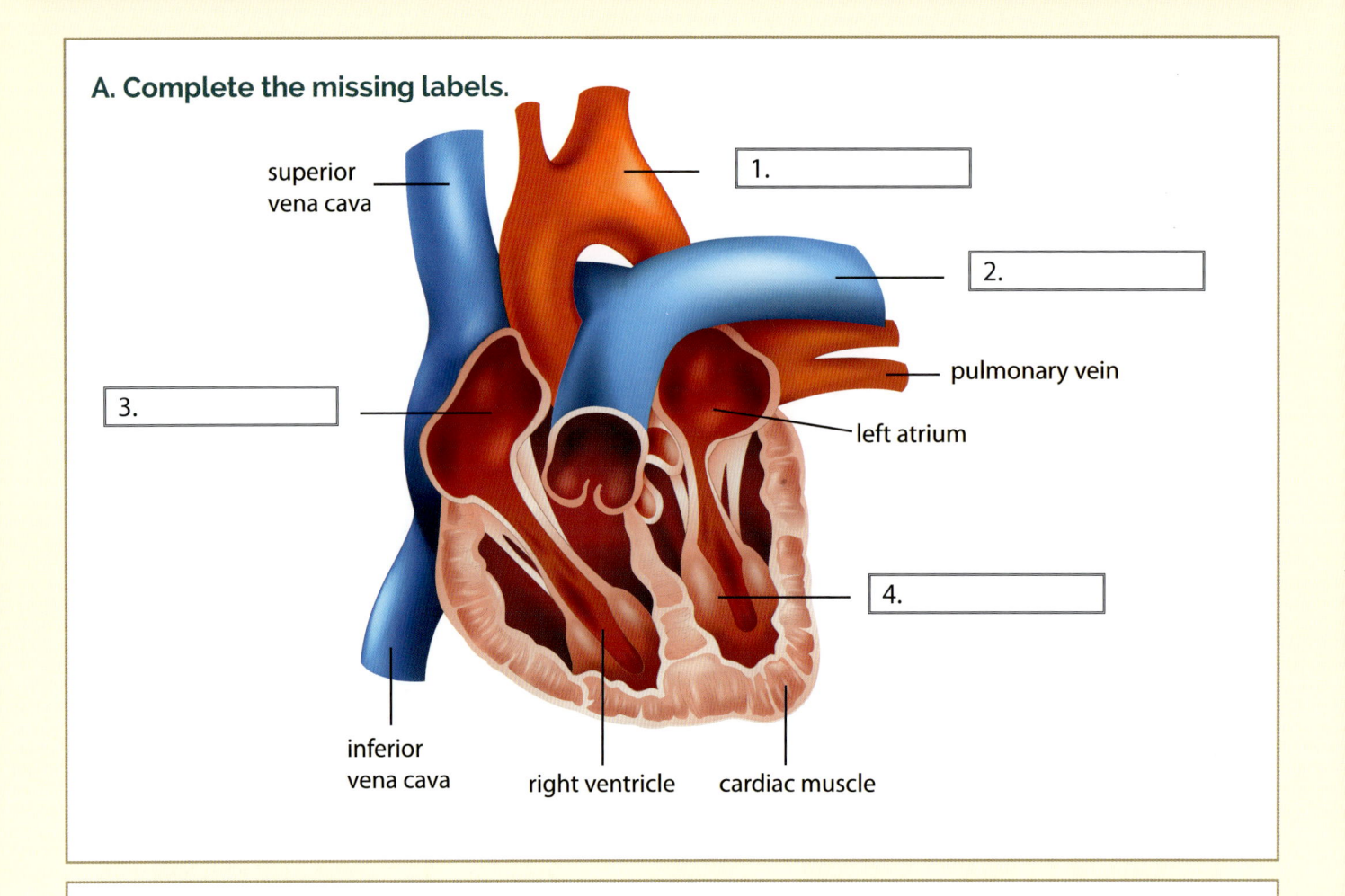

A. Complete the missing labels.

- superior vena cava
- 1.
- 2.
- pulmonary vein
- 3.
- left atrium
- 4.
- inferior vena cava
- right ventricle
- cardiac muscle

B. Answer the following questions.

1. Describe the primary purpose of the circulatory system.
2. What are the major items moved to the body tissues by the circulatory system?
3. Name the major items removed from the body tissues by the circulatory system.
4. What is plasma?
5. Describe red blood cells.
6. What do white blood cells do?
7. What is the importance of hemoglobin?
8. What are platelets and what is their main contribution to the body?
9. Describe the importance of capillaries.
10. Which blood vessels have valves? Why are valves important?
11. What is the purpose of coronary circulation?
12. What causes a heart attack?
13. Identify systolic and diastolic blood pressure.
14. What is normal blood pressure?

Chapter 11: "Words to Remember" Crossword

ACROSS

7 a protein that solidifies a clot
8 vessels that carry blood away from the heart.
11 chemicals that allow cells to maintain the correct electrical voltage to work properly.
13 __ pressure is the pressure that remains throughout the circulatory system when the left ventricle is relaxing and not pumping blood.
15 __ circulation provides oxygen and nutrients to the cardiac muscle (heart muscle) itself.
16 __ muscle is a specialized muscle that contracts without stimulation from nerves.
17 A __ valve separates the left atrium from the left ventricle to prevent blood from flowing backwards.

DOWN

1 the largest artery of the circulatory system located on the top of the heart
2 __ blood cells are responsible for fighting infection.
3 small cell fragments responsible for blood clotting to protect the body from excessive blood loss
4 vessels that carry blood from the body tissues back to the heart
5 The __ system includes the heart, blood vessels, and the blood.
6 a tough fibrous sac that protects the heart
9 the very important molecule that carries oxygen throughout the body
10 specialized tissue composed of living cells in a liquid environment
12 __ circulation brings oxygenated blood from the heart to the rest of the body.
14 the muscular organ at the center of the circulatory system that pumps the blood through the blood vessels to the body tissues

Life Science for Young Catholics

12 THE HUMAN DIGESTIVE SYSTEM

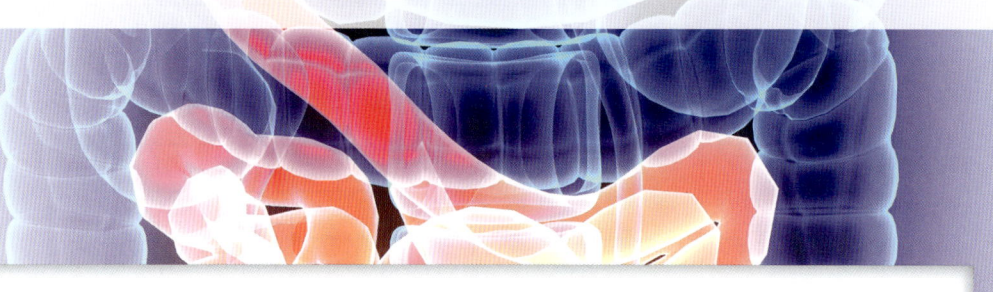

12.1 Introduction

12.2 The Human Digestive System

12.3 The Processes of Digestion
- A. Ingestion
- B. Secretion
- C. Mixing and Movement
- D. Digestion
- E. Absorption
- F. Excretion

12.4 Related Systems to Digestion
- A. Blood Vessels
- B. The Endocrine System
- C. The Nervous System

12.5 Structures and Functions of the Alimentary Canal
- A. The Mouth
    1. The Teeth
    2. Salivary Glands
    3. The Tongue
- B. The Esophagus
- C. The Stomach
- D. The Small Intestine
- E. The Large Intestine

12.6 Structure and Function of the Liver
- A. Structure of the Liver
- B. Function of the Liver
- C. Portal Circulation

12.7 Oxidation and Assimilation
- A. Oxidation
- B. Assimilation

12.8 Summary

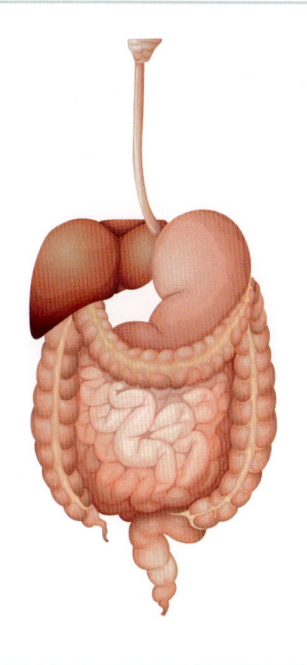

Chapter 12

The Human Digestive System

12.1 Introduction

Do you know the story of St. Peter's vision about food? The Jewish people believed that certain animals were "unclean" and therefore they were forbidden to eat them. However, God sent St. Peter a vision that declared that all things God made were clean and proper to eat. A voice from Heaven spoke to Peter three times, "What God hath cleansed, do not call that unclean."

Jesus taught, "What goes into someone's mouth does not defile him, but what comes out of his mouth, that is what defiles him."

Jesus fed 5,000 people with five loaves of bread and two fish. On another occasion, He fed 4,000 people with seven loaves of bread and a few fish. Clearly, these miracles indicate the importance of food in our lives, and of spiritual food in our more important spiritual life. Jesus said that without the Holy Eucharist, we would not have life within us, meaning we would not have eternal life.

Since God made food so important for this life, He gave us a marvelous system to process food to give us the energy and the materials that we need to grow and to live in good health. This system is one of the countless gifts for which we can thank God for His marvelous love for us.

Let's learn about this wondrous gift, the human digestive system.

12.2 The Human Digestive System

God created plants with the ability to produce their own food, so that they could be a source of food for His other creatures, especially for His greatest creation, man:

> God also said: See, I give you every seed-bearing plant on all the Earth and every tree that has seed-bearing fruit on it to be your food; and to all the wild animals, all the birds of the air, and all the living creatures that crawl on the earth, I give all the green plants for food. And so it happened. (Genesis 1:29-30)

Just as God created the plants with the ability to produce their own nutrition, He provides nutrition for all of His creatures. As has been illustrated throughout the previous chapters, all living organisms require nutrition, and all have the means, given by the Creator, to obtain it. Animals must ingest their food and digest it internally. God has equipped each animal with a source of food, but also with a means of obtaining food, breaking it down into its usable parts, distributing the nutrients throughout the organism, and ridding the organism of unusable wastes.

The human **digestive system** is the organ system responsible for breaking down food into carbohydrates, proteins, fats, vitamins, and other small nutrients which are used by the human body for energy to fuel all the life processes.

CHAPTER 12: THE HUMAN DIGESTIVE SYSTEM

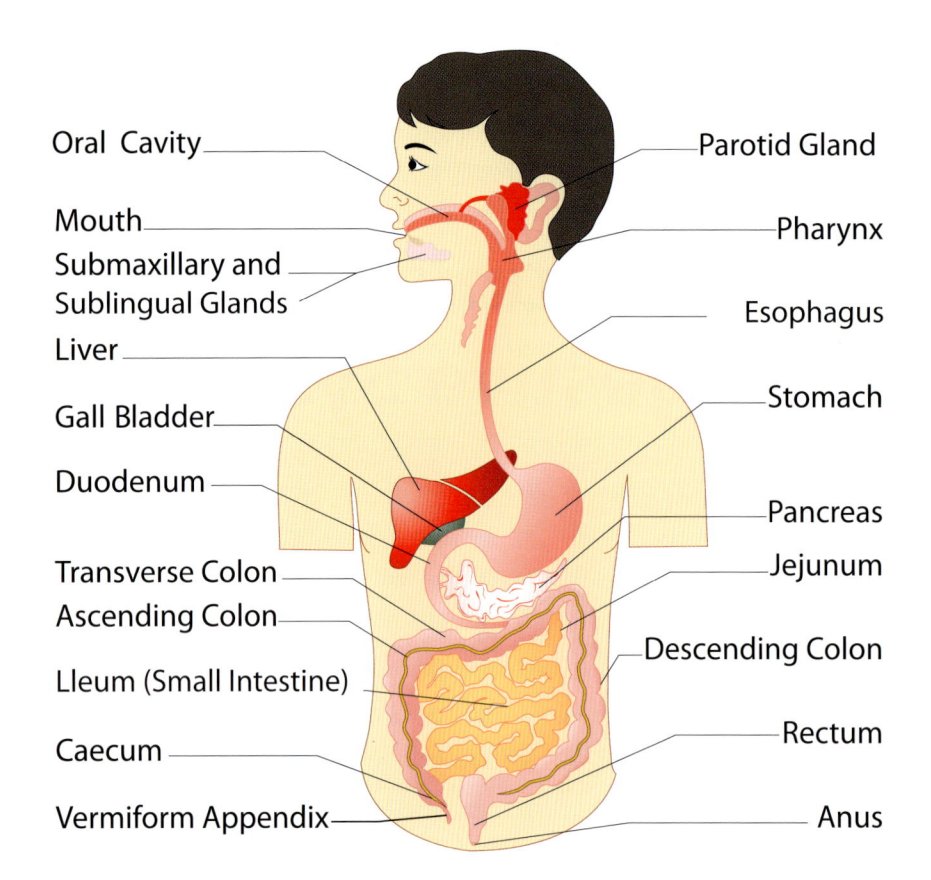

The Human Digestive System

- Oral Cavity
- Mouth
- Submaxillary and Sublingual Glands
- Liver
- Gall Bladder
- Duodenum
- Transverse Colon
- Ascending Colon
- Lleum (Small Intestine)
- Caecum
- Vermiform Appendix
- Parotid Gland
- Pharynx
- Esophagus
- Stomach
- Pancreas
- Jejunum
- Descending Colon
- Rectum
- Anus

The human digestive system includes all the tissues, structures, and organs that work together to break down food into simple substances, or **nutrients**, used by the cells to keep us in good health.

The human digestive system includes the **alimentary** (*al-uh-**men**-tar-ee*) canal, a long, hollow, twisted, and coiled tube extending from the mouth to the anus, or exit of waste from the body. The alimentary canal is sometimes referred to as the **gastrointestinal** (*gas-tro-in-**tes**-tin-al*) **tract**, or **GI tract**.

The alimentary canal includes the **mouth**, **throat**, **esophagus** (the tube from the throat to the stomach), **stomach**, **small intestine**, **large intestine, rectum, and anus**. The digestive system also includes the **teeth**, **tongue**, **salivary glands**, **liver**, **pancreas**, and **gallbladder**. Each of these organs contributes to digestion.

> **Section Review --
> 12.2 The Human Digestive System**
>
> 1. Briefly describe the purpose of the digestive system.
>
> 2. Identify the alimentary canal. Include the organs and tissues that compose it.
>
> 3. Draw and label the human digestive system.

12.3 The Processes of Digestion

Digestion occurs within the entire gastrointestinal tract or region. Complete digestion, however, involves not only the entire digestive system, but also the nervous system, and even the circulatory system.

There are six individual processes that lead to complete digestion of food. These are **ingestion**, **secretion**, **mixing and movement**, **digestion**, **absorption**, and **excretion**.

Life Science for Young Catholics

A. Ingestion

Ingestion is the means by which food enters the digestive system. Ingestion is simply eating and drinking. Food enters the digestive system through the mouth.

B. Secretion

Secretion is the process by which a substance, such as a hormone, chemical, or enzyme, is released from an organ or gland to perform a particular function.

In the process of digestion, the human digestive system secretes or releases, on the average, almost two gallons of digestive fluids per day. These fluids include **saliva** (*sa·lie·vah*), **mucus**, **hydrochloric** (*high·droe·klor·ik*) **acid**, and **bile**.

Saliva is produced by salivary glands in the mouth. The function of saliva is to moisten the food and begin breaking it down. Saliva is a watery mixture produced in the mouth, containing digestive enzymes. Enzymes are proteins that speed up a chemical reaction in the body without being used up in the process. Digestive enzymes are proteins that speed up the breakdown of food into simpler substances for easy digestion.

Hydrochloric acid is produced in the stomach; it is a strong acid that helps break down food, particularly proteins in food.

Bile is a thick green fluid that is produced by the liver, stored in the gallbladder, and released into the small intestine. Bile breaks down large fat droplets into small droplets for easier digestion and absorption into the blood stream.

C. Mixing and Movement

Mixing and movement of food occurs through the entire digestive tract, beginning in the mouth. The **muscles of chewing** begin the mixing process in the mouth. Four major muscle groups are involved in biting and chewing. The chewing muscles all have points of attachment to the skull and to the jawbone.

The tongue, a large muscular structure on the floor of the mouth, is the primary organ of **taste**, but also forms the chewed food into a **bolus**, a soft, rounded mass. The tongue helps move the food to the **throat**, or **pharynx** (*fair·inx*), so it can be swallowed and enter the esophagus.

The **alimentary tract**, from the esophagus through the large intestine, is a hollow tube with muscular walls. The muscles in the walls of the alimentary canal are involuntary, smooth muscles. Contraction of these smooth muscles of the alimentary tract occurs in waves, thus propelling food materials through the alimentary canal.

WORDS TO REMEMBER

digestive system: the organ system responsible for breaking down food into carbohydrates, proteins, fats, vitamins, and other small nutrients which are used by the human body for energy to fuel all the life processes

nutrients: include food, or other nourishing substances, assimilated by an organism and required for growth, repair, and normal metabolism

alimentary canal (GI tract): a long, hollow, twisted, and coiled tube extending from the mouth to the anus

small intestine: the largest digestive organ of the human intestinal tract, measuring between 18 and 23 feet in length

large intestine: the final part of the digestive tract, where any remaining water and electrolytes are re-absorbed for use in the body; so named because it is larger in diameter, or wider, than the small intestine

ingestion: the means by which food enters the digestive system

secretion: the process by which a substance, such as a hormone, chemical, or enzyme, is released from an organ or gland to perform a particular function

saliva: produced by salivary glands in the mouth to moisten the food

hydrochloric acid: produced in the stomach; a strong acid that helps break down food, particularly proteins in food

bile: a thick green fluid that is produced by the liver, stored in the gallbladder, and released into the small intestine. Bile breaks down large fat droplets into small droplets for easier digestion and absorption into the blood stream.

Life Science for Young Catholics

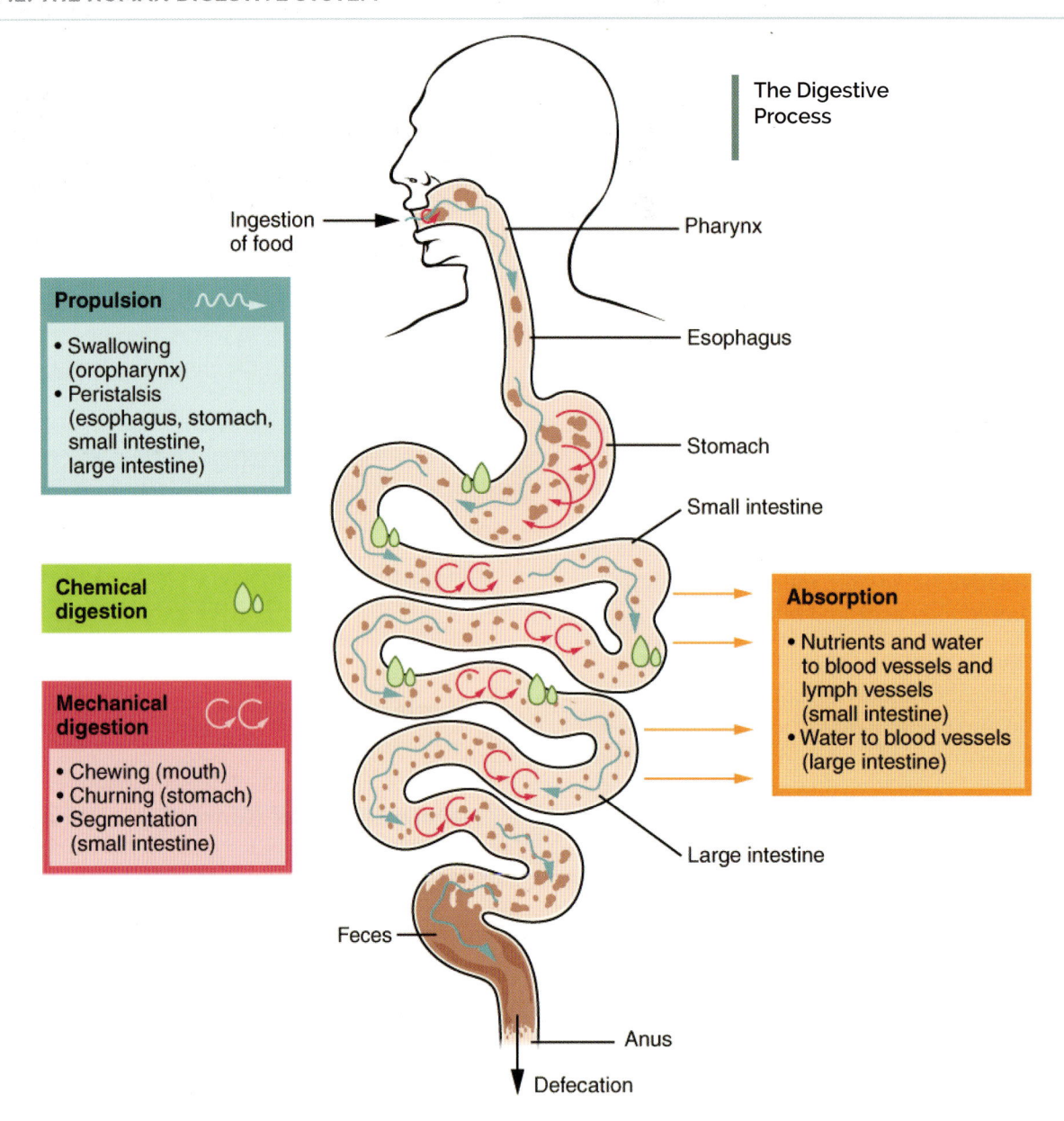

CHAPTER 12: THE HUMAN DIGESTIVE SYSTEM

The Digestive Process

- Ingestion of food
- Pharynx
- Esophagus
- Stomach
- Small intestine
- Large intestine
- Feces
- Anus
- Defecation

Propulsion
- Swallowing (oropharynx)
- Peristalsis (esophagus, stomach, small intestine, large intestine)

Chemical digestion

Mechanical digestion
- Chewing (mouth)
- Churning (stomach)
- Segmentation (small intestine)

Absorption
- Nutrients and water to blood vessels and lymph vessels (small intestine)
- Water to blood vessels (large intestine)

Although mixing begins in the mouth and occurs to some extent through the entire digestive tract, most **mixing of food** occurs in the **stomach**. In the stomach, the partially mixed and partially digested food materials are mixed with **gastric juice**, which contains mucus, hydrochloric acid, and enzymes. A protease is an enzyme which breaks down proteins. **Pepsin** is the principal protease found in gastric juice.

D. Digestion

Digestion is the actual breaking down of complex food into the basic building blocks of carbohydrates, proteins, fats, vitamins, and other small nutrients.

Mechanical digestion is the physical breaking down of larger pieces of food into smaller particles. Mechanical digestion begins with chewing in the mouth, but continues through the entire digestive tract.

Chemical digestion is the breakdown of food particles by chemical means, through the action of enzymes, into simpler substances. Chemical digestion also begins in the mouth and continues in the stomach and small intestine. Saliva contains an enzyme that breaks down starches and other carbohydrates. Chemical digestion continues in the stomach where protease, an enzyme, and hydrochloric acid begin the digestion of proteins.

Most digestion, about 90%, occurs in the small intestine. Three substances meet in the small intestine: first, a thick fluid of partly digested food and stomach juices from the stomach; second,

Life Science for Young Catholics

digestive enzymes from the pancreas; and third, bile from the gallbladder. The pancreas produces enzymes that break down carbohydrates, proteins, and lipids for use by the body.

A very small amount of chemical digestion occurs in the large intestine through the actions of **gut flora**, or symbiotic bacteria. The gut flora are symbiotic bacteria, or mutually helpful bacteria, because the gut flora bacteria are able to break down some materials that the human digestive system alone cannot break down. The human digestive system provides a suitable living environment for the gut flora.

E. Absorption

Absorption is the process by which digested food substances are passed from the digestive tract into the blood where these food substances are transported to the remainder of the body. Almost all absorption of digested materials occurs in the small intestine.

Most nutrients are absorbed into the blood of the circulatory system. Absorption from the gut occurs into the gastrointestinal cells, and, from the gastrointestinal cells the nutrients are absorbed into nearby capillaries. Water and a few vitamins are absorbed into the blood in the large intestine.

F. Excretion

Excretion is the final step in the process of digestion. Excretion is the removal of waste products from the digestive tract. Digestive wastes accumulate in the large intestine, where water is absorbed from them into circulation. As a result, liquid waste is transformed or reduced to solid waste in the large intestine, temporarily stored in the **rectum**, and eliminated through the **anus**. Thus, undigested materials are removed from the body.

Now that the six processes of complete digestion have been introduced, an in-depth look at each process as it occurs within each structure and organ will be discussed. Proper emphasis will be given to the structure of each organ and how each was created in accord with its function.

> **Section Review – 12.3 The Processes of Digestion**
>
> 1. Identify the following: digestion, ingestion, secretion, absorption, & excretion.
> 2. Describe bile and its importance.
> 3. Describe the function and importance of both the large and small intestines.

12.4 Related Systems to Digestion

Like all the body's systems, the digestive system is not independent, but works closely with other organs. The circulatory system carries the nutrients supplied by the digestive system to the rest of the body. Together, the nervous system and the endocrine system control various functions of the digestive system.

A. Blood Vessels

Blood vessels play an essential role in the process of digestion. They supply each digestive organ with nutrients and oxygen to ensure the constant supply of energy for proper functioning. Blood vessels also absorb the digested nutrients and distribute them throughout the rest of the body.

> **WORDS TO REMEMBER**
>
> **gastric juice**: a thin, strong acid; a nearly colorless liquid that is secreted by the glands in the lining of the stomach; contains mucus, hydrochloric acid, and enzymes
>
> **pepsin**: the principal protease found in gastric juice
>
> **digestion**: the actual breaking down of complex food into the basic building blocks of carbohydrates, proteins, fats, vitamins, and other small nutrients
>
> **gut flora**: symbiotic bacteria that break down some materials that the human digestive system alone cannot break down
>
> **absorption**: the process by which digested food substances are passed from the digestive tract into the blood, where these food substances are transported to the remainder of the body
>
> **excretion**: the final step in the process of digestion. Excretion is the removal of waste products from the digestive tract.

B. The Endocrine System

The **endocrine system** is composed of ductless glands which secrete hormones that regulate many body functions. Hormones related to the digestive tract can make a person feel hungry or thirsty. Other digestive hormones can start or stop the production of digestive juices, and control the strength and rate of contraction of the muscles in the stomach. Other hormones from the endocrine system control the rate of absorption of nutrients in the small intestine.

C. The Nervous System

The **nervous system** prepares the body for the upcoming meal. For example, when a person is hungry, he may hear or feel his stomach "grumbling." This feeling is caused by increased muscle contractions in anticipation of the incoming food. Likewise, even the thought of food can cause one's mouth to "water." This is because the nervous system triggers the salivary glands to produce and release more saliva, again in preparation for the meal. With preparation underway, the work of the digestive system begins as the food enters the alimentary canal through the mouth.

> **Section Review —**
> **12.4 Related Systems to Digestion**
> 1. How do blood vessels aid the digestive system?
> 2. Give three ways the endocrine system interacts with the digestive system.
> 3. Discuss the role of the nervous system in digestion.

12.5 Structures and Functions of the Alimentary Canal

The alimentary canal is also called the **digestive tract**; it is the place where food passes through so that nutrients are digested and absorbed into the blood, and where the indigestible or nonessential portion is eliminated as waste. The alimentary canal is a tubular structure of muscle and mucous membrane lining that begins at the mouth and ends at the anus. The organs of the alimentary canal include the **mouth, esophagus, stomach, small intestine,** and **large intestine**. Other organs, such as the liver, pancreas, and the gallbladder, are related to digestion, but are not part of the alimentary canal.

A. The Mouth

The mouth includes the **teeth**, the **tongue**, and the openings from the ducts of the **salivary glands**. Food containing nutrients enters the mouth and the teeth start the process of digestion by mechanically breaking down the food into smaller pieces, while the salivary glands start the digestive process of breaking down the food by chemical means.

1. The Teeth

The adult mouth contains 32 **secondary teeth,** with 16 in the upper jaw and 16 in the lower jaw. These teeth begin to form in the jaw under the gums before a baby is born. By ages eleven to thirteen years, the typical human mouth contains 28 secondary teeth. The remaining four are known as **wisdom teeth** and erupt in the late teens to early twenties; sometimes wisdom teeth do not appear at all.

Four types of teeth are found in the human mouth: **incisors, cuspids, bicuspids,** and **molars**. Different teeth are characterized by different shapes and different functions.

Incisors are the most centrally located teeth; four incisors are in the upper jaw, and four are in the lower jaw. Incisors are chisel-shaped teeth used primarily for biting off relatively large pieces of food.

Next to the incisors are the cuspids, or **canine teeth**. There are two upper canines and two lower canines; all are cone-shaped and used for grasping and tearing food.

At the side of the canines are the bicuspids, or **premolars**. There are four premolars in each jaw. These teeth have relatively flat surfaces and are used for grinding food.

The **molars** have flattened surfaces for grinding food. The molars, however, are generally larger than the premolars and farther back in the mouth. There are three pairs of molars in each jaw, including the wisdom teeth.

CHAPTER 12: THE HUMAN DIGESTIVE SYSTEM

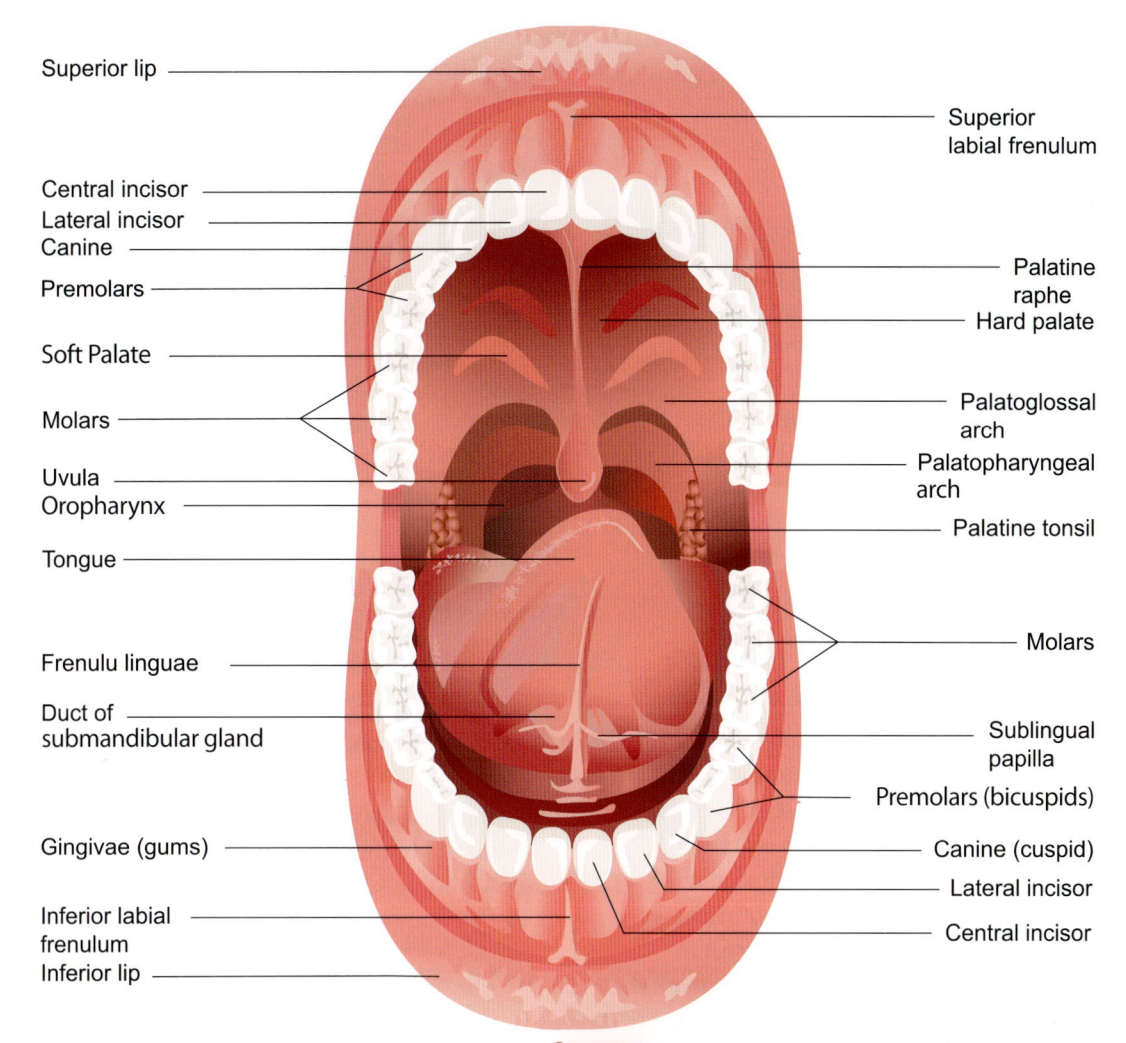

[Diagram of the mouth with labels: Superior lip, Superior labial frenulum, Central incisor, Lateral incisor, Canine, Premolars, Palatine raphe, Hard palate, Soft Palate, Molars, Palatoglossal arch, Palatopharyngeal arch, Uvula, Oropharynx, Palatine tonsil, Tongue, Molars, Frenulu linguae, Duct of submandibular gland, Sublingual papilla, Premolars (bicuspids), Gingivae (gums), Canine (cuspid), Lateral incisor, Inferior labial frenulum, Central incisor, Inferior lip]

Teeth are made of many types of tissues. **Enamel** covers the **crown**, or the part of the tooth above the gum. The **root** extends into the jaw socket to anchor the tooth; roots are covered by a bony material called **cementum** (*see*-**men**-*tum*).

Beneath the enamel is the largest component of the tooth, a hard bone-like tissue called **dentin**. The centermost part of each tooth is called the **pulp**. The pulp contains nerves, blood vessels, and connective tissue; the pulp is the living, sensitive part of the tooth. Injury to the pulp leads to a toothache. Besides taking part in chewing and in the digestion of food, the teeth give shape to the face and help in **articulation**, or speaking clearly.

2. Salivary Glands

Chemical digestion begins in the mouth, with saliva beginning the breakdown of carbohydrates or starches in the food. Saliva is produced and secreted by salivary glands. Humans have three main pairs of **salivary** (*sal*-*uh*-*ver*-*ee*) **glands**.

WORDS TO REMEMBER

cementum: a thin layer of bony material that fixes teeth to the jaw

enamel: one of the four major tissues that make up the tooth. It makes up the hard, mineralized surface of teeth.

dentin: the largest component of the tooth, a hard, bone-like tissue found beneath the enamel

pulp: the centermost part of each tooth. The pulp contains nerves, blood vessels, and connective tissue; the pulp is the living, sensitive part of the tooth.

chemical digestion: the breakdown of food particles by chemical means, through the action of enzymes, into simpler substances

Life Science for Young Catholics

CHAPTER 12: THE HUMAN DIGESTIVE SYSTEM

3. The Tongue

The tongue is the primary organ of taste. It is covered with **taste buds**, which send taste information to the brain where it is processed and perceived as taste, or flavor.

Once the food is moistened by saliva, and mixed by the chewing of the teeth, the tongue shapes the mixture into a **bolus**, and directs it to the **pharynx**, or throat. The pharynx is a muscular tube that helps the food bolus move from the mouth to the esophagus. Three constrictor muscles are wrapped like rubber bands around the tube-like throat. These throat muscles move the food to the esophagus.

B. The Esophagus

With swallowing, each of the three muscles of the throat contracts in sequence from the top down to push the bolus into the **esophagus** (*eh·soff·ah·gus*), or the tube through which the food must pass to the stomach. The esophagus is simply a muscular-walled tube through which the food bolus passes from the mouth to the stomach. The lowest of these constrictor muscles also prevents air from the respiratory tract from entering the esophagus.

Swallowing triggers the epiglottis, the flap that covers the trachea during swallowing, to protect the airway from food.

C. The Stomach

Once the food bolus passes through the lower esophagus, it enters the **stomach**. The stomach is the organ in which a large amount of mixing and digestion occurs. It is also an organ of food storage.

The structure of the stomach fully supports its function. The human stomach is a single-chambered, hollow, muscular, sac-like organ found just under the diaphragm on the left side of the body, between the esophagus and the small intestine. The inner lining of the stomach is made of thick folds. These folds give the stomach the ability to expand to accommodate up to two or more liters of food at any given time.

Once the food bolus enters the stomach, it remains there for approximately one to two hours during the digestion process. A muscle located at the lower end of the stomach contracts to prevent the food from moving into the intestine before it is ready.

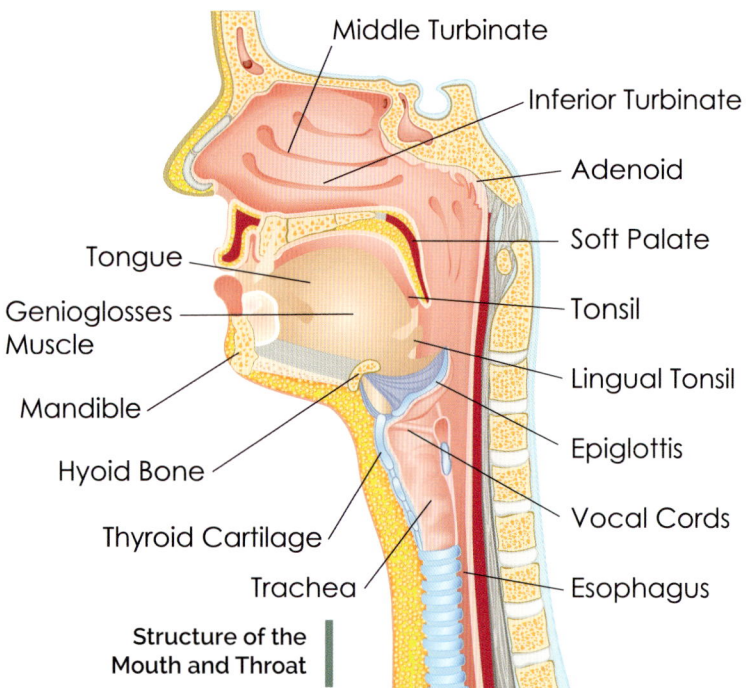

During this time, digestion, which had started in the mouth, continues. The food bolus is mixed by strong contractions of the muscles in the walls of the stomach.

While the mixing occurs, the cells lining the stomach secrete gastric juice containing **hydrochloric acid**, **mucus**, and **digestive enzymes** that speed up the chemical reactions of digestion. In this process, **lipids or fats** are broken down into fatty acids and triglycerides that can be absorbed by the blood, and **proteins** are broken down into smaller amino acids that can be absorbed.

Hydrochloric acid is responsible for activating the enzymes and for beginning the breaking down of proteins in the food bolus. Mucus produced by some stomach cells creates a thick protective surface over the lining of the stomach; this prevents damage to the stomach from the hydrochloric acid and the digestive enzymes.

Little by little, chyme (usually pronounced "kime"), the semi-liquid food mass, is released into the small intestine for further digestion and absorption.

Structure of the Mouth and Throat — labels: Middle Turbinate, Inferior Turbinate, Adenoid, Soft Palate, Tonsil, Lingual Tonsil, Epiglottis, Vocal Cords, Esophagus, Tongue, Genioglosses Muscle, Mandible, Hyoid Bone, Thyroid Cartilage, Trachea

Life Science for Young Catholics

Structure of the Stomach

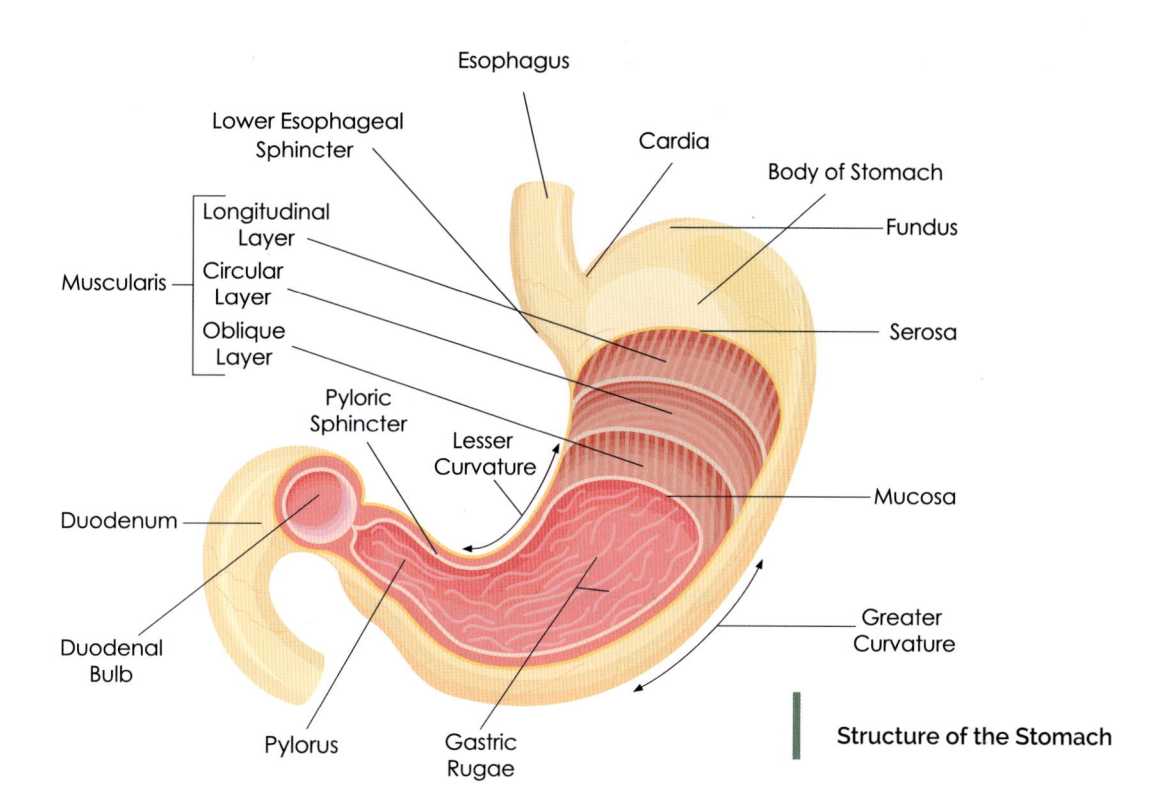

D. The Small Intestine

The **small intestine** is the largest digestive organ of the human intestinal tract, measuring between 18 and 23 feet in length! The great length of the small intestine is necessary to provide enough time and surface area for the necessary processing and absorption of nutrients. The lining of this long, hollow, muscular tube has thick, permanent **circular folds** throughout its length; each fold has thousands of small finger-like folds called **villi** on its surface.

Each of the **villi** folds is supplied with a tiny artery, vein, lymph vessel, and capillaries **to provide adequate oxygen and nutrients** to the intestinal lining, as well as **to absorb nutrients** for distribution throughout the rest of the body. **Peristalsis** (per-uh-**stal**-sis), the wave-like contractions of the intestines, continues the mixing of the chyme, or mass of partially digested food, with more digestive enzymes as the process moves along the length of the intestine.

The **duodenum** (dew·uh·**dee**·num) is the first of three segments of the small intestine extending directly from the stomach. The duodenum receives the partially digested food from the stomach; it also receives digestive enzymes and chemicals from the **pancreas** (**pan**·cree·us) and the **gallbladder**.

WORDS TO REMEMBER

enzymes: large biological molecules responsible for the thousands of metabolic processes that sustain life; catalysts that make a chemical reaction work faster, or better, without being used up themselves; accelerate or increase the rate of metabolic reactions, like the digestion of food

villi: folds in the small intestine that are supplied with a tiny artery, vein, lymph vessel, and capillaries to provide adequate oxygen and nutrients to the intestinal lining, as well as to absorb nutrients for distribution throughout the rest of the body

peristalsis: the wave-like contractions of the intestines that continue the mixing of the chyme, or mass of partially digested food, with more digestive enzymes as the process moves along the length of the intestine

duodenum: the first of three segments of the small intestine extending directly from the stomach; receives the partially digested food from the stomach

Life Science for Young Catholics

Structure of the Intestines

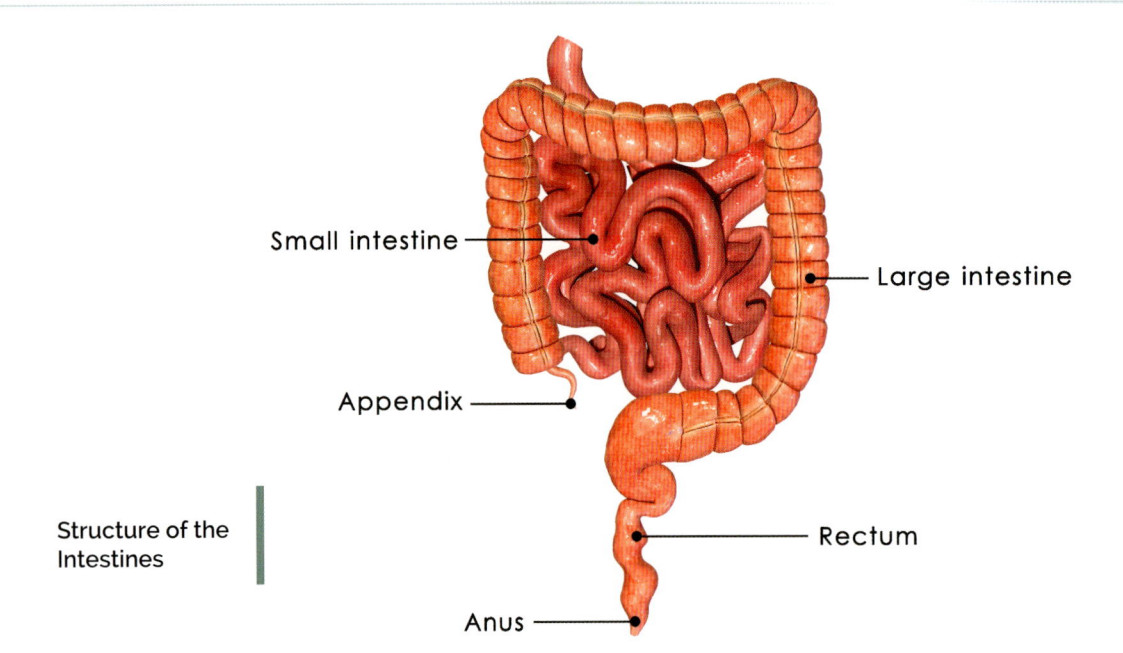

The pancreas is an elongated gland found beneath the stomach. The pancreas produces **pancreatic juice**, which is a mixture of water, salts, bicarbonate, and digestive enzymes.

Bicarbonate neutralizes the hydrochloric acid from the stomach to protect the lining of the intestine, while pancreatic enzymes complete much of the digestion.

The gallbladder is a pear-shaped, muscular-walled organ that stores and releases bile into the duodenum to aid in digestion by breaking down fats. Bile travels from the gallbladder to the small intestine in the **common bile duct**.

While most digestion is completed in the duodenum, most absorption of the nutrients occurs in the second portion of the small intestine. A smaller amount of absorption continues in the third part of the small intestine.

The third section of the small intestine is the only location in the digestive tract in which **vitamin B12** and the components of bile are absorbed into the blood circulation. A muscular valve is found at the end of the small intestine. This valve helps maintain the one way flow of digested materials from the small intestine into the large intestine.

E. The Large Intestine

The **large intestine** is so named because it is larger in diameter than the small intestine. However, it is much shorter. Typically, the adult large intestine is just under 5 feet long.

The large intestine is divided into several parts. The **colon** makes up most of the large intestine, about 4.25 of the 5-foot-long large intestine. The primary function of the entire colon is to absorb any remaining water and electrolytes. **Vitamin K**, **thiamine**, and **riboflavin** are essential vitamins that are absorbed in the colon.

The other function of the large intestine is to remove the undigested waste products from the body.

The final absorption of water and the compaction of waste into **feces** takes approximately 32 hours. When this is complete, the **rectum** stores the waste until it can be expelled from the body through the **anus**.

Section Review – 12.5 Structures and Functions of the Alimentary Canal

1. Identify the alimentary canal.
2. What is the structure and function of the esophagus?
3. What is the role of mucus in the stomach?
4. How long is the small intestine?
5. Why does the small intestine require that length?

CHAPTER 12: THE HUMAN DIGESTIVE SYSTEM

Structure of the Liver

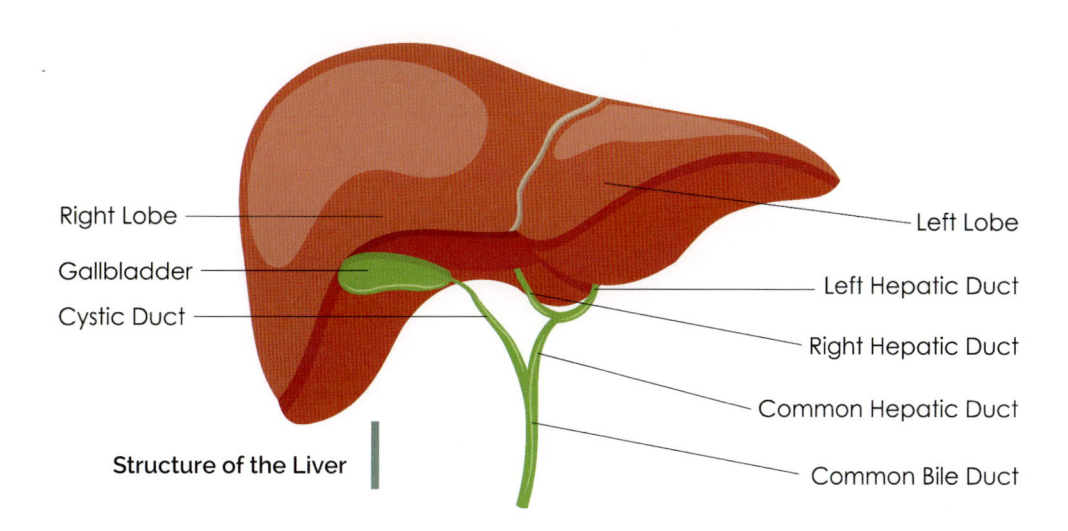

- Right Lobe
- Gallbladder
- Cystic Duct
- Left Lobe
- Left Hepatic Duct
- Right Hepatic Duct
- Common Hepatic Duct
- Common Bile Duct

12.6 Structure and Function of the Liver

The **liver** is an accessory organ or assisting organ for digestion, which means it helps or assists with digestion but is not part of the actual digestive tract, or alimentary canal. The salivary glands in the mouth, the liver, and the gallbladder, which is located right under the liver, are not parts of the digestive system, but they help with digestion.

The liver has many important functions that not only aid in digestion, but are vital to life. The liver has its own special circulation. Unlike any other organ in the human body, the liver has the **unique ability to regenerate itself** after severe injury or even after surgical removal of some parts. The liver is responsible for many essential functions related to digestion, to metabolism or bodily chemical processes, to immunity from disease, and to the storage of nutrients within the body.

A. Structure of the Liver

You probably did not realize that the liver is the **second largest organ** in the human body! The skin is the largest organ! The liver typically weighs about three pounds and is found in the abdominal cavity immediately **under the right side of the rib cage** and the diaphragm. The liver is a solid organ.

Rows of liver cells are arranged like spokes on a wheel into small lobules. A lobule is a hexagonally shaped group of liver cells arranged around a central vein. The lobules are the functional units of the liver. Groups of lobules are organized into the larger left and right lobes, and two smaller lobes.

The right and left lobes of the liver are separated by a ligament. The lobes are held together by a smooth fiber capsule to comprise the whole liver.

The gallbladder is located under one of the small lobes. The gallbladder stores the bile secreted by the liver.

WORDS TO REMEMBER

pancreas: an elongated gland beneath the stomach; produces pancreatic juice, a mixture of water, salts, bicarbonate, and digestive enzymes

gallbladder: a pear-shaped muscular-walled organ that stores and releases bile into the duodenum to aid in digestion by breaking down fats. Bile travels from the gallbladder to the small intestine in the common bile duct.

liver: a solid organ that assists in digestion. The liver is responsible for many essential functions related to digestion, to metabolism or bodily chemical processes, to immunity from disease, and to the storage of nutrients within the body.

Life Science for Young Catholics

B. Function of the Liver

Liver cells are responsible for performing all the functions of the liver: **synthesis**, **metabolism**, **detoxification**, **excretion**, and **storage**.

Synthesis is the production of bile. Bile is a mixture of water, bile salts, lipids, and **bilirubin** produced in the liver cells and transferred to the gallbladder through bile ducts for storage until needed for digestion.

Bilirubin is a pigment formed from the breakdown of hemoglobin from old red blood cells. This gives the bile its green color.

The liver cells produce many important proteins, including **albumin** and proteins necessary for proper blood clotting. Albumin is the protein primarily responsible for maintaining fluid balance inside and outside of cells.

Liver cells are responsible for many vital metabolic processes that support the rest of the body. These include the absorption and release of **glucose** into the blood to maintain a constant blood sugar level. The liver is also responsible for the production of **ATP**, the main source of energy at the level of the cell.

C. Portal Circulation

Because of its importance in the health and proper functioning of the human body, the liver has been created by God with a **unique** circulation system that receives blood from two sources. **Oxygenated blood** is carried to the liver, as to all organs, by the **arteries** which are supplied directly by the aorta from the heart.

However, the liver also receives all the **deoxygenated** blood which must be returned to the heart from the stomach, intestines, pancreas, and spleen before it returns to the heart. The word portal means entrance or gate. So before the oxygen-depleted blood from the digestive organs returns to the heart, it must go through the gate or portal of the liver **to remove toxins** that were absorbed from the digestive system, before the blood can be delivered back to the heart and then on to other tissues. This is called **portal circulation**.

After the toxins are removed from the blood, the liver returns the blood to the regular part of the circulatory system to go to the heart, and then to the lungs for more oxygen.

Portal circulation, therefore, ensures that the blood is detoxified by the liver before being re-distributed via the heart throughout the remainder of the body.

> ### Section Review – 12.6 Structure and Function of the Liver
>
> 1. Provide three main functions of the liver.
> 2. Describe the structure of the liver.
> 3. What is the functional unit of the liver?
> 4. What is unique about the liver's portal circulation?
> 5. What is the purpose of portal circulation?

12.7 Oxidation and Assimilation

Digested food supplies the body with energy and with the building blocks to form new cell structures as needed in repair and growth. Carbohydrates and fats are primarily used for energy production, whereas proteins are primarily used for repair and growth.

The digestive system converts all the ingested food into one of four types of organic molecules: **glucose**, **glycerol**, **fatty acids**, or **amino acids**. These organic molecules are absorbed into the circulatory system, processed at times by the liver, and distributed throughout the tissues of the entire body for use.

A. Oxidation

Oxidation is a vital process in which the body uses the digested nutrients. Oxidation is the chemical process by which oxygen is added to the nutrients to produce water, carbon dioxide, and energy in the form of heat. **Enzymes** in the body help these reactions to proceed at normal body temperature, normal body conditions, and in the presence of water.

Enzymes are large biological molecules responsible for the thousands of metabolic processes

CHAPTER 12: THE HUMAN DIGESTIVE SYSTEM

that sustain life. Enzymes are catalysts; they make a chemical reaction work faster, or better, without being used up themselves. Enzymes accelerate or increase the rate of metabolic reactions, like the digestion of food.

The carbon dioxide produced by oxidation is largely exhaled by the respiratory system; the water is used by the body. The heat produced by oxidation is important in the maintenance of a constant internal body temperature which, in turn, is required for the normal healthy functioning of all organ systems.

B. Assimilation

Assimilation is the process by which the digested food materials **become a part of the cells** in the human body. The food cells are assimilated into or become part of the body cells. **Fatty acids** and **glycerol** are processed for cell membranes. **Amino acids** are used in protein synthesis to build many hormones, enzymes, and tissues throughout the body. These processes are continually in action to keep the human body alive and healthy, and none could occur without a constant supply of nutrients from the digestive system.

> **Section Review –**
> **12.7 Oxidation and Assimilation**
>
> 1. Describe oxidation and its relationship to the digestive system.
> 2. What are enzymes?
> 3. Identify the role of assimilation.

12.8 Summary

Along with His words in the Bible permitting us to eat both plants and animals, God gave the human body the digestive system to do so properly. This digestive system is a marvel of design, to provide the simple nutrients needed by every cell in the human body, from the complex organic chemicals in plants and animals.

In Genesis 1:29, God gave mankind the plants to eat.

God also said: See, I give you every seed-bearing plant on all the Earth and every tree that has seed-bearing fruit on it to be your food; and to all the wild animals, all the birds of the air, and all the living creatures that crawl on the earth, I give all the green plants for food. (Genesis 1:29-30)

After the Flood, God gave Noah, and all men, permission to add animals to the human diet.

Then God blessed Noah and his sons, saying to them, "Be fruitful and increase in number and fill the earth. The fear and dread of you will fall upon all the beasts of the earth and all the birds of the air, upon every creature that moves along the ground, and upon all the fish of the sea; they are given into your hands. Everything that lives and moves will be food for you. Just as I gave you the green plants, I now give you everything. (Genesis 9:1-3)

> **WORDS TO REMEMBER**
>
> **bile:** a mixture of water, bile salts, lipids, and bilirubin produced in the liver cells and transferred to the gallbladder through bile ducts for storage until needed for digestion.
>
> **albumin:** the protein primarily responsible for maintaining fluid balance inside and outside of cells
>
> **bilirubin:** a pigment formed from the breakdown of hemoglobin from old red blood cells.
>
> **glucose:** a carbohydrate; the most important simple sugar in human metabolism.
>
> **glycerol:** a simple sugar-alcohol compound; a colorless, odorless liquid; soluble in water; a central component of triglycerides
>
> **assimilation:** the process by which digested food materials become a part of the cells in the human body
>
> **fatty acids:** the building blocks of the fat in food and in the body; fatty acid molecules are usually joined together in groups of three, forming a molecule called a triglyceride.

Life Science for Young Catholics

Chapter 12 Review

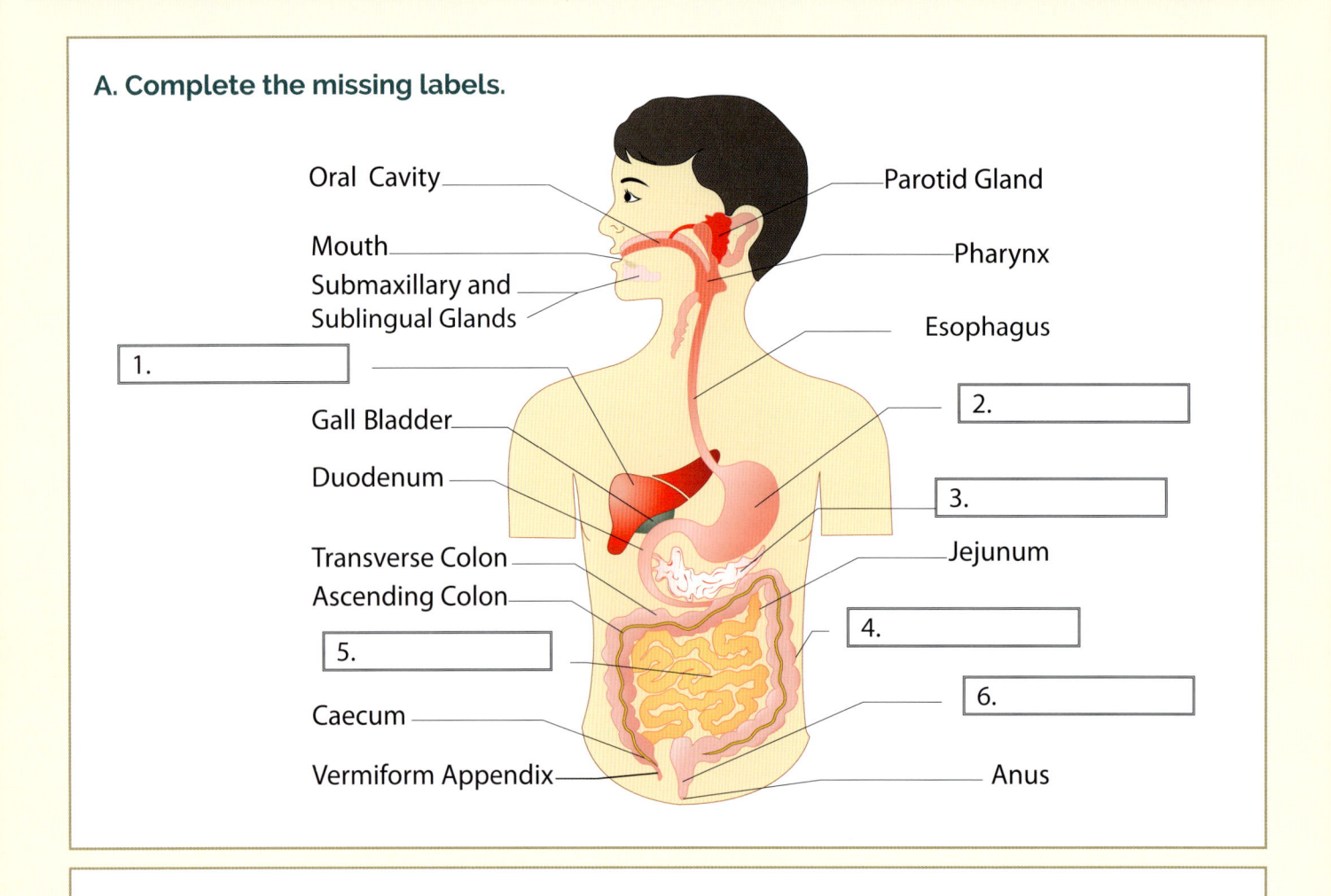

A. Complete the missing labels.

Oral Cavity
Mouth
Submaxillary and Sublingual Glands
1. _____
Gall Bladder
Duodenum
Transverse Colon
Ascending Colon
5. _____
Caecum
Vermiform Appendix

Parotid Gland
Pharynx
Esophagus
2. _____
3. _____
Jejunum
4. _____
6. _____
Anus

B. Answer the following questions.

1. Identify the alimentary canal. Include the organs and tissues that compose it.
2. Identify parts of the digestive system that are not part of the alimentary canal.
3. Describe the function and importance of both the large and small intestines.
4. Briefly distinguish between chemical and mechanical digestion.
5. How do blood vessels aid the digestive system?
6. How long is the small intestine?
7. Provide three main functions of the liver.
8. What is the functional unit of the liver?
9. Describe oxidation and its relationship to the digestive system.
10. What are enzymes?

Chapter 12: "Words to Remember" Crossword

ACROSS

3 the centermost part of each tooth
6 the largest component of the tooth, a hard bony-like tissue found beneath the enamel
7 produced by salivary glands in the mouth
8 the removal of waste products from the digestive tract
10 the process by which a substance, such as a hormone, chemical, or enzyme, is released from an organ or gland to perform a particular function
14 a thin layer of bony material that fixes teeth to the jaw
15 the protein primarily responsible for maintaining fluid balance inside and outside of cells
16 the wave-like contractions of the intestines that continue the mixing of the chime, or mass of partially digested food, with more digestive enzymes as the process moves along the length of the intestine
18 a pear-shaped muscular-walled organ that stores and releases bile into the duodenum to aid in digestion by breaking down fats
19 __ digestion is the breakdown of food particles by chemical means, through the action of enzymes, into simpler substances.

DOWN

1 __ juice is a thin, strong acid.
2 the principal protease found in gastric juice
3 an elongated gland found beneath the stomach
4 a pigment formed from the breakdown of hemoglobin from old red blood cells
5 Gut __ are symbiotic bacteria that break down some materials that the human digestive system alone cannot break down.
6 the first of three segments of the small intestine extending directly from the stomach
9 makes up the hard mineralized surface of teeth
11 accelerate or increase the rate of metabolic reactions, like the digestion of food
12 thick green fluid that is produced by the liver, stored in the gallbladder, and released into the small intestine
13 The __ canal is a long, hollow, twisted, and coiled tube extending from the mouth to the anus, or exit of waste from the body.
17 The __ intestine is the largest digestive organ of the human intestinal tract, measuring between 18 and 23 feet in length! Most of the digestive process occurs here.

Life Science for Young Catholics

13 THE HUMAN URINARY AND REPRODUCTIVE SYSTEMS

13.1 Introduction

13.2 Structures and Functions of the Urinary Tract

13.3 The Kidney: Structure and Functions
   A. Structure and Primary Function of the Kidney
   B. Other Functions of the Kidney

13.4 The Collecting System

13.5 Summary

13.6 Human Reproductive Systems

Chapter 13
The Human Urinary and Reproductive Systems

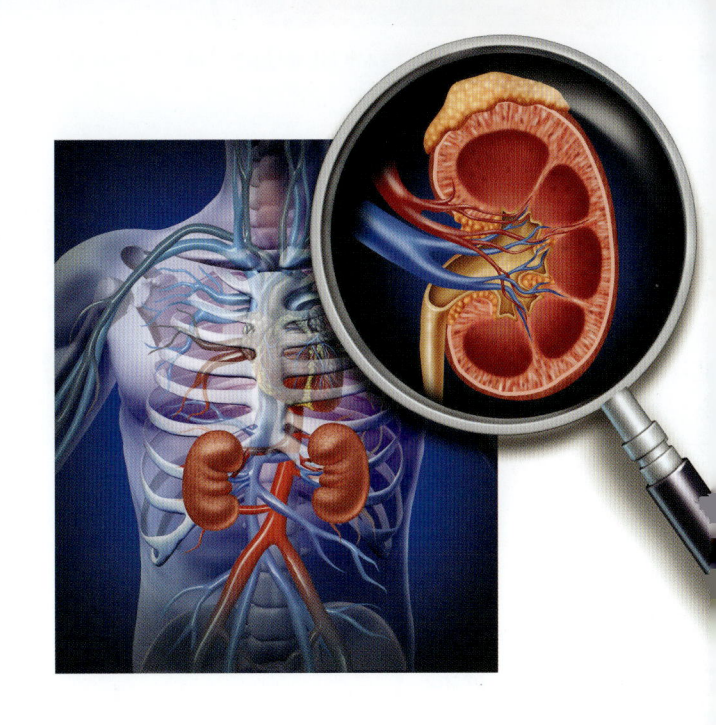

13.1 Introduction

The kidneys are an important part of the body's system that keeps our bodies free of harmful waste products. As confession helps us to keep our souls clean, the kidneys help us to keep our bodies clean on the inside. Let's now study the important kidneys and the urinary system of the body.

The urinary system removes wastes from the body. As with other organ systems, the urinary system does not operate independently, but it relies heavily on the circulatory, nervous, and endocrine systems for proper functioning. The other systems also depend on the urinary system to maintain the proper chemical balance in the body's cells.

In much of today's popular culture, the wonder and awe of God's creation has been lost. The urinary system is as amazing in its design as all other body systems. To think that an organ the size of a fist has the capacity to maintain the balance of fluids and chemicals for the entire body is truly amazing.

13.2 Structures and Functions of the Urinary Tract

The human body has been created with the gastrointestinal tract for eliminating solid digestive wastes, with the respiratory system for eliminating carbon dioxide, with the skin for dissipating excess heat from the body, and another extraordinary system for eliminating metabolic wastes from the blood: the urinary system.

The **urinary system** has been created to filter all the blood in the body and to remove metabolic wastes from it in a liquid form called **urine**. This system, however, is not simply a waste removal system, but a complex system that maintains the delicate balance of fluids and **electrolytes** throughout the body. Electrolytes are minerals in the blood and in other human body fluids that carry an electric charge.

Four organs comprise the urinary system: the kidneys, the ureters (*you-**ree**-ters*), the urinary (***your**-in-a-ree*) bladder, and the urethra (*you-**ree**-thruh*).

Like the other organ systems discussed thus far, the urinary system does not accomplish its functions independently. The nervous system not only provides input to the various organs of the urinary system, but the brain also receives information from the urinary system, which, in turn, has an impact on almost every other organ system in the human body.

The circulatory system is the system that is most closely connected to the urinary system. Not only does the kidney monitor blood volume, blood pressure, and to a large degree, blood content, but the kidney's structure contains millions of very tiny capillaries and arterioles necessary for the function of the kidneys.

Life Science for Young Catholics

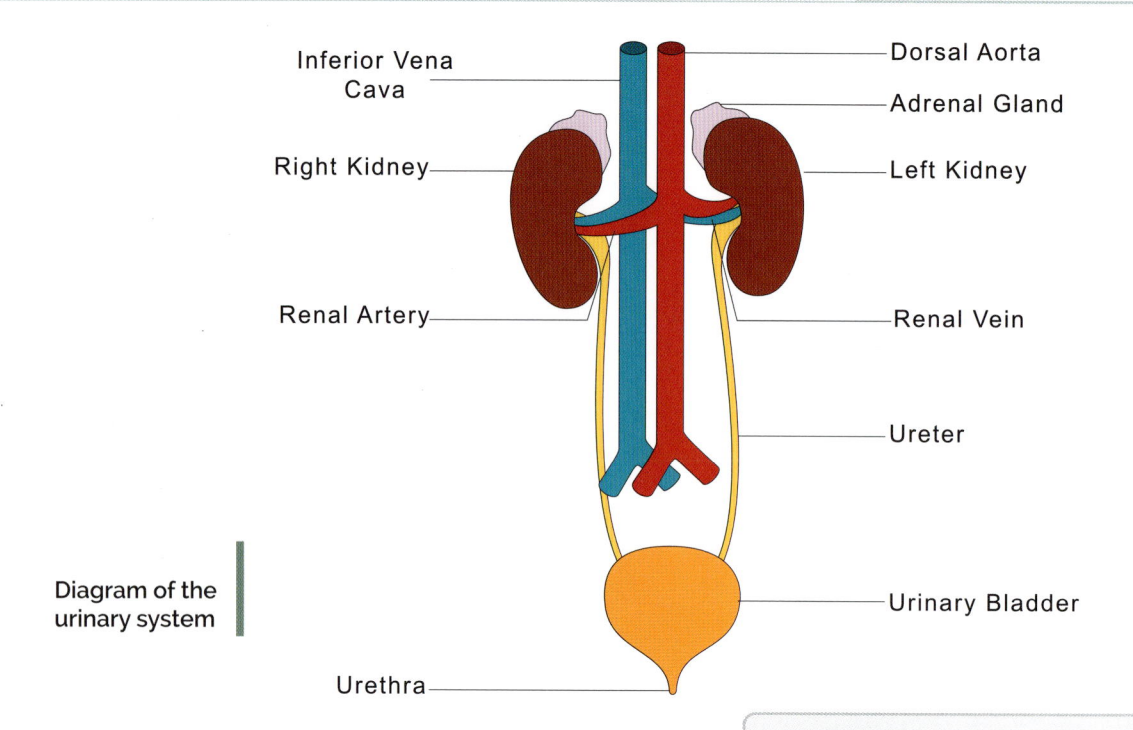

CHAPTER 13: THE HUMAN URINARY AND REPRODUCTIVE SYSTEMS

Diagram of the urinary system

Labels: Inferior Vena Cava, Right Kidney, Renal Artery, Urethra, Dorsal Aorta, Adrenal Gland, Left Kidney, Renal Vein, Ureter, Urinary Bladder

The endocrine system affects and is affected by the actions of the urinary system. The endocrine system monitors glands. Together with the circulation and other organ systems, the urinary system filters blood to remove wastes. It also maintains the balance of electrolytes (sodium and potassium, for example), as well as water, calcium, and acid/base levels in the blood and body tissues. In addition, the urinary system maintains a healthy blood pressure and ensures an adequate supply of red blood cells.

> **Section Review – 13.2 Structures and Functions of the Urinary Tract**
> 1. Which other system is the most directly related to the urinary system?
> 2. Describe the four specific functions of the urinary system.
> 3. List the four organs of the urinary system.
> 4. Briefly explain what electrolytes are.
> 5. Draw and label the organs of the human urinary system.

13.3 The Kidney: Structure and Functions

The most important and complex organ of the urinary system is the **kidney**. Two kidneys are located behind the abdominal cavity, behind the digestive organs against the muscles of the back, one on the right and one on the left. Each kidney is surrounded and protected by a layer of fatty tissue and a separate layer of fiber tissue. The ribs and the muscles of the back also protect the paired, bean-shaped kidneys.

The adrenal gland is not a part of the urinary system. However, one adrenal gland sits on top of each kidney. The adrenal glands secrete hormones that help the kidneys maintain fluid and electrolyte (salts and minerals) balance in the body.

A. Structure and Primary Function of the Kidney

As we look at the structure of a kidney, we see that each kidney is about the size of a fist and is divided into three major regions. The outermost region along the convex, or outwardly curved, side of the organ is known as the **renal cortex**. The middle region beneath the cortex is known as the **renal medulla**. The area at the concave, or inwardly curved, side of the kidney is known as the **renal pelvis**.

The **renal cortex** is the part of the kidney where the blood is filtered. The **renal medulla** is divided into tiny tubes or tubules that transport the filtered

Life Science for Young Catholics

CHAPTER 13: THE HUMAN URINARY AND REPRODUCTIVE SYSTEMS

liquid from the cortex to the **renal pelvis**, the enlarged upper end of the **ureter**.

The **ureter** is a thin, muscular tube through which urine is transported away from the kidney. Along with the **renal artery** and the **renal vein**, the ureter passes through an area known as the **renal hilum** (**high**-lum). Each kidney is immediately surrounded by a tough, fibrous **renal capsule** that provides a layer of protection.

As we look at the function of the kidney, we see that the **nephron** (**nef**-ron) is the basic functional unit of the kidney. Approximately one million nephrons are neatly and tightly packaged into each human kidney, along with millions of tiny networks of arterioles, venules, and capillaries. Each of the one million nephrons independently filters blood and produces urine. The nephron is a tubular structure made of two distinct parts: the **renal corpuscle** and the **renal tubule**.

The **renal corpuscle** is the site at which blood is filtered. The filtered liquid then passes through the **renal tubule** to collecting tubules. Electrolytes and water are re-absorbed into the cells of the tubules and then pass into the blood by way of capillaries.

Re-absorption occurs along the entire length of the renal tubule. **Collecting tubules** from nearby nephrons join to form larger **collecting ducts**, which carry the filtered **urine** to the **renal pelvis**. The renal pelvis acts like a funnel to bring urine into the ureter.

Each nephron (which filters blood and produces urine) is approximately 2.2 inches long, and is situated in such a way that part of its structure is within the cortex and part is within the medulla. With 2.2 inches of tubule in each nephron, 1 million nephrons in each kidney, and two kidneys in each body, there are about 69.4 miles of renal tubules packaged into two fist-sized organs!

The blood supply of the kidney is essential to the **kidney's filtering function**. To filter the wastes from the blood efficiently, the kidney has been created with a unique system of arterioles and capillaries.

Oxygenated blood enters the kidney through the **renal artery**. The arteries branch as they travel through the structure of the kidneys.

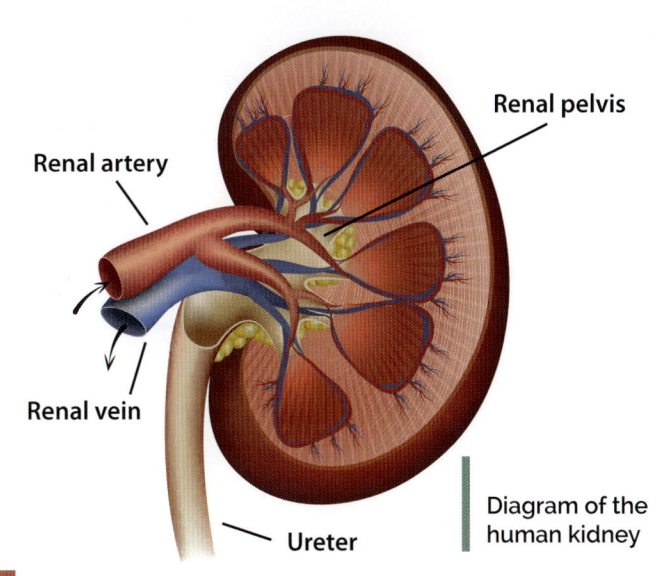

Diagram of the human kidney

WORDS TO REMEMBER

urinary system: filters all the blood in the body by removing metabolic wastes from it; maintains the delicate balance of fluids and electrolytes

urine: a liquid that consists of the waste products filtered out of the blood

kidneys: the most important and complex organs of the urinary system; remove wastes from the blood; through re-absorption, put water and electrolytes back into the blood; monitor and help control blood pressure.

renal cortex: the part of the kidney where the blood is filtered

renal medulla: consists of tiny tubes or tubules that transport the filtered liquid from the renal cortex to the renal pelvis

renal pelvis: acts like a funnel to bring urine into the ureter

ureter: a thin, muscular tube through which urine is transported away from the kidney

nephron: the basic functional unit of the kidney; a tubular structure made of two distinct parts: the renal corpuscle and the renal tubule

renal corpuscle: the site at which blood is filtered

renal capsule: a tough, fibrous layer surrounding the kidney and covered in a thick layer of adipose tissue (fat); provides a layer of protection for the kidney.

Life Science for Young Catholics

Functions of the Kidney

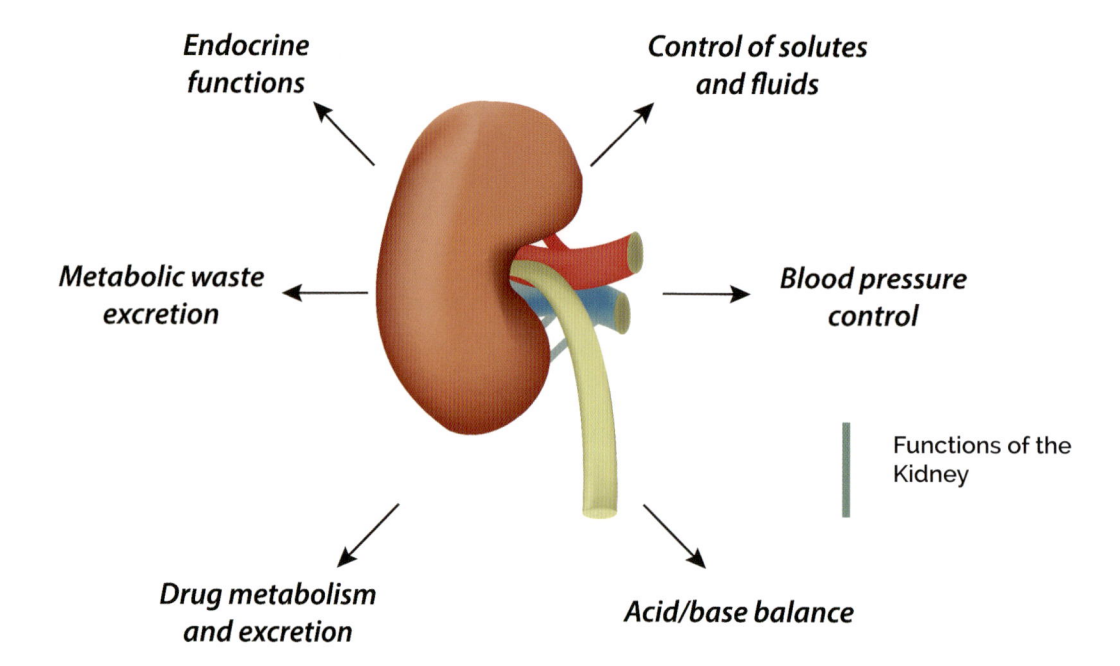

- Endocrine functions
- Control of solutes and fluids
- Metabolic waste excretion
- Blood pressure control
- Drug metabolism and excretion
- Acid/base balance

From the capillaries, the blood enters the venous system, or blood vessels returning to the heart.

The **urine**, which consists of the waste products filtered out of the blood, passes through the collecting tubules to be temporarily stored in the bladder.

B. Other Functions of the Kidney

Through filtration, the kidneys remove wastes from the blood. Through re-absorption, the kidneys put water and **electrolytes** back into the blood.

Most of the waste is a nitrogen-based compound called **urea**. Urea is generated from the breakdown of the amino acids in proteins. However, the kidneys also filter other substances from the blood, including electrolytes, such as potassium, sodium, and chloride.

The kidney monitors the concentrations of electrolytes in the blood. It adjusts the amount of each electrolyte that is excreted in the urine by re-absorbing fresh electrolytes back into the circulatory system.

For example, if a person has too much potassium in his blood, the kidneys detect this and increase the amount of potassium lost in the urine. Similarly, if the kidneys detect a low concentration of potassium in the blood, they reduce the amount of potassium lost in the urine.

In much the same way, the kidneys help control the acidity of the blood.

The kidneys monitor and help control **blood pressure**. Blood pressure is determined, largely, by the amount of fluid circulating through the blood vessels. The kidneys are able to monitor the blood pressure in a collection of special cells.

If the pressure of the flow of blood is a little high, the kidneys respond by excreting more water and salt into the urine. Conversely, if the blood pressure is a little low, the kidneys are able to decrease the filtration of water, and to increase the re-absorption of water as it passes through the tubules.

In blood pressure regulation, the kidneys work as an endocrine gland with the endocrine system. An endocrine gland is a gland that secretes its products directly into the blood stream where the products travel to other organs to affect a change.

Likewise, the kidneys work with several other parts of the human body. They work with the endocrine glands, and the **parathyroid** (*par-uh-thigh*-roid) **glands**, the skin, the gastrointestinal tract, and the bones. The kidneys also work to maintain the proper amount of calcium in the blood.

Besides monitoring blood pressure and the volume of electrolytes (potassium, sodium, and chloride) in the body, the kidneys also monitor

CHAPTER 13: THE HUMAN URINARY AND REPRODUCTIVE SYSTEMS

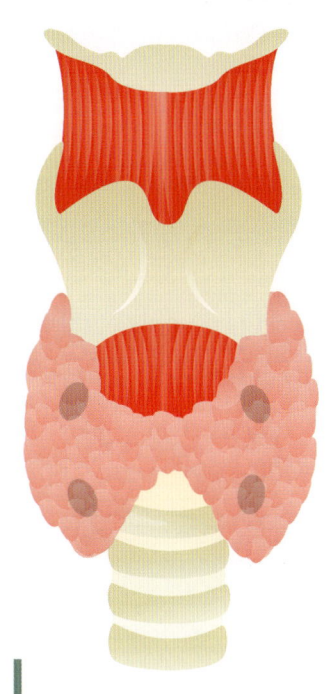

Diagram of the parathyroid gland

the concentration of oxygen in the blood. If blood oxygen levels are low, the bone marrow is stimulated to increase production of red blood cells. By increasing the red blood cells, the oxygen-carrying capacity of the blood is increased, and oxygen levels in the blood are maintained at a healthy level.

> **Section Review — 13.3 The Kidney: Structure and Primary Function**
>
> 1. Identify the most complex organ of the urinary system.
> 2. Identify three major regions of the kidney.
> 3. What is the relationship of the renal hilum to the renal artery, renal vein, and ureter?
> 4. Identify and describe the functional unit of the kidney.
> 5. What is the function of the renal corpuscle?
> 6. Identify re-absorption. Where does re-absorption occur?
> 7. How do the kidneys affect blood pressure?
> 8. Name three electrolytes that are monitored by the kidneys.
> 9. What is the function of the renal pelvis?
> 10. What is the purpose of the filtration function of the kidney?
> 11. Draw and label the main parts of the human kidney.

13.4 The Collecting System

The collecting system is the plumbing of the urinary system. It consists of two **ureters**, one **urinary bladder**, and one **urethra**.

One ureter exits from the renal pelvis of each kidney. The ureter is a slender but muscular tube about 10-12 inches long that acts as an exit for urine to leave the kidney. Urine moves through the ureter by the force of gravity, as well as by waves of muscle contraction. Each ureter ends within the muscular wall of the urinary bladder.

WORDS TO REMEMBER

renal artery: an artery that branches off the abdominal aorta to supply the kidney with blood

urinary bladder: a hollow muscular organ that acts as a reservoir to store urine until it is released from the body

urethra: the tube at the lower end of the bladder. When the bladder is full, urine passes through the urethra and finally out of the body.

Life Science for Young Catholics

The smooth muscle in the bladder wall, and the angle at which the ureter enters the bladder, prevent urine from running back up into the ureter. The urinary bladder is a hollow muscular organ that acts as a reservoir to store urine until it is released from the body. The bladder is made of very elastic tissue and smooth muscle that expand to hold up to a pint of urine. Once the bladder is distended to near its maximum capacity, nerves are activated to signal the need to empty the bladder.

The urethra is the tube at the lower end of the bladder. When the bladder is full, urine passes through the urethra and finally out of the body.

> **Section Review — 13.4 The Collecting System**
>
> 1. What is the purpose of the collecting system of the urinary system?
> 2. Identify the organs of the collecting system.
> 3. Briefly describe the ureters.
> 4. What is the purpose of the bladder?
> 5. Briefly describe the urethra.
> 6. Draw and label the organs of the collecting system.

13.5 Summary

The kidneys function to purify the blood. The Biblical view of the blood is that the blood contains the life of the person. In Jeremiah 17:10, we read, "I the Lord search the heart and test the mind [lit., "kidneys" in Hebrew], to give every man according to his ways, according to the fruit of his deeds." There are other Biblical references to God's examining the kidneys to evaluate the soul of a person.

This is fitting: since the kidneys purify the blood, and the blood is the life of the person, God would examine the kidneys to see if they are purifying the life of that person. This is an example of using physical processes to explain spiritual realities.

The kidneys not only purify the blood by removing wastes, but also control the body's fluid balance and regulate the balance of electrolytes to keep all of the body's organs functioning properly.

13.6 Human Reproductive Systems

Man and woman were created for each other. They were created to be loving, supporting, and nurturing to each other, as God is with them. Together, man and woman were created in such a way as to continue the human race, and to "fill the earth," according to God's command in Genesis 1.

> God created mankind in his image; in the image of God he created them; male and female He created them. God blessed them and God said to them: Be fertile and multiply; fill the earth and subdue it. (Genesis 1:27-28)

In the document *Donum Vitae* ("The Gift of Life"), the Church teaches that, like Jesus Christ, the Son of God, all humans are "begotten, not made." While men and women are called to share in God's creation by "begetting" a child, or bringing a child into life, they do not create life. Only God creates life.

God has endowed the human race with the means to **participate** in the creation of new life, but all life ultimately comes from Him. While it is the bodily material from the mother and father that join at the moment of conception and develop into a new human being, it is God Who creates the unique and individual soul that animates the physical body and gives it life. Every human life is a gift from God, and as a gift from God, every human life is sacred from the moment of conception until the moment of death.

The Church teaches that husband and wife "procreate" children through their intimate act of love. This could be termed "co-create" since the human parents can produce a new human body. God cooperates with the husband and wife by creating the new human soul that He designs just for that particular body and that particular family.

God, in His justice and mercy, gives each new child the best possible chance to go to Heaven, through the parents, the time in history, and the location on Earth that He chooses. We must all thank God for our parents, and for all of the blessings of life that He provides each of us through His Diving Providence.

The male and female reproductive systems were created in such a way that each performs a complementary function to the other in the production of new offspring. The female reproductive organs are created to ensure that a young girl matures into a woman with reproductive abilities, to procreate human babies with immortal souls, and to provide a nurturing environment in which the children can grow into holy people of God. Likewise, the organs of the male reproductive system are made to ensure that a young boy matures into a man with reproductive abilities so that new life may begin, for the glory of God.

In his Apostolic Exhortation *Familiaris Consortio*, Pope John Paul II said that the education about human reproduction "is a basic right and duty of parents, [which] must always be carried out under their attentive guidance." (Paragraph 37)

The Catholic Church's traditional teaching about reproductive education, especially as formulated by Popes Pius XI and Pius XII, is that it should not be primarily a matter of giving explicit "information" at all, but rather of inculcating modesty, purity, chastity, and morality, a matter of teaching the Sixth and Ninth Commandments. Moreover, it should be primarily a matter for the parents to impart privately in the home, not something to be discussed in mixed classrooms of boys and girls at various stages of life.

Based on these teachings of the Catholic Church, the specific biology of the human reproductive systems will not be covered in this course. Fathers are urged to review these materials with their sons as each son matures and is ready for this information in the judgment of his parents. Mothers are urged to cover human reproduction with their daughters, as each one matures and is ready to understand this information in the judgment of the parents.

CHAPTER 13: THE HUMAN URINARY AND REPRODUCTIVE SYSTEMS

Chapter 13 Review

A. Complete the missing labels.

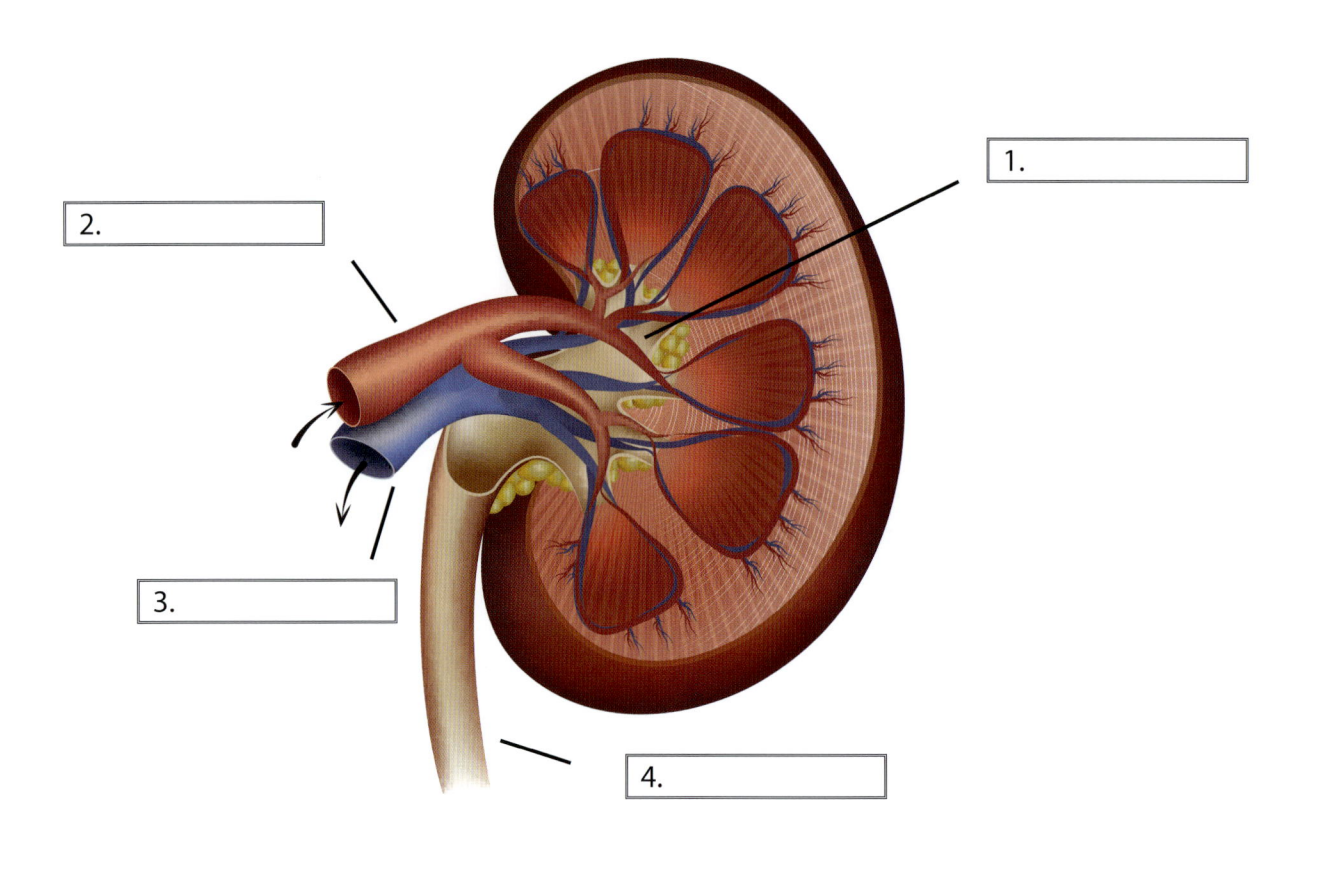

1.
2.
3.
4.

B. Answer the following questions.

1. Name two main functions of the urinary system.
2. Identify three other systems that coordinate with the urinary system.
3. Describe the four specific functions of the urinary system.
4. Identify the four organs of the urinary system.
5. Identify three major regions of the kidney.
6. Identify and describe the functional unit of the kidney.
7. What is the function of the renal corpuscle?
8. What is urea?
9. How do the kidneys affect blood pressure?
10. What is the function of the renal pelvis?
11. What is the purpose of the collecting system of the urinary system?
12. Identify the organs of the collecting system.
13. Briefly describe the ureters.
14. What is the purpose of the bladder?
15. Briefly describe the urethra.

Life Science for Young Catholics

Chapter 13: "Words to Remember" Crossword

ACROSS

2. a liquid that consists of the waste products filtered out of the blood
3. The renal ___ acts like a funnel to bring urine into the ureter.
5. the basic functional unit of the kidney
6. The renal ___ is the part of the kidney where the blood is filtered.
7. The renal ___ is the site at which blood is filtered.
9. The urinary ___ is a hollow muscular organ that acts as a reservoir to store urine until it is released from the body.
10. a thin muscular tube through which urine is transported away from the kidney
11. The ___ system filters all the blood in the body and removes metabolic wastes from it, and maintains the delicate balance of fluids and electrolytes.

DOWN

1. the most important and most complex organ of the urinary system. It remove wastes from the blood.
2. the tube at the lower end of the bladder
4. The renal ___ consists of tiny tubes or tubules that transport the filtered liquid from the renal cortex to the renal pelvis.
7. The renal ___ is a tough fibrous layer surrounding the kidney and covered in a thick layer of adipose tissue (fat). It provides a layer of protection for the kidney.
8. The renal ___ is an artery that has branched off of the abdominal aorta to supply the kidney with blood.

14 THE HUMAN IMMUNE SYSTEM

14.1 Introduction

14.2 Defense Mechanisms

14.3 The Immune System
    A. Leukocytes – White Blood Cells
        1. White Cells of the Blood
        2. White Cells of the Lymph System
            a. T-cells
            b. B-cells
            c. Natural Killer cells
    B. The Lymph System
        1. Lymph
        2. Lymph Vessels
        3. Lymph Nodules
        4. Lymph Nodes
    C. Other Lymph Organs

14.4 Allergies

14.5 Illness and the Goodness of God

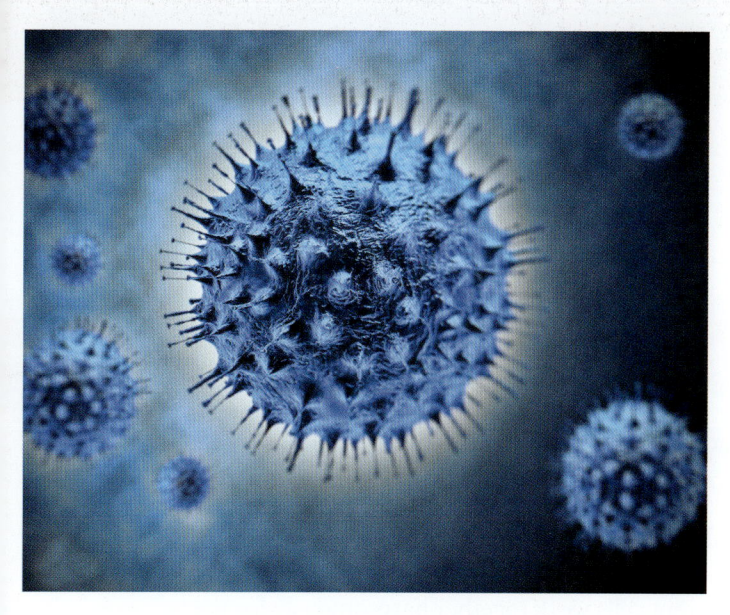

Chapter 14

The Human Immune System

14.1 Introduction

Do you remember the Gospel story of Our Lord curing the mother-in-law of St. Peter (Luke 4:38-40)? In that story, she had a fever, and Jesus cured her, and she immediately got up and started to wait on St. Peter and his guests. After healing St. Peter's mother-in-law, Our Lord cured many others in that town.

Have you heard about St. John Vianney, the Curé of Ars? He is the patron saint of parish priests. He was a friend of Miss Pauline Jaricot. In 1835, Miss Jaricot was publicly cured of an extremely serious heart condition by the newly discovered relics of a young woman called Philomena. Miss Jaricot's cure would lead to the canonization of Philomena, who became St. Philomena.

When God wants us to recognize a saint, He will perform miracles like the cure of Pauline Jaricot. However, God does not miraculously cure everyone. Instead, He has provided our bodies with marvelous systems to fight disease and injury. He did this to keep us healthy so that we can live on this Earth to grow as Jesus did, in wisdom, age, and grace.

14.2 Defense Mechanisms

God created the human body with the remarkable ability to repair, heal, and protect itself from harmful agents in the environment. Each organ system has some unique, and some shared, characteristics and mechanisms to protect the body.

For example, the structure of the skin provides a physical barrier to external attacks. The skin is covered with hairs to trap and remove foreign materials that may cause injury to the skin itself, to the eyes, and to the body as a whole.

Likewise, the digestive system produces mucus and hydrochloric acid, both of which prevent injury to the lining of the digestive system and prevent harmful microorganisms from entering the body.

The respiratory system, too, has its mechanisms to protect itself and the rest of the body from potentially dangerous invaders. Mucus and cilia trap and remove particles throughout the respiratory system; coughs and sneezes remove those that have made it past the cilia.

Each of the major organ systems of the human body has been designed by God to provide a line of defense against harmful agents from the environment. Each major organ system of the human body, then, provides some form of **immunity**. Immunity is the body's ability to prevent or resist **infection** or **illness** caused by a **germ**.

These defense mechanisms, though, are not the only protectors of the human body. God, in

CHAPTER 14: THE HUMAN IMMUNE SYSTEM

His infinite wisdom, created a special system, the **immune system**, whose only function is to protect the body and rid it of germs. This system, however, is not restricted to one area. Instead, it is located throughout the entire body, making it most efficient at detecting germs wherever they may be.

> **Section Review – 14.2 Defense Mechanisms**
>
> Identify features in the body's organ systems (skin, digestive, and respiratory) that act as defense mechanisms for the body.

14.3 The Immune System

The **immune system** is composed of the following: **leukocytes** (*lu-co-sites*) or **white blood cells**, the **lymph system**, the **thymus gland**, the **spleen**, and other specialized tissues.

The immune system is the body's strongest **defense** against germs and parasites, including viruses, bacteria, protists, and fungi. (Recall that parasites are organisms that live off of, and sometimes harm, a host organism). The immune system also rids the body of abnormal, damaged, and dead cells. To do so, the immune system must be able to distinguish such unwanted cells from the body's own normal cells. This remarkable task is accomplished by very specialized immune system cells, along with very complex proteins, which no one could have created except the Almighty God Himself.

A. Leukocytes – White Blood Cells

The name "leukocyte" comes from Greek word roots, *leukos,* which means white, and *kytos,* which means cell. Leukocytes are simply white blood cells.

The **leukocytes** are made in the **bone marrow**, the soft tissue inside bones. They are then stored in the blood and lymph tissues. Leukocytes make up about 1% of the blood volume in the human body.

Leukocytes are the immune cells. These white blood cells are the agents, like police agents, of the immune system. These white blood cells locate and destroy enemy germs and prevent illness. When you start to feel sick, and then feel better the next day, you should offer a prayer of thanks to God for giving you such a great immune system to protect you, to help your body automatically fight off germs and diseases.

There are several types of white blood cells or leukocytes. Each type of cell has a unique and specific function, but like a well-trained orchestra, all the different cells work together harmoniously for the overall health of the whole body.

There are special white cells in the blood and other special white cells in the lymph system, which are both part of the immune system.

1. **White Cells of the Blood**

There are two types of white cells in the blood. One type is a **phagocyte** (*fag-o-site*) or "cell-eating" white blood cell. "Phago" is a form of the Greek word that means "to eat," and "cyte" means cell. So a phagocyte is a "cell-eater."

Phagocytes, or cell-eating white cells, find cells, like germs, that do not belong in the human body. The phagocyte cell-eater surrounds the germ cell and "eats" it, thus destroying it.

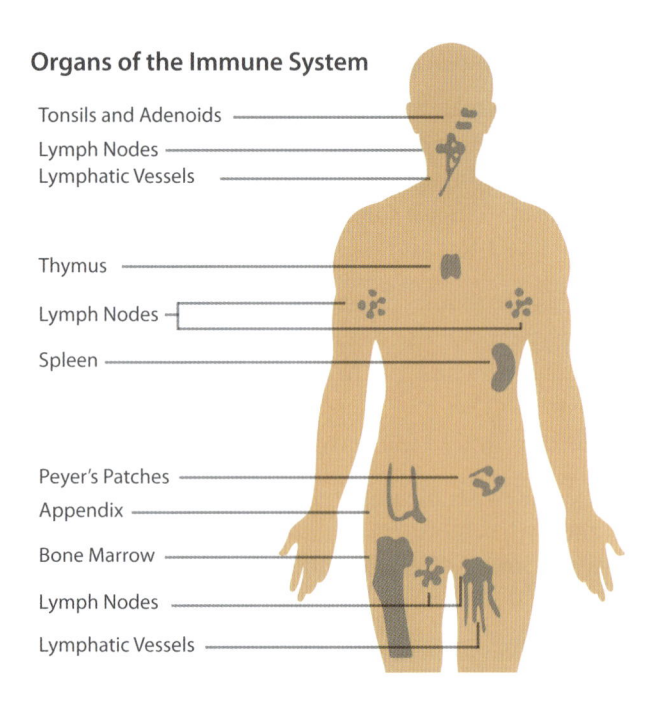

Organs of the Immune System

- Tonsils and Adenoids
- Lymph Nodes
- Lymphatic Vessels
- Thymus
- Lymph Nodes
- Spleen
- Peyer's Patches
- Appendix
- Bone Marrow
- Lymph Nodes
- Lymphatic Vessels

CHAPTER 14: THE HUMAN IMMUNE SYSTEM

Another type of white cell in the blood is the **granulocyte** (*gran*-u-lo-site), or **granular white cells,** which have tiny granules, or grains.

Believe it or not, some granular white blood cells have **red** granules which target parasites in the blood, that is, they eat and destroy parasites.

Other granular white blood cells have dark **blue** granules which attack foreign substances, like pollen. During their attack on foreign substances, these cells are responsible for the signs and symptoms of inflammation. Inflammation is the development of redness, heat, swelling, and pain at the site of an injury or infection. The signs of inflammation during the attack are caused by **histamine** found in the blue granule cells. The histamine is used as a weapon to fight the foreign substances.

When **histamine** is released from the blue granules, it causes the blood vessels in the immediate area to dilate. The dilated blood vessels cause blood flow to increase in the area which, in turn, increases the temperature of the tissue involved. Heat and increased blood flow, then, can cause leaking of fluid into the nearby tissues from the capillaries. This results in swelling. The heat and swelling, together with other chemicals in the tissues, cause pain. While the pain is uncomfortable, the result of inflammation is that large numbers of white blood cells are delivered to help control the infection in the area invaded by the germ.

2. White Cells of the Lymph System

T-cells, **B-cells**, and **natural killer cells** are **white lymph cells**, that is, cells of the lymph system. White blood cells live alone, not together in an organ, such as the liver. However, there are enough of these kinds of cells in the blood that, if they were grouped together, they would form an organ the size of the liver.

   a. T-cells

T-cells directly kill germ-infected cells. The "T" in T-cells stands for the thymus gland, where the T-cells are generated and "trained."

As unwanted foreign cells travel through the blood stream, some are "captured" by the thymus gland. The foreign cells have antigens on their surfaces. An antigen is a unique protein on the surface of a cell that identifies that cell, like a name tag.

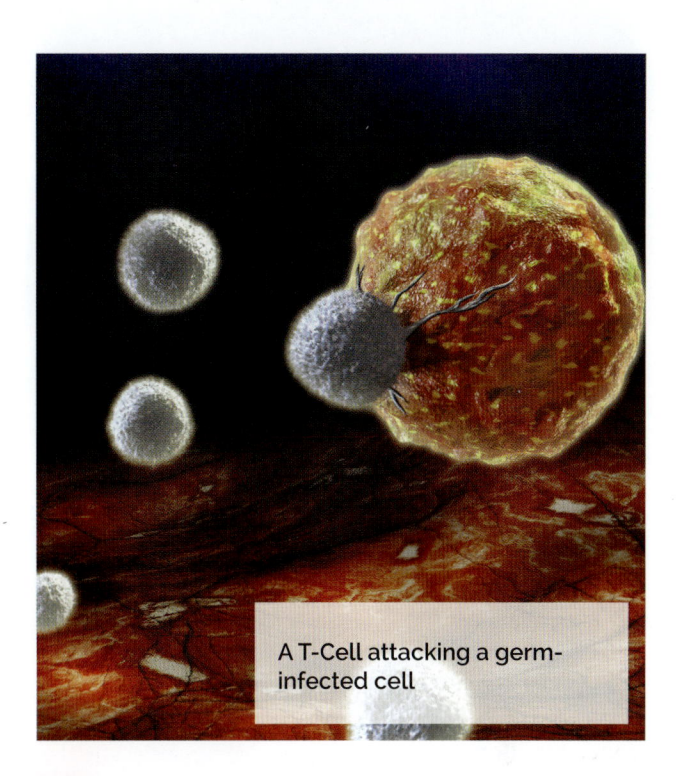

A T-Cell attacking a germ-infected cell

WORDS TO REMEMBER

immunity: the body's ability to prevent or resist infection or illness caused by germs

immune system: has the function to protect the body and rid it of germs; composed of leukocytes or white blood cells, the lymph system, the thymus gland, the spleen, and other specialized tissues

leukocytes: white blood cells which locate and destroy enemy germs and prevent illness

lymph system: the system within the immune system that absorbs fluid from the body's tissues and returns it into circulation

thymus gland: located just in front of the heart, develops T-cells and stores them for when they are needed

phagocyte: "cell-eating" white blood cell; surrounds the germ cell and "eats" it, thus destroying it

granulocytes: white cells which have tiny granules, or grains

histamine: used as a weapon to fight foreign substances; causes the blood vessels in the immediate area to dilate

Life Science for Young Catholics

T-cells stay in the thymus for their "schooling." In the thymus gland, the T-cells come in contact with antigens from foreign cells. There the T-cell will "learn" the antigens of foreign cells and develop a "memory" of these antigens. When the T-cell has learned its "lessons," it "graduates," leaving the thymus and re-entering the blood stream and body tissues. If and when it encounters a cell with one of those antigens, it attacks the foreign cells.

Basically, once the body's T-cells have fought off a disease, they learn the antigens associated with that disease and will attack those disease cells. This is God's way of providing the body with a built-in defense system if the same germs or disease strike again!

b. B-cells

B-cells are similar to T-cells, but these B-cells are made in the bone marrow. The "B" in B-cell stands for "**b**one marrow."

B-cells also learn about the antigens of foreign cells and attack cells with the antigens they recognize. B-cells produce **antibodies** to destroy the foreign cells. Antibodies are complex molecules that attach to infected cells in order to kill the germs.

Note: B-cells work within the blood stream, while T-cells work more inside the tissues.

c. Natural Killer cells

Natural killer cells kill abnormal cells. Natural killer cells are **nonspecific**. This means that they do not require activation, that is, needing to "learn" about specific foreign cells. Natural killer cells do not have memory, but are active against many different virus-infected cells, as well as abnormal or diseased cells.

Natural killer cells are the body's major defense against all types of cancer cells. Cancer is the term used to describe a large group of diseases. These diseases develop when cells from a certain part of the body or organ keep dividing and increasing without control, and even invade other tissues. Cancer can begin in any tissue or organ of the body. The type of cancer is usually named for the tissue in which the cancer began. For example, cancer that begins in the lung is referred to as lung cancer.

Natural killer cells release chemical "messengers" that attract T-cells and B-cells to come to the area to help destroy the abnormal cells. Remarkably, natural killer cells are able to distinguish between normal and abnormal body cells, and avoid disturbing the normal cells nearby.

The amazing immune system gives us an idea of the God-given working of the human body, which could exist only because of the great love and perfect intellect of our loving God. We should pray for those suffering from diseases. Many saints who have suffered from specific diseases are often called upon to help the suffering person recover quickly.

Types of White Blood Cells

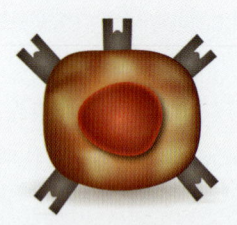

T-Cell
T-Cells attack invaders **inside** the cells.

B-Cell
B-Cells attack invaders **outside** the cells.

Natural killer
NK Cells require no activation and are the major defense against cancer.

CHAPTER 14: THE HUMAN IMMUNE SYSTEM

B. The Lymph System

The cells of the immune system work <u>within tissues</u> to destroy germs. In addition, the immune system is also responsible for destroying germs in the fluid <u>between tissues</u>, or in the **extracellular** fluid, that is, <u>in the fluid outside the cells</u>. This is the fluid found outside of the cells, tissues, and circulatory system. God has provided a remarkable system within a system that provides immune oversight to the fluid outside the cells.

The **lymph** system is the system within the immune system that absorbs fluid from the body's tissues and returns it into circulation. In doing so, the lymph system circulates the lymph fluid through a series of **nodes** (knot-shaped tissues) where <u>the lymph fluid</u> is filtered, and where germs, damaged cells, and abnormal cells are removed from the body.

1. Lymph

Lymph is a clear to white, somewhat milky liquid that contains extracellular (out of a cell) fluid called plasma, which has left the circulatory system by way of capillaries in the tissues. These capillaries collect the plasma and empty it into larger lymph vessels.

2. Lymph Vessels

Lymph vessels are <u>similar to veins</u>. Like veins, lymph vessels have valves that prevent the lymph from flowing back toward the tissues. Also, like blood returning to the heart, the lymph is pushed through its vessels by the contraction of the surrounding muscles.

The lymph vessels empty lymph into two ducts. Tissue fluid, collected from the right arm and from the right side of the head, neck, and chest cavity, empties into the right lymph duct. Tissue fluid collected from both legs, the abdomen, the left arm, and the left side of the head, neck, and chest cavity, empties into the thoracic (thor-**as**-ick) duct.

3. Lymph Nodules

Lymph nodules are small <u>collections of lymph tissue</u>, usually <u>located in the loose connective tissue beneath wet membranes, as in the digestive system, respiratory system, and urinary bladder</u>. Lymph nodules are located in areas of exposure to germs, and the nodules contribute to the defense against germs. The nodule differs from a **lymph node** in that the nodule is much smaller than the node and does not have a well-defined connective-tissue capsule as a boundary. The lymph nodule also does not function as a filter, because it is not located along a lymph vessel.

Several groups of lymph nodules are located in the body outside of the lymph circulation. Many lymph nodules are <u>located in the linings of the mouth</u> and in the small intestine to protect the body from germs that may enter through the mouth, the nose, or the digestive tract.

WORDS TO REMEMBER

T-Cells: directly kill germ-infected cells; T stands for the thymus gland where T-cells are generated and "trained," T-cells work inside tissues

B-Cells: directly kill germ-infected cells; made in the bone marrow; B stands for "bone marrow"; B-cells work within the blood stream

antibodies: destroy foreign cells; complex molecules that attach to infected cells in order to kill germs

natural killer cells: kill abnormal cells; nonspecific; active against many different virus-infected cells, as well as abnormal or diseased cells; the body's major defense against cancer cells

extracellular fluid: fluid outside the cells

lymph fluid: a clear to white, somewhat milky liquid that contains extracellular fluid called plasma, which has left the circulatory system through capillaries in the tissues

lymph vessels: similar to veins; have valves that prevent the lymph fluid from flowing back towards the tissues; empty lymph fluid into two lymph ducts

lymph nodules: small collections of lymph tissue, usually located in the loose connective tissue beneath wet membranes, as in the digestive system, respiratory system, and urinary bladder

Life Science for Young Catholics

The tonsils are actually lymph nodules in the throat. God designed our five tonsils to ward off germs that enter through the mouth. There are two palatine tonsils, two lingual tonsils, and one adenoid, or pharyngeal, tonsil.

4. Lymph Nodes

As the lymph returns from the tissues to the circulatory system, it is filtered through approximately 600-700 lymph nodes. **Lymph nodes** are made up of grouped lymph nodules that are held together by connective tissue. These lymph nodules are surrounded and held together by a tough fibrous capsule, to define the lymph node.

Lymph nodes are distributed throughout the body, but are particularly numerous in the underarm and groin. Lymph enters a node through lymph vessels. As the lymph passes through these vessels, the immune cells remove and destroy several substances, namely germs, damaged cells, abnormal cells, and other debris that gets caught in the surrounding connective tissue. The filtered lymph leaves the node through lymph vessels, and thus the clean lymph continues its way back to the blood stream free of harmful agents.

C. Other Lymph Organs

The **appendix** functions as a lymph organ in adults. It assists with the maturing of B-cells, that is, immune cells made in bone marrow. The appendix is also involved in the production of molecules that help to direct the movement of lymphocytes, the small white cells of the immune system, to various other locations in the body.

Another lymph organ, the **spleen**, filters the blood to rid it of germs and other debris. The spleen is a red-brown, somewhat flattened organ located in the abdominal cavity just under the ribs on the left side of the body. The spleen can be considered to be the largest lymph node in the body.

The spleen is composed of both red and white pulp. The white pulp makes up only about 25% of the spleen. This is the part of the spleen in the lymph system. The red pulp has a different function. The white pulp produces antibodies that recognize and neutralize harmful bacteria and viruses in the blood. It also produces and stores white blood cells.

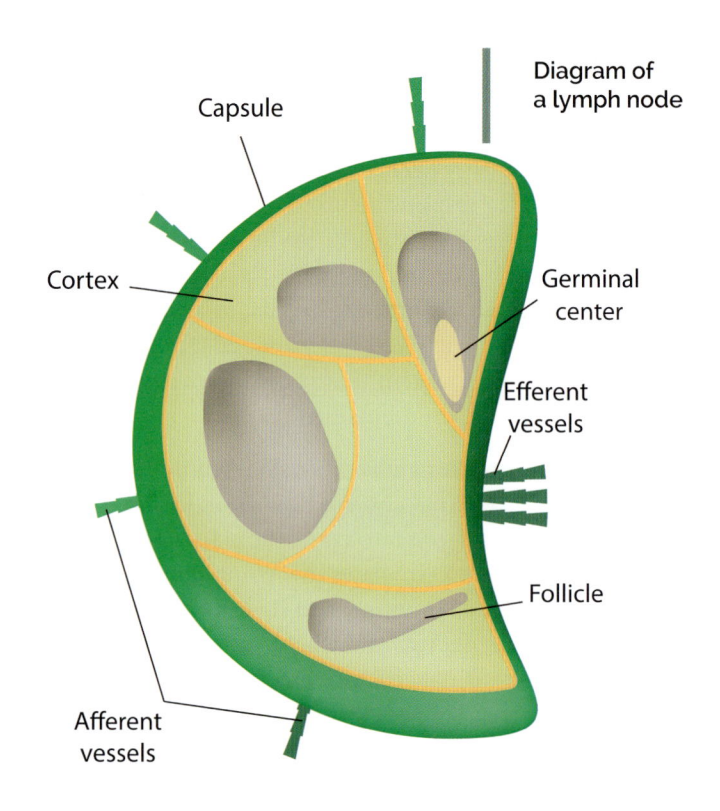

Diagram of a lymph node

Capsule • Cortex • Germinal center • Efferent vessels • Follicle • Afferent vessels

Peyer's Patches are lymph tissues associated with the small intestine. Peyer's Patches filter out harmful organisms from the digestive tract. Both T-cells and B-cells are found in significant numbers in Peyer's Patches lymph tissues to eliminate germs.

The **thymus gland**, located just in front of the heart, develops T-cells and stores them for when they are needed.

> **Section Review –
> 14.3 The Immune System**
>
> 1. List the major components of the human immune system.
> 2. Identify red and blue granulocytes.
> 3. Where do T-cells acquire "memory"?
> 4. What makes natural killer cells so important?
> 5. What are lymph nodes?

14.4 Allergies

Sometimes maturing lymph cells react to seemingly harmless antigens (things which don't belong in the human body) from the environment such as pollen, or cat or dog dander. Remember that lymph cells retain memory for the harmless antigens just as they would for true germs.

Every time the lymph cells, then, are re-exposed to the "harmless" antigens, an immune reaction ensues. This is known as an **allergic reaction**, or **allergy**. An allergy is a hypersensitivity disorder of the immune system. The symptoms of allergies, such as itchy, watery eyes, runny nose, and sneezing, are all caused by the actions of the immune cells that release histamine, a local immune response factor.

> **Section Review – 14.4 Allergies**
> 1. What is an allergy?
> 2. Describe the mechanism for an allergic response.

14.5 Illness and the Goodness of God

One of the truths of creation is summarized in Genesis 1:31, "And God saw everything that he had made, and it was very good." This is not only a truth of creation, but a basic truth of our faith: all that comes from God is good.

All life comes from God and all life is good. The human body was created by God and is good. Look back at the creation story. Is there any mention of illness? Did God, in those "seven days," create illness?

No, God created life. He created perfect life in all of its forms, especially that of man. He created the human body as whole, complete, and in a state of physical perfection. God created the human body and all of its systems to be in perfect harmony within itself and with all of creation. How, then, did sickness and death enter into His perfect creation?

Sickness and death entered into God's creation through Original Sin. Adam and Eve disobeyed God and ate the fruit that was forbidden. Because of this sin of pride and disobedience, Adam and Eve and all of their descendants lost the gift of perfect health and immortality.

This sin of Adam and Eve destroyed the perfect harmony in all creation. The Catechism explains that each person inherits Original Sin and, as a result, is subject to suffering, sickness, and death. God did not create sickness nor death, but these entered the world along with Original Sin.

In His goodness, however, God is the Healer of the body and of the soul. He created the human body with a wonderfully complex immune system to protect and heal itself. He also gave the sacraments as a means to overcome the tendency to sin and to heal the soul. Most importantly, He gave His only Son, to restore us from death to perfect life, in body and in soul, for all eternity.

WORDS TO REMEMBER

lymph node: made up of grouped lymph nodules that are held together by connective tissue. These lymph nodules are surrounded and held together by a tough, fibrous capsule, to define the lymph node.

appendix: assists with the maturing of B-cells, that is, immune cells that are made in bone marrow; involved in the production of molecules that help to direct the movement of lymphocytes to various other locations in the body

spleen: filters the blood to rid it of germs; a red-brown, somewhat flattened organ, located in the abdominal cavity under the ribs on the left side of the body

Peyer's Patches: lymph tissues associated with the small intestine; filter out harmful organisms from the digestive tract

thymus gland: located in front of the heart; develops T-cells and stores them for when they are needed

allergy: a hypersensitivity disorder of the immune system; allergic reaction occurs when maturing lymph cells react to seemingly harmless antigens

Chapter 14 Review

A. Complete the statements below.

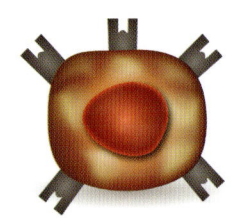

T-Cell
T-Cells attack invaders _____ the cells.

B-Cell
B-Cells attack invaders _____ the cells.

Natural killer
NK Cells require no activation and are the major defense against _____.

B. Answer the following questions.

1. List the major components of the human immune system.
2. How is the immune system different from the normal defense mechanisms of the body?
3. What are leukocytes, and where are they produced?
4. Explain what phagocytes are.
5. Identify red and blue granulocytes.
6. Identify four features of inflammation.
7. Where do T-cells acquire "memory?"
8. What makes natural killer cells so important?
9. What are lymph nodes?
10. Provide three facts about tonsils.
11. Provide three facts about the spleen.
12. Explain the importance to the immune system of each of the following:
    a. the appendix
    b. the spleen
    c. the thymus gland
    d. Peyer's Patches
13. What is an allergy?
14. Describe the mechanism for the allergic response.

Chapter 14: "Words to Remember" Crossword

ACROSS

4 functions as a lymph organ in adults
5 Natural ___ cells kill abnormal cells. They are the body's major defense against all types of cancer cells.
8 the body's ability to prevent or resist infection or illness caused by germs
9 The ___ system is the system within the immune system that absorbs fluid from the body's tissues and returns it into circulation.
10 complex molecules that attach to infected cells in order to kill the germs
11 small collections of lymph tissue, usually located in the loose connective tissue beneath wet membranes

DOWN

1 filters the blood to rid it of germs and other debris
2 causes the blood vessels in the immediate area to dilate
3 granular white cells which have tiny granules, or grains
4 a hypersensitivity disorder of the immune system
6 white blood cells
7 The ___ gland is located just in front of the heart, develops T-cells, and stores them for when they are needed.

15 THE HUMAN NERVOUS SYSTEM

15.1 Introduction

15.2 Distinctly Human

15.3 The Nervous System

15.4 Cells and Tissues of the Nervous System
  A. Neurons
  B. Glial Cells

15.5 The Brain
  A. The Forebrain
  B. The Midbrain
  C. The Hindbrain

15.6 The Spinal Cord

15.7 Protection of the Nervous System

15.8 The Peripheral Nervous System

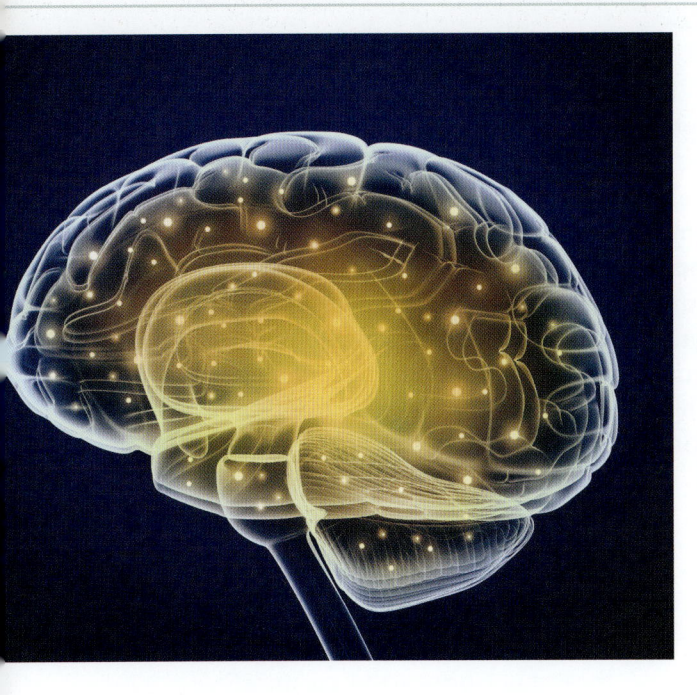

Chapter 15

The Human Nervous System

15.1 Introduction

Did you know that there are three stories in the Bible about women who save God's people from the head of the army of Israel's enemy? These stories can be found in the books of Judges and Judith. You may ask, "Why is this important?" The women in these stories are types of the Mother of God, Mary Most Holy.

Immediately after the Fall of Adam and Eve, God told the Serpent, the Devil, that He "will put enmities between thee and the woman, and thy seed and her seed: she shall crush thy head, and thou shalt lie in wait for her heel." This translation comes from the Latin Vulgate Bible, that the pope asked St. Jerome to write. The Church has declared the Vulgate to be without error.

Satan's first sin was pride, which led to disobedience. He said "I will not serve." Satan encouraged the sin of pride in Adam and Eve. They desired to "be like God" and so they disobeyed and ate the forbidden fruit.

The virtue that opposes pride, like the sin of Adam and Eve, is humility. Mary is most humble, and wanted a minimum mention of her in the Gospels. The Bible talks about Mary keeping things in her heart; she wanted to keep her thoughts to herself.

It would be less damaging to Satan's pride if he could say, "I was defeated, but it took the All-Powerful God to beat me!" But Satan's pride would be deflated by being defeated by a simple, humble woman. He was defeated not by a great general with his army, but by a humble woman from Nazareth.

Our Blessed Mother is often depicted crushing the head of a serpent, which represents the Devil. The blow to Satan is figurative in that the vice of pride is centered in the head, so it is fitting that God told Satan that the woman would strike at his head.

The head is the location of the brain that controls everything in the human body. In this chapter, let's learn about the brain, and the nervous system that brings the commands of the brain to the body.

15.2 Distinctly Human

Man is different from all other creatures. Angels are pure spirits who do not have bodies. Animals have bodies, and when their bodies die, they will no longer exist. Animals are not rational, so they cannot think like humans to control their behavior; they react only with the instincts that God gave them. Man is the only creature that is created in the "image of God" with a body and a rational soul, and with an amazingly complex mind capable of rational thought.

Life Science for Young Catholics

The Church teaches that man is different from the rest of God's creation because human beings are the only creatures on Earth that are able to *know* and *love* both their Creator and other people. Man is the only creature that God calls to share in His own life through knowledge and love. Man is the only creature capable of choosing to know, love, and serve God in this life and in the next. Indeed, God created man for the glorious life in Heaven, with the earthly life as a pathway to Heaven.

The human mind makes each person, according to the *Catechism of the Catholic Church*, "capable of self-knowledge, of self-possession, and of freely giving himself and entering into communion with other persons." Man was created to live with God forever, in Heaven, in eternal happiness.

The human mind, or **brain**, is the unique creation of God that enables a person to be aware of himself and of others. The human brain enables a person to think, to reason, to sense, to judge, to understand, to learn, to know, and to choose.

The human brain, like the brain of animals, is responsible for all **lower functions,** including heart rate, respiration, blood pressure, and digestion, and for all voluntary movement. However, unlike the animal brain, the human brain is capable of **higher functions**, including consciousness, memory, planning, language, creativity, emotion, personality, expression, problem solving, and reasoning. The human brain, capable of these higher functions, along with the soul, separates man from all the rest of God's creatures.

> **Section Review –
> 15.2 Distinctly Human**
>
> 1. What two facts separate mankind from the rest of God's earthly creatures?
>
> 2. List ten of the higher functions of the human brain.

15.3 The Nervous System

The **nervous system** includes the **brain**, the **spinal cord**, the **sensory organs**, and the **nerves**. Together, the brain and spinal cord make up the **central nervous system**. The sensory organs and nerves make up the **peripheral nervous system**.

The peripheral nervous system is further divided into, first, the **autonomic nervous system**, which controls involuntary body functions through smooth muscle, cardiac muscle, and glands; and second, the **somatic nervous system**, which controls voluntary body functions through skeletal muscles.

The brain is the central and most complex organ of the human nervous system. Together with the other components of the nervous system, the brain controls and regulates all functions of the human body through electrical impulses sent through the neurons, or nerves.

The atom is the basic building block of all physical things. Atoms are made up of three basic particles: protons, electrons, and neutrons. Protons and neutrons join to form the central part of an atom. The central part is called a nucleus.

All atoms contain identical numbers of both electrons and protons. Protons have positive electrical charges, and electrons have negative charges. Electrical impulses have to do with the movement of negative charges, or electrons.

Electrons are tiny moving particles that orbit the nucleus of an atom, like the Moon moves around the Earth. The tiny electrons can be "freed" from the atom, giving the remaining part of the atom a positive charge (because it now has more positive protons than negative electrons). When a significant number of electrons are moving, these negatively charged particles cause an "electrical impulse." These impulses are not a continuous flow of electrons, but a pulse, like a lightning bolt.

Chemical reactions can "excite" the nerve cell and cause the electrical impulse, which moves through the cell like an electric current through a wire. The electrical impulse that propagates, or travels, down a nerve cell, called an "action potential," is caused by charged particles moving across the cell membrane in a wave from one end of the cell to the other.

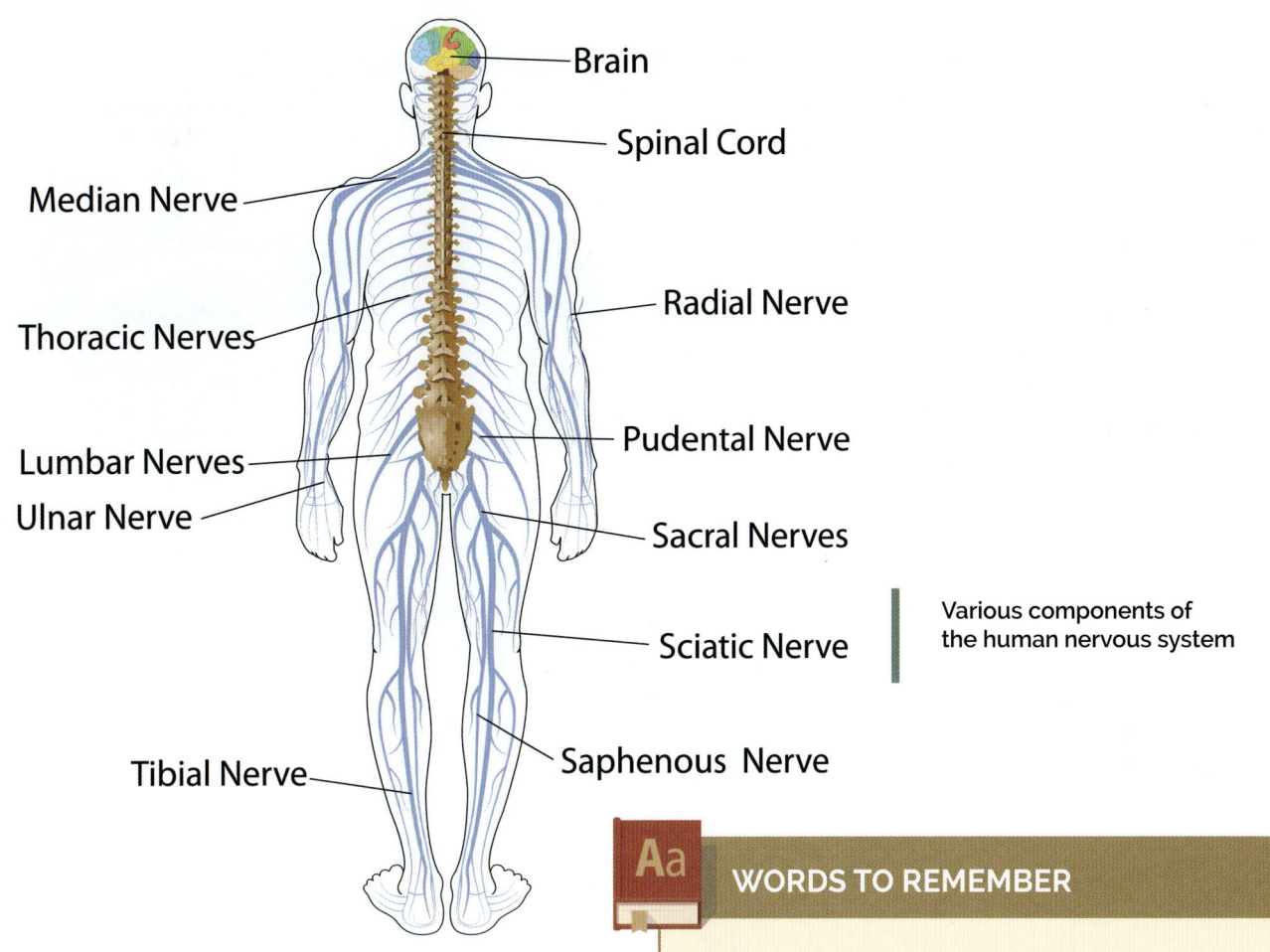

CHAPTER 15: THE HUMAN NERVOUS SYSTEM

- Brain
- Spinal Cord
- Median Nerve
- Radial Nerve
- Thoracic Nerves
- Pudental Nerve
- Lumbar Nerves
- Ulnar Nerve
- Sacral Nerves
- Sciatic Nerve
- Saphenous Nerve
- Tibial Nerve

Various components of the human nervous system

The nervous system also regulates body functions through control of the **endocrine system**. The endocrine system includes the **glands** that produce and secrete **hormones** directly into the blood to help the body maintain homeostasis, that is, the proper healthy internal environment of the body. <u>Together, both the nervous system and the endocrine system regulate, control, and maintain the human body.</u>

Section Review – 15.3 The Nervous System

1. List four components of the nervous system.
2. Describe the central nervous system.
3. Describe the peripheral nervous system.
4. Identify the autonomic nervous system.
5. Identify the somatic nervous system.

WORDS TO REMEMBER

brain: the organ that controls most of the functions of the body

nervous system: the part of the body that coordinates its voluntary and involuntary actions and transmits signals between different parts of the body; includes the brain, the spinal cord, the sensory organs, and the nerves

central nervous system: includes the brain and spinal cord

peripheral nervous system: is composed of the sensory organs and nerves

autonomic nervous system: part of the peripheral nervous system which controls <u>involuntary</u> body functions through smooth muscle, cardiac muscle, and glands

somatic nervous system: part of the peripheral nervous system which controls <u>voluntary</u> body functions through skeletal muscles

Life Science for Young Catholics

15.4 Cells and Tissues of the Nervous System

The nervous system contains two major types of cells: **neurons** and **glial cells**.

Neurons, or nerve cells, are the functional cells of the nervous system. Neurons have three functions: (1) to transmit sensory information to the central nervous system; (2) to process, integrate, and interpret incoming sensory information; and (3) to transmit motor impulses to muscles and glands to affect a change as a result of the sensory information.

Glial (**glee**-al) **cells** are the supporting cells of the nervous tissue, which protect, nourish, and insulate the neurons.

A. Neurons

Neurons, or nerve cells, are surrounded by a cell membrane. Neurons contain cytoplasm, organelles, and a nucleus. However, neurons differ from other body cells in two major ways.

1. Differences from other cells

The first difference from other body cells is that neurons stop reproducing shortly after they come into existence, and do not repair or heal well after injury. If and when a neuron dies, it is not replaced. However, nerve cells are among the longest-living cells in the human body.

The second difference from other body cells is that neurons can transmit, or send and receive, information both **chemically** and through **electrical impulses**. Neurons receive information through chemical messengers, then generate an electrical impulse from the receiving end to the transmitting end. Finally, they release a chemical messenger to activate the next neuron, or muscle cell. No other cell in the human body has this ability.

2. Parts of a Neuron

Neurons have several distinct parts. The central part of the neuron is the nerve cell body. The nucleus and cellular organelles are located within the **nerve cell body**.

There are two types of membrane-bound extensions at the ends of the nerve body. These are **dendrites** and **axons**.

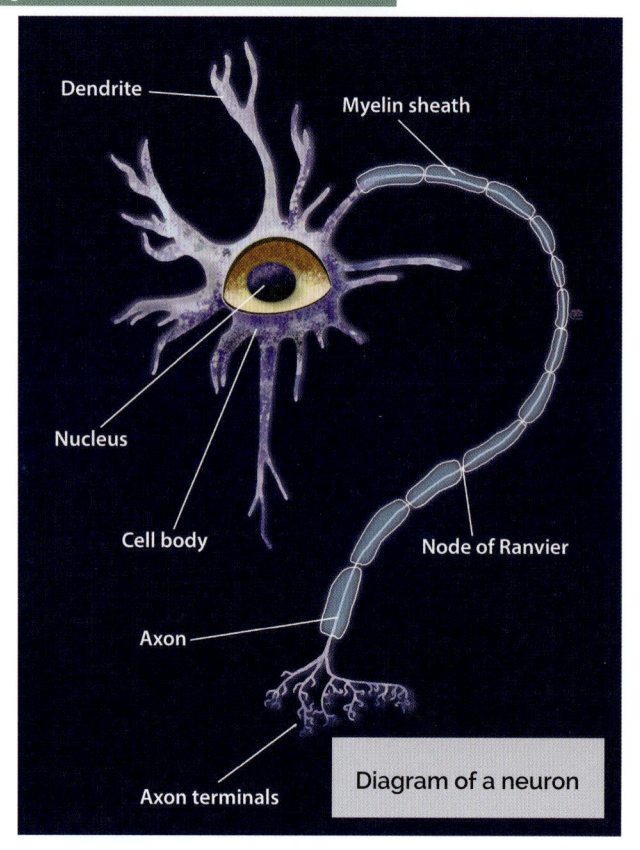

Diagram of a neuron

Dendrites are short, highly branched extensions that help increase the surface area of the nerve cell body. Dendrites **receive impulses** from other cells. Most neurons have many dendrites extending from the cell body, but some have only one. Dendrites are located at the beginning or top of a nerve cell body.

The second type of membrane-bound extension is the **axon**. An axon is the extension from the nerve cell body at the bottom or end of the cell. Each neuron has only one axon. An axon carries impulses away from the cell body and transmits them to other cells.

Axons have several characteristics which determine the speed with which an impulse is transmitted through an axon. First, surprisingly, the longer the axon is, the faster it transmits information. Second, axons that are covered by a **myelin sheath** also transmit impulses faster, up to 200 miles per hour, than axons without a myelin sheath. Myelin is an insulating material made of lipids and proteins that not only protects the axons but also speeds up the transmission of impulses.

Cells containing myelin wrap themselves around the axon in many layers, forming the myelin sheath. Axons protected by a myelin sheath are collectively referred to as **white matter**, and axons without myelin are referred to as **gray matter**.

3. Types of Neurons

There are three basic types of neurons: **motor neurons**, **sensory neurons**, and **interneurons**.

Motor neurons relay information from the brain, through the spinal cord, and to the muscles to produce movement.

Sensory neurons are the neurons which convert external stimuli from the environment, from outside the body, into an impulse, and then transmit that information to the central nervous system.

The **interneuron** is the third functional type of neuron. It forms connections or serves as a link between sensory and motor neurons. Interneurons are smaller neurons whose axons, nerve cell bodies, and dendrites are found completely within the central nervous system.

B. Glial Cells

There are three times more glial cells than neurons in the human body. Although glial (**glee**-al) cells do not transmit impulses, they are critical to the health and proper functioning of the neurons.

In the central nervous system, the glial cells have several functions:

1) Glial cells are responsible for providing nutrients for the neurons, and thus promote healing after injury.

2) Glial cells produce myelin for the neurons of the brain and spinal cord. Thus, they protect and insulate the axons.

3) Glial cells circulate brain and spinal fluid throughout the nervous tissue, carry nutrients to the neurons, and carry cellular waste away from the neurons.

4) Glial cells serve as the immune cells of the central nervous system. These specialized glial cells constantly "survey" the brain and spinal cord to rid it of pathogens or any disease-causing organism.

In conclusion, from the several functions as listed above, you can see that glial cells ensure the care and protection of the very sensitive neurons. Without this extremely high level of protection for the neurons by the numerous glial cells, the nervous system would not be able to function properly.

Section Review – 15.4 Cells and Tissues of the Nervous System

1. How do neurons use electrical impulses?
2. How do neurons transmit and receive information?
3. Describe the difference between "white matter" and "gray matter."
4. Identify four functions of glial cells.

WORDS TO REMEMBER

neurons: the functional cells of the nervous system

glial cells: supporting cells of the nervous tissue; protect, nourish, and insulate the neurons

nerve cell body: the central part of a neuron (nerve cell); the nucleus and cellular organelles are located within the nerve cell body.

dendrites: short, highly-branched extensions that help increase the surface area of the nerve cell body; receive impulses from other cells

axon: the extension from the nerve cell body at the bottom or end of the cell; carries impulses away from the cell body and transmits impulses to other cells

myelin sheath: an insulating material made of lipids and proteins, which protects the axons and speeds up the transmission of impulses

motor neurons: relay information from the brain, through the spinal cord, and to the muscles to produce movement

sensory neurons: the neurons which convert external stimuli from the environment, from outside the body, into an impulse, and then transmit that information to the central nervous system

interneurons: form connections or serve as a link between sensory neurons and motor neurons

Anatomy of the human brain

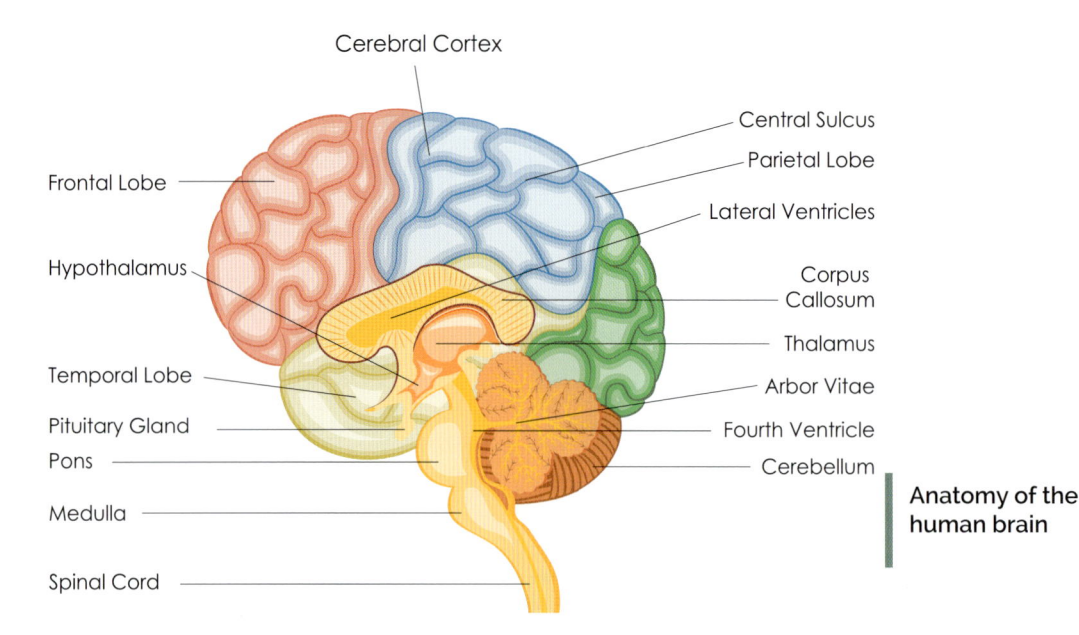

15.5 The Brain

The brain is the most complex organ in the human body. The human brain weighs approximately 3 pounds. It contains about **100 billion neurons** and up to **three times as many glial cells**. Despite its relatively small size, the brain consumes 20% of the body's glucose and 20% of the body's available oxygen, and requires a constant flow of blood at the rate of about 1 quart of blood per minute to ensure its survival. (Remember that glucose is a form of sugar in the blood; glucose is the main source of energy for the body's cells.)

The 100 billion neurons in the brain are organized into distinct areas or regions, with each area responsible for a particular function. However, all areas are connected and communicate in a remarkable way to control all aspects of the human body, from emotion and personality to voluntary muscle movement.

The brain is organized into distinct areas of gray and white matter, and can be divided into three regions: the **forebrain**, the **midbrain**, and the **hindbrain**.

A. The Forebrain

The forebrain includes the **cerebrum** (*sir·***ree**·*brum*), two **thalami** (***thal***·*uh·my*), and the **hypothalamus** (*high-puh-***thal**-*uh-muss*).

1) The **cerebrum** is the outermost portion of the forebrain and is made up of two areas called hemispheres. The right and left cerebral hemispheres are connected by a tract of white matter.

The cerebrum is the largest region of the brain and is where higher functions occur, including thought, language, logic, reasoning, and creativity.

a) The **left hemisphere** is where language processing, logic, and mathematical computation occur.

b) The **right hemisphere** is largely responsible for visual imagery, processing music, and interpreting the tone and context of what is seen and heard.

c) The outer surface of the two cerebral hemispheres is called the **cerebral cortex**. The cerebral cortex is a convoluted surface made of folds and fissures of gray matter. Different areas of the cerebral cortex are responsible for different functions. The **motor cortex** controls voluntary movement of skeletal muscles. The **sensory cortex** receives sensory information from receptors throughout the body, processes that information, and develops perceptions.

The **right hemisphere** controls muscles and receives sensory input from the left side of the body. Conversely, the **left hemisphere** controls the movements and sensory perceptions from the right side of the body. Both hemispheres work together in a highly coordinated way.

CHAPTER 15: THE HUMAN NERVOUS SYSTEM

Beneath the cerebral cortex is a <u>layer of white matter</u> that provides connections between the brain and the spinal cord. White matter in the brain consists of brain neurons that are protected by myelin sheaths, for protection and to increase signal speed.

Deep within the cerebral hemispheres are two important regions of gray matter. <u>One region</u> regulates and controls muscle movements associated with muscle tone and posture. The <u>other</u> helps control emotions, memory, and emergency responses of other internal organs.

2) Two **thalami** (singular: **thalamus**) are located beneath the regions of gray matter. The two thalami send incoming sensory information to the proper sensory area of the cerebral cortex for processing. The thalami play an important role in learning and memory.

3) The **hypothalamus** is the tiny area directly beneath the thalami; it is about the size of a pea. Despite its tiny size, the hypothalamus controls the body's metabolism, that is, the biochemical processes in the body that maintain life, through a number of hormones which it produces and releases.

B. The Midbrain

The midbrain sits beneath the cerebral hemispheres. The midbrain conveys movement information between the brain and the rest of the body. The midbrain also processes visual and auditory information. The midbrain is part of the brainstem.

C. The Hindbrain

The hindbrain includes the cerebellum, the medulla oblongata, and the pons. The medulla oblongata and the pons are also included in the brainstem, along with the midbrain.

The **brainstem** is the portion of the brain connecting the brain to the spinal cord. The brainstem is mostly white matter from motor neurons and sensory neurons traveling between the brain and spinal cord. The brainstem coordinates motor signals sent from the brain to the body.

The **medulla oblongata** is the portion of the brainstem that regulates autonomic, or automatic, functions, that is, those functions that do not require conscious control, such as blood pressure, oxygen levels, heart rate, and respiratory rate.

WORDS TO REMEMBER

forebrain: the largest part of the brain; has roles within perception, memory, and all higher thought processes; involved in regulating skeletal movement and other higher motor functions

cerebrum: the largest region of the brain, responsible for higher functions of the brain, including thought, language, logic, reasoning, and creativity

left hemisphere: the left half of the cerebrum; responsible for language processing, logic, and mathematical computation

right hemisphere: the right half of the cerebrum; responsible for processing imagery, music, and interpreting the tone and context of what is seen and heard

cerebral cortex: outer surface of the two cerebral hemispheres; a convoluted surface made of folds and fissures of gray matter

motor cortex: part of the cerebral cortex that controls voluntary movement of skeletal muscles

sensory cortex: part of the cerebral cortex that receives sensory information from receptors throughout the body, processes that information, and develops perceptions

thalamus: one of two glands that send incoming sensory information to the proper sensory area of the cerebral cortex for processing; plays an important role in learning and memory

hypothalamus: a gland that controls the body's metabolism, that is, the biochemical processes in the body that maintain life

brainstem: the portion of the brain connecting the brain to the spinal cord; coordinates motor signals sent from the brain to the body

medulla oblongata: the portion of the brainstem that regulates autonomic, or automatic, functions, that is, those functions that do not require conscious control

Life Science for Young Catholics

The **pons**, which means "bridge," is the part of the brain that connects or serves as a bridge between the cerebral cortex and the medulla oblongata. The pons helps to provide communication between the cerebral cortex and the medulla oblongata. The pons also relays sensory information between the cerebrum and the cerebellum. In addition, the pons helps regulate autonomic or automatic functions.

The **cerebellum**, or "little brain," is the part of the hindbrain situated beneath the occipital lobes (round projections). The cerebellum is important for coordinating motor functions, including those involved in maintaining posture and balance, and muscle coordination in activities such as speaking, walking, and writing.

> ### Section Review – 15.5 The Brain
> 1. How many neurons does the brain contain?
> 2. List three major regions of the brain.
> 3. List the three parts of the forebrain.
> 4. Describe the cerebrum.
> 5. Name the higher functions of the cerebrum.
> 6. List the three major parts of the hindbrain.

15.6 The Spinal Cord

The brainstem connects the brain to the **spinal cord**. The spinal cord is a cylindrical or circular collection of nervous tissue that begins at the base of the brainstem and extends to the second lumbar vertebra in the spine, one of the five large vertebrae below the rib cage. The spinal cord is extremely important because it provides the connection for sensory and motor pathways from the brain to all areas of the body below the neck.

White matter in the spinal cord makes up many different bundles of nerve fibers that ascend and descend through the spinal cord.

Ascending tracts are pathways that carry sensory impulses *to* the spinal cord from the skin.

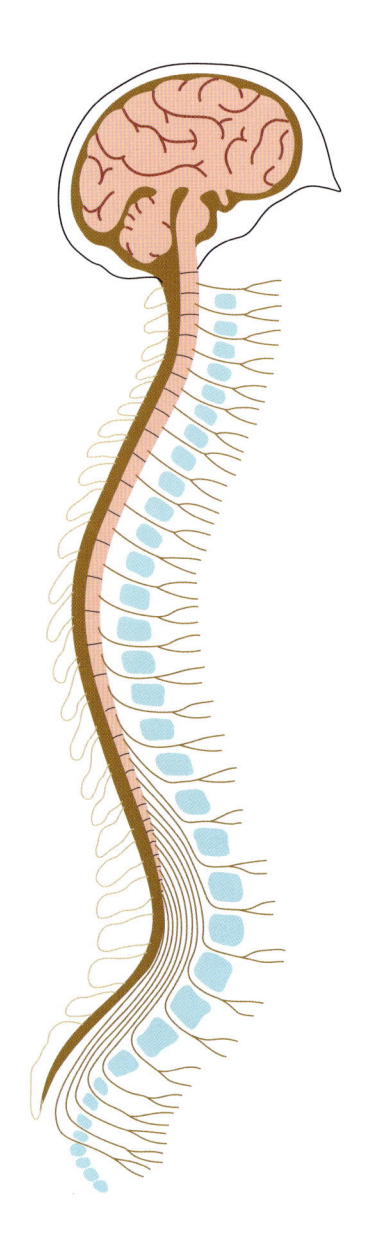

Descending tracts are pathways that carry motor impulses *from* the spinal cord to the muscles.

> ### Section Review – 15.6 The Spinal Cord
> 1. Of what are the bundles in the spinal cord made?
> 2. Identify the ascending and descending tracts of the spinal cord.

Life Science for Young Catholics

15.7 Protection of the Nervous System

In general, nerve cells of the brain and spinal cord are not replaced after nerve cell death. Therefore, the human nervous system was created by God with multiple mechanisms and layers of protection to keep it healthy and functioning.

A. Special fluid cushions and protects the brain and spinal cord from injury, often due to movement within their bony cases.

B. Glial cells support, protect, and nourish neurons throughout the nervous system.

C. Specialized cells protect the neurons of the central nervous system from germs.

D. Blood-brain barrier: Designated cells form part of the **blood-brain barrier**, which protects the brain from harmful substances in the blood.

E. Several external layers of tissues protect the brain and spinal cord.

F. The skin and the skull, or cranium, form the outermost layers of tissues and bone to protect the brain.

G. The bones of the spine, the muscles of the back, and the skin also protect the spinal cord.

Section Review – 15.7 Protection of the Nervous System

1. Identify three things that provide protection for the brain and spinal cord.
2. Identify two things that form the outermost layers around the brain.

15.8 The Peripheral Nervous System

The nerves, together with the sensory or sense organs, comprise the **peripheral nervous system.**

Nerves are bundles of axons outside of the central nervous system. These nerves carry impulses between the brain and the spinal cord and the remainder of the body.

The axons are bundled together by connective tissue in much the same way that muscle fibers are bundled to form a muscle. A collection of nerve cells outside of the central nervous system is known as a **ganglion**.

Sensory nerves are made exclusively of axons from sensory neurons; these transmit sensory information to the central nervous system.

Motor nerves are made exclusively of axons from motor neurons. Motor nerves transmit information away from the central nervous system to the rest of the body, specifically to muscles and glands.

Section Review – 15.8 The Peripheral Nervous System

1. What are nerves?
2. What is a ganglion?
3. Identify sensory and motor nerves.

WORDS TO REMEMBER

pons: means "bridge"; the part of the brain that connects or serves as a bridge between the cerebral cortex and the medulla oblongata.

cerebellum: or "little brain," is the part of the hindbrain for coordinating motor functions, such as those involved in maintaining posture and balance, and muscle coordination in activities such as speaking, walking, and writing.

spinal cord: a circular collection of nervous tissue that begins at the base of the brainstem and extends to the second lumbar vertebra in the spine; provides the connection for sensory and motor pathways from the brain to areas of the body below the neck

ascending tracts: pathways that carry sensory impulses to the spinal cord from the skin

descending tracts: pathways that carry motor impulses from the spinal cord to the muscles

nerves: bundles of axons outside of the central nervous system; carry impulses between the brain and spinal cord and the remainder of the body

Chapter 15 Review

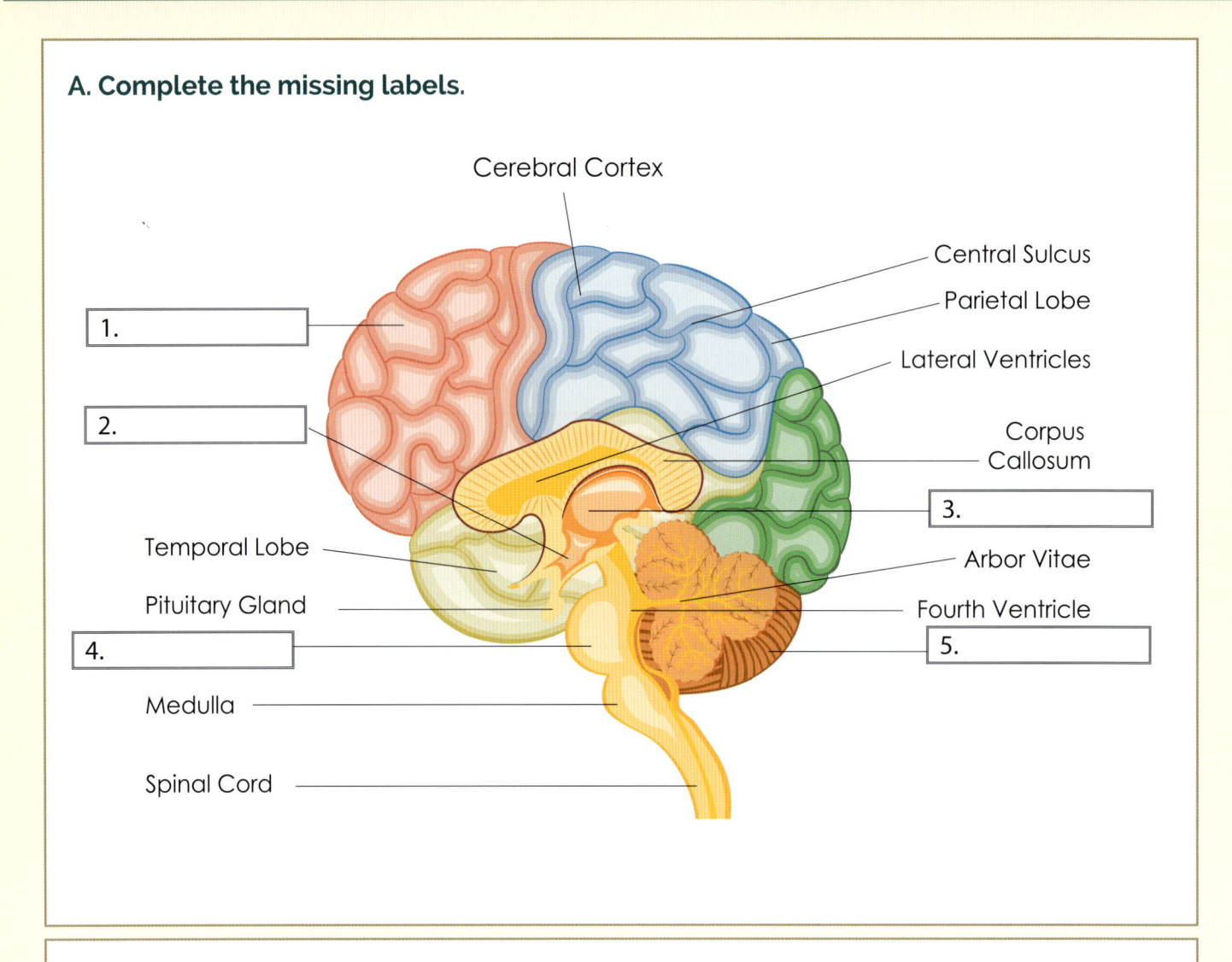

A. Complete the missing labels.

Cerebral Cortex
Central Sulcus
Parietal Lobe
Lateral Ventricles
Corpus Callosum
Arbor Vitae
Fourth Ventricle
Temporal Lobe
Pituitary Gland
Medulla
Spinal Cord

1.
2.
3.
4.
5.

B. Answer the following questions.

1. Describe the central nervous system.
2. Describe the peripheral nervous system.
3. Identify the autonomic nervous system.
4. Identify the somatic nervous system.
5. How do neurons transmit and receive information?
6. Identify and describe the three basic types of neurons.
7. Briefly describe dendrites, axons, and interneurons.
8. Identify four functions of glial cells.
9. List the three major regions of the brain.
10. What is the cerebrum? Name the higher functions of the cerebrum.
11. Explain the importance of the hypothalamus.
12. What are nerves?

Chapter 15: "Words to Remember" Crossword

ACROSS

1. form connections or serve as a link between sensory neurons and motor neurons
3. is the extension from the nerve cell body at the bottom or end of the cell.
6. the portion of the brain connecting the brain to the spinal cord. It coordinates motor signals sent from the brain to the body.
9. means "bridge." It is the part of the brain that connects or serves as a bridge between the cerebral cortex and the medulla oblongata.
10. the largest region of the brain and is responsible for higher functions of the brain, including thought, language, logic, reasoning, and creativity.

DOWN

2. one of two glands that send incoming sensory information to the proper sensory area of the cerebral cortex for processing
4. or "little brain," is the part of the hindbrain that is important for coordinating motor functions, including those involved in maintaining posture and balance, and muscle coordination in activities such as speaking, walking, and writing.
5. short, highly-branched extensions that help increase the surface area of the nerve cell body.
7. or nerve cells, are the functional cells of the nervous system.
8. bundles of axons outside of the central nervous system. These carry impulses between the brain and the spinal cord, and the remainder of the body.

16 THE HUMAN SENSE ORGANS AND ENDOCRINE SYSTEM

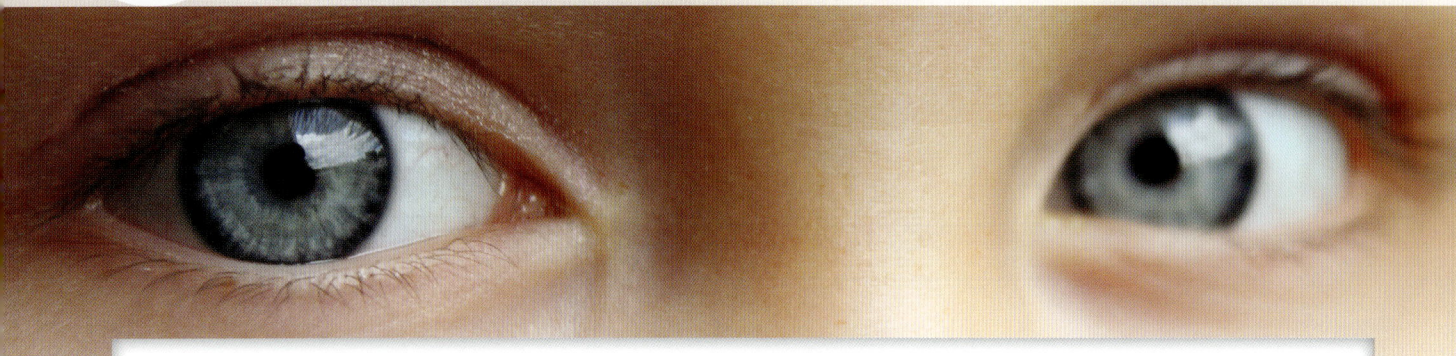

16.1 Introduction

16.2 The Sense Organs
    A. The Eye
    B. The Ear
    C. The Tongue
    D. The Nose
    E. The Skin

16.3 Making Connections and Putting It All Together

16.4 The Endocrine System
    A. The Hypothalamus Gland
    B. The Pituitary Gland
    C. The Thyroid Gland
    D. The Parathyroid Glands
    E. The Thymus Gland
    F. The Adrenal Glands
    G. The Pineal Body
    H. The Gonads
    I. The Pancreas

16.5 Endocrine Summary

16.6 What is Man?

Chapter 16
The Human Sense Organs and the Endocrine System

16.1 Introduction

In the Gospel of St. John, the story is told of how Jesus cured the man born blind. Jesus "spat on the ground, and made clay of the spittle, and spread the clay on his eyes, and said to him: Go, wash in the pool of Siloe." The blind man was then cured.

The Bible talks about the human senses and God's concern for them. Jesus gives sight to the blind man to heal him, for He came to give life and give it abundantly. That abundance is really a super-abundance.

Have you read St. Paul's first letter to the Corinthians? This is the one where he states that "eye hath not seen, nor ear heard, neither hath it entered into the heart of man, what things God hath prepared for them that love him" (1 Corinthians 2:9). St. Paul tells us that our eyes have never seen anything as wonderful as we will find Heaven to be. The eternal life that God has prepared is wonderful beyond what we can even imagine.

Nevertheless, the eyes and ears and other sense organs are wonders of God's love to us that we can see and appreciate. In this chapter, we will learn about the sense organs, and other wonders of the bodies that God gave us.

16.2 The Sense Organs

Along with the brain, spinal cord, and nerves, the human nervous system includes five **sensory organs**. Each of the five senses of sight, hearing, taste, smell, and touch is connected with sensory organs that take in information from the environment. That information is processed in the brain, and then we can act upon the information. The five sense organs are the eyes, ears, tongue, nose, and skin.

Each sensory organ captures information from the environment through **sensory receptors**. A sensory receptor is a sensory nerve ending in an organ or tissue that responds to a particular stimulus by sending an electrical impulse toward the central nervous system.

There are seven basic types of sensory receptors in the human body. These receptors inform the body about: 1) pressure, 2) pain, 3) light and color, 4) smell and taste, 5) temperature, 6) osmotic pressure to maintain fluid balance, and 7) position and motion of the body or limbs.

A. The Eye

The **eye** is the organ of **sight**. The eye is responsible for vision.

Light enters the eye through the **pupil**, but the amount of light that enters is controlled by the **iris**, the pigmented portion of the eye associated with eye color. The light is focused through a **lens** that sits behind the pupil, and directed to the back of the eye.

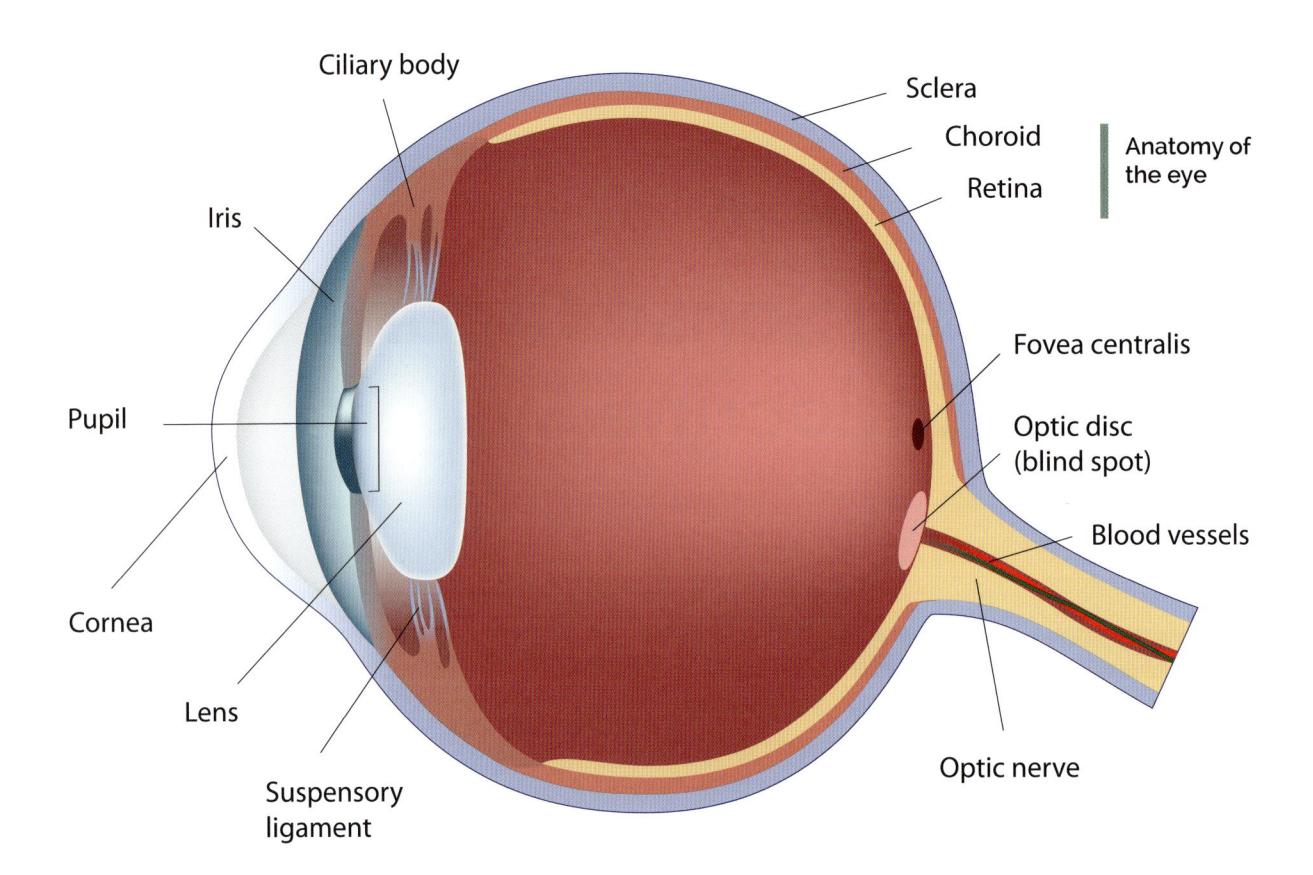

CHAPTER 16: THE HUMAN SENSE ORGANS AND ENDOCRINE SYSTEM

Anatomy of the eye

(Labels: Ciliary body, Sclera, Choroid, Retina, Iris, Fovea centralis, Optic disc (blind spot), Pupil, Blood vessels, Cornea, Optic nerve, Lens, Suspensory ligament)

In the back of the eye, the light strikes the lining, or the **retina**, which contains **photoreceptors**, receptors for light and color.

When photoreceptors are stimulated by the light, the retina begins to send the sensory information to the brain for processing. The sensory impulses are carried to the brain by the **optic nerve**.

B. The Ear

The ear is the organ of hearing. The ear has three basic parts: the **outer ear**, the **middle ear**, and the **inner ear**. All three parts play a role in gathering and processing sound.

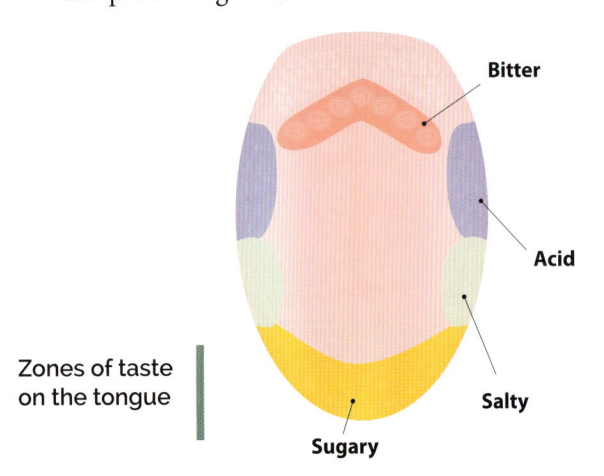

Zones of taste on the tongue

(Labels: Bitter, Acid, Salty, Sugary)

The outermost portion of the ear is known as the pinna. The pinna (**pin·uh**) gathers sound waves and funnels them through the external auditory canal to the middle ear. The sound waves strike the eardrum in the middle ear, causing it to vibrate.

Vibrations are next transmitted through the eardrum to three small bones, or **middle ear ossicles**: the **malleus**, the **incus**, and the **stapes**, in that order. The vibrations are then passed through the oval window from the stapes to enter the fluid-filled inner ear.

The **cochlea** (**cok·lee-uh**) is the portion of the inner ear that contains **hair cells**, which are the sensory receptors for sound. Different frequencies of vibrations cause fluid waves within the cochlea to stimulate various groups of hair cells, and the nerve impulse, generated by the hair cells, is sent to the brain by way of the auditory nerve.

C. The Tongue

The **tongue** is the major organ of **taste**. The tongue is a muscular organ covered by thousands of **papillae** (**puh·pill-ee**), each of which surrounds and protects the **taste buds**.

Anatomy of the Ear

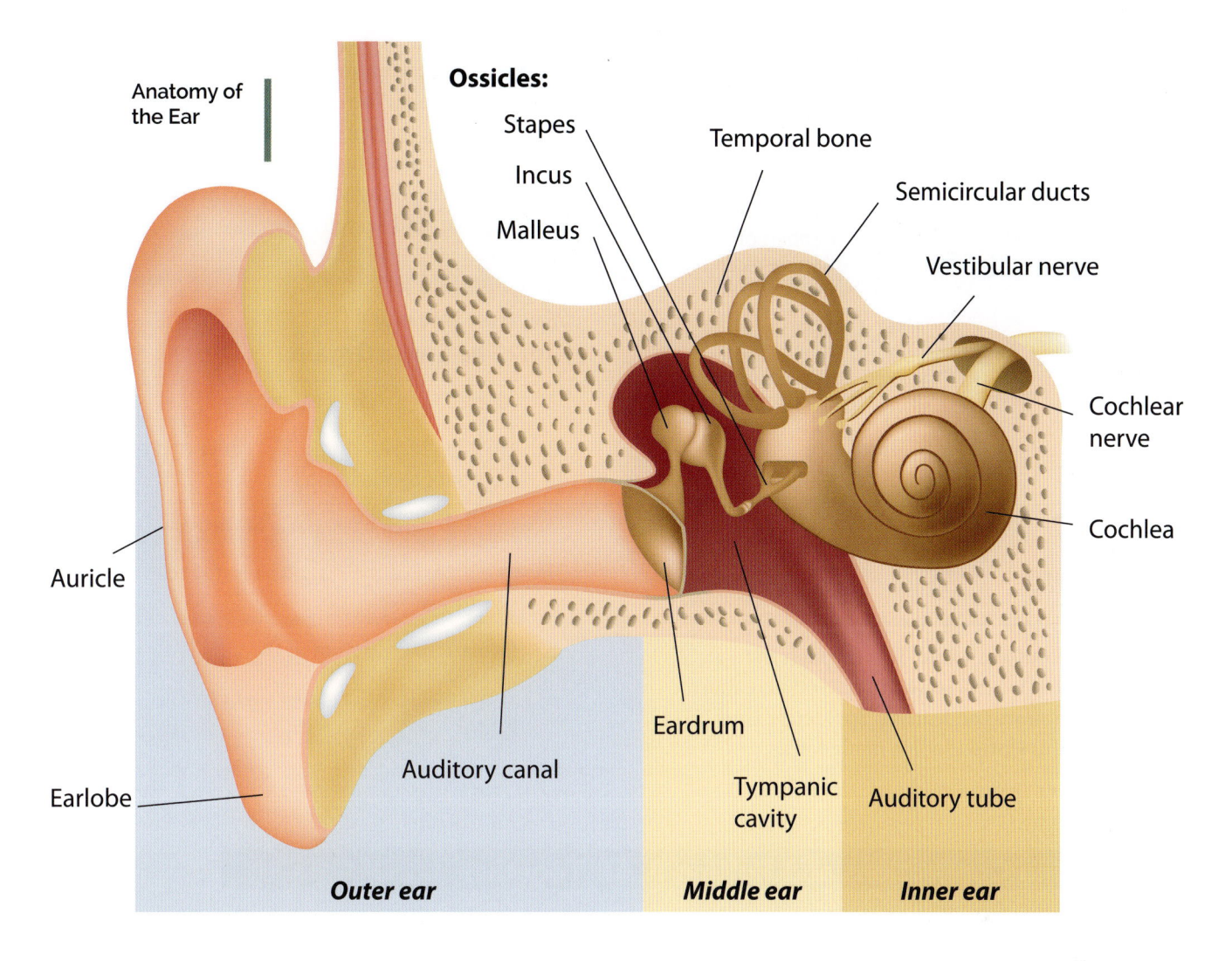

- Ossicles:
  - Stapes
  - Incus
  - Malleus
- Temporal bone
- Semicircular ducts
- Vestibular nerve
- Cochlear nerve
- Cochlea
- Auricle
- Earlobe
- Auditory canal
- Eardrum
- Tympanic cavity
- Auditory tube

Outer ear | *Middle ear* | *Inner ear*

Taste buds are also found on the palate and in the upper esophagus. Taste buds contain **taste receptor cells**, which are chemoreceptors, and have thin extensions known as taste hairs. The **taste hairs** detect chemicals from food dissolved in the saliva.

There are five basic tastes detected by the taste receptors: salty, sweet, sour, bitter, and savory. Other factors, including the smell, texture, and temperature, influence the overall taste perception of food.

D. The Nose

The **nose** is the organ of **smell**. The nose is part of the respiratory system and responsible for drawing in air to the lungs, but it is also responsible for **olfaction**, or the sense of smell.

Olfactory receptors are located within a small patch of tissue high up in the nasal cavity. The olfactory receptors are stimulated by **odor** molecules in the air, and the sensory information is transmitted to the brain by way of the **olfactory nerve**.

E. The Skin

The **skin** is the major organ of **touch**. While considered one of the five basic senses, touch is more a composite sensation produced from sensory information gathered by a number of different sensory receptors in the skin.

The skin contains receptor cells to detect pressure and vibration, temperature, and painful stimuli. The skin has nerve fibers that are able to detect position in space and position of one body part with respect to others.

The skin also has nerve endings sensitive to light touch. Nerve impulses, generated by stimulation of the sensory receptors, travel first to the spinal cord and then to the brain.

Life Science for Young Catholics

CHAPTER 16: THE HUMAN SENSE ORGANS AND ENDOCRINE SYSTEM

Olfactory analyzer bulb
Olfactory epithelium
Nasal cavity
The fibers of olfactory receptors
Nostrils
Hard palate Tongue
Nose and olfactory system

The sense organs work in conjunction with the human nervous system. The complicated combined interactions between the sense organs and the nervous system provide delightful evidence of the intellect of God, Who designed them so that we can learn to know, love, and serve Him.

> **Section Review – 16.2 The Sense Organs**
>
> 1. Identify five sense organs.
> 2. How are sensory impulses generated by light sent to the brain?
> 3. Identify three basic parts of the ear.
> 4. What part of the ear vibrates due to sound waves?
> 5. Explain the function of the papillae.
> 6. How is odor information sent to the brain?

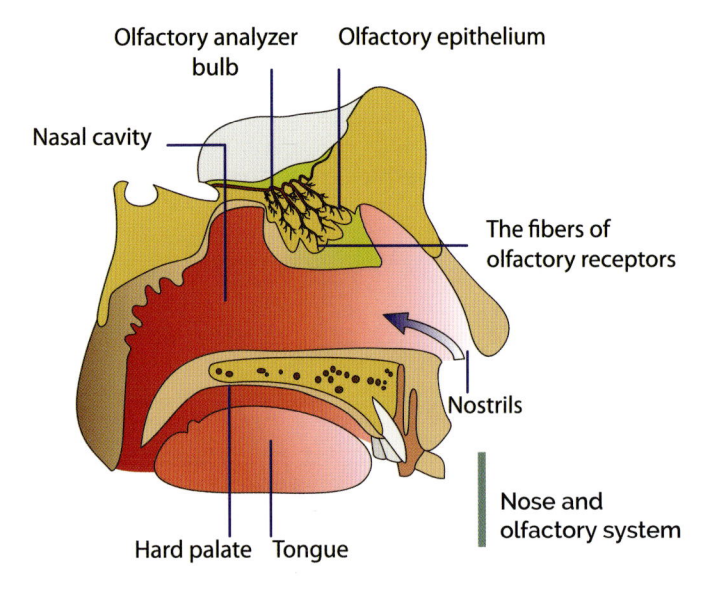

F. Summary

In summary, the sense organs provide our input from the outside world. It is through the sense organs that we can learn about God's creation. Through creation we can learn to appreciate God and the beautiful world that He made for us.

16.3 Making Connections and Putting It All Together

Neurons or nerve cells generate electrical impulses and thus transmit information to other neurons, to muscles, and to glands. Information from a neuron is transmitted to another cell across a **synapse** (*sin·aps*). Synapses are gaps between the end of one nerve cell and the beginning of another nerve cell, or muscle cell or gland.

The nerve impulse crosses the gap in a chemical way, not in an electrical way. The electrical impulse travels from one end of the nerve cell to the other. When a dendrite is excited through a chemical reaction, the impulse is generated and travels through the nerve cell to the other end, the axon. There the impulse generates a release of chemicals that travel across the synapse to the dendrite of the next nerve cell. These chemicals excite the next dendrite, causing a new electrical impulse that travels through that cell.

All activity directed and controlled by the brain and the nervous system is routed or directed and transferred between billions of synapses or gaps.

1. Sensory information, from receptors in the skin or in other sense organs, travels through sensory nerves and synapses within the central nervous system where the message is processed.

2. Interneurons connect the sensory fibers to motor neurons through more synapses.

3. Finally, motor neurons transmit the information to muscles and glands to produce an action or response.

Reflexes are actions controlled by the cells in the spinal cord rather than in the brain. Spinal reflexes allow a much more rapid response by the human body to a stimulus. For example, the instant withdrawal of a hand from a burning hot object is a spinal reflex. The nerve pathway that controls a reflex is called a **reflex arc**. The brain is not involved in the reflex arc, but is aware of the painful stimuli and can override and suppress the reflex action.

Life Science for Young Catholics

CHAPTER 16: THE HUMAN SENSE ORGANS AND ENDOCRINE SYSTEM

> **Section Review – 16.3 Making Connections and Putting It All Together**
>
> 1. Identify synapses.
> 2. Briefly describe reflexes.

16.4 The Endocrine System

The **endocrine system** is responsible for maintaining the body's proper functions, including all aspects of metabolism, reproduction, growth, and development. The endocrine system is a system of glands. Glands are responsible for producing hormones which are important for good health and development of the human body. **Hormones** are chemical messengers. These chemicals are secreted directly into the blood and affect specific tissues, often distant from the gland in which they were produced.

The major endocrine glands that make up the human endocrine system include: the **hypothalamus gland**, the **pituitary gland**, the **thyroid gland**, the **parathyroid glands**, the **thymus gland**, the **adrenal glands**, the **pineal gland**, the **gonads**, and the **pancreas**.

The **endocrine system** controls and regulates body processes that happen slowly over time, such as growth. The **nervous system**, on the other hand, controls and regulates body processes that change quickly, or moment to moment. However, the nervous system controls the endocrine system.

WORDS TO REMEMBER

sense organs: take in information from the environment. That information is processed in the brain; the five sense organs are the eyes, ears, tongue, nose, and skin.

sensory receptor: a sensory nerve ending in an organ or tissue that responds to a particular stimulus by sending an electrical impulse toward the central nervous system. Types of sensory receptors in the human body: 1) pressure, 2) pain, 3) light and color, 4) smell and taste, 5) temperature, 6) osmotic pressure to maintain fluid balance, and 7) position and motion of the body or limbs

synapse: a gap between the end of one nerve cell and the beginning of another nerve cell, or muscle cell or gland

reflexes: actions controlled by the cells in the spinal cord rather than in the brain; spinal reflexes allow rapid response to a stimulus.

endocrine system: a system of glands responsible for maintaining the body's proper functions, including metabolism, reproduction, growth, and development.

glands: responsible for producing hormones which are important for good health and development of the human body

hormones: chemical messengers secreted directly into the blood and affect specific tissues

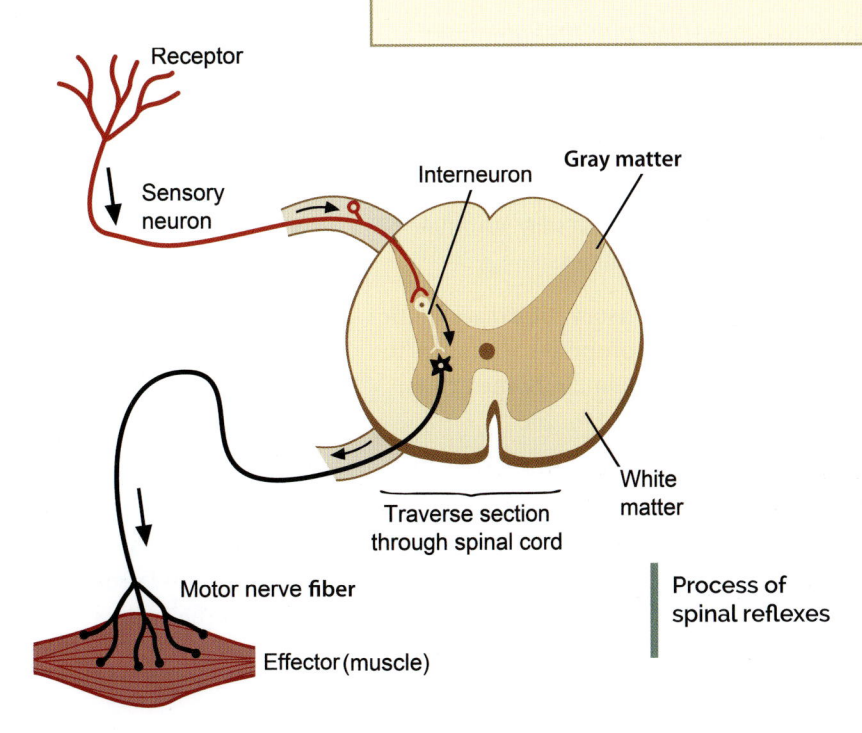

Process of spinal reflexes

Life Science for Young Catholics

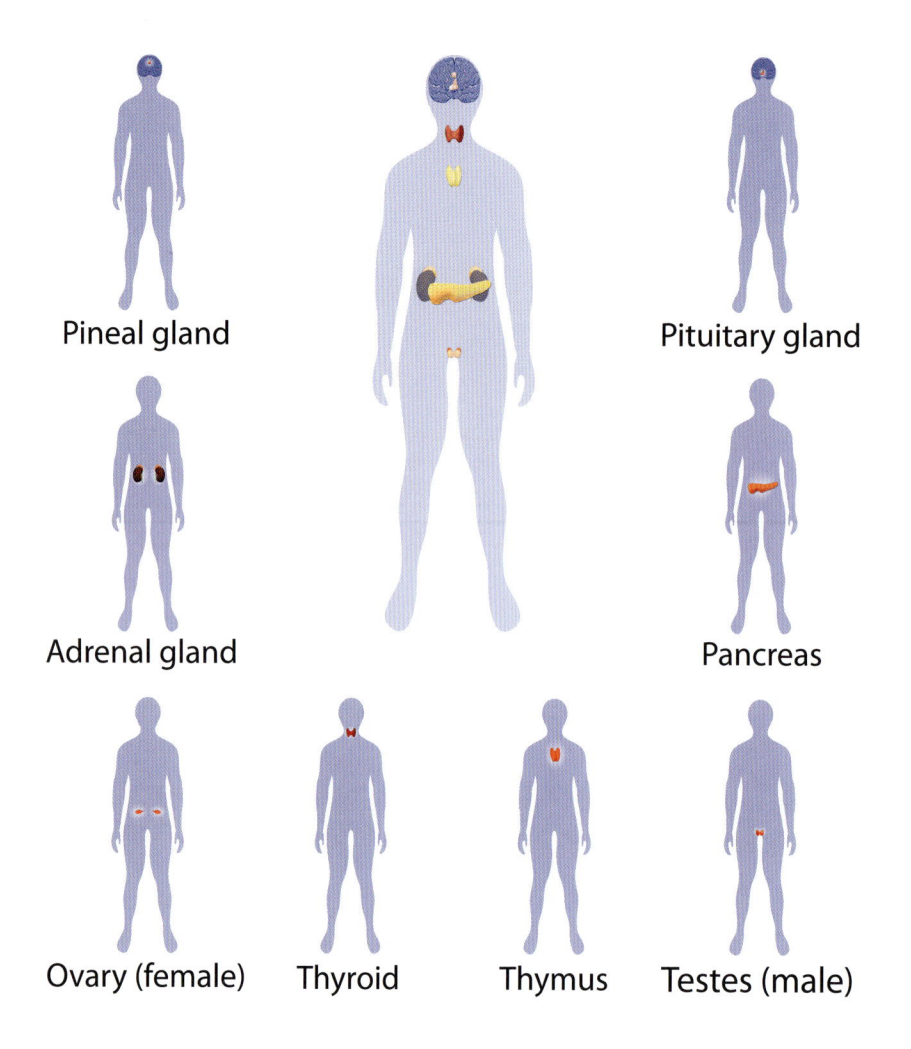

CHAPTER 16: THE HUMAN SENSE ORGANS AND ENDOCRINE SYSTEM

Location of some glands of the endocrine system

Pineal gland | Pituitary gland
Adrenal gland | Pancreas
Ovary (female) | Thyroid | Thymus | Testes (male)

A. The Hypothalamus Gland

The hypothalamus (*high-puh-**thal**-uh-muss*) gland is located in the forebrain. The hypothalamus gland controls most of the endocrine system.

Neurons in the hypothalamus gland produce hormones that affect the release of other hormones. Hormones from the hypothalamus may stimulate or block the release of other hormones.

Under the influence of sensory information, the hypothalamus releases the appropriate hormones to affect the change needed to maintain homeostasis, the proper internal environment for life.

The hormones produced by the hypothalamus control body temperature, thirst, hunger, sleep, and the release of other hormones in the body.

Hormones from the hypothalamus are released through axons to the pituitary gland.

B. The Pituitary Gland

The pituitary gland is a tiny gland that sits just under the hypothalamus in the brain. The pituitary gland is made of an anterior lobe, or rounded projection, and a posterior lobe.

The pituitary gland is called the "master gland" because it produces hormones that influence the activities of many of the major endocrine glands.

The **anterior lobe** of the pituitary gland produces "stimulating hormones" that influence the activity of the **thyroid gland** and the **adrenal glands**.

The anterior pituitary gland also produces the **human growth hormone**, which regulates growth and development of all tissues in the human body. The pituitary gland also produces **prolactin**, which regulates milk production in the **mammary glands** for a mother with a nursing baby.

Life Science for Young Catholics

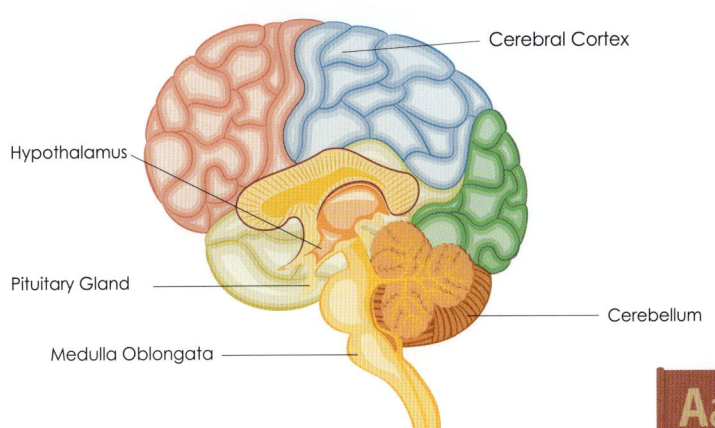

CHAPTER 16: THE HUMAN SENSE ORGANS AND ENDOCRINE SYSTEM

Location of the hypothalamus and the pituitary glands in the brain

The posterior lobe of the pituitary does not produce hormones. However, some hormones produced by the hypothalamus are sent to the posterior pituitary, which releases them into the bloodstream.

C. The Thyroid Gland

The thyroid gland is a butterfly-shaped gland found in the neck overlying the trachea, the tube carrying air to the lungs. The thyroid gland produces two hormones which regulate the body's metabolic rate, or the rate at which body cells use energy. The metabolic rate is important for every life process of every type of cell in the human body. It is also important for growth and normal development of the nervous system in infants and young children.

D. The Parathyroid Glands

Embedded within the lobes of the thyroid gland are four small **parathyroid glands**. The parathyroid glands produce a hormone which is important in calcium balance.

E. The Thymus Gland

The thymus gland is only active in children. After puberty, the thymus shrinks and is replaced by fat. The thymus is located between the lungs. It is important for the production of T-cells, disease-fighting white blood cells. Even after the thymus is no longer active, the T-cells it produced help to keep us healthy.

F. The Adrenal Glands

The **adrenal glands** are paired structures that sit on top of the kidneys. Each adrenal gland is made of an outer **cortex** and an inner **medulla**. The adrenal cortex controls salt and water balance in the body. The adrenal medulla controls the body's response to stressful events, controls metabolism, and influences sexual development.

WORDS TO REMEMBER

pituitary gland: a gland that sits under the hypothalamus in the brain and is made of an anterior lobe and a posterior lobe; called the "master gland" because it produces hormones that influence the activities of many of the major endocrine glands

anterior lobe: part of the pituitary gland that produces "stimulating hormones" that influence the activity of the thyroid gland and the adrenal glands; produces the human growth hormone, which regulates growth and development of all tissues in the human body; also produces prolactin, which regulates milk production in the mammary glands for a mother with a nursing baby

posterior lobe: part of the pituitary gland that releases some of the hormones produced in the hypothalamus into the bloodstream.

thyroid gland: a butterfly-shaped gland found in the neck overlying the trachea; produces two hormones which regulate the body's metabolic rate, or the rate at which body cells use energy

adrenal glands: paired structures that sit on top of the kidneys; made of an outer cortex and an inner medulla. The adrenal cortex controls salt and water balance in the body; the adrenal medulla controls the body's response to stressful events, controls metabolism, and influences sexual development.

adrenaline: the "fight or flight" hormone responsible for preparing the body to withstand stressful events; the hormone responsible for the increased heart rate, blood pressure, and shakiness that a person experiences when frightened, nervous, or excited

pineal gland: located within the brain, is important in regulating the sleep cycle through a hormone called melatonin

Life Science for Young Catholics

CHAPTER 16: THE HUMAN SENSE ORGANS AND ENDOCRINE SYSTEM

The adrenal glands produce **adrenaline**, the "fight or flight" hormone responsible for preparing the body to withstand stressful events. **Adrenaline** is the hormone responsible for the increased heart rate, blood pressure, and shakiness that a person experiences when frightened, nervous, or excited.

G. The Pineal Gland

The **pineal** (*pin-ee-uhl*) **gland**, located within the brain, is important in regulating the sleep cycle through a hormone called **melatonin** (*mel-uh-tone-in*). Increased amounts of melatonin are released as light is decreased; the increased melatonin helps a person fall asleep. Decreased release of melatonin in the morning with increasing light triggers a person to awaken.

H. The Gonads

The gonads are the reproductive glands. The **testes** in males are endocrine organs that produce **testosterone** and other hormones that are responsible for sexual development. The **ovaries** in females are also endocrine organs that produce **estrogen** and **progesterone**, which are responsible for female sexual development and maintaining pregnancy.

I. The Pancreas

The pancreas is both an endocrine gland, or ductless gland, and an exocrine gland, or gland with a duct.

The ductless endocrine portions of the pancreas are known as the **islets of Langerhans**. The islets of Langerhans produce three hormones: **somatostatin**, **insulin**, and **glucagon**. These three hormones are extremely important in maintaining normal glucose levels, or blood sugar levels, in the human body.

Insulin is the hormone that <u>decreases</u> blood glucose levels. **Glucagon** is the hormone that <u>increases</u> blood glucose levels. Together, insulin and glucagon maintain an appropriate level of sugar in the blood so that the body has a constant supply of energy. Somatostatin regulates insulin and glucagon.

WORDS TO REMEMBER

melatonin: the hormone produced by the pineal gland that regulates the sleep cycle.

gonads: the reproductive glands. Male gonads are called testes, and female gonads are called ovaries.

testes: the reproductive glands in males. They produce testosterone and other hormones that are responsible for sexual development.

ovaries: the reproductive glands in females. They produce estrogen and progesterone, which are responsible for female sexual development and maintaining pregnancy.

parathyroid glands: located on the thyroid; produce a hormone which is important in calcium balance.

pancreas: is both an endocrine gland, or ductless gland, and an exocrine gland, or gland with a duct. The ductless, endocrine portions of the pancreas are known as the Islets of Langerhans. The islets of Langerhans produce three hormones: somatostatin, insulin and glucagon. These three hormones are extremely important in maintaining normal glucose levels, or blood sugar levels, in the human body.

insulin: the hormone that decreases blood glucose levels.

glucagon: the hormone that increases blood glucose levels.

somatostatin: the hormone that regulates insulin and glucagon

Section Review – 16.4 The Endocrine System

1. Identify four areas of the body's internal environment that are controlled by the endocrine system.
2. List the nine major parts of the endocrine system.
3. What are hormones?
4. What gland controls most of the endocrine system?
5. Identify adrenaline. Include where it is produced and how it helps the body.

16.5 Endocrine Summary

Together with the nervous system, the endocrine system helps maintain the proper functions of the human body. The endocrine system influences the way the body grows, develops, and uses and stores energy through chemical messengers, the hormones.

The hormones of the endocrine system coordinate and control many functions throughout the human body. Both the nervous system and the endocrine system are intimately related to all other organ systems. Together, they maintain the delicate balance needed for growth, life, and the continuation of God's creative earthly masterpiece, the human being, made of soul and body.

> **Section Review – 16.5 Endocrine Summary**
>
> 1. The nervous system and the endocrine system work together for what purpose?
> 2. Which other organ systems are influenced by these two systems?

16.6 What is Man?

"What is man that thou art mindful of him? Or the son of man that thou visitest him? Thou hast made him a little less than the angels, thou hast crowned him with glory and honor: and hast set him over the works of thy hands. Thou hast subjected all things under his feet, all sheep and oxen: moreover the beasts also of the fields. The birds of the air, and the fishes of the sea, that pass through the paths of the sea. O Lord our Lord, how admirable is thy name in all the earth!" (Psalm 8:4-9)

"Blessed are all they that fear the Lord: that walk in his ways. For thou shalt eat the labors of thy hands: blessed art thou, and it shall be well with thee. Thy wife as a fruitful vine, on the sides of thy house. Behold, thus shall the man be blessed that fear the Lord. May the Lord bless thee out of Sion: and may thou see the good things of Jerusalem all the days of thy life. And may thou see thy children's children." – Psalm 127

The Church and the Bible make it clear that God deeply loves each and every person He ever created. In its own way, the study of the human body confirms God's care for mankind, and gives us some insight into the wonder of God Himself.

From the smallest atoms and the workings of physical creation, to the smallest single-celled creatures, through the magnificence and beauty of the plants and animals of the world, we can see God's Providence, and feel a sense of awe that He gave us dominion over all of the earthly world.

God made us wonderfully. God made us to grow, and He provided the food for growth. He gave us the means to consume that food and change it into the energy and materials that our bodies need for growth. He gave us the ability to reproduce, and provide Him the vehicle to create new, eternal human souls. He gave us minds to learn to know Him, and the means to love Him and to serve Him.

Let us all thank God for the wonder of Himself, and for creating us to share in His eternal family life on Earth and in Heaven.

CHAPTER 16: THE HUMAN SENSE ORGANS AND ENDOCRINE SYSTEM

Chapter 16 Review

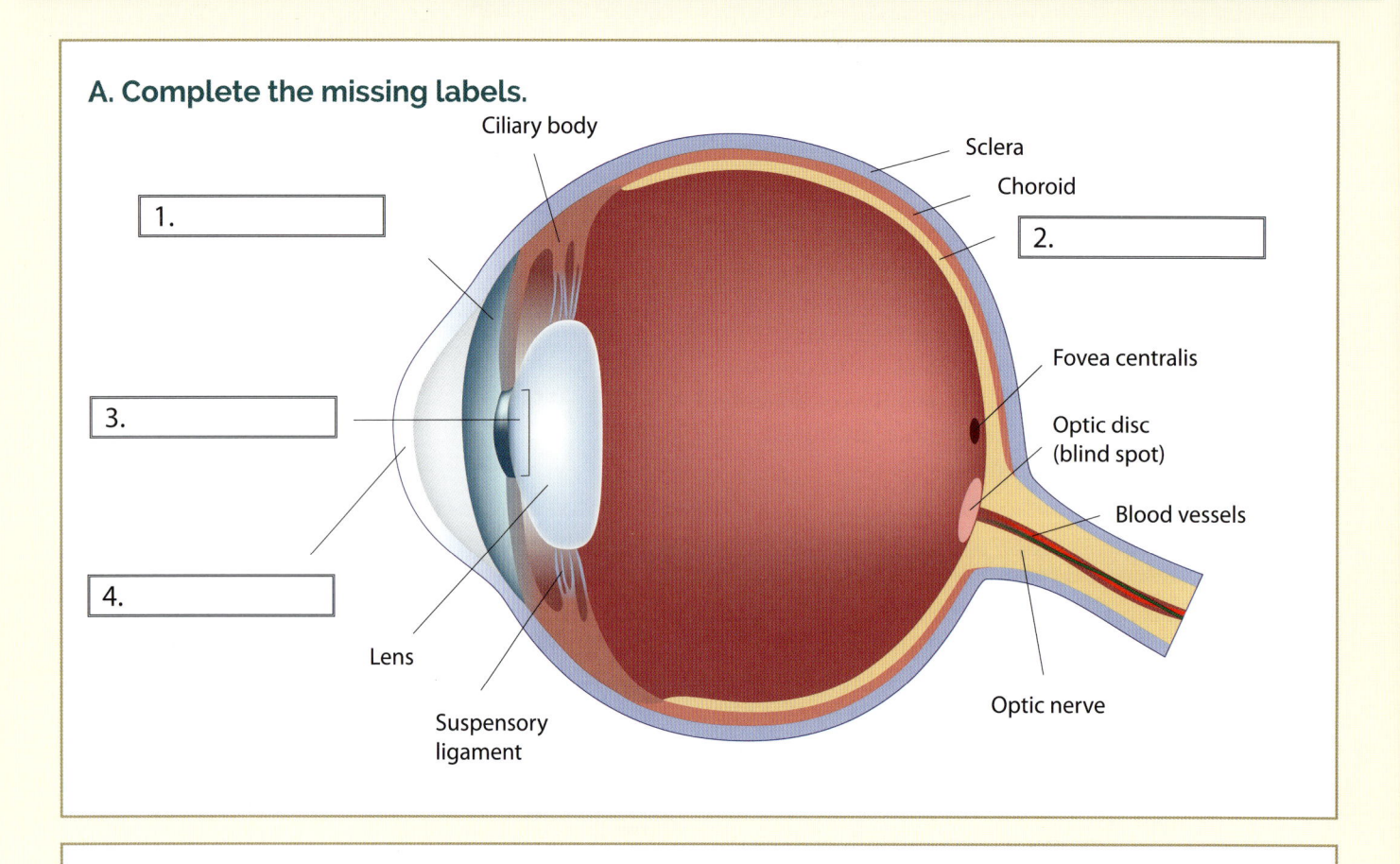

A. Complete the missing labels.

Labels shown on diagram: Ciliary body, Sclera, Choroid, Fovea centralis, Optic disc (blind spot), Blood vessels, Optic nerve, Lens, Suspensory ligament

1. ____
2. ____
3. ____
4. ____

B. Answer the following questions.

1. Identify five sense organs.
2. Identify the senses related to each sense organ.
3. How are sensory impulses generated by light sent to the brain?
4. Identify three basic parts of the ear.
5. What part of the ear vibrates due to sound waves?
6. How does "sound" get transmitted to the brain?
7. Explain the function of the papillae.
8. What is the major organ of touch?
9. Identify four bodily functions that are controlled by the endocrine system.
10. What are hormones?
11. What gland controls most of the endocrine system?
12. Explain the function of melatonin, and where it is produced.
13. Identify adrenaline. Include where it is produced and how it helps the body.
14. Identify insulin. Include where it is produced and how it helps the body.
15. The nervous system and the endocrine system work together for what purpose?

Life Science for Young Catholics

Chapter 16: "Words to Remember" Crossword

ACROSS

6. The system is responsible for maintaining the body's proper functions including all aspects of metabolism, reproduction, growth, and development.
7. the hormone produced by the pineal gland that regulates the sleep cycle
9. responsible for producing hormones which are important for good health and development of the human body
10. the hormone that decreases blood glucose levels
11. actions controlled by the cells in the spinal cord rather than in the brain
12. the reproductive glands

DOWN

1. the hormone that increases blood glucose levels
2. both an endocrine gland, or ductless gland, and an exocrine gland, or gland with a duct
3. chemical messengers. They are secreted directly into the blood and affect specific tissues, often distant from the gland in which they were produced.
4. the reproductive glands in males. They produce testosterone and other hormones that are responsible for sexual development.
5. the "fight or flight" hormone responsible for preparing the body to withstand stressful events
8. the reproductive glands in females. They produce estrogen and progesterone which are responsible for female sexual development, and maintaining pregnancy.

Glossary

Absorption: the process by which digested food substances are passed from the digestive tract into the blood where these food substances are transported to the remainder of the body

Acellular slime molds: eukaryotic organisms that have a streaming phase in which the separate organisms merge and produce spore-bearing fruiting bodies

Acidophiles (a-**sid**·o·files): extremophiles that live in very acidic environments

Active transport: requires the use of energy to get substances to cross the cell membrane, either because their chemical properties do not permit diffusion, or because they must be transported from an area of lesser concentration to an area of greater concentration.

ADP: adenosine diphosphate (*die*-**fos**-*feyt*). ADP is involved in the synthesis and breakdown of ATP. ADP has only two phosphates.

Adrenal glands: paired structures that sit on top of the kidneys. Each adrenal gland is made of an outer **cortex** and an inner **medulla**. The adrenal cortex controls salt and water balance in the body. The adrenal medulla controls the body's response to stressful events, controls metabolism, and influences sexual development.

Adrenaline: the "fight or flight" hormone responsible for preparing the body to withstand stressful events. Adrenaline is the hormone responsible for the increased heart rate, blood pressure, and shakiness that a person experiences when frightened, nervous, or excited.

Aerobic (ay·**row**·bik): organisms or processes that require oxygen

African sleeping sickness: a disease caused by trypanosomes. Symptoms include fever, severe headaches, irritability, extreme fatigue, body aches, and confusion. If the person is not quickly and properly treated, the infection will cause death within months.

Airways: tube-like structures that carry oxygen-containing air into the respiratory system and carry carbon dioxide out of the system

Albumin: the protein primarily responsible for maintaining fluid balance inside and outside of cells

Algae (**al**·jee): a plantlike organism that lives in water, contains chlorophyll

Alimentary (al-uh-**men**-tar-ee) **canal**: a long, hollow, twisted, and coiled tube extending from the mouth to the anus, or exit of waste from the body. The alimentary canal is sometimes referred to as the gastrointestinal (gas-tro-in-**tes**-tin-al) tract, or GI tract.

Allergy: a hypersensitivity disorder of the immune system. Another name for an allergy is an allergic reaction. An allergic reaction occurs when maturing lymph cells react to seemingly harmless antigens (things which don't belong in the human body) just as they would for true germs.

Alveoli (al·vee·**oh**·lee): tiny balloon- or sac-like structures made of endothelial cells that are only one cell layer thick. The alveoli are the location of gas exchange in the lungs.

Amino (*uh*-**mee**-*noh*) **acids**: organic molecules that are the building blocks of proteins. There are twenty-two amino acids that occur naturally in nature.

Amoeba: unicellular, or single-celled, protozoa that move by means of pseudopods. Pseudopods, also known as false feet, are extensions of cytoplasm that reach out and then retract to pull the organism along a surface. They live on land and in water environments.

Amphibians (am-**fib**-ee-ans) cold-blooded, vertebrate animals that live part of their life cycle in the water and part on the land. Amphibians include frogs, toads, salamanders, and caecilians (sa·**sill**·ee·ans).

Anaerobic (**an**·a·row·bik): organisms or processes that do not require oxygen

Anaerobic fungi: only found in the digestive tracts of certain plant-eating animals. These fungi do not require oxygen, hence the name anaerobic – without oxygen. These fungi are necessary for the larger animals to break down plant materials in the digestive process.

Angiosperms (**an**·jee·o·sperms): flowering plants which produce seeds protected by a cover

Animal-like protists: known as protozoa. Protozoa are single-celled eukaryotes that share some traits with animals. Animal-like protists can move, and they obtain nutrition from outside of themselves instead of producing their own food.

Anterior lobe (of the pituitary gland)**:** produces "stimulating hormones" that influence the activity of the thyroid gland and the adrenal glands. The anterior pituitary gland also produces the human growth hormone, which regulates growth and development of all tissues in the human body, and prolactin, which regulates milk production in the mammary glands for a mother with a nursing baby.

Antibiotics (ant·i·by·**ah**·tiks): powerful medicines that fight bacterial infections. Antibiotics either stop the growth of or directly kill bacteria.

Antibodies: destroy foreign cells. Antibodies are complex molecules that attach to infected cells in order to kill the germs.

Aorta: the largest artery of the circulatory system, located on the top of the heart

Aortic valve: allows blood pumped by the left ventricle to pass into the aorta and to the rest of the body, but does not permit blood to flow back from the aorta into the left ventricle.

Appendicular (app·en·**dik**·you·lar) **skeleton**: consists of the 126 bones that attach from the central axis, that is, the spinal column, and includes all the bones of the shoulder and hip girdles, that is, the arms, legs, hands, fingers, feet, and toes.

Appendix: functions as a lymph organ in adults. The appendix assists with the maturing of B-cells, that is, immune cells made in bone marrow. The appendix is also involved in the production of molecules that help to direct the movement of lymphocytes, the small white cells of the immune system, to various other locations in the body.

Arachnids: arthropods that have bodies comprised of two segments and eight legs. Those eight legs help them to move very quickly! Arachnids, including spiders, mites, scorpions, and ticks, have an abdomen and a cephalothorax (**seff**·ah·low·**thor**·ax). A cephalothorax means the head and the thorax are joined. Thus, the arachnids have only two body segments.

Archaea (ar-**key**-uh): single-celled organisms that lack a membrane-bound nucleus and membrane-bound organelles

Aristotle: a Greek scientist, lived in the third century B.C., that is, Before Christ. Aristotle devised a classification system or scheme based on similarities between organisms and based on a hierarchy from "lowest to highest," with humans being the highest. Aristotle is considered to be the ancient "Father of Taxonomy."

Arteries: vessels that carry blood away from the heart. Arteries have thick muscular walls with much elastic connective tissue and a smaller central cavity because they carry blood pumped under high pressure from the heart.

Arterioles (are·**teer**·ee·oles): small arteries. Arterioles downsize the blood flow so that it can be handled by the tiny capillaries.

Arthropods (**arth**-ro-pods): the largest group of the whole animal kingdom; this group includes myriapods (**meer**·ee·ah·pods) **or multi-foots, insects, arachnids** (a·**rack**·nids), and crustaceans (crus·**tay**·shuns). All arthropods are bilaterally symmetrical, with similar parts on each side of their bodies. Arthropods also have jointed appendages, or jointed limbs.

Ascending tracts: pathways that carry sensory impulses to the spinal cord from the skin

Assimilation: the process by which the digested food materials become a part of the cells in the human body

Asymmetric body symmetry: describes bodies with no orderly repeating parts

Atom: the basic unit of all matter

Atomic mass: the mass of an element that is derived from the mass of both the protons and neutrons in the nucleus of that atom

Atomic number: unique for each type of atom, or element. It is determined by the number of protons in that element.

ATP: adenosine triphosphate (*uh-**den**-uh-sin try-**fos**-feyt*). ATP is the molecule of energy in living cells. ATP transports the chemical energy required for metabolism. ATP has three phosphates.

Atria (**ay**-tree-ah): two smaller chambers at the top of the heart that pump blood into the larger ventricles.

Atrioventricular node (AV node): located in the floor of the right atrium

Autonomic nervous system: part of the peripheral nervous system which controls involuntary body functions through smooth muscle, cardiac muscle, and glands

Autotrophs (**au**-to-trofs): organisms that make their own food supply

Axial (**ax**-ee-ahl) **skeleton:** is made of 80 bones and includes all the bones of the body's axis: the spinal column, head, and ribs

Axon: the extension from the nerve cell body at the bottom or end of the cell. Each neuron has only one axon. An axon carries impulses away from the cell body and transmits impulses to other cells.

Bacteria: the second of the prokaryotic domains. Bacteria are single-celled organisms that lack a membrane-bound nucleus and membrane-bound organelles.

Ball and socket joint: like that of the shoulder or the hip, is the only type of joint that allows movement in a full circle around a fixed point

Basidia: the spore-bearing or spore-producing organs on mushrooms that form on the gills

B-cells: directly kill germ-infected cells. B-cells are made in the bone marrow. The "B" in B-cell stands for "bone marrow." B-cells work within the blood stream.

Biaxial joints: allow movement in two planes, as in the knuckles of the hand

Bicarbonate: neutralizes the hydrochloric acid from the stomach to protect the lining of the intestine, while pancreatic enzymes complete much of the digestion.

Bilateral symmetry: describes animals that have bodies that can be divided into two identical halves.

Bile: a thick green fluid that is produced by the liver, stored in the gallbladder, and released into the small intestine. Bile breaks down large fat droplets into small droplets for easier digestion and absorption into the blood stream.

Bilirubin: a pigment formed from the breakdown of hemoglobin from old red blood cells.

Binomial nomenclature (*bahy-**noh**-mee-uhl noh-muhn-**kley**-cher*): a two-part naming system for living things. In this system, organisms are identified according to the genus and species.

Biochemistry (by-oh-**kem**-is-tree): the study of all the chemical reactions occurring in living organisms

Birds, or Aves (**ay**·vees): warm-blooded, egg-laying vertebrates that have feathers, wings, and a beak, and can usually fly

Blight: a disease or injury of plants, caused by fungi, and marked by the formation of lesions, withering, and death of parts

Blood-brain barrier: protects the brain from harmful substances in the blood.

Blood pressure: the force needed to keep blood flowing through the vessels to the whole body. Blood pressure must be high enough so that all the tissues are adequately supplied, but also low enough so that the tissues are not damaged.

Blood vessels: the "pipes" that carry blood throughout the body. The major types of blood vessels include arteries, veins, and capillaries. Blood vessels have walls made of smooth muscle cells and elastic connective tissue, and are lined with endothelial cells.

Life Science for Young Catholics

Blood: a specialized tissue composed of living cells in a liquid environment

Body symmetry: in animals is characterized by exactly similar body parts organized facing each other.

Bone marrow: a jelly-like substance that contains red blood cells

Bony fish: comprise the largest group of vertebrates, with approximately 30,000 different species of fish divided into two major subgroups: the ray-finned fish and the lobe-finned fish. Over 99% of all bony fish are ray-finned; there are only eight living species of lobe-finned fish.

Botanists: scientists who study plants.

Brain functions: the brain is the organ that controls most of the functions of the body. Lower functions controlled by the brain include heart rate, respiration, blood pressure, and digestion, and all voluntary movement. Higher functions controlled by the human brain include consciousness, memory, planning, language, creativity, emotion, personality, expression, problem solving, and reasoning.

Brainstem: the portion of the brain connecting the brain to the spinal cord. The brainstem is mostly white matter from motor neurons and sensory neurons traveling between the brain and spinal cord. The brainstem coordinates motor signals sent from the brain to the body. It consists of the **medulla oblongata** and the **pons**.

Bread Molds: a type of fungus that live on land, in soil, and on decaying organic matter. Bread molds are a major cause of spoiled fruits and vegetables.

Bronchi (*bron*-keye): the tubes at the end of the trachea that bring air into the lungs. The bottom of the trachea divides into two main bronchi, these divide again into smaller and smaller tubes.

Bronchioles (bron·kee·oles): the smallest tubes of the bronchi

Capillaries (cap·ill·air·ees): the smallest of blood vessels, with walls that are only one cell-layer thick. In the capillaries, oxygen and carbon dioxide are able to freely move in and out of the blood by diffusion.

Carbohydrate: an organic macromolecule which is an important source of energy for your body. All **sugars** and **starches** and fibers are carbohydrates.

Carbon: the basic element of life

Cardiac muscle: specialized muscle of the heart that contracts without stimulation from nerves

Carolus Linnaeus (*kar*-uh-luhs li-*nee*-uhs): a Swedish botanist who devised a system of classification and naming of organisms that remains the basic framework of the modern system used today. Carolus Linnaeus is considered to be the modern "Father of Taxonomy."

Cartilage: firm but rubbery tissue that serves as a cushion at the joints

Cartilaginous fish: fish whose internal structure is not bone but cartilage, which is like a tough elastic tissue, and they do not have ribs to protect internal organs. Cartilaginous fish include sharks, rays, and chimaeras (kim·*ear*-as).

Cell division: the process by which a cell divides into two or more cells. Cell division is the source or cause of tissue growth and repair in multicellular organisms.

Cell membrane: a biological membrane, made up of proteins and lipids, that separates the interior of all cells from the outside environment and protects the cell from its surroundings.

Cell theory: living organisms are composed of living cells that are organized according to specific laws. Cell theory has three main points: 1) All living organisms are composed of one or more cells; 2) the cell is the basic unit of life; 3) new cells are reproduced from pre-existing, living cells, through cell division.

Cell wall: the rigid structure on the outside of plant cells that provides their basic structure.

Cell: the basic unit of structure and function of all living organisms

Cellular respiration: the process by which a cell turns the energy stored in food into energy that is used by the cell. More specifically, cellular respiration is the process by which the sugar, which is glucose ($C_6H_{12}O_6$), is broken down to produce ATP.

Cellular slime molds: eukaryotic organisms that exist as free-living amoeboid cells in the soil and under certain conditions aggregate into a large colonial mass

Cellulose (*sel-yuh-lohs*): a complex carbohydrate that gives cells strength and support

Cementum (see-**men**-tum): a thin layer of bony material that fixes teeth to the jaw

Central nervous system: includes the brain and spinal cord.

Centrioles (**sent**-ree-oles): organelles in animal cells, they are small paired cylindrical structures that help to pull apart the two halves of a cell during cellular reproduction

Cerebellum: or "little brain," is the part of the hindbrain situated beneath the occipital lobes (round projections). The cerebellum is important for coordinating motor functions, including those involved in maintaining posture and balance, and muscle coordination in activities such as speaking, walking, and writing.

Cerebral cortex: the outer surface of the two cerebral hemispheres. The cerebral cortex is a convoluted surface made of folds and fissures of gray matter.

Cerebrum (sir·**ree**·brum): the outermost portion of the forebrain, made up of two areas called hemispheres. The right and left cerebral hemispheres are connected by a tract of white matter. The cerebrum is the largest region of the brain and is responsible for higher functions, including thought, language, logic, reasoning, and creativity.

Chemical digestion: the breakdown of food particles by chemical means, through the action of enzymes, into simpler substances

Chemistry: the study of matter, its composition and properties.

Chitin (**ky**·tin): a complex, large sugar molecule that makes up the cell walls of fungi. Chitin is also found in the hard outer shell of insects and mollusks.

Chlorophyll (**klor**·o·fill): the green pigment in plant cells where photosynthesis takes place

Chloroplasts (**klor**·o·plasts): membrane-bound organelles that contain stacks of chlorophyll

Cholesterol (*kol·es·ter·all*): an important component of cell structure and a building block for other steroids

Chordates (**kor**-dates): have bilateral symmetry or duplicate body parts on both sides, a body cavity, and segmented bodies. All chordates are animals with a digestive tract that has an intake opening or mouth, and an exit opening or anus.

Chytrids (**ky**·trids): fungi shaped like "little pots." Chytrids are some of the simplest of fungi. They exist mainly in aquatic environments, including both fresh water and salt water.

Cilia (**sill**·ee·ah): short hair-like structures that extend from the surface of some cells

Circulatory system: includes the heart, blood vessels, and blood. Another name for the circulatory system is the cardiovascular system. This system brings oxygen and nutrients to the cells in the body, and brings waste products, like carbon dioxide, to the lungs and other organs of waste disposal for elimination from the body.

Club fungi: have club-shaped spore-producing structures, and are important decomposers of decaying materials in the soil. Club fungi are also symbiotic partners, providing mutual benefits for many plants.

Cochlea (**kok**·lee·uh)**:** the portion of the inner ear that contains **hair cells,** which are the sensory receptors for sound

Colon: another name for the large intestine. It is the final part of the digestive tract, where any remaining water and electrolytes are re-absorbed for use in the body.

Commensalism (com·**men**·sal·ism): a symbiotic relationship that benefits one organism, but neither helps nor harms the other organism

Compact bone: the hard, smooth bone tissue that forms the surface of bones

Complementary muscles: muscles that operate in pairs, but in opposite directions. When one muscle of the pair contracts, the other relaxes.

Compound: a combination of two or more elements. The ratio of the elements in any compound is always the same for the molecules of that particular compound.

Conifers (con·eh·furs): cone-bearing, woody gymnosperms that are found in a wide variety of climates on all continents except Antarctica.

Connective tissue: is made up of cells and fibers distributed throughout a fluid environment. Connective tissue supports and connects other tissue types within organs, serves as a barrier between different layers of tissues within organs, provides structure to organisms, and serves to transport materials from one part of the organism to another.

Coronary (**core**·on·air·ee) **circulation:** provides oxygen and nutrients to the cardiac muscle (heart muscle) itself.

Cotyledons (kot·o·**lee**·dons): seed leaves that develop within the seed

Cristae (**kris**·tay): the folded, fingerlike projections of the inner wall of mitochondria. Cristae are important in the making of ATP during cellular respiration.

Crustaceans: mostly aquatic arthropods that typically have the body covered with a hard shell or crust. Crustaceans include lobsters, crabs, crayfish, shrimp, krill, barnacles, and pill bugs.

Cuticle (**kyoo**·tik·al): the waxy layer on a leaf that protects the leaf from outside injury and from excessive water loss

Cytoplasm (**sigh**·toe·plaz·m): clear, gel-like substance outside the nucleus of the cell of plants and animals

Decomposers (dee·com·**pose**·ers): organisms that break down dead organisms and organic matter into simpler organic compounds so they can release carbon and minerals back into the environment.

Dehydration (dee-hi-**dray**-shun): excessive loss of water from the body

Dendrites: short, highly-branched extensions that help increase the surface area of the nerve cell body. Dendrites receive impulses from other cells.

Dentin: the largest component of the tooth, a hard bony-like tissue found beneath the enamel

Deoxyribose (dee-ok-si-**rahy**-bohs**):** the sugar in DNA

Dermis: the middle layer of skin that contains the base of the hair follicles and the base of the sweat glands

Descending tracts: pathways that carry motor impulses from the spinal cord to the muscles

Diaphragm (**die**·uh·fram): a large muscle at the bottom of the chest cavity. The contraction and relaxation of this muscle controls the movement of air into and out of the lungs.

Diastolic (di·as·**taul**·ik) **pressure:** the forces remaining in the arteries when the ventricles are resting and refilling

Diatomaceous (di-at-o-**may**-shus) **earth:** made of the hard outer layer of the outer cell wall of diatoms that collect on the sea floors over many years. It is used in filtering systems, abrasives, cleansers, and paint.

Diatoms (**die**·uh·toms): single-celled organisms, a type of algae, that can be found in fresh water, salt water, moist soil, and on moist surfaces of some plants. Diatoms are a component or a part of **plankton**.

Dicots: seed-bearing plants that contain two embryonic seed leaves. Dicots produce flowers with petals in multiples of four and five. Dicot leaves have veins that form a branching, or netted, pattern from a central mid-vein.

Diffusion (dih-**fyoo**-shun): the movement of molecules across a membrane from an area of higher concentration to an area of lower concentration. Diffusion does not require the use of the cell's energy.

Digestion: the actual breaking down of complex food into the basic building blocks of carbohydrates, proteins, fats, vitamins, and other small nutrients

Digestive system: the organ system responsible for breaking down food into carbohydrates, proteins, fats, vitamins, and other small nutrients which are used by the human body for energy to fuel all the life processes

DNA: deoxyribonucleic (*dee-ok-si-rahy-boh-noo-klee-ik*) acid. DNA carries the genetic code of the organism.

Domain: classifies organisms based on the complexity of their cell structure. Modern scientists now consider this to be the broadest classification category of living things.

Double helix (*hee-liks***):** the "twisted ladder" shape of the DNA molecule

downy mildew: fungi-like, parasitic organisms that produce whitish masses of sporangiophores or conidiophores on the undersurface of the leaves of host plants

Ducts: tubes surrounded by tissue to conduct liquids

Duodenum (dew·oh·**dee**·num): the first of three segments of the small intestine extending directly from the stomach. The duodenum receives the partially digested food from the stomach.

Ear: the organ of hearing

Eardrum (tympanic membrane): a thin membrane that separates the external ear from the middle ear. Its function is to transmit sound vibrations from the air to the ossicles inside the middle ear.

Electrical impulses: are part of the method that nerve cells use to send information from one end of the cell to the other. Neurons receive information through chemical messengers, then generate an electrical impulse from the receiving end to the transmitting end.

Electrolytes (ee·**lek**·tro·lites): include sodium, potassium, chloride, and other substances. Electrolytes are chemicals that allow cells to maintain the correct electrical voltage to work properly.

Electrons: tiny, negatively charged sub-units of an atom that orbit about the nucleus

Element: a pure substance, that is, a substance in its simplest form, which cannot be broken down further by normal chemical means

Enamel: one of the four major tissues that make up the tooth. It makes up the hard mineralized surface of teeth.

Endocrine system: responsible for maintaining the body's proper functions, including all aspects of metabolism, reproduction, growth, and development. The endocrine system is a system of glands.

Endocytosis (end·o·sigh·**toe**·sis): a type of **active transport** involving the proteins in cell membranes. Endocytosis brings materials **into the cell**.

Endoplasmic reticulum (end·o·**plaz**·mik re·**tick**·you·lum): the network of membranes and pockets of the nuclear membrane that extends and branches into the cytoplasm. This network is involved in the production and movement of proteins. There are two types of endoplasmic reticulum: **rough** and **smooth**.

Enzymes: large biological molecules responsible for the thousands of metabolic processes that sustain life. Enzymes are catalysts; they make a chemical reaction work faster, or better, without being used up themselves. Enzymes accelerate or increase the rate of metabolic reactions, like the digestion of food.

Epidermis (ep·uh·**der**-mis) (root): the outermost tissue of a root, which protects the root and helps prevent water loss.

Epidermis (ep·uh·**der**-mis) (layer of the skin): the outer layer, or top layer, of the skin. It is made up of epithelial cells.

Epiglottis (ep·uh·**glott**·iss): a small flap of tissue at the base of the throat. The epiglottis is a protective feature of the respiratory system. The epiglottis flap automatically closes over the voice box, that is, the opening of the windpipe, when a person swallows, to prevent choking.

Life Science for Young Catholics

Epithelial (ep-eh-**thee**-lee-al) **cells**: flat, scale-like cells on the outermost layer of the skin. Vitamin D is produced in these cells.

Epithelial (ep-eh-**thee**-lee-al) **tissue:** is made of groups of cells tightly packed together in sheets or clusters and assembled on a **membrane**. Epithelial tissue is important in protection, secretion, absorption, and transportation of materials between cells.

Euglena (you-**glee**-na): single-celled protists that contain chlorophyll and are capable of photosynthesis. Euglena do not have cell walls. Some species of euglena have a red eye spot that helps them detect and move toward light.

Eukaryotes (you-**kar**-ee-oats): multicellular organisms with cells that have an organized nucleus as well as tiny, membrane-protected organelles, which are specialized parts of a cell

Eukaryotic (**you**·kar·ee·ot·ik) **cells**: complex cells. Eukaryotic cells have a true, organized nucleus, usually located near the center of the cell. This nucleus has a protective membrane around it to separate it from the cytoplasm within the cell. Eukaryotic cells also have membrane-enclosed organelles as well as ribosomes.

Excretion (*ek-**skree**-shuhn*): an active process through which living organisms remove byproducts of metabolism, or waste products, from themselves. Excretion is the final step in the process of digestion.

Exocytosis (**ex**·o·sigh·**toe**·sis): active transport of materials out of cells, a process that involves proteins. Exocytosis is the process by which waste is removed from cells; it is a means of excretion.

Exoenzymes (ex-o-**en**-zimes): enzymes that are secreted out of a fungus cell, and that work outside of the cell directly in decaying matter to digest it

External auditory canal: passageway that leads from the outer ear to the tympanic membrane, or eardrum

Extracellular fluid: the fluid outside the cells

Extremophiles (ex·**treem**·o·files): types of archaea that live and thrive in extreme conditions where other organisms could not. For example, some extremophiles live in volcanoes and hot springs, while others can thrive in the Dead Sea and the Great Salt Lake.

Eye: the organ of **sight**. The eye is responsible for vision.

Fats: are important in long-term energy storage in animals, and provide much nutritional energy. In fact, one gram of fat stores nine times as much energy as the same amount of carbohydrate.

Fatty acid: a very long chain of carbon and hydrogen molecules. Fatty acids are the building blocks of the fat in food, and in the body. Fatty acid molecules are usually joined together in groups of three, forming a molecule called a triglyceride.

Fermentation (fur·men·**tay**·shun): the process by which yeasts turn sugars into alcohols

Fibrin: a protein that solidifies a blood clot

Fibrous root system: the network of secondary roots that develops by replacing an embryonic taproot with a great number of smaller roots. These smaller roots grow into a highly intertwined network that spreads throughout the soil. This type of fibrous root system is seen in grasses and in plants used to prevent surface erosion by holding the soil so it does not wash away in a rain storm.

Flagella (fla·**gel**·uh): whip-like structures, similar to tails, that extend from the cell body and enable those cells to move through their environment

Fleshy roots: taproots that enlarge and store sugars and starches. Carrots and beets are two common examples of fleshy roots.

Flowers: house the reproductive structures of angiosperms.

Forebrain: the largest part of the brain. It is located at the front and top of the brain cavity. The forebrain has roles within perception, memory, and all higher thought processes. It is also involved in regulating skeletal movement and other higher motor functions. The forebrain includes the cerebrum, two thalami, and the hypothalamus.

Fronds: the leaves of ferns

Fructose (*frook-tohs*): "fruit sugar"

Fruit: forms from a mature fertilized ovary in an angiosperm plant. A fruit acts as a means of protection and dispersal for the seeds.

Fruiting bodies: the part of a fungus that forms on the surface of the soil. The fruiting bodies are the structures most commonly recognized as fungi and are found in a wide variety of shapes, sizes, and colors. The part of the common mushroom that you can see on your lawn is a fruiting body. The fruiting bodies are specialized to produce and release spores, which are the reproductive cells of fungi.

Fungus: (plural: **fungi**): a large group of eukaryotic organisms, including molds, mildews, mushrooms, rusts, and smuts, which are parasites on living organisms or feed upon dead organic material. Fungi lack chlorophyll, true roots, stems, and leaves, and they reproduce by means of spores.

Fungus-like protists: obtain food outside themselves. They also have cell walls and reproduce by forming spores, just like fungi. Fungus-like protists usually do not move on their own. Two major types of fungus-like protists are slime molds and water molds.

Gallbladder: a pear-shaped muscular-walled organ that stores and releases bile into the duodenum to aid in digestion by breaking down fats. Bile travels from the gallbladder to the small intestine in the common bile duct.

Ganglion: a collection of nerve cell bodies outside of the central nervous system

Gastric juice: a thin, strong acid. It is a nearly colorless liquid that is secreted by the glands in the lining of the stomach, which contains mucus, hydrochloric acid, and enzymes.

Gastrointestinal (gas-tro-in-tes-tin-al) **tract:** or **GI tract**, is also called the alimentary canal. It is a long, hollow, twisted, and coiled tube extending from the mouth to the anus, or exit of waste from the body.

Genetic code: contains all information needed to build and maintain a complete organism, and to pass on traits from parents to offspring.

Genus: a group or organisms or species that are structurally similar.

Geotropism (gee·o·trope·ism): the growth of parts of a plant towards or away from the source of gravity. For example, roots grow down towards gravity, and stems grow up away from gravity.

Gills: the feather-like structures under the cap of a mushroom. The spore-bearing or spore-producing organ called basidia form on the gills.

Ginkgo trees: the oldest of all known living trees. They produce unprotected seeds at the tips of short branches of the female trees.

Glands: are responsible for producing hormones, which are important for good health and development of the human body.

Glial (*glee*-al) **cells:** the supporting cells of the nervous tissue which protect, nourish, and insulate the neurons

Gliding joints: two bone plates that glide against one another. The joints in your ankles and wrists are gliding joints.

Glucagon: the hormone that increases blood glucose levels.

Glucose (*gloo-kohs*): the basic sugar made in plants by photosynthesis. Glucose is a carbohydrate, and is the most important simple sugar in human metabolism.

Glycerol (*glis·er·all*): a three carbon molecule. Glycerol is a simple sugar-alcohol compound. It is a colorless, odorless liquid. Glycerol is soluble in water. Glycerol is a central component of triglycerides.

Glycogen (*glai-kuh-jen*): a complex molecule found in the muscles of the human body that stores energy

Golgi (*goal*·jee) **bodies:** organelles made of stacks of membrane pouches organized throughout the cytoplasm of a cell. Golgi bodies are the "post office" of the cell. Here, newly made proteins are sorted and packaged according to type.

Gonads: the reproductive glands. Male gonads are called testes, and female gonads are called ovaries.

Granulocytes (**gran**-you-lo-sites): white cells which have tiny granules, or grains.

Gray matter: axons without myelin

Growth: the gradual increase in size of an animal or vegetable body over time, the development of an organism, e.g., of a plant from a seed to full maturity.

Growth plate: zones of cartilage at each end of the long bones. New bone forms at the growth plate.

Gut flora: symbiotic bacteria that break down some materials that the human digestive system alone cannot break down

Gymnosperms (**jim**·no·sperms): vascular plants that produce "naked" or exposed seeds

Halophiles (**hal**·o·files): extremophiles that live in extremely salty, or saline, environments, such as the Dead Sea and the Great Salt Lake

Heart chambers: There are four chambers in the heart, two atria and two ventricles.

Heart: the muscular organ at the center of the circulatory system that pumps the blood through the blood vessels to the body tissues

Hemoglobin (*hee-muh-gloh-bin*)**:** a protein in the blood cells of humans that carries oxygen throughout the body.

Heterotrophs: organisms that cannot make their own food supply

Hindbrain: the third major region of the brain. The hindbrain is at the bottom of the skull and connects to the spinal cord. The hindbrain includes the medulla oblongata, the pons, the brainstem, and the cerebellum.

Hinge joint: allows movement back and forth in only one plane; the elbow is a hinge joint.

Histamine: is used as a weapon to fight foreign substances. Histamine causes the blood vessels in the immediate area to dilate. The dilated blood vessels cause blood flow to increase in the area which, in turn, increases the temperature of the tissue involved.

Homeostasis (*hoh-mee-uh-***stey***-sis*): a stable internal environment which can be maintained despite changes in the external environment.

Hormones: chemical messengers. Hormones are secreted directly into the blood and affect specific tissues, often distant from the gland in which they were produced.

Host cell: an animal or plant cell on or in which a parasite or virus lives

Hydrochloric (high·droe·**klor**·ik) **acid**: a strong acid produced in the stomach; helps break down food, particularly proteins in food.

Hyphae: long filaments of cytoplasm surrounded by a cell membrane and cell wall of fungi.

Hypothalamus (**hi**-po-**thal**-a-mus)**:** a gland located directly beneath the thalamus. The hypothalamus controls the body's metabolism, that is, the biochemical processes in the body that maintain life, through a number of hormones which it produces and releases.

Hypothesis (hi-**poth**-uh-sis): an idea, or explanation, based on the currently known facts about something. The hypothesis tries to explain how those facts fit together and how the "something" works.

Immune system: has the function to protect the body and rid the body of germs. The immune system is composed of the following: leukocytes or white blood cells, the lymph system, the thymus gland, the spleen, and other specialized tissues.

Immunity: the body's ability to prevent or resist infection or illness caused by germs

Ingestion: the means by which food enters the digestive system. Ingestion is simply eating and drinking.

Inorganic chemistry: the study of nonliving matter

Insects: the largest and most diverse group of arthropods.

Insertion: the point of attachment to the bone that moves

Insulin: the hormone that <u>decreases</u> blood glucose levels

Integumentary (in-te-gu-**men**-tar-ee) **system**: the skin, which protects the body from the outside. The skin is the largest organ of the body and includes the epidermis, dermis, subcutaneous tissue, hair, nails, sweat glands, sebaceous glands, and specialized sensory nerves, along with related muscles and blood vessels.

Intercostal muscles: those muscles between the ribs that aid the diaphragm to control normal respiration, or breathing

Interneurons: form connections or serve as a link between sensory neurons and motor neurons

Interphase: the phase of the cell cycle in which the cell spends the majority of its time and performs the majority of its purposes including preparation for cellular division. During the interphase, the cell takes in nutrients, grows, and duplicates its chromosomes.

Invertebrates: animals that do not have a backbone. Invertebrates make up over 95% of all species of animals. The invertebrates include sponges, flatworms, mollusks, roundworms, and many other groups.

Iris: the pigmented portion of the eye, associated with eye color. The iris is responsible for controlling the diameter and size of the pupil and thus the amount of light reaching the retina.

Irregular bones: bones of a variety of shapes and sizes that do not fit into the other categories of bones. Irregular bones include the middle ear bones, the vertebrae, some facial bones, and the jaw bone. The skull is made up of flat bones and irregular bones.

Joint: the location at which bones connect. Most joints allow movement and provide mechanical support.

Keratin: a protein that makes up hair, nails, and parts of the skin

Kidney: the most important and complex organ of the urinary system. The kidneys remove wastes from the blood and, through re-absorption, put water and electrolytes back into the blood. Each kidney is divided into three major regions. The kidneys monitor and help control blood pressure.

Lampreys (**lam**·prays): long, eel-like, jawless fish with smooth skin and no scales. They are distinguished by having a round, sucker-like mouth without jaws.

Lancelets (**lance**·ah·lets): invertebrate chordates shaped like a knife blade. They are salt water, or marine, animals that are only a few centimeters long with elongated, segmented bodies.

Large intestine: the final part of the digestive tract, where any remaining water and electrolytes are re-absorbed for use in the body

Larynx (**lair**·inx): a tube-shaped organ in the neck that contains the vocal cords; it is also called the voice box.

Lateral growth: the increasing girth, or thickness, of some plant stems. Lateral growth is evident in the rings which can be seen on the cross section of a fallen tree trunk.

Lateral line: a system of sensory organs unique to fish that detects vibrations in the water, and even helps the fish determine the position of their own bodies.

Leaves: the organs in which photosynthesis occurs. The leaves are involved also in excretion and in homeostasis, that is, maintaining healthy functioning, particularly in water balance. Leaves are generally made of flat, thin structures called blades that catch the sun's rays.

Left hemisphere: the left half of the cerebrum, largely responsible for language processing, logic, and mathematical computation.

Life Science for Young Catholics

Lens: a transparent structure in the eye that helps to refract light to be focused on the retina. The lens, by changing shape, functions to change the focal distance of the eye so that it can focus on objects at various distances, thus allowing a sharp, real image of the object of interest to be formed on the retina.

Leprosy: a chronic infectious disease caused by bacteria, affecting especially the skin and peripheral nerves and characterized by the formation of nodules or macules that enlarge and spread, accompanied by loss of sensation with eventual paralysis, wasting of muscle, and deformities.

Leukocytes: white blood cells. These white blood cells locate and destroy enemy germs and prevent illness.

Lichen (lie·kin): is a symbiotic combination of fungus with algae. The algae provide carbohydrates for the fungus, and the fungus protects the algae and helps to collect and retain minerals and water from the surroundings that are needed by the algae for growth and development.

Ligaments: thick bands of connective tissue that join two bones together

Lipids: large organic molecules. Lipids are made of glycerol and fatty acids.

Liver: a solid organ that assists in digestion. It helps with digestion but the liver is not part of the actual digestive tract. The liver is responsible for many essential functions related to digestion, to metabolism or bodily chemical processes, to immunity from disease, and to the storage of nutrients within the body.

Lobe-finned fish: have fins supported by more fleshy rays that are attached to the body with a single bone.

Lock jaw: or tetanus, is a disease caused by a bacterial toxin. Lock jaw is a serious disease, and as many as one-third of all people who contract lock jaw die from it.

Lungs: two air-filled, spongy internal organs located on either side of the chest

Lyme disease: the most common tick-borne illness in North America and Europe. Lyme disease is caused by the bacterium Borrelia burgdorferi. Deer ticks, which feed on the blood of animals and humans, can harbor the bacteria and spread it when feeding.

Lymph: a clear to white, somewhat milky liquid that contains extracellular (out of a cell) fluid called plasma, which has left the circulatory system by way of capillaries in the tissues

Lymph nodes: are made up of grouped lymph nodules that are held together by connective tissue. These lymph nodules are surrounded and held together by a tough fibrous capsule, to define (hold together and give shape to) the lymph node.

Lymph nodules: small collections of lymph tissue, usually located in the loose connective tissue beneath wet membranes, as in the digestive system, respiratory system, and urinary bladder

Lymph system: the system within the immune system that absorbs fluid from the body's tissues and returns it into circulation

Lymph vessels: are similar to veins. Like veins, lymph vessels have valves that prevent the lymph from flowing back towards the tissues. The lymph vessels empty lymph into two lymph ducts.

Lysosomes (lice·o·somes): vesicles or small sacs made from the Golgi bodies that contain enzymes (substances that cause a reaction) that help to digest and remove debris from the cell.

Macromolecules (mak-ruh-mol-uh-kyools): large organic molecules. There are four basic groups of macromolecules: carbohydrates, proteins, lipids, and nucleic acids.

Malaria: a serious illness in humans that, if left untreated, can lead to death. People with malaria experience high fevers, shaking chills, and flu-like symptoms. Malaria is transmitted to humans through the bite of an Anopheles mosquito and is common in tropical and subtropical areas where these mosquitoes are found.

Mammals: warm-blooded animals with a four-chambered heart that breathe exclusively with lungs, have hair, and nourish their young with milk produced in mammary glands. Mammals may be divided into three large groups based on the development of their offspring: monotremes, marsupials, and placental mammals.

Mammary glands: a unique trait found in both male and female mammals. However, they develop fully only in females to produce milk to feed the young.

Marsupials: mammals that give birth to very undeveloped young, called joeys, that develop in a pouch usually located on the mother's abdomen. The marsupials include opossums, kangaroos, wallabies, wombats, koalas, and some others.

Mass: a property of a physical body which determines resistance to being accelerated by a force, and the strength of its mutual gravitational attraction with other bodies

Matter: anything that has mass and takes up space

Mechanical digestion: the physical breaking down of larger pieces of food into smaller particles. Mechanical digestion begins with chewing in the mouth, but continues through the entire digestive tract.

Medulla oblongata: the portion of the brainstem that regulates autonomic, or automatic, functions, that is, those functions that do not require conscious control, such as blood pressure, oxygen levels, heart rate, and respiratory rate.

Medullary cavity: the marrow cavity in the shaft of a long bone

Melanin (**mel**·ah·nin): a brown pigment produced in the epidermis, which gives the skin its color and protection from the ultraviolet radiation from the sun

melatonin (mel-a-**tone**-in): the hormone produced by the pineal gland that regulates the sleep cycle

Metabolic (met-uh-**bol**-ik) **processes:** the processes necessary for life, such as the intake of nutrients and respiration, for the growth, repair, and reproduction of the organism

Metabolism (muh-**tab**-uh-liz-uhm): the sum of all chemical reactions occurring within the cells of living organisms

Methanogens (me·**than**·o·jens): extremophile archaea that require anaerobic conditions, that is, conditions without oxygen. These microorganisms live in the intestinal tracts of termites, cows, and humans where they use the available carbon dioxide and hydrogen for energy and produce methane gas as a byproduct.

Micro fungi: the smallest and the simplest fungi in organization. The micro fungi are parasites in larger animals.

Midbrain: the smallest region of the brain. The midbrain sits beneath the cerebral hemispheres. The midbrain conveys movement information between the brain and the rest of the body. The midbrain also processes visual and auditory information.

Mitochondria (might·o·**con**·dree·a): the powerhouses of a cell. The ATP that fuels cell processes is made in mitochondria.

Mitosis: the process in which the nucleus divides during the process of cell division

Mitral (**my**·trill) **valve:** separates the left atrium from the left ventricle to prevent blood from flowing backwards.

Molecule (**mol**·e·kyool): the functional substance of most of creation. A molecule is a combination of two or more atoms of either the same kind, or of two or more kinds.

Mollusks: have a soft body without a backbone and usually live in a shell. The mollusk group includes over 80,000 different species of snails, squids, oysters, and octopuses.

Monocots: seed-bearing plants that contain one embryonic seed leaf. Monocots produce flowers with petals in multiples of three. Monocot leaves have veins that are parallel to each other and run the length of each leaf.

Monotremes (**mon**-o-tremes): the mammals that lay eggs

Motile: capable of moving on its own

Motor cortex: part of the cerebral cortex that controls voluntary movement of skeletal muscles

Life Science for Young Catholics

Motor nerves: are made exclusively of axons from motor neurons. Motor nerves transmit information away from the central nervous system to the rest of the body, specifically to muscles and glands.

Motor neurons: relay information from the brain, through the spinal cord, and to the muscles to produce movement.

Motor units: consist of a nerve and all the muscle fibers that the nerve activates.

Multicellular organisms: organisms that are made up of many cells. Some of these cells may be specialized, for example bone cells, or skin cells.

Muscle tissue: is made of interconnected, elongated cells that have the ability to contract and relax. Muscle tissues are responsible for movement in almost all animals. There are three basic types of muscle tissue: skeletal (or voluntary) muscle tissue, smooth (or involuntary) muscle tissue, and cardiac muscle tissue.

Muscles: support and protect other body organs, but most importantly, muscles are the agents or the cause of movement for the body. Muscles are soft tissues composed of hundreds of thousands of muscle fibers.

Musculoskeletal system: the system of skeletal bones and the muscles that move them

Mushrooms: fungi that have fruiting bodies shaped like umbrellas

Mutualism (**myoo**·tyul·ism): a symbiotic relationship that helps both organisms

Mycelium (my·**sea**·lee·um): the underground structure of fungi. It is a network of hyphae spread out under the soil

Myelin sheath: an insulating material made of lipids and proteins that protects the axons and speeds up the transmission of impulses

Myriapods: have "myriads," or a great number, of legs. The myriapods have multiple body segments that bear the legs. Centipedes have one pair of legs per body segment, while millipedes have two pairs of legs per body segment.

Natural killer cells: kill abnormal cells. Natural killer cells are nonspecific; they are active against many different virus-infected cells, as well as abnormal cells or diseased cells. Natural killer cells are the body's major defense against all types of cancer cells.

Nephron (**nef**-ron) the basic functional unit of the kidney. The nephron is a tubular or tube structure made of two distinct parts: the renal corpuscle and the renal tubule.

Nerve cell body: the central part of a neuron (nerve cell). The nucleus and cellular organelles are located within the nerve cell body.

Nerve tissue: is responsible for: brain activity, sensory input, integration, control of muscles and glands, and homeostasis. Nerve tissue is composed of neurons, or impulse-conducting cells, and glial cells, or supporting cells.

Nerves: bundles of axons outside of the central nervous system. These nerves carry impulses between the brain and the spinal cord, and the remainder of the body.

Nervous system: the part of an animal's body that coordinates its voluntary and involuntary actions and transmits signals between different parts of its body. The human nervous system includes the brain, the spinal cord, the sensory organs, and the nerves.

Neurons: or nerve cells, are the functional cells of the nervous system. Neurons have three functions: (1) to transmit sensory information to the central nervous system; (2) to process, integrate, and interpret incoming sensory information; and (3) to transmit motor impulses to muscles and glands to affect a change as a result of the sensory information.

Neutrons (**noo**·trons): uncharged, neutral sub-units within the nucleus of an atom

Nipple: an area of fleshy skin on mammals to allow milk to exit when feeding the young

Nitrogen fixation: the process by which some bacteria are able to remove nitrogen gas from air and convert it into ammonia for use in the growth and metabolism of plants and animals

Non-vascular plants: the group of plants which do not have vessels which carry fluid; includes mosses, liverworts, and hornworts. Non-vascular plants have cell walls containing cellulose and contain chlorophyll. These plants also produce sugars through photosynthesis.

Nose: the organ of smell

Nuclear membrane: the double membrane around the nucleus of a cell. The nuclear membrane contains large pores which allow the RNA to pass into the cytoplasm.

Nucleic (noo·klay·ik) acids: the large organic molecules which store the genetic code

Nucleolus (new·klee·o·lus): a part of the nucleus of a cell which is involved in making proteins

Nucleotides (noo·klee·o·tides): the basic units of nucleic acids. Each nucleotide is made up of three parts: a five-carbon sugar in the shape of a ring, a phosphate group of molecules, and a nitrogen base.

Nucleus: the center of an atom, made up of protons and neutrons. The large part of the mass of the atom is in the nucleus. The nucleus is also the control center of the cell, separated from the cytoplasm by two membranes.

Nutrients: used by the cells to keep us in good health

Nutrition: the process by which all organisms organisms take in nutrients from their environment and use the energy from the nutrients for life processes

Olfaction: the sense of smell

Olfactory nerve: brings odor sensations from the nose to the brain

Olfactory receptors: are located within a small patch of tissue high up in the nasal cavity. The olfactory receptors are stimulated by odor molecules in the air, and the sensory information is transmitted to the brain by way of the olfactory nerve.

Optic nerve: a special nerve that brings sensory impulses from the eye to the brain

Organs: groups of tissues that work together to perform a specific function, such as the liver, brain, and heart.

Organ systems: are made of two or more organs that work together to perform a specific function, such as the skeletal system, nervous system, and circulatory system

Organic chemistry: the study of carbon-containing matter, the matter of organisms

Organisms: living things composed of various levels of cellular organization, such as human beings, animals, and plants

Origin: the point of muscle attachment to the bone that does not move

Osmosis (os·mo·sis): a special form of diffusion that allows larger substances to pass through the pores in the cellular membrane

Ossicles: three small bones in the middle ear that transmit sound vibrations through the oval window from the stapes to enter the fluid-filled inner ear. The middle ear ossicles are the malleus, the incus, and the stapes, in that order.

Ovaries (human): the reproductive glands in females. They produce estrogen and progesterone, which are responsible for female sexual development and maintaining pregnancy.

Ovary (plant): the organ that contains the ovule; it is the organ in which fertilization occurs and the seed is produced. The ovary matures around a seed to form the fruit.

Pacemakers: specialized cells in the heart that control the electrical system of the heart to cause it to beat

Palisade cells: long, relatively narrow cells that have the highest content of chlorophyll and are responsible for most of the plant's photosynthesis.

Pancreas (pan·cree·us): an elongated gland found beneath the stomach. The pancreas produces pancreatic juice, which is a mixture of water, salts, bicarbonate, and digestive enzymes.

Life Science for Young Catholics

Papillae: cover the tongue and surround and protect the taste buds.

Paramecium (pair·a·**mee**·see·um): an animal-like protist that is covered in short hair-like organelles called cilia, which are used for movement, for attachment to surfaces and other organisms, for feeding, and for sensation. Paramecia are found in all water habitats and soils.

Parasitism (**pair**·a·site·ism): a symbiotic relationship where one species takes advantage of the other and does it harm.

Parathyroid glands: are located on the thyroid gland. They produce a hormone which is important in calcium balance.

Passive transport: the movement of materials through the cell membrane without energy being used

Pathogen (**path**·o·jen): a bacteria or virus that causes disease

Peat moss: a non-vascular plant that can absorb up to twenty times its weight in water

Penicillin: a familiar antibiotic used to treat strep throat and many other diseases

Pepsin: the principal protease found in gastric juice

Pericardium: a tough, fibrous sac that protects the heart.

Periodic Table of the Elements: a table, or chart, that organizes and classifies all of the known elements.

Periosteum (pear·ee·**ost**·ee·um): a thick, fibrous, two-layered covering of bone containing blood vessels and nerves.

Peripheral nervous system: is comprised of the sensory organs and nerves.

Peristalsis (per·uh·**stal**·sis): the wave-like contractions of the intestines, continues the mixing of the chyme, or mass of partially digested food, with more digestive enzymes as the process moves along the length of the intestine

Peyer's Patches: lymph tissues associated with the small intestine. Peyer's Patches filter out harmful organisms from the digestive tract. Both T-cells and B-cells are found in significant numbers in Peyer's Patches lymph tissues to eliminate germs.

Phagocyte (**fag**-o-site): or "cell-eating" white blood cell. The phagocyte cell-eater surrounds the germ cell and "eats" it, thus destroying it.

Pharynx (**fair**·inx): or throat, a hollow section of the body that connects the oral cavity to the esophagus.

Phloem (flo-em): carries sugars back to the root from the remainder of the plant.

Photoreceptors: specialized cells that are sensitive to light. They respond to light and color.

Photosynthesis (foh-tuh-**sin**-thuh-sis): the process that plants use to convert the energy of sunlight, and the nutrients picked up from the soil by the roots, to make food in the forms of sugar and starches.

Phototropism (foh·toe·**trope**·ism): the growth or movement of a plant towards light

Pineal (pi-**nee**-al) **body:** or pineal gland, located within the brain, is important in regulating the sleep cycle through a hormone called melatonin.

Pinna: the outermost portion of the ear. The pinna gathers sound waves and funnels them to the middle ear.

Pistil: the female reproductive structure of an angiosperm

Pituitary gland: a tiny gland that sits just under the hypothalamus in the brain. The pituitary gland is made of an anterior lobe, or rounded projection, and a posterior lobe.

Pivot joint: enables turning in a circle, like that between the two bones of the forearm, which allows the forearm to rotate so that the palm can face up or down. Likewise, the pivot joint in the neck allows turning of the head from left to right.

Placental mammals: bear live young which develop in the mother's uterus, nourished by a special organ known as the placenta, which is connected to the developing offspring by an umbilical cord.

Plankton: a group of organisms, including diatoms and a variety of single-celled organisms, which live together in a body of water. Plankton are known as drifters. Plankton are the basic source of nutrition for many aquatic organisms, ranging from newly hatched fish to large fish and whales.

Plant-like protists: a large and diverse group that produce their own food. They perform photosynthesis to produce sugar by using carbon dioxide and water, and the energy from sunlight, just like plants. Unlike plants, however, plant-like protists do not have true stems, roots, or leaves.

Plasma: the liquid part of blood, makes up over half of the volume of the blood. Plasma is composed of water, as well as many different proteins, dissolved nutrients, and electrolytes.

Plasmids (**plaz**·mids): small sections of DNA in the cytoplasm of bacteria

Plasmodium (plaz·**moe**·dee·um): sporozoans. There are over 200 species of plasmodia, with eleven species that cause disease in the human body, including **malaria**, which is caused by Plasmodium Malariae.

Platelets: small cell fragments responsible for blood clotting to protect the body from excessive blood loss

Pleura: a thin tissue layer that protects the lungs

Pneumonia: an infection that inflames the air sacs in one or both lungs. The air sacs may fill with fluid or pus, causing cough with phlegm or pus, fever, chills, and difficulty breathing. A variety of organisms, including bacteria, viruses, and fungi, can cause pneumonia. Pneumonia can range in seriousness from mild to life-threatening.

Pons: means "bridge." It is the part of the brain that connects, or serves as a bridge between, the cerebral cortex and the medulla oblongata. The pons also relays sensory information between the cerebrum and the cerebellum, and helps regulate autonomic or automatic functions.

Pores: portholes made of proteins that span the width of a membrane. These pores function like little tunnels to allow larger molecules passage into and out of the cell.

Portal circulation: a special part of the circulatory system that brings deoxygenated blood from the digestive system through the liver for cleansing before it returns to the heart. Portal circulation, therefore, ensures that the blood is detoxified by the liver before being re-distributed via the heart throughout the remainder of the body.

Primary growth: the increase in the length or height of all plants by cell division. Primary growth occurs as a plant grows upward toward the sun, and as it extends roots downward into the soil.

Primary root, or **taproot**: the structure that grows downward directly from the seed. Taproots are single structures that grow straight down into the soil. From the primary roots, secondary, or lateral, roots develop. Lateral roots grow out from the taproot in a sideways direction. Primary and secondary roots may develop root hairs, which are fine hair-like projections that grow near the root tip.

Prokaryotic (pro·kar·ee·ot·ik) **cells**: the simplest cells. Prokaryotic cells lack an organized nucleus. They have cell walls, and are filled with cytoplasm. Prokaryotic cells do not have membrane-enclosed organelles, the tiny organ-like structures in some cells that perform specific functions. Prokaryotic cells do contain ribosomes.

Protease: an enzyme which breaks down proteins

Proteins: large molecules composed of amino acids. Proteins make up the muscles and other structural parts of the human body.

Protist: any eukaryotic organism that is not a fungus, a plant, or an animal but is fungus-like, or plant-like, or animal-like

Protons: positively charged sub-units within the nucleus of an atom

Pulmonary circulation: brings deoxygenated blood to the lungs to discard carbon dioxide and to pick up oxygen. The right side of the heart is responsible for pulmonary circulation.

Pulmonary valve: regulates the blood flow from the

right ventricle into the pulmonary artery for the lungs and prevents blood from flowing backward to the heart.

Pulp: the centermost part of each tooth. The pulp contains nerves, blood vessels, and connective tissue; the pulp is the living, sensitive part of the tooth.

Pupil: the part of the eye where light enters

Radial symmetry: describes animals that have bodies that are symmetrical in several directions about a central point like a spoked bicycle wheel.

Ray-finned fish: have bony rays, or spines, that support their fins.

Recyclers: prokaryotes that recycle carbon, nitrogen, phosphorus, iron, and other elements in the environment

Red blood cells: tiny flexible cells without a nucleus that contain hemoglobin. These make up about 45% of the blood volume. Red blood cells carry oxygen throughout the body.

Reflexes: actions controlled by the cells in the spinal cord rather than in the brain. Spinal reflexes allow a much more rapid response by the human body to a stimulus. For example, the instant withdrawal of a hand from a burning hot object is a spinal reflex. The nerve pathway that controls a reflex is called a reflex arc.

Regeneration: the ability of an injured or fragmented organism to grow back into a full intact organism. For example, if a stinger loses part of its body, it automatically regrows that missing part.

Renal artery: an artery that has branched off of the abdominal aorta to supply the kidney with blood. There is one renal artery for each kidney.

Renal capsule: a tough fibrous layer surrounding the kidney and covered in a thick layer of adipose tissue (fat). It provides a layer of protection for the kidney.

Renal corpuscle: the site at which blood is filtered

Renal cortex: the part of the kidney where the blood is filtered

Renal hilum (**high**·lum): a depression or pit on the concave part of the kidney that gives entrance and exit to blood vessels and nerves

Renal medulla: consists of tiny tubes or tubules that transport the filtered liquid from the renal cortex to the renal pelvis.

Renal pelvis: acts like a funnel to bring urine into the ureter.

Renal tubule: a tube through which filtered liquid passes to collecting tubules

Renal vein: drains the kidney. Renal veins connect the kidney to the inferior vena cava. They carry the blood purified by the kidney.

Reproduction: the ability of organisms to produce offspring similar to themselves. Non-living things are not capable of reproducing themselves.

Reptiles: cold-blooded vertebrates that have dry, scaly skin and usually lay soft-shelled eggs on land. Snakes, turtles, crocodiles, and lizards are reptiles.

Respiration (res-puh-**rey**-shuhn): All living organisms have the capacity to take in, transform, and use energy. The process by which all living organisms take in, transform, and use energy is known as cellular respiration. In cellular respiration, living organisms take in "food" for the energy needed to perform the processes of life, and carbon dioxide is produced.

Retina: a light-sensitive layer of tissue on the inner surface of the eye, which serves much the same function as the film in a camera. Light striking the retina triggers nerve impulses to the brain through the fibers of the optic nerve.

Rhizoids (**rye**·zoyds): root-like structures that anchor non-vascular plants to the ground, but do not absorb water or other nutrients

Ribosomes: organelles inside cells that synthesize proteins

Right hemisphere: the right half of the cerebrum, it is largely responsible for visual imagery, processing music, and interpreting the tone and context of what is seen and heard.

RNA: ribonucleic (rahy-boh-noo-klee-ik) acid. RNA is a single-stranded molecule that is responsible for making proteins by coding and decoding the genetic information held in the DNA molecules.

Root fungi: live *only* in mutualistic symbiotic relationships. It is estimated that over 80% of all land plants have root fungi living in and among their roots.

Roots: the organs that anchor the plants in the soil, and which absorb water and minerals from the soil. In some plants, roots store food produced by the plant.

Rough endoplasmic reticulum (RER): is studded with ribosomes.

Respiratory system: composed of every organ and structure that is involved in bringing oxygen into the blood.

Sac fungi: fungi that have bag-shaped spore-forming structures. There are over 64,000 varieties.

Saddle joints: joints where one of the bones forming the joint is shaped like a saddle, with the other bone resting on it like a rider on a horse. Saddle joints provide stability to the bones while providing more flexibility than a hinge or gliding joint. The best example of a saddle joint in the body is at the base of the thumb.

Saliva: produced by salivary glands in the mouth. The function of saliva is to moisten the food.

Sarcodines: protozoa that move and capture food by means of their pseudopods (false feet)

Scientific Method: consists of procedures involving systematic observation, measurement, and experiment, of some object or event or phenomena. The scientific method includes formulating some ideas, testing them, and modifying the ideas, thus developing a hypothesis about that object or event or phenomena.

Sebaceous (see-bay-shus) glands: glands in the skin that produce a waxy substance called sebum

Sebum (see-bum): a thick substance secreted by sebaceous glands. Sebum consists of fat and cell fragments; it lubricates and waterproofs the hair in your skin.

Secretion: the process by which a substance, such as a hormone, chemical, or enzyme, is released from an organ or gland to perform a particular function

Segmentation: describes a body plan in which an animal has distinct body segments. For example, insects are animals with three body segments: the head, the thorax, and the abdomen; each of these segments has special organs and systems to serve a specific purpose in the overall functioning of the animal.

Semipermeable (sem·ee·per·mee·a·ble) membrane: a membrane that protects a cell, or part of a cell, and that only allows certain substances to pass through it

Sense organs: take in information from the environment. This information is then processed in the brain and then we are able to act on the information. The five sense organs are the eyes, ears, tongue, nose, and skin.

Sensitivity: the ability of organisms to detect changes in their environment and to respond to stimuli, such as heat or cold

Sensory cortex: part of the cerebral cortex that receives sensory information from receptors throughout the body, processes that information, and develops perceptions

Sensory nerves: made exclusively of axons from sensory neurons; these transmit sensory information to the central nervous system.

Sensory neurons: the neurons which convert external stimuli from the environment, from outside the body, into an impulse, and then transmit that information to the central nervous system

Sensory receptor: a sensory nerve ending in an organ or tissue that responds to a particular stimulus by sending an electrical impulse toward the central nervous system

Septa (singular **septum**): filaments within the hyphae of fungi that divide the hyphae into smaller compartments, like walls in a building to make rooms

Sesamoid (sess·a·moyd) bones: bones that develop after birth to protect the tendons. The kneecap is a sesamoid bone.

Shells: the different levels that electrons inhabit about the nucleus of an atom

Shoot system: the part of a plant made up of the stems and leaves

Sinoatrial node (SA node): the primary pacemaker and is located in the right atrium. The SA node generates the electrical signal for the heart to beat about 70-80 times per minute in a healthy adult heart. The electrical impulse from the SA node travels to the two atria and to the AV node.

Skeletal muscle: the striated muscles that move the bones in the skeleton.

Skin: the major organ of **touch**. The skin contains receptor cells for pressure and vibration, temperature, and painful stimuli.

Small intestine: the largest digestive organ of the human intestinal tract, measuring between 18 and 23 feet in length. Most of the digestive process occurs here.

Smooth endoplasmic reticulum (SER): does not have ribosomes. Smooth endoplasmic reticulum is the site of lipid, or fat, and carbohydrate production.

Smooth muscle: the specialized muscles inside arteries and organs. These muscles carry out involuntary movements.

Soft rot: a mushy, watery, or slimy decay of plants or their parts caused by bacteria or fungi

Somatic nervous system: part of the peripheral nervous system which controls voluntary body functions through skeletal muscles

Species: a group of organisms having common characteristics and capable of mating with one another to produce fertile offspring

Spinal cord: a cylindrical or circular collection of nervous tissue that begins at the base of the brainstem and extends to the second lumbar vertebra in the spine, one of the five large vertebrae below the rib cage. The spinal cord is extremely important because it provides the connection for sensory and motor pathways from the brain to all areas of the body below the neck.

Spleen: filters the blood to rid it of germs and other debris. The spleen is a red-brown, somewhat flattened organ located in the abdominal cavity just under the ribs on the left side of the body. The spleen can be considered to be the largest lymph node in the body.

Spongy bone: the tissue that makes up the interior of bones. Spongy bone has air pockets and may look like a kitchen sponge.

Spongy cells: found in plant leaves, packed loosely and separated by large air spaces. The air spaces allow the diffusion of carbon dioxide into each cell so that it is readily available for photosynthesis. The air spaces also allow for the diffusion of oxygen, a byproduct of photosynthesis, out of the cells.

Spore-bearing plants: vascular plants that reproduce by spores, not seeds

Sporozoans: animal-like protists. Sporozoans get part of their name, "sporo," from the fact that they produce spores, like some plants. The other part of the name is from "zoo" which means "animal." So sporozoans are spore-producing, animal-like organisms.

Stamen (stay·men): the male reproductive structure of a flower where pollen is formed

Starches: complex carbohydrates produced in plants for energy storage for an emergency

Stems: the organs through which the water and minerals are transported to other parts of a plant. Stems also allow plants to grow upward toward the sun to better capture the sun's energy for photosynthesis, the process by which plants make energy.

Steroids: lipids with the carbon atoms arranged in rings instead of chains. Steroids, like some small proteins, function as hormones.

Stingers: a diverse group of aquatic animals that includes jellyfish, corals, anemones, and hydras. Stingers have special stinging cells they use for defense. Their stingers are also used like harpoons, sending out poison to immobilize little creatures in the water, which are then captured and eaten by the Stingers.

Strep throat: a bacterial throat infection that can make your throat feel sore and scratchy.

Striated (**stry**-ay-ted) **muscle cells:** are called "striated" because they look like long bands or stripes.

Subcutaneous (sub-cue-**tane**-nee-us) **layer** (skin): the third and deepest layer of the skin. It lies below the middle layer, or the dermis. The subcutaneous layer contains mostly fat and support tissues.

Sucrose (**soo**-krohs): common table sugar. It is a carbohydrate made up of two other, simpler sugars, glucose and fructose.

Sugars: usually simple carbohydrates

Symbiotic (sim·by·**ot**·ik) **relationships:** close and long-term relationships between two different species that benefit one or both of the organisms. There are three basic types of symbiotic relationships: mutualism, commensalism, and parasitism.

Symmetry: the characteristic of having exactly similar parts facing each other, or similar parts around an axis

Synapse: a gap between the end of one nerve cell and the beginning of another nerve cell, or muscle cell or gland

Synovial (syn-**o**-vee-ole) **fluid:** a thick fluid that lubricates joints to reduce the friction with movement of the bones. The joints that this fluid lubricates are called synovial joints.

Synthesis: the process of making proteins in ribosomes

Systemic circulation: brings oxygenated blood from the heart to the rest of the body. The left side of the heart is responsible for systemic circulation.

Systolic (sis·**taul**·ik) **pressure:** the force generated when the ventricles are contracting and pushing blood through the arteries.

Taproot, or **primary root:** the structure that grows downward directly from the seed. Taproots are single structures that grow straight down into the soil. From the primary roots, secondary, or lateral, roots develop. Lateral roots grow out from the taproots in a sideways direction. Primary and secondary roots may develop root hairs, which are fine hair-like projections that grow near the root tip.

Taste buds: contain taste receptor cells, which are chemoreceptors, and have thin extensions known as taste hairs. The taste hairs detect chemicals from food dissolved in the saliva. There are five basic tastes detected by the taste receptors: salty, sweet, sour, bitter, and savory.

Taxonomy (tak-**son**-uh-mee): the scientific classification and naming of God's living creatures for purposes of study through an organized approach

T-cells: directly kill germ-infected cells. The "T" in T-cells stands for the thymus gland where the T-cells are generated and "trained." T-cells work inside the tissues.

Tendon: a very strong band of fibrous tissue that connects a muscle to a bone.

Testes: the reproductive glands in males. They produce testosterone and other hormones that are responsible for sexual development.

Tetanus: see **Lock jaw.**

Tetrapods (*tetra* meaning four, *pod* meaning feet): animals that have four limbs

Thalamus (plural: **thalami**): glands located beneath the regions of gray matter. The two thalami send incoming sensory information to the proper sensory area of the cerebral cortex for processing. The thalami play an important role in learning and memory.

Thermophiles (**therm**·o·files): extremophiles that prefer extreme heat, often above 100° C, which is the boiling point of water

Thigmotropism (**thig**·moe·trope·ism): the growth of parts of a plant in response to touch. The tendrils (thin, often winding stems) of climbing plants grow around the main stem, trunk, or trellis they touch.

Thoracic (thor-as-ic) **cavity:** the chest cavity that contains the heart and lungs

Life Science for Young Catholics

Thymus gland: located just in front of the heart, develops T-cells and stores them for when they are needed.

Thyroid gland: a butterfly-shaped gland found in the neck overlying the trachea, the tube carrying air to the lungs. The thyroid gland produces two hormones which regulate the body's metabolic rate, or the rate at which body cells use energy.

Tissues: are groups of cells that work together to serve a specific function. There are four basic types of tissues found in animals: epithelial tissue, connective tissue, muscle tissue, and nerve tissue.

Tongue: the major organ of taste

Toxin: a poison produced by a bacterium that harms the host

Trachea (**tray**·key·ah): a tube-like pipe supported by rings of cartilage and lined with cilia. The trachea connects the voice box to the lungs.

Tricuspid (tri-**cus**-pid) **valve**: separates the right atrium from the right ventricle to prevent blood from flowing backwards when the heart is beating.

Triglyceride (try·**glis**·er·ide)**: a basic unit of fat, formed when three fatty acids bond to one glycerol. Both fats and oils are triglycerides.

Trypanosomes (tri·**pan**·o·somes): an example of the harmful category of zooflagellates. Trypanosomes are protozoa with a single elongated flagellum attached to and extending from the cell membrane like the fin and tail of a fish. The arrangement of the flagellum causes the trypanosome to move in corkscrew-like motion. Trypanosomes are parasites that live primarily in mammals.

Tuberculosis (TB): a potentially serious infectious disease, caused by bacteria, that mainly affects your lungs. These bacteria can be spread from one person to another through tiny droplets released into the air via coughs and sneezes.

Tubers (**too**·bers): specialized stems that grow underground. Potatoes are actually tubers.

Tunicates (**tune**·i·kates): immobile, invertebrate chordates with a tunic-like covering that gives the animal its name

Unicellular organisms: single-celled organisms that function wholly and independently from other organisms

Ureter (you-**ree**-ter): a thin muscular tube through which urine is transported away from the kidney.

Urethra (you-**ree**-thrah): the tube at the lower end of the bladder. When the bladder is full, urine passes through the urethra and finally out of the body.

Urinary (**your**-in-a-ree) **bladder**: a hollow muscular organ that acts as a reservoir to store urine until it is released from the body

Urinary system: filters all the blood in the body and removes metabolic wastes from it, and maintains the delicate balance of fluids and electrolytes

Urine: a liquid that consists of the waste products filtered out of the blood

Valves: fibrous flaps that control blood flow to keep it from going backwards

Vascular plants: have vascular tissues, which are like pipes or blood vessels, which conduct water and nutrients throughout the plant. Vascular plants are divided among spore-bearing and seed-bearing.

Vascular tissue: specialized tissue in the central cylinder of a root or stem that transports water and minerals throughout the remainder of the plant

Vegetable: any edible part of a plant. Vegetables may be the leaves of the plants, such as lettuce, kale, spinach, collard greens, and chard. Specialized leaves called bulbs form the vegetables known as onions, garlic and shallots. Vegetables may be stems or modified stems, such as asparagus, ginger, potatoes, sweet potatoes, and yams. Carrots, turnips, beets, and radishes are root vegetables. Broccoli and cauliflower are actually flower buds.

Veins: vessels that carry blood from the body tissues back to the heart. Veins have thinner walls with less elastic and smooth muscle and a larger lumen, or hole in the tube, because they receive blood from the tissues that is not under pressure.

Ventricles: two large chambers that pump blood out of the heart to the lungs and to the body.

Venules (**ven**-yulls): small veins that connect to capillaries. Venules bring deoxygenated blood from the capillaries to larger veins, which eventually return the blood to the heart.

Vertebrates: animals of the chordate group which have backbones, or vertebrae columns. The backbone is also known as the spine, and is made of individual bony units called vertebrae (singular, vertebra). Vertebrates have a well-developed brain and a dorsally located (dorsal means on the back), hollow nerve cord (spinal cord), comprising a central nervous system.

Vesicle: a capsule that has pinched off from a cell membrane after surrounding some substance.

Villi: folds in the small intestine that are each supplied with a tiny artery, vein, lymph vessel, and capillaries to provide adequate oxygen and nutrients to the intestinal lining, as well as to absorb nutrients for distribution throughout the rest of the body.

Virus: a very tiny particle, made up of some of the same components, proteins and genetic material as living cells. Viruses are not composed of cells; they are less than cells, of a category which we call subcellular particles. They do not move on their own, nor do they reproduce on their own, but only through a cell. Viruses carry on only some life processes, and only when in association with a true living cell, or host cell. Viruses, then, are non-living by strict definition.

Vitamin D: is made in the skin with help from sunlight. Vitamin D helps the body to absorb calcium to keep bones strong, and is an important factor in fighting some diseases.

Water molds: fungi-like organisms that live in water or soil, and may be parasitic on plants.

Waxes: are lipids. Waxes form the protective covering over the leaves of plants and in the ears of animals; bees produce wax used to build honeycombs in which to store pollen and provide a place for young bees to develop and grow.

White blood cells: are responsible for fighting infection. They are a part of the immune system.

White matter: axons protected by a myelin sheath

Whooping cough (pertussis): a highly contagious respiratory tract infection. In many people, it's marked by a severe hacking cough followed by a high-pitched intake of breath that sounds like "whoop."

Wilts: plant diseases characterized by permanent wilting, usually caused by fungal parasites attacking the roots

Xylem (**zy**·lem): carries water and minerals to the plant from the root.

Yeasts: a variety of sac fungi that are extremely important in the food industry. Yeasts are typically single-celled fungi that reproduce by budding and metabolize or change sugars into both alcohols and carbon dioxide by the process of fermentation.

Zooflagellates (**zoh**·oh·**flaj**·ell·ates): single-celled protozoa that move by means of flagella. The prefix "zoo" means animal, and "flagella" is a small tail-like appendage that allows the organism to move.

Zoospores (**zoh**·oh·spores): chytrids that contain a single flagellum, a long thread-like or whip-like organ extending from one end of the cell that enables the spores to disperse by swimming, a distribution method appropriate for an aquatic fungus.

Index

A

abdomen, 103
absorption, 82, 157-159, 163-164, 215
acid, 23, 157-162, 222-224
acidophiles, 49, 215
active transport, 34-35, 44, 215
ADP, 24, 215
adrenal glands, 209, 215
adrenaline, 209-210, 215
aerobic, 49, 215
aggregate, 90
albumin, 166, 215
algae, 53-56, 61, 71, 215, 226
alimentary, 156-160, 164, 168, 215
allergy, 187, 215
alveoli, 135-138, 215
amino acids, 21, 215
amoeba, 59-61, 215
amphibians, 107, 215
anaerobic, 49, 73, 216
angiosperms, 87-92, 216
antibiotics, 52-53, 216
antibodies, 184-185, 216
anus, 156
aorta, 146-149, 216
appendix, 186-187, 216
arachnids, 103, 216
Aristotle, 9, 216
arteries, 143-148, 174, 216
arterioles, 143-144, 173, 216
arthropods, 103, 216
assimilation, 154, 167, 216
atom, 16-17, 217
atomic number, 16, 217
ATP, 24, 37, 217
atria, 145, 217
autonomic nervous system, 193, 217
axial, 124, 217
axons, 194-195, 199, 217, 228

B

B-cells, 184-186, 217
biceps, 128
bile, 157-159, 164-167, 217, 223
bilirubin, 166-167, 217
binomial nomenclature, 9-12, 217
blood, 9, 58, 117-119, 124-128, 135-152, 157-161, 166, 171-176, 180-186, 196-199, 207-211, 215-219, 224-237
blood pressure, 149-152, 174-175, 217
blood vessels, 142-144, 159-161, 174, 183, 217-218, 224, 232
body symmetry, 100, 218
bolus, 162
bone marrow, 108, 124-125, 184-185, 217, 218
brain, 105, 137, 191-199, 203-207, 212, 217-222, 227-232
brainstem, 197-198, 218
bronchioles, 135, 218
bronchus, 135, 218

C

cap, 73-76
capillaries, 135-137, 143-145, 163, 173-174, 185, 218, 237
capsule, 50, 173
carbohydrates, 20-21, 71, 158-159, 218, 221, 226
carbon, 6, 15-18, 22-23, 34, 38, 49-51, 85, 133-137, 144, 218, 231-234
Carolus Linnaeus, 9, 218
carrageenan, 53
cartilage, 107, 125-126, 135, 218
cell cycle, 39-40
cell division, 39-41, 81, 218
cell membrane, 33-35, 39, 50, 59
cells, 8-9, 20-24, 29-50, 55, 61, 65-70, 75, 80-86, 98-101, 117-119, 124-127, 135, 140-145, 149-152, 159-167, 175, 180-190, 194-199, 204-209, 215-237
Cell Theory, 28-32, 218
cell wall, 38, 50, 56-57, 66, 218
cellulose, 51, 57, 87, 219
cementum, 161, 219
central nervous system, 105, 193-195, 199, 219, 228, 233
centrioles, 37, 219
cephalothorax, 103, 216
cerebellum, 198, 219
cerebral cortex, 196-198, 219
cerebrum, 196-200, 219
chemistry, 14-18, 219
chitin, 66-67, 219
chlorophyll, 38-39, 55-58, 80, 85-87, 219, 229
chloroplasts, 38, 219
cholesterol, 22, 219
chordates, 96, 104-105, 112, 219
chytrids, 68-71, 219
cilia, 60, 135, 181, 219
circulatory system, 140-143, 149-152, 159, 166, 171, 185, 219
class, 10
club fungi, 64, 72-73, 219
cochlea, 204, 219
colon, 164, 219
colonies, 49
commensalism, 51, 219
complementary muscles, 128, 220
compound, 17, 220
cones, 89
conifers, 89-94, 220
connective tissue, 98-99, 127, 143, 161, 185-186, 220, 226

coronary arteries, 148
coronary circulation, 148, 220
cortex, 84, 172-173, 196-198, 209, 215, 219, 227, 232-233
cristae, 37, 220
crustaceans, 103, 220
cuticle, 85, 220
cytoplasm, 31-39, 50, 59, 220, 224, 229-231

D

daughter cells, 39
decomposers, 51, 57, 74, 220
dendrites, 194-195, 220
dentin, 161, 220
deoxygenated blood, 144-148, 231
dermis, 117, 220
descending tracts, 198, 220
diaphragm, 136-138, 220
diastolic pressure, 149, 220
diatoms, 55-59, 220
dicots, 87, 91-92, 220
diffusion, 34-35, 85, 221, 234
digestion, 154-167, 217, 221, 226-227
digestive system, 154-160, 166-168, 181, 185, 221, 224
DNA, 23, 31, 221
duodenum, 163-164, 221

E

eardrum, 204, 221
electrolytes, 142-143, 171-175, 221, 225
electrons, 16-17, 192, 221
element, 16-18, 217, 221
embryo, 88
enamel, 161, 221
endocrine system, 117, 160, 172, 193, 202, 207-212, 221
endocytosis, 34-35, 221
endoplasmic reticulum, 36-37, 221, 234
enzyme, 157-158, 221
epidermis, 84-86, 117-119, 221
epiglottis, 134-135, 222
epithelial tissue, 98-99, 222
esophagus, 156-157, 162
euglena, 56-59, 222
eukaryotic cells, 32-33, 40, 44, 222
excretion, 7, 35, 39, 159, 222
exocytosis, 35, 222

extracellular fluid, 185, 222
extremophiles, 48-49, 222
eye, 29, 203, 222-226, 232

F

fats, 22, 222
fatty acids, 22, 167, 222
fermentation, 72-73, 222
ferns, 88-89
fibers, 20-21, 127-128, 145, 228
fibrous root system, 82-85, 222
fiddleheads, 88
flagella, 49, 58-60, 222, 237
flat bones, 124
flowers, 5, 90-91, 222
forebrain, 196-197, 222
fronds, 88, 222
fructose, 20-21, 223
fruit, 1, 89-91, 223
fruiting bodies, 67-73, 223
fungus, 64-71, 76, 223-226

G

gallbladder, 157, 164-165, 223
ganglion, 199, 223
gastric juice, 158-159, 223
genus, 9-10, 223
geotropism, 81, 223
germ, 183
gills, 73, 223
glands, 109, 117-119, 156-161, 172-174, 193, 202, 206-211, 216, 223-228, 233-235
glial cells, 195, 223
gliding joints, 223
glucagon, 210-211, 223
glucose, 20-21, 37, 80, 166, 196, 210-211, 223
glycerol, 22-23, 167, 223
glycogen, 20, 223
Golgi bodies, 36-37, 223
gray matter, 195-197, 224
group, 9, 22-24, 55-56, 82, 87-88, 101-110, 216, 223, 231-234
growth plate, 125, 224
gymnosperms, 87-89, 224

H

hair cells, 204
heart, 109, 136, 140-150, 166, 216-218, 224, 229-237
hemoglobin, 142-143, 224
hindbrain, 197-198, 224
histamine, 183, 224
homeostasis, 7, 84, 224
Homo sapiens, 10
hormones, 117, 160, 207-211, 224
hornworts, 87
host, 9, 52, 224
human growth hormone, 209
hydrochloric acid, 157-158, 162, 224
hyphae, 66-72, 224, 233
hypothalamus, 197, 208-209, 224
hypothesis, 4-5, 224

I

immune system, 180-188, 224
immunity, 165, 181, 224
infection, 149, 183, 237
ingestion, 156-157, 224
inner ear, 204
inorganic, 15-18, 225
insulin, 210-211, 225
integumentary system, 114-119, 225
intercostal muscles, 136-137, 225
Interneurons, 195, 225
interphase, 39-41, 225
invertebrates, 100-101, 225
iris, 225
irregular bones, 124, 225
islets of Langerhans, 210

J

joeys, 110

K

kidneys, 171-176, 209, 225
Kingdom, iii, 10, 46, 54, 61-68, 74, 78-80, 87, 96-99, 103
Kingdom Animalia, 99
Kingdom Fungi, 68
Kingdom Protista, 54

L

lampreys, 105, 225
large intestine, 157-159, 164, 225
leaves, 55, 78, 82-92, 220-225, 236
lens, 226, 226

leukocytes, 182-183, 226
lichen, 71, 226
lipids, 22-23, 226
liver, 154-157, 165-168, 183, 226, 231
liverworts, 87
long bones, 124-125
lymph, 163, 180-187, 226, 230
lymph node, 186-187, 226
lymph nodules, 185-187, 226
lymph system, 180-185, 226
lysosomes, 36-37, 226

M

macromolecules, 18, 31, 40, 226
malaria, 60, 226
mammary glands, 109, 209, 227
marrow, 108, 124-125, 184-185, 217
mass, 16-18, 65, 163, 217, 227
matter, 15-17, 31, 51, 66-69, 177, 195-197, 218-219, 227, 229
medulla, 173, 197-198, 209, 215
medulla oblongata, 197-198, 227
melanin, 118-119, 227
melatonin, 210-211, 227
membrane, 31-39, 50, 59, 98, 218-224, 229, 233
metabolic processes, 166, 227
metabolism, 24, 50, 165, 197, 207, 227
methanogens, 49, 227
Micro Fungi, 64, 73, 227
midbrain, 197, 227
middle ear, 204, 221, 229
millipedes, 103
mitochondria, 37, 227
mitral valve, 147, 227
mixing and movement, 157
molds, 55-57, 69-71, 76, 218, 223
molecule, 17-18, 23-24, 223, 227
mollusks, 96, 102, 227
monocots, 87, 91-92, 227
monotremes, 110, 227
mosses, 80, 87
motor nerves, 199, 228
motor neurons, 195, 206, 228
movement, 5, 34-35, 80-82, 86, 98, 126-128, 137, 157, 192-197, 217, 221, 227-230
multicellular organisms, 40-41, 75, 228
muscle tissue, 98-99, 228
mushrooms, 6, 65, 72-73, 228
mutualism, 51, 228

mycelium, 66-68, 228
myelin sheath, 194-195, 228
myriapods, 103, 228

N

Natural killer cells, 184-185, 228
nephron, 173, 228
nerves, 145, 161, 192-193, 199, 228-232
nerve tissue, 98-99, 228
nervous system, 98, 105, 160, 171, 190-195, 199-210, 217, 228, 233-234
neutrons, 16-17, 192, 228
nitrogen fixation, 50, 228
node, 145, 185-187, 217, 234
non-vascular plants, 87-88, 229
nuclear membrane, 36-37, 229
nucleic acids, 23-26, 229
nucleolus, 36, 229
nucleus, 16-17, 31-39, 48-49, 54, 98, 192-194, 217, 222, 228-231
nutrients, 6-7, 66, 87-88, 93, 142-144, 149, 155-167, 195, 221, 229-230, 237
nutrition, 6-7, 38, 54, 59, 66, 80, 98, 155, 229

O

odor, 229
olfactory nerve, 229
olfactory receptors, 205, 229
order, 9-10, 15-16, 40, 79
organelles, 32-39, 48-49, 59, 98, 194, 219-222
organs, 41-42, 78, 82-86, 98-99, 106-107, 117, 125, 134, 142, 156, 160, 166, 171-172, 176-178, 192-193, 202-210, 220, 225-229, 233-234
organ systems, 41, 117, 150, 171, 210, 229
organic chemistry, 15-17, 229
organism, 7, 23, 40-42, 51-53, 59-61, 75, 98-101, 155, 215, 220, 229, 232
osmosis, 34-35, 82, 229
ovary, 90-91, 229
oxidation, 154, 166-167
oxygenated blood, 145-147

P

pacemakers, 145, 229
palisade cells, 85, 229
pancreas, 159, 164-165, 210-211, 229
paramecium, 59-60, 230
parasite, 52
parathyroid glands, 209, 230
parent cell, 39
passive transport, 34-35, 230
pericardium, 146, 230
Periodic Table of the Elements, 16, 230
periosteum, 124, 230
peripheral nervous system, 192-193, 199, 230
peristalsis, 163, 230
petals, 91
Peyer's Patches, 186-187, 230
phagocyte, 182-183, 230
pharynx, 162, 230
phloem, 84-86, 230
photosynthesis, 6-7, 20-21, 38-39, 54-59, 70, 80-90, 219-225, 229-234
phototropism, 81, 230
phylum, 10
pinna, 204, 230
pistil, 90-91, 230
pituitary gland, 208-209, 216, 230
placenta, 110
plankton, 56-59, 104, 231
plasma, 142, 185, 231
plasmids, 49-50, 231
plasmodium, 60, 231
platelets, 125, 142, 231
pons, 197-198, 231
pores, 34-35, 86, 229-231
portal circulation, 166, 231
prokaryotic, 31-33, 40, 44-48, 231
prolactin, 209
protease, 158, 231
proteins, 21-26, 31-37, 157-162, 166, 221-224, 231-232
protists, 46, 53-62, 216, 223, 231
protons, 16-18, 192, 217, 231
protozoa, 51, 55-59, 216
pseudopods, 59-61, 215
pulmonary artery, 147
pulmonary circulation, 147, 231
pulmonary valve, 147, 231-32
pulp, 161, 186, 232
pupil, 203, 232

R

radial symmetry, 100, 232
receptor, 205
red blood cells, 125, 142-143, 175, 232
reflex arc, 206, 232
renal artery, 173-175, 232
renal corpuscle, 173, 232
renal cortex, 173, 232
renal medulla, 173, 232
renal pelvis, 173-175, 232
renal tubule, 173, 232
reproduction, 6-7, 28, 37-39, 82, 207, 232
respiration, 5-7, 37-38, 66, 133-137, 219, 232
retina, 226, 232
rhizoids, 87, 232
ribosomes, 32-37, 50, 232
RNA, 23, 36, 65, 232
root fungi, 70, 233
roots, 55, 78-86, 90, 222-223, 231-235

S

sac fungi, 64, 70-72, 233
saddle joints, 127, 233
saliva, 157, 161, 233
salivary glands, 157-161, 233
Scientific Method, 4-5, 233
sea anemone, 101
sebaceous glands, 119, 233
sebum, 119, 233
secretion, 157, 233
segmentation, 100, 233
sensory neurons, 195, 233
sensory organs, 192-193, 203
sensory receptors, 203-205, 233
septa, 66-70, 233
short bones, 124
sight, 203
skeleton, 108, 124-125, 130
small intestine, 156-164, 234
somatic nervous system, 193, 234
soul, 116, 176, 187
species, 9-10, 51, 60, 87, 100, 107-110, 218, 231, 234
spinal cord, 105, 192-199, 218, 228, 234
spleen, 186-188, 234
spores, 6, 67-73, 88, 223, 234-237
sporozoans, 60-61, 234
stamen, 90-91, 234
stapes, 204, 229
stems, 78-88, 92, 223, 234-236

steroids, 22-23, 234
stomach, 156-164, 221
storage, 165-166
sucrose, 20, 235
sugars, 20-21, 73, 84-87, 222, 235
symbiotic relationships, 51-54, 235
symmetry, 100-104, 217, 235
synapse, 206, 235
synthesis, 166-167, 235
systemic circulation, 147-148, 235
systolic pressure, 149, 235

T

taproot, 82, 235
taste buds, 205, 235
taste hairs, 205, 235
taxonomy, 9-12, 235
T-cells, 183-188, 209, 235
teeth, 160-161
testes, 211, 235
thalamus, 197, 235
thallus, 87
thermophiles, 48, 235
thigmotropism, 81, 235
thoracic cavity, 136, 235
thorax, 103
throat, 52, 134-135, 156, 162, 230, 234
thymus gland, 183, 209, 236
thyroid, 209, 236
tissues, 41-42, 55, 78, 82-87, 98-99, 117-118, 123, 133-134, 138-152, 156, 161, 166, 182-186, 199, 207-209, 217, 224-230, 235-236
tongue, 157, 162, 204, 236
toxins, 52, 166, 236
trachea, 135-137, 209, 218, 236
triceps, 128
trypanosomes, 58-59, 236
tsetse fly, 58
tubers, 85, 236

U

urea, 174
urethra, 175-176, 236
urinary bladder, 175, 185, 236
urinary system, 171-178, 182, 236
urine, 173-176, 236

V

vacuoles, 36
vascular plants, 87-89, 236
vascular tissue, 84-87, 236
vectors, 60
vegetable, 92, 236
veins, 85-86, 91, 144-147, 185, 226, 236-237
ventricles, 145, 237
venules, 144-145, 237
vertebrae, 105, 237
vertebrates, 105-109, 237
vesicle, 35, 237
villi, 163, 237
virus, 8-9, 237

W

water molds, 57, 237
white blood cells, 142-143, 149, 182-183, 226, 237
white matter, 195-197, 237

X

xylem, 84-86, 237

Z

zooflagellates, 58, 236, 237
zoospores, 68, 237

Image Attributions

Chapter 1
Balcony of Scientists: tpsdave, CC0 Public Domain, pixabay
Flower: shijingsjgem, CC0 Public Domain, pixabay
Fossil: PublicDomainPictures, CC0 Public Domain, pixabay
Dog: Patrice_Audet, CC0 Public Domain, pixabay
Rocks: schober, CC0 Public Domain, pixabay
Eagle: skeeze, CC0 Public Domain, pixabay
Carnivorous plant, Flytrap: Copyright: Hayati Kayhan, Shutterstock
Mushroom: Royalty Free: Mary Rizzo, pics.tech4learning.com
Illustration of Child Running: Copyright: Matthew Cole, Shutterstock
Plant Sequence: Copyright: divvector, dollarphotoclub.com
Vista Microscopica Virus y Células: Copyright: Giovanni Cancemi: dollarphotoclub
Aristotle: Public Domain: WikiCommons
Carolus Linnaeus: Public Domain: WikiCommons
Domain Archae: Public Domain: Pixgood
Domain Bacteria: Public Domain: Pixgood
Elephant: cocoparisienne, CC0 Public Domain, pixabay
Flower: zdenet, CC0 Public Domain, pixabay
Fungi: TomaszProszek, CC0 Public Domain, pixabay
Protists: CC0 Public Domain, pixabay
Tipsoo Lake Sunset: Copyright: aaron_huang86: dollarphotoclub

Chapter 2
Green chemistry with reaction formula : Copyright: Garsya, Shutterstock
Ripe peppers and tomatoes and chemistry: Copyright: photodsotiroff: dollarphotoclub
Fossil: PublicDomainPictures, CC0 Public Domain, pixabay
Atom: Wikimedia: CC-BY-SA-3.0, Shizhao
Water in glass with water splash: Copyright: somchaij, Shutterstock
Water Molecule: Nemo, CC0 Public Domain, pixabay
Molecule, atoms and particles in motion: Copyright: Laurent Renault, Shutterstock
Periodic Table of Elements: Copyright: goldaur: dollarphotoclub
High Glycaemic Index Foods - carbohydrates which have a high glycaemic index rating, on a white background.: Copyright: travellight, Shutterstock
spoon of protein powder and food with protein, isolated on white: Copyright: Africa Studio, Shutterstock
Butter and Oil: Copyright: Multiart: dollarphotoclub
DNA: PublicDomainPictures, CC0 Public Domain, pixabay
Structure of RNA & DNA: Copyright: Designua, Shutterstock
ATP Molecule: Copyright: chromatos, Shutterstock
Image of DNA strand and doctor: Copyright: Sergey Nivens, Shutterstock

Chapter 3
Bacteria background: Copyright: Lonely11, Dreamstime
Cell: PublicDomainPictures, CC0 Public Domain, pixabay
Magnifying Glass: HebiPics, CC0 Public Domain, pixabay
DNA Background: Copyright: SunnySideUp, Shutterstock
Cell Division: Copyright: O2creationz, Shutterstock
DNA Background 2: Copyright: Leigh Prather, Shutterstock
Prokaryotic Cell Diagram: Copyright: Mark Rasmussen: dollarphotoclub
Eukaryotic Cell Diagram: Copyright: Mark Rasmussen: dollarphotoclub
Prokaryotic Cell (3D): Copyright: Decade3D: dollarphotoclub
Eukaryotic Cell (3D): Copyright: Naeblys: Shutterstock
Cell Diffusion: Wikimedia: Public Domain, LadyofHats
Endocytosis / Exocytosis: Illustration by Dr. Wendy Ripple
Endoplasmic Reticulum: Wikimedia: CC-BY-3.0, BruceBlaus
Plant Cell: Copyright: Snapgalleria: dollarphotoclub
Photosynthesis: Copyright: casaltamoiola: dollarphotoclub
Cell Division (3D): Copyright: klss: Shutterstock
Cell Division: Illustration by Dr. Wendy Ripple
The Giving of the Keys to St. Peter by Perugino

Chapter 4
Bacteria background: geralt, CC0 Public Domain, pixabay
E Coli Bacteria: WikiImages, CC0 Public Domain, pixabay
Cheeses: Hans, CC0 Public Domain, pixabay
Thermophile Lake: Copyright: KKimages, Shutterstock
Salmonella Bacteria: WikiImages, CC0 Public Domain, pixabay
Average Prokaryote Cell: Wikimedia: Public Domain, LadyofHats
Spiral-like Bacteria: Wikimedia: Public Domain, PDH (Original: ARS)
Rod-shaped Bacteria: Copyright: beawolf: dollarphotoclub
Round Bacteria: Copyright: Dmitry Knorre: dollarphotoclub
Penicillin: Copyright: Olha Rohulya: Shutterstock
Tetanus Bacteria: Copyright: decade3d: dollarphotoclub
Bee: JamesDeMers: CC0 Public Domain, pixabay
Barnacles: salmonboy: CC0 Public Domain, pixabay
Tick: Catkin: CC0 Public Domain, pixabay
Algae: B.Ash: CC0 Public Domain, pixabay
Diatoms: Copyright: Jubal Harshaw, Shutterstock
Coral Reef: Copyright: Ethan Daniels, Shutterstock
Euglena: Copyright: snapgalleria: dollarphotoclub
Zooflagellate: Wikimedia: CC-BY-SA-3.0, Zephyris
Amoeba Diagram: Copyright: snapgalleria, dollarphotoclub
Paramecium Diagram: Copyright: snapgalleria, dollarphotoclub

Chapter 5
Mushroom background: Nikiko, CC0 Public Domain, pixabay
Mushrooms: stevepb, CC0 Public Domain, pixabay
Single Mushroom: Death_Proof, CC0 Public Domain, pixabay
Mycelium Illustration: Copyright: Designua, Shutterstock
Mycelium Photograph: Copyright: Kichigin, Shutterstock
Mushroom Diagram: DomenicBlair, CC0 Public Domain, pixabay
Chytrid: Wikimedia: CC-BY-3.0, CSIRO
Bread mold closeup: Copyright: Armando Frazao, dollarphotoclub
Root mushrooms: Copyright: jessicahyde, Shutterstock
Sac fungi: Wikimedia: CC-BY-3.0, Sasata
Club fungi: TomaszProszek, CC0 Public Domain, pixabay
Micro fungi: Wikimedia: Public Domain, Masur
Mushrooms: lichtwerk2, CC0 Public Domain, pixabay
Mushrooms: Copyright: hakase420, dollarphotoclub

Chapter 6
Tree leaves background: cocoparisienne, CC0 Public Domain, pixabay
Tree leaf: cocoparisienne, CC0 Public Domain, pixabay
Flowers: HolgersFotografie, CC0 Public Domain, pixabay
Plant Cell: Copyright: Snapgalleria: dollarphotoclub
Moss on wall: Nacymac, CC0 Public Domain, pixabay
Roots: Copyright: Casther: dollarphotoclub
Leaf structure: Copyright: sciencepics, Shutterstock
Leaf anatomy: Copyright: Designua, Shutterstock
Leaves: Copyright: Rostislav Sedlacek, dollarphotoclub
Moss: Nacymac, CC0 Public Domain, pixabay
Liverwort: Copyright: Henrik Larsson, dollarphotoclub
Hornwort: Wikimedia: CC-BY-2.0, Jason Hollinger
Ferns: Copyright: Scisetti Alfio, dollarphotoclub
Horsetails: Copyright: padu_foto, Shutterstock
Club Moss: Copyright: Uryadnikov Sergey, dollarphotoclub
Ginkgo tree: punch_ra, CC0 Public Domain, pixabay
Conifer branch: kapa65, CC0 Public Domain, pixabay
Flower anatomy: Copyright: 7activestudio, dollarphotoclub
Vegetables: tonton9, CC0 Public Domain, pixabay
Foxglove: imbrouwer, CC0 Public Domain, pixabay

Chapter 7
Cat background: Amandad, CC0 Public Domain, pixabay
Group of Animals: Copyright: Angela Waye, Shutterstock
Anatomy of Animal Cell: Copyright, blueringmedia, dollarphotoclub
Types of Muscles: Copyright, blueringmedia, dollarphotoclub
Coral: Copyright, aquapix, Shutterstock
Sponge: fabiopiccini, CC0 Public Domain, pixabay
Crab: xu_ming-xm, CC0 Public Domain, pixabay
Jellyfish: klawson, CC0 Public Domain, pixabay
Snail: Huskyherz, CC0 Public Domain, pixabay
Spider: 631372, CC0 Public Domain, pixabay
Pets: Copyright: ots-photo, dollarphotoclub
Lancelet: Copyright: 7activestudio, dollarphotoclub
Lamprey: Copyright: bit24, dollarphotoclub
Sharks: Copyright: storm, dollarphotoclub
Lobe-finned fish: Copyright: 7activestudio, dollarphotoclub
Ray-finned fish: skeeze, CC0 Public Domain, pixabay
Snake: Copyright: Alexandr Satoru, dollarphotoclub
Turtle: benscherjon, CC0 Public Domain, pixabay
Lizard: PublicDomainPictures, CC0 Public Domain, pixabay
Crocodile: Copyright: underworld, dollarphotoclub
Bird skeleton diagram: Copyright: roadrunner, dollarphotoclub
Baby pigs, Copyright: anoli, dollarphotoclub
Cow: zdenet, CC0 Public Domain, pixabay
Possum: Copyright: nicolaselowe, dollarphotoclub
Platypus: Copyright: worldswildlifewonders, Shutterstock
Noah's Ark, Brueghel the Elder

Chapter 8
Baby background: jelly, CC0 Public Domain, pixabay

Life Science for Young Catholics

Baby feet: Frankbeckerde, CC0 Public Domain, pixabay
Skin anatomy: Copyright: 7activestudio, dollarphotoclub

Chapter 9

3D Skeleton: Copyright: Sebastian Kaulitzki, Shutterstock
Foot X-Ray: Copyright: wonderisland, Shutterstock
Bone Structure: Copyright: 7activestudio, dollarphotoclub
Skull / Brain diagram: Copyright: 7activestudio, dollarphotoclub
Joint types: Copyright: ellepigrafica, Shutterstock
Skeletal Muscle: Copyright: Designua, Shutterstock
Structure of a motor neuron: Copyright, Designua, shutterstock
Anatomy of the Elbow: Copyright, blueringmedia, dollarphotoclub

Chapter 10

Lungs background: Copyright: Sergey Nivens, dollarphotoclub
Lungs: Copyright: hywards, dollarphotoclub
Respiratory System: Copyright: snapgalleria, dollarphotoclub
Diaphragm and Respiration: Copyright: rob3000, dollarphotoclub

Chapter 11

Heart background: Copyright: Sergey Nivens, dollarphotoclub
Heart: Copyright: CLIPAREA.com, dollarphotoclub
Blood cells in vein: Copyright: adimas, dollarphotoclub
Arteries & Veins: Copyright: Matthew Cole, dollarphotoclub
Anatomy of the Human Heart: Copyright, blueringmedia, dollarphotoclub
Systemic circulation: Copyright: Matthew Cole, dollarphotoclub

Chapter 12

Digestive system background: Copyright: 7activestudio, dollarphotoclub
Digestive system: Copyright, blueringmedia, dollarphotoclub
The Human Digestive System: Copyright, snapgalleria, dollarphotoclub
The Digestive Process: Wikimedia: CC-BY-3.0, OpenStax College
Mouth Anatomy: Copyright: stockshoppe, dollarphotoclub
Throat Anatomy: Copyright, snapgalleria, dollarphotoclub
Stomach Anatomy: Copyright: stockshoppe, Shutterstock
Intestines: Copyright: 7activestudio, dollarphotoclub
Liver Anatomy: Copyright: stockshoppe, dollarphotoclub

Chapter 13

Urinary System background: Copyright: hywards, dollarphotoclub
Urinary System / Kidney: Copyright: Lightspring, Shutterstock
Human Urinary System: Copyright: Mr High Sky, Shutterstock
The Kidney: Copyright: GunitaR, Shutterstock
Kidney Functions: Copyright: joshya, dollarphotoclub
Parathyroid Gland: Copyright: zuzanaa, dollarphotoclub

Chapter 14

T-Cell background: Copyright: Andrea Danti, dollarphotoclub
Cell virus: Copyright: Vitstudio, dollarphotoclub
Blood stream: Copyright: Decade3d, dollarphotoclub
T-Cell: Copyright: Andrea Danti, dollarphotoclub
Types of White Blood Cells: Copyright: extender_01, shutterstock
Lymph Node diagram: Copyright: joshya, shutterstock

Chapter 15

Brain background: Copyright: shumpc, dollarphotoclub
Brain: Copyright, Alexandr Mitiuc, dollarphotoclub
Nervous System: Copyright, snapgalleria, dollarphotoclub
Neuron: Copyright: kateryna zakorko, dollarphotoclub
Brain: Copyright: stockshoppe, dollarphotoclub
Spinal Cord: Copyright: Olexiy Voloshyn, dollarphotoclub

Chapter 16

Eyes background: Copyright: alexmac, dollarphotoclub
Human Eye Anatomy: Copyright: Alila Medical Media, Shutterstock
Zones of taste on the tongue: Copyright: Designua, Shutterstock
Anatomy of the Ear: Copyright: Alila Medical Media, Shutterstock
Olfactory System: Copyright: p6m5, dollarphotoclub
Spinal Reflexes: Copyright: Balint Radu, dollarphotoclub
Human Endocrine System: Copyright: Designua, shutterstock
Brain: Copyright: stockshoppe, dollarphotoclub

Front Cover

Family Gardening: Copyright: Andresr, Shutterstock
Squirrel: Elli60, CC0 Public Domain, pixabay
Flower: metadog, CC0 Public Domain, pixabay
Cell: PublicDomainPictures, CC0 Public Domain, pixabay

Back Cover

Basilica of Covadonga: Copyright: Marques, Shutterstock